(Re-)Reading Bede

Bede's *Ecclesiastical History* is the most important single source for early medieval English history. Without it, we would be able to say very little about the conversion of the English to Christianity, or the nature of England before the Viking Age.

Bede wrote for his contemporaries, not for a later audience, and it is only by an examination of the work itself that we can assess how best to approach it as a historical source. N. J. Higham shows, through a close reading of the text, what light the *Ecclesiastical History* throws on the history of the period and especially on those characters from seventh- and early eighth-century England whom Bede either heroised, such as his own bishop, Acca, and kings Oswald and Edwin, or villainised, most obviously the British king Cædwalla but also Oswiu, Oswald's brother.

In *(Re-)Reading Bede*, N. J. Higham offers a fresh approach to how we should engage with this great work of history. He focuses particularly on Bede's purposes in writing it, its internal structure, the political and social context in which it was composed and the cultural values it betrays, remembering always that our own approach to Bede has been influenced to a very great extent by the various ways in which he has been both used, as a source, and commemorated, as man and saint, across the last 1300 years.

N. J. Higham is Professor of Early Medieval and Landscape History at the University of Manchester. His publications include *King Arthur: Myth-Making and History* (Routledge, 2002) and the edited collection *Edward the Elder* (Routledge, 2001).

(Re-)Reading Bede

The *Ecclesiastical History* in context

N. J. Higham

Routledge
Taylor & Francis Group

LONDON AND NEW YORK

First published 2006
by Routledge
2 Park Square, Milton Park, Abingdon, Oxon OX14 4RN

Simultaneously published in the USA and Canada
by Routledge
270 Madison Ave, New York, NY 10016

Routledge is an imprint of the Taylor & Francis Group, an informa business

Typeset in Garamond Three by
RefineCatch Limited, Bungay, Suffolk
Printed and bound in Great Britain by
Antony Rowe Ltd, Chippenham, Wiltshire

British Library Cataloguing in Publication Data
A catalogue record for this book is available from the British Library

Library of Congress Cataloging in Publication Data

Higham, N. J.
(Re-)reading Bede : the ecclesiastical history in context / N.J. Higham.
p. cm.
Includes bibliographical references and index.
ISBN13: 978–0–415–35367–0 (hbk)
ISBN10: 0–415–35367–X (hbk)
ISBN13: 978–0–415–35368–7 (pbk)
ISBN10: 0–415–35368–8 (pbk)
1. Bede, the Venerable, Saint, 673–735. Historia ecclesiastica gentis
Anglorum. 2. England—Church history —449–1066. 3. Church
history—Middle Ages, 600–1500. 4. Civilization, Anglo-Saxon. I.
Title.
BR746.H54 2006
274.2'02—dc22

2006006584

ISBN10: 0–415–35367–X (hbk)
ISBN10: 0–415–35368–8 (pbk)
ISBN10: 0–203–30710–0 (ebk)

ISBN13: 978–0–415–35367–0 (hbk)
ISBN13: 978–0–415–35368–7 (pbk)
ISBN13: 978–0–203–30710–6 (ebk)

For Cheryl

Contents

Figures

Tables

Acknowledgements

I should like to record my thanks to the University of Manchester for the year's sabbatical leave (in 2004–5), which has enabled me actually to write this book, sections of which I have been working on for some years. Assistance with continental sources and other aspects was very kindly provided by Professor Paul Fouracre, who has also been quietly supportive in any number of other ways. Staff of the John Rylands University Library have, as ever, assisted in the provision of appropriate literature with their customary goodwill and patience. Professor Richard Coates (Sussex) very kindly commented in correspondence on the origins of several personal names recorded by Bede. Jamie Wood helped with references to Isidore. I owe a very considerable, indeed incalculable, debt to Dr Martin Ryan, who acted as part-time research assistant to this project across the academic year 2004–5, as well as undertaking teaching replacement between February and June 2005, to free me to devote myself to research. My thanks too to the many groups of students who have studied Bede with me over the last thirty years at either or both of undergraduate and postgraduate level.

To all go my grateful thanks for a mix of stimulation and kindness the absence of which would have seriously detracted from the end product. All opinions expressed, however, and likewise all mistakes made, remain exclusively my own.

As ever, I owe my greatest thanks to my wife, Cheryl, whose patience has been tested repeatedly by the self-absorption, mood-swings and neuroses which have been a consequence of undertaking this project. This work is dedicated, therefore, to her, in gratitude for the quality she brings to my life: without her I should be poor indeed.

Introduction

How Bede is remembered and how we choose to commemorate him today both remain contentious areas. In the year 2000, a national campaign came to fruition, with a petition supported by some 20,000 signatures and championed by Fraser Kemp, MP for Houghton and Washington East. The proposal was to secure the then long-vacant plinth in Trafalgar Square for a permanent memorial to Bede. The pleas failed, however, to move London's mayor, Ken Livingstone, who reportedly felt that Bede's *Ecclesiatical History*, which he recalled having read some decades previously, was 'politically incorrect' in ignoring King Arthur and just 'the Church's airbrushed version of British history, because he ignores our pagan past'.[1]

The mayor's remarks brought a not unexpected response from sections of the academic community and from the North-East into the letter pages of what were then still the broadsheets, predominantly in favour of the proposal and/or scornful of his objections, but Livingstone stuck to his guns. A series of temporary exhibitions had begun in July 1999 with Mark Wallinger's '*Ecce Homo:* Behold the Man' – a portrayal of Christ at the moment of condemnation – and continue to the present, with the controversial but 'politically correct', 3.6m high marble sculpture, 'Alison Lapper Pregnant', by Marc Quinn, erected in September 2005.

Had his statue been placed here, however, one might pause to wonder how Bede himself might have viewed this initiative, had he the opportunity, to site a memorial to his own scholarship, and his role as national icon, some 300 miles (484 km) south of his normal stamping grounds, and in a thoroughly secular space originally designed to commemorate victory by the Protestant 'British' – two terms with which he would have had enormous difficulty identifying – in a bloody sea battle against Catholic opponents off the coast of Spain almost 1100 years after his own demise. Admittedly, the original design by Charles Barry in 1832 was intended to provide scope for the Arts, but the centrepiece was always to be the great war-hero, Nelson, atop his column. Today, Trafalgar Square serves as something of a communal open space, particularly at times of great celebration or tragedy, for a Metropolis which has a reputation for materialism, consumerism and hedonism, as well as a mix of peoples as broad as any to be found in a single community anywhere in the world. Whether or not Bede might have appreciated any aspect of the proposed commemoration must remain in doubt, but the desire to give him such a memorial which that petition demonstrated reflects claims on national identity today by groups within society who feel less than central to current notions of either 'Englishness' or 'Britishness', including elements of the religious establishment, the academic world, and a regional community in the North-East which has often felt itself to be peripheral to the nation state. A statue of Bede established permanently on the long-vacant plinth in Trafalgar Square had some potential to assuage these senses of difference, therefore, and establish 'Geordie' claims on the nation, even while offering a symbol of Christian learning and authorship to the intelligentsia as a whole.

That said, one might add that we have no idea what Bede actually looked like, so the sculpting of a statue (supposing such was intended) might have been somewhat problematic from the perspective of both artist and commissioning committee alike. A tonsure? Yes, that seems unproblematic, and we could probably manage the right one: but for the rest?

Nor was this the only such instance of a project designed to commemorate Bede in very recent years, for 1996 saw grandiose proposals brought forward by Northumberland County Council for what was termed a 'millennium cathedral' to be sited at Cramlington, close to the A1 and almost midway between Newcastle and Morpeth, to celebrate 'the parts played by the British saints, Cuthbert and Bede in bringing Christianity to England'.[2] What either might have made of his putative 'Britishness' in this press release is perhaps best unexplored (for once again one can imagine Bede near boiling point), but this was an ambitious proposal for a building designed, in plan, to recall the jewel in St Cuthbert's Cross, which was recovered from his coffin in Durham Cathedral. It was to include an exhibition, a museum, state-of-the-art interactive computer systems and a chapel, but eventually foundered owing to the failure of the Millennium Commission to find the necessary £53,000,000 of funding.

Whether or not either of these projects would have provided an appropriate means of commemorating the late seventh- and early eighth-century scholar and monk of Wearmouth/Jarrow is very largely a matter of personal taste, but both reveal the memory of Bede to be still a live issue even at the close of the second millennium AD and on into the next. Indeed, one such project was brought to a successful conclusion: Tyneside now has Bede's World, constructed at Jarrow close to where he was buried in 735, the main exhibition centre of which was opened by Her Majesty the Queen in December 2000. Perhaps the whole issue of Bede's commemoration is best served there.

This book begins by exploring the ways in which later generations have remembered Bede and valued his works, starting with his immediate followers and running right up to the twentieth century, then homes in on the conception of the *Ecclesiastical History* to explore his purposes in writing his

Figure 1 The commemoration of Bede in an insular context

longest and best-known 'historical' work and review how he expected his immediate audience to respond thereto.

Why this particular focus? Because these are arguably the most important single issues in determining how today we should read Bede, and it is how our own generation can best appreciate and take from the *Ecclesiastical History* that lies at the heart of this project. Necessarily, how we envisage Bede's own agenda as he set about the task of writing should affect how we read the *EH*, the authority we confer on the work, and the ways in which we explore it both as a piece of literature and as an historical source for the period.

1 (Re-)Reading Bede: an author and his audience

> The present looks back at some great figure of an earlier century and wonders,
> Was he on our side? Was he a goodie?[1]

Each year, hundreds – perhaps thousands – read Bede's *Ecclesiastical History* for the first time. Others reread it, perhaps after a lengthy break, or turn to another of his numerous works which they had not before opened. For the vast majority, the initial experience will be via a modern translation into English. In the case of the *Ecclesiastical History*, which is today by far the most widely read of his works, this will almost certainly be in one of the two paperback translations published respectively by Penguin and Oxford University Press.[2]

Why read Bede? Most present-day readers approach his work as an entrée to investigation of early Anglo-Saxon England, be that primarily in areas historical, literary, archaeological or ecclesiastical. Bede's writings, taken together, dwarf those of any contemporary or near-contemporary, insular author,[3] and his breadth of interests and depth of scholarship are incomparable. It is with good reason that he is commonly termed 'the Father of English History', or even 'Master of the Middle Ages',[4] albeit both terms carry connotations that may be less than helpful to our understanding of his work. The *Ecclesiastical History* is a set text on many university history syllabuses, so a work which is studied both in different ways and at various levels: some passages may be explored in considerable detail, as a 'source' for broader discussion of the period and/or in order to cast light on the author's purposes in writing what and how he did. So too, on occasion, are several of his other works on course reading lists, in a wide variety of disciplinary studies, although some of these are more likely to appear as secondary or optional reading than as set texts, to be consulted in detail in support of a specific issue,[5] rather than read as a whole. Other modern readers will approach Bede's works as a consequence of a variety of stimuli received from different media, including magazine articles, television and books, in accordance with their own agendas. In each instance, their purpose will, at least initially, direct the way that the individual chooses to read. Some will find it sufficient to use key words or names and the modern index, so never gain much impression of the overall shape of the work. Others will focus exclusively on particular books or specified chapters, while some will start at the beginning and attempt the whole, using modern commentaries and notes. A comparative few will approach Bede in the original language, which is a very different experience again, although it is worth noting that the Latin of the *Ecclesiastical History* is far easier to read than that of much of his exegesis – his biblical commentaries.

In what ways can we – even should we – read Bede's work in the twenty-first century? How can we react to it? What does Bede mean to us, and what did he intend his work to mean? How does the early eighth century address the twenty-first, and how should the twenty-first respond? These questions, and many others in like vein, are important issues that are likely to spring to mind as we begin to turn the pages and (re-)read Bede's *History*, or others of his works, and all are better addressed early in the process.

It is important to bear in mind that every reader opening Bede does so with some preconception of the author, which derives, however distantly, from the ways in which he has been commemorated and his work utilised over the following twelve to thirteen centuries. Who has not been exposed to his 'venerability', for example, so his reputation as a holy man and truth-teller? The purpose of this book is to help the twenty-first-century reader with an interest in the history of the period at whatever level to interpret Bede's *Ecclesiastical History*, by exploring primarily why and in what circumstances he wrote it. In furtherance of this objective, we need first to explore the interface between Bede, as author, and ourselves as the ultimate consumers of his works but following successive generations of consumption and commentary, all of which has impacted on modern traditions of Bedan scholarship.

Bede's persona

We know very little about any individual living around 700. Bede is arguably among the better known, but it is important to recognise just how limited our knowledge actually is. Excepting only Acca's letter to Bede which has survived as a preface to *On Luke*, his life passed unnoticed, by name at least, in any surviving text written by anyone other than himself until after his death. Although we can safely assume that he was male, was born c.672–3 and almost certainly died in 735, having only quite recently finished his *Ecclesiastical History*, we have little further information about his person. He was a monk at an eccentrically double-sited monastery dedicated to SS Peter and Paul, at Wearmouth/Jarrow,[6] but we cannot reconstruct the Rule under which he lived in any detail,[7] and so the precise pattern of his life and the daily round of the monastic office to which he submitted himself. He claimed to have joined that community at the age of seven, to have been ordained deacon at what we might think the precocious age of nineteen,[8] and priest at the canonical age of thirty, but we have no independent means of verification of the dates of any of these milestones in his life. We have no idea of his appearance, other than the assumption that his hair was cut according to the Petrine tonsure – he may have been fair or dark, short or tall, we just do not know. We have no knowledge of his family or wider kin, other than the presumption that they were neither royal, at one end of the spectrum, nor members of the rural proletariat at the other.[9] He claimed to have been born on lands which were later granted to the monastery, so most probably in the Tyne–Wear lowlands (but that is an assumption), and seems always to have identified himself as 'English', so from that part of the community which believed itself, at least, to be descended from fifth/sixth-century immigrants, primarily from north-west Germany. But this is hardly a very rounded portrait.

Archaeological excavations have done much to provide a picture of Wearmouth and Jarrow at this date,[10] through which to contextualise Bede as author in a particular and most unusual space. St Peter's at Wearmouth (now Monkwearmouth: the place-name is self-explanatory) was constructed close to the estuary on or adjacent to a pre-existing burial ground on sloping ground close to a natural harbour. The work was undertaken by Gaulish/ Frankish craftsmen and was sufficiently far advanced for consecration to occur in 674. They erected a church of a kind with which they were familiar in Merovingian Gaul, of coarsely shaped stone rubble rendered externally by yellow and internally with pink mortar and with coloured glass in the windows.[11] The associated cemetery contained exclusively male burials, suggesting that women were not normally resident here.

The name 'Jarrow' refers to 'fen' or 'bog', which had been used to construct the name of a local group or tribe, 'the Gyrwe', comparable to the similarly named community around Peterborough whom Bede mentioned on occasion (*EH* III, 20; IV, 6, 19). Jarrow was likewise adjacent to good harbourage but built on a more restricted site, on the north bank of the River Don, a tributary of the Tyne, on the lesser of two slight rises (the other was later occupied by Jarrow Hall): whether the lesser elevation was preferred *ab initio*, or the higher one unavailable for some reason, is not clear. Construction was apparently undertaken without assistance from overseas, using coursed blocks of stone apparently robbed from so far unlocated Roman buildings and constructed on foundations of cobblestones and clay laid in trenches – a technique not present at Wearmouth but known on some Roman sites in the region, so perhaps copied from the buildings which this spoliation had demolished.

Architectural remains on both sites include numerous lathe-turned shafts, which reflect continental architectural influences. That they were already present by the early eighth century finds a somewhat surprising confirmation in Bede's reference to them in his commentary on the Song of Songs.[12] As a youth, he would presumably have witnessed Jarrow church's construction and consecration in the early 680s,[13] and also the building of two related buildings of similar construction and on the same alignment some 16.7m to the south, the larger of which was over 29m long and probably of two storeys, with an *opus signinum* floor derivative of Roman practice (of cement coloured by broken brick), plus window glass and a stone slate roof. It has been suggested that this building was the monastic refectory, and the rather smaller but similarly equipped, subdivided building to the east on the same alignment may have served both as a hall and for more private functions. Another large stone building on the terracing to the south, with wall-plaster and coloured window glass, was an elaborate hall which has been interpreted as a late seventh-century guest-house. Both sites were clearly very different in conception and execution from the Irish-inspired monastic sites of the period in this region, as exemplified by the timber building tradition at Lindisfarne reported by Bede himself, but similarities existed with Wilfrid's foundations in stone at Ripon and Hexham.

This 'man-made environment' has been interpreted as 'the visible expression of an ideal' – and a particularly 'Roman' ideal at that – to which Bede himself is assumed to have been party, and the central part played in both foundations by King Ecgfrith as patron highlights the extent to which 'imperial' aspirations may have underlined allusions to Rome.[14] The virtual absence in the excavations of finds reminiscent of personal items contrasts with their profusion at Whitby, for example, suggesting that the monks were discouraged from having personal possessions, although Cuthbert's letter on the death of Bede may require us to reconsider this impression (see below).

Archaeology can tell us something of Bede's physical environs, therefore, but what of his person? To what extent might he have been infirm by the time he wrote the EH? Cuthbert's description of his final days has Bede dictating rather than writing, and modern experience would suggest that his eyesight may well already have deteriorated to the point that he could neither read nor write at latest by around 720, when he would have been in his late forties, so it is quite likely that his later works were dictated, and even composed with assistants – perhaps even a close team of helpers. On this reading, the revision (Retractatio) of his earlier Commentary on the Acts of the Apostles on the basis of improved access to a Greek text of the Bible perhaps required at least one other of his brethren to have had a reading knowledge of Greek. Bede was certainly later considered to be virtually blind at the end of his life, hence the apocryphal story of his being tricked by his brethren into delivering a sermon to an audience of stones, only for the angels to reply, 'Amen, very venerable Bede',[15] but this story derives from the thirteenth century and is clearly of a type which we experience elsewhere, designed to reinforce the holiness of the individual by rebutting the scepticism of putative companions. Otherwise, there is no real evidence of ill health and, on balance, we should probably think of Bede as comparatively fit throughout the bulk of his life.

To my knowledge, Bede's sexuality has not been discussed in the modern period, but it is a legitimate issue if we are interested in his person, even if we can make virtually no progress here, for there is very little evidence. As already noted, the cemetery evidence implies a single-sex community and, as a priest, we might assume that Bede had relatively little personal contact with women, yet in his Commentary on the Seven Catholic Epistles he wrote as if he were married.[16] There is otherwise virtually no means of exploring his own perception of his sexuality, other than to note that his addresses to male correspondents were far less effusive than those of his fellow Northumbrian, Alcuin, two generations later,[17] and there is even less cause to postulate a queer personal history in Bede's case than in that of his contemporary in the Fen country, St Guthlac.[18] It may be worth noting in addition that, even where Scripture offered respectable female personae capable of a gendered interpretation, Bede generally presented them to his audience typologically in a fashion far removed from their literal selves; so, for example, in *On Tobias*, Sara, Tobias's bride, became the type of the Gentiles as a counterweight to his father Tobit, who was presented as the type of the Jews.[19] In his exegesis, he followed the prevailing tradition of presenting Christ on occasion in feminine terms and the Wisdom of God via maternal rhetoric,[20] but this does not really get us very far. Bede may be best represented as either effectively asexual or to have been so preoccupied with other matters that issues regarding his own sexuality were excluded or suppressed, but this can only be an interim position on our part.

Even Bede's name is problematic: there are two entries in the list of priests in the *Liber Vitae* of Durham, one of which is presumably not our Bede;[21] it occurs as a marginal addition to some manuscripts of Bede's prose *Life of Cuthbert*, as the name of Cuthbert's priest,[22] who may perhaps, but need not, be the other Bede in the *Liber Vitae*. There is in addition a certain Bede son of Bubba in the genealogy of the kings of Lindsey in the Anglian collection, and a Bieda in the *Anglo-Saxon Chronicle*,[23] but that is all. The name almost certainly derives from the OE *bēd*, meaning 'prayer' or 'supplication', and is connected also with *bēodan*, 'to bid, command'.[24] If this was his birth-name, then it may imply that it was always his family's intention that this offspring should follow a monastic or clerical career, so contextualising his kinsmen's surrender of the young boy to monastic care, which he later described as if both responsible and purposeful.[25] Otherwise, it is conceivable that the name was given him at the point of entry to Wearmouth by Benedict Biscop, whose own name is presumably other than that which he received at birth.[26]

The name by which he is now often known is equally problematic: 'the Venerable Bede'. Use of the definite article threatens to convert Bede into a common noun. We do not normally speak of 'the prolific Margaret Drabble', for example, or 'the telegenic David Attenborough', although the construction is not unique in modern vernacular. It reflects somewhat clumsy efforts in English to retain the sense of Latin *venerabilis*, which frequently accompanied reference to Bede from the central Middle Ages onwards, when it was eventually attributed to angelic authority (as above). This first appears in the ninth century, when Bede was among several figures described as 'venerable' in the records of the Church Councils held at Aix/Aachen in 816 and 836,[27] and the term was applied to him shortly thereafter by Paul the Deacon in a homily.[28] The connection eventually became commonplace, then virtually obligatory. A concluding sentence appears to have been added at an unknown but comparatively early date to copies of the letter by his protégé Cuthbert: 'Here ends Cuthbert's letter on the death of the venerable priest, Bede' – which cannot have been part of the original. It recurs in the earliest versions of his life (see below, p. 28) and also in Simeon's early twelfth-century *History of the Church of Durham*,[29] and then in much later transcriptions of his epitaph at Durham, but there is neither contemporary nor near-contemporary evidence for Bede's 'venerability'. The word is not used in the early epitaphs.[30] Alcuin similarly did not use the term of Bede in his poem, *On the Bishops, Kings, and Saints of York*, although he did of Gregory the Great, Archbishop Egbert of York and the hermit Echa.[31] Rather, he described Bede variously as 'a famous priest and teacher' (line 685), 'a priest of outstanding merits' (1289), *magister* ('master': 1207, 1305, 1315), *doctor* ('teacher': 1307) and 'blessed father' (1317–18). Bede was included in several eleventh-century calendars but always as 'St Bede', with or without 'priest'.[32] Bede's 'venerability' is, therefore, very much a later construct, originating apparently in the ninth and gaining hold in the eleventh–twelfth centuries, but it is a powerful one. While the term has on occasion been used of many individual churchmen, it has long been linked quite specifically with this particular figure, for who today does not think of Bede when the expression 'the venerable' is used? It has become part of his modern-day persona, a central feature of his mythology, part of the tough hide which keeps at bay the arrows and spears of historical huntsmen. It must be said that 'saint' would work better in English but that might at various stages have risked losing the very 'Englishness' of this icon of insular scholarship by intruding what could have seemed an unpalatably papist term.

So far so good, but we need to be very cautious regarding the vehicles by which much of this very limited information has reached us. Although we can make reasonable judgements about some aspects of Bede's person on the basis of his surviving work – his Latinity and scholarship for example, his religious and cultural positioning and vision of ethnicity, his place of domicile – we are very dependent for personal details on two short texts from the 730s. One is the brief vignette that he himself provided at the close of the *Ecclesiastical History*, sandwiched between his recapitulation of events in chronicle form and a list of his own works which, in turn, forms the natural corollary of a life given over to his 'delight to learn or to teach or to write'. The second is the letter describing his death written, ostensibly at least, by his pupil Cuthbert, probably the later abbot of that name of Wearmouth/Jarrow, to the otherwise unknown Cuthwin.[33] Most later discussions of Bede as a person begin with long quotations from either or both texts, or at least lengthy paraphrases of their contents, with little discussion of the nature of either.[34] It is worth stressing that both pieces are highly rhetorical and should be read with an awareness of the genres and conventions to which each conforms.

Let us begin with Bede's own comments, which provide slightly the earlier of our two passages. His decision to insert an autobiographical paragraph in the last chapter of the final book of the final draft of the *Ecclesiastical History* may have been prompted by his reading of pre-existing histories. Gregory of Tours's provision of a similar piece at the close of his *History* has some similarities but also major differences, as has Jerome's final autobiographical sketch in his *Concerning Illustrious Men*, but neither even begin to rival the plenitude of personal and family information provided by Josephus at the close of his *Judean Antiquities*.[35] Bede's needs to be read very much in combination with the Preface with which the work starts, since, taken together, these frame the entirety of his narrative, and provide Bede with important opportunities both to position and to reinforce the authority of his own voice, as author, as he completed the work.

The Preface begins with the dedication, *Gloriosissimo regi Ceoluulfo Beda famulus Christi et presbyter* ('To the most glorious king Ceolwulf, Bede, servant of Christ and priest'). While the immediate juxtaposition of the names of recipient and author occurs in preceding histories which Bede had read,[36] and was comparatively common in contemporary epistolary convention, Bede's normal practice varied in the opening lines of his own narrative works. Take, for example, the first lines of the Prologue to his prose *Life of Cuthbert*, in which he and Bishop Eadfrith both appear but in comparative isolation from one another: *Domino sancto ac beatissimo patri Eadfrido episcopo, sed et omni congregationi fratrum qui in Lindisfarnensi insula Christo deseruiunt, Beda . . .* ('To the holy and most blessed father, Bishop Eadfrith, and also to the whole congregation of brethren who serve Christ on the island of Lindisfarne, Bede . . .'[37]). In *Concerning Ezra and Nehemiah*, written perhaps within the same half-decade as the *Ecclesiastical History*, dedication to Bishop Acca only occurs in line 10 of the modern edition, without juxtaposition of his own name,[38] and the dedicatee of *Concerning the Reckoning of Time*, written *c.*725, is buried in line 39.[39]

A similar tactic could easily have been adopted in the *Ecclesiastical History*. That it was not may suggest that Bede here sought the rhetorical impact which juxtaposition of his own name with that of the king offered, as an assertion both of his right to a presence in this august company and of the equality of his own identity vis-à-vis the secular social fabric personified by the king, based on his priestly rank and claims on Christ's patronage. Although the Preface is to an extent conditioned by the expressions of humility conventional in the opening lines of a piece of hagiography of the period, this aspect is comparatively low key and it is in other respects a masterpiece of positioning which sets out his own self-perception as an historian. Bede portrayed the king as if dependent on himself as author, eager to acquaint himself with the work both in its first draft (which he had already seen) and in its present state, and as its enthusiastic recipient and consumer. He presented himself, in contrast, as a gracious benefactor to the king, then as if a wise teacher to his royal pupil and shepherd to his sheep.[40] This offers a comparatively elevated self-perception, although there are modesty formulae included in later passages: so only Albinus's encouragement led him 'to dare to undertake' the task and he closed with a plea to his audience to request God's mercy for 'my weaknesses both of mind and body', but these are only a very minor part of this opening, framing section of the text and there is no apology for any inadequacies of style, which convention might have suggested.

Otherwise the Preface consists of a long but retrospective account of the nature of the *History* and its meaning, and of Bede's methods and the limits of his own responsibility, to which we shall return in chapter 2. On balance, it betrays his confidence in his status as author and, implicitly at least, claims the role of moral guide to both court and country. Despite the conventions of humility which it adopts and the single superlative attached to the king, the authorial position is one which is far from subservient towards his royal patron, whose position and power do not in any sense seem to overawe Bede. Rather, he was putting forward his own deeply held vision of his personal role with considerable confidence.

The final narrative passage opens: *Haec de historia ecclesiastica Brittaniarum, et maxime gentis Anglorum . . . Domino adiuuante digessi Baeda famulus Christi et presbyter monasterii beatorum apostolorum Petri et Pauli . . .* ('This ecclesiastical history of Britain, and particularly of the people of the English . . . Bede, servant of Christ and priest of the monastery of the blessed apostles Peter and Paul has put together with the aid of God . . .'). Although now separate from the overt proximity of king Ceolwulf and the court, this passage reintroduces Bede's person and his self-positioning, his vision of the status of his work and his own authority as author, resting on all of God, Christ and SS Peter and Paul. This message was reinforced once more by the final words of both chapter and *History* after the list of his own works, which reverts to the first person and is framed as a prayer *bone Iesu* ('to the good Jesus') in thanks for receipt of 'the Word which tells of Thee' (the Scriptures), with which his own words just written are thereby connected, and acknowledges once again the divine aid vouchsafed the author in closing his *Ecclesiastical History of the English People*. Repetition of the phrase *famulus Christi et presbyter* at the opening of this passage connects back to its previous use in the context of his self-positioning in the Preface, and to his perception of his own, divinely aided work. It is in this context that we need to read the remainder of this passage.

The brief personal history that follows is not provided merely as an autobiographical sketch to satisfy the casual interest of the reader. In very general terms, this passage seems to have been included as a necessary part of the summation of the whole work in a fashion similar to his extended treatments of clerical heroes at the close of their roles within his history, as a fitting point at which to underline their authority as individuals beloved by God, and so to emphasise the validity and authority of their deeds. Both his personal details and the list of his works were arguably appended as a means of reinforcing his own authority as author. More specifically, it emphasises his personification of the greater authority and identity of the monastery of Wearmouth/Jarrow, its patron saints and the God they represented,[41] in whose glorious presence they now sat. Figuratively at least, Bede was claiming an exceptional ownership of that identity from even before the monastery was actually founded, by his birth on what would become its estates, then via his formal removal into the community as at an age pregnant with symbolic meaning.[42] He positioned himself as an early acolyte of the 'most reverend' founder, Benedict Biscop, whose praises he had already sung both in his *History of the Abbots*, to which he referred, of course, later in this chapter, and in a homily which was presumably read within the monastery on the annual festival associated with his death.[43] Benedict Biscop had been an important figure in royal circles up to his last illness, *c.*686 (he died in 689), and was perhaps remembered as such in 731, particularly given that he was presented earlier in this same text (IV, 18 (16)) in honorific terms. Bede's second association here was with Ceolfrith, who likewise appears herein (as the author of a letter to the Picts on the Paschal controversy, V, 21) and more substantially in the *History of the Abbots*, who was the subject of a separate and anonymous *Life* written at Wearmouth/Jarrow,[44] and who had departed for Rome only to die *en route* in 716. These authoritative figures Bede claimed as responsible for his own education, so he was presenting himself, metaphorically at least, as their representative in the context of his authorship of the *Ecclesiastical History*. He was, therefore, in 731 positioning himself as a unique embodiment of the traditions and sanctity of his own house and as the spiritual successor to its founders.

This self-positioning might gain something from a reading of the anonymous *Life of Ceolfrith*, which outlines the consequences of plague deaths at the nascent monastery at Jarrow in the 680s, following which only 'the abbot himself and one little boy, who had been brought up and taught by him, and who now at this day, being in priest's orders in the same monastery, duly commends the abbot's praiseworthy acts both by his writings and his discourse to all desiring to know them,'[45] were available to maintain the monastic office. This 'little boy' has often been assumed to have been the young Bede, and the connection is certainly feasible – perhaps even attractive, albeit problems of authorship and date plus the failure to name him should restrain us from too confident an opinion regarding his identity.[46] Whether or not this was Bede, however, the dramatic plague deaths surely did bulk large in the story of Jarrow's foundation, serving to divide recollection of its initial story from what was in most respects its later re-establishment with an almost entirely new intake of brethren. An individual who could claim to represent in his own person the pre-plague community and its first but now-deceased abbot, Ceolfrith, *ab initio*, was in a very special position of authority in 731 when composing a historical commentary.

Bede's next remark, that 'I have spent all my life in this monastery', is too easily read as an indication that he had hardly, if ever, left Wearmouth/Jarrow, as modern accounts frequently suggest, but this once again needs to be read in context and with a degree of caution. This comment is part of his wider self-positioning as author which encompasses all of the education provided him by Benedict Biscop and Ceolfrith, his own consequent delight in learning, his commitment to the monastic office, his successive ordinations, in dutiful obedience to the authority of Abbot Ceolfrith, at the hands of a well-reputed, putatively saintly and canonically appointed bishop, plus the impressive and, as far as can be judged, comparatively inclusive listing of his works, which follows. These few words regarding his domicile should not be read too literally. Rather, they once again emphasise his claim on the monastery and its authority, but this time in terms of the regularity of his behaviour as a member of its brethren and in obedience to its Rule.

First of all, we need to remember that Bede's monastery existed on two sites, 5 or 6 miles – so perhaps two hours' travelling time – apart. There is no indication whether both had *scriptoria* or manuscript collections, but it seems very likely. Ceolfrith had great gospels (termed 'pandects') written for each of the two churches and it seems difficult to imagine that the books which he and Benedict Biscop had collected were arranged in such a way as to deny many inmates easy access to a proportion, at least, at any one time. Indeed, the need to duplicate works may well have been an important stimulus to the undoubted energy of Wearmouth/Jarrow as a centre of manuscript production. Although Bede is generally associated quite specifically with Jarrow, this is primarily because, on his own admission, he was swept up as a youth in Ceolfrith's initial establishment of the house there *c.*681, soon after his entry to Wearmouth, and he was then reputedly buried there in 735. But during other stages of his life there is no particular reason to prefer this site's claims on Bede's person to Wearmouth's, any more than we should particularly associate Ceolfrith with Jarrow, given that he was long abbot of both and set out from Wearmouth on his final journey to the continent. Wearmouth was the founding site and always seems to have been the larger as well as the senior.[47] Given the dogged insistence on the unity of the double monastery expressed in his *History of the Abbots*, Bede may well have taught the young brethren of both communities – we simply do not know. So, supposing his scholarship and teaching to have required frequent reference to manuscripts held at both sites, we should probably imagine Bede as regularly travelling between them, perhaps by road and trackway, perhaps by sea. Others of his numerous brethren presumably did likewise,[48] as so too, one imagines, did the managers and senior operatives of their estates and the abbot himself. The monks may even have had regular carriers back and forth, to allow them to order up texts and other small items. We read in contemporary correspondence of messengers carrying books and manuscripts between more distant houses. Both sites were relatively accessible by ship, and a stray remark by Bede, in his *Commentary on the Acts of the Apostles*, betrays his familiarity with the use of 'millstone-sized stones behind the stern of ships in the British sea to hold a ship back in high wind'.[49] While he could, of course, have gained this detail from a visitor or one of his brethren whom we know to have journeyed abroad, it just might indicate that Bede was himself a seasoned sea-voyager, at least on in-shore vessels.

The sedentary impression engendered by too literal a reading of Bede's comment in *Ecclesiatical History* V, 24 is, in practice, dispersed by various other of his writings, which reveal that, by the end of his life, he had travelled on at least one occasion to Bishop Egbert's monastery, which commentators have generally assumed to have been at York (around 75 miles (120 km) direct and much further by road or sea), and had intended so to do again had not infirmity intervened.[50] He had earlier visited Lindisfarne at least once (around 60 miles (95 km) direct), perhaps by sea.[51] These are the only journeys to known destinations, but a letter to the otherwise unknown Wicthed, priest,[52] reveals that Bede had also recently visited his monastery. The text assumes Wicthed's ability to follow a complex series of references to existing authorship, which implies a well-established library, such as may, of course, have encouraged Bede's visit. Others of his letters combined with notice of his sources in the Preface of the *Ecclesiastical History* reveal a wide-flung acquaintance, stretching as far as Kent, Wessex, East Anglia and Lindsey as well as throughout Northumbria, and his forms of address often suggest that these literary connections were built upon face-to-face meetings and friendships established at first hand: take, for example, his letter to the otherwise unknown Helmwald, 'his most beloved brother in Christ', whose unnamed monastery was 'such vast distances of land and sea' away,[53] so perhaps outside Northumbria, or his comparatively numerous and intimate addresses to Bishop Acca, with whom Bede clearly shared his delight in exegesis even despite his diocesan's fundamental misunderstanding of one of his commentaries, as revealed in his extended letter, *On What Isaiah Says*.[54] Several recent commentators have assumed, reasonably enough, that Bede had visited Hexham, although that is nowhere made explicit. But not all this acquaintance is likely to have derived entirely from the visits of others to Wearmouth/Jarrow, nor from connections which owed their inception and maintenance to purely literary mechanisms. The fact is, Bede knew significant numbers of individuals at other houses and he had arguably become acquainted with some of them, at least, while staying with them.

It is worth bearing in mind just how mobile seventh- and early eighth-century society actually was. Kings, their families, companions and servants regularly travelled so as to consume the produce of their estates, show themselves to society at large, adjudicate in disputes, visit friends and associates, fight, hunt and otherwise manage their affairs, and most of the landed classes probably behaved similarly. Youths, in particular, seem to have spent much time away from their immediate families, in fosterage, journeying, seeking patronage or serving as military retainers. Early episodes in the lives of Wilfrid, Cuthbert and Guthlac all provide illustration. And even the poor seem to have journeyed, be it on the business of their superiors, to escape exactions, to seek cures or merely to take flocks and herds to distant pastures in the summer months, all of which are evidenced in the same works. So too did priests and monks travel widely: Bede's own work provides numerous examples of religious and clerics from Northumbria crossing the seas to Ireland or the continent, as well as conducting many journeys closer to home, and others from neighbouring regions clearly paid extended visits. Several brethren at Wearmouth/Jarrow had begun their religious careers in other houses and Bede was arguably distinguishing himself from such herein, and claiming credit thereby as a member of the hard core of monks within his own house who had been there since taking monastic vows. Bede inhabited a world, therefore, in which men (and women) did travel extensively, for a wide variety of social, religious, economic or military reasons. His comments need indicate nothing more than that he had never been a member of another monastery but had been a member of Wearmouth/Jarrow throughout his life. Bede may well have travelled extensively as a young man – we cannot be sure.

We may well conclude, therefore, with Dorothy Whitelock, that Bede may have been absent from his monastery rather more than is immediately evident from his brief comment in *Ecclesiastical History* V, 24,[55] and that had more of his correspondence survived we would probably have been presented with a very different picture. That said, there is no reason to suppose that he ever travelled outside England, let alone to Rome as was once supposed.[56] On the contrary, there is no sign that he joined those of his brethren who visited the Holy See at the turn of the century, of whom his friend and eventual abbot Hwætberht was one, or those who shared Ceolfrith's last journey, then variously carried on to visit the pope, remained with his body at Langres on the upper Marne, and/or returned.[57] Bede was clearly not the type of Anglo-Saxon, clerical tourist represented a little later by St Willibald, whose ten-year peregrination of the Holy Land was later to be described by his relative, Huneberc of Heidenheim.[58] Rather, his principal journeys were imaginative ones, framed variously by his reading and his authorship, or his own passage through life and onwards into death, to which we must now turn, but he was probably much less sedentary than he has, perhaps inadvertently, led us to suppose.

We have seen that Bede's brief account of himself in the last chapter of his *Ecclesiastical History* was not developed as an objective, autobiographical note intended to satisfy the curiosity of some later reader regarding its author. Read in combination with expressions of his own self-perception and his purposes within the Preface, it is clear that the personal information which he offered was selected and presented primarily so as to sustain a particular interpretation of his own authorial status, so by extension that of the work which it both defends and concludes. His listing of his previous works there-after reinforces the point, starting as they do with works of exegesis arranged in their biblical order, then his letters, histories of the saints, of his abbots and of the English Church, and lastly his works as a monastic teacher. However, our over-dependence on Bede's own autobiographical comments should alert us to the dangers of uncritical treatment. It is poor history to take this passage out of context and present it as a neutral and objective account of Bede's life and as if invested with some universal validity capable of speaking literally to the present regarding the innermost thoughts of its author on himself.[59]

The second of our accounts is that contained in a letter written by Cuthbert, describing himself as 'deacon', to the otherwise unknown Cuthwin.[60] Bede's recent death (late on 25, or on 26 May 735) forms the context of the letter, and Cuthbert expressed his satisfaction at having already learned that

Cuthwin's community had offered 'masses and devout prayers' for his soul. The bulk of this work is given over to a comparatively detailed account of his last weeks, and more particularly his last few days, his repeated rendition of an Old English poem concerning death (now generally known as *Bede's Death Song*), his continuing routine as teacher of Cuthbert and other pupils, his attention to, and delight in, the monastic office, and his efforts to complete both a translation of the first part of the Gospel of St John and a critical collection of annotated excerpts from Isidore of Seville's *Concerning Natural Things*. Although there has been an attempt to cast doubt on the authenticity of this letter,[61] this has not generally found favour: the details regarding the works in progress and Bede's preoccupations at this point seem plausible in the light of his recent *Letter to Egbert*, the author is probably identifiable as a later abbot of Wearmouth/Jarrow, and Cuthbert's concern to share his recollections with a friend at another monastery where Bede was known and valued provides a credible context. In general terms, therefore, it seems safer to accept the letter as an authentic account by an eyewitness of Bede's death than to suppose it to be a later fabrication.

That said, this letter should not be read uncritically or taken too literally. Within it are embedded well-established literary forms of the day, including conventional expressions of authorial humility which are registered at both the opening and the close. It should be recognised additionally that it was not written immediately after Bede's death but only after a comparatively complex series of events: following his decease and burial, news had reached Cuthwin's brethren by some unknown mechanism, who had reacted by remembering Bede in the mass and in their prayers; then Cuthwin had written to Cuthbert, apparently predominantly on unrelated matters, all before Cuthbert wrote the letter which survives. It seems likely that several weeks had elapsed, at least, and perhaps more, during which the experience of witnessing Bede's death presumably resonated at Wearmouth/Jarrow, and the significance of particular aspects of his last days was developed in discussion or personal reflection. The letter was the work of a witness who saw Bede very much as his own 'father' and 'master', so was very closely involved with events on an emotional level and was prone to investing his death with a particular set of culturally determined meanings. He wrote 'from love of him'. Read literally, the letter tells of the death of an elderly and infirm individual who recognised that he was approaching his end and sought comfort in well-tried religious behaviours which he had embraced throughout his long life – so in singing the psalms, hymns and antiphons. Several of Bede's works suggest, understandably enough, that he was habitually nervous regarding death and the interface it represented with the afterlife.[62] His distress was apparent in his repeated bursting into tears, which upset onlookers. It tells also of his concern to complete the work of translating into English the *Gospel according to St John* from the beginning to VI, 9 (the opening of the story of the Feeding of the Five Thousand), and to finish his book of extracts from Isidore's work, which he was keen to annotate for the benefit of his pupils. His concern for the pastoral care of those incapable of Latin, plus an eagerness to establish the veracity of reading matter available to his younger brethren, both form a natural part of Bede's self-positioning as teacher and scholar, or *doctor*.

This narrative is accompanied in the letter, however, by layers of interpretation: it was Cuthbert's purpose to present his teacher as one who was *pro Deo dilecto* – 'chosen by God' and peculiarly 'blessed'; his work of translation was not reported neutrally but was 'to the great profit of the Church'; all witnesses to his death were cited as in collective agreement that Bede had approached his death in a state of 'incomparable holiness and peace' (which does not sit entirely comfortably with other internal comment, which points rather to his anxiety); direct speech was used extensively and consists largely of quotation from or allusion to sacred text. It is unclear whether we should presume this to have been Bede's responsibility or Cuthbert's, but the latter, as author, is obviously a real possibility. Cuthbert sought to develop his master's sanctity, by reporting, for example, that he and all his companions believed that he had known when his end would be, a feature which is commonly attributed to saints at this date,[63] and that they were all confident of his entry in triumph to the sacred realm: 'without doubt we may believe that, since he always laboured here in praise of God, so his soul was carried by angels to the joys of heaven of which he was desirous'. Again, the carriage by angels of the soul of the departed into the afterlife was a literary device common within hagiography, to be found for example in Bede's own accounts of St Cuthbert as witness to the ascension of St Aidan,[64] and Begu of St Hild,[65] and dependent ultimately on the ascensions of Elijah and Christ. While Cuthbert did not claim to have witnessed such, as in these reported instances, his letter does present Bede's case within these conventions, and both he and his audience obviously knew these and other examples of the type.

Nor was the physicality of this death fully shared by Cuthbert with his friend. Bede's initial illness was characterised by 'frequent attacks of breathlessness but almost without pain'. On the penultimate day, his breathing became 'very much worse, and a slight swelling had appeared in his feet' but at that point his corporality passed behind a veil and the focus is entirely on the 'great holiness and peace' with which he spent his last hours: chanting 'songs to the glory of God, and spreading out his hands he ceased not to give God thanks'. Cuthbert's account was less about Bede's actual death, therefore, than about its Christian meaning to those who witnessed it.

Bede's distribution of his possessions raises similarly major issues. Cuthbert wrote: 'he said to me: "I have some precious things in my box, namely some pepper, cloths and incense. Run quickly and fetch the priests of our monastery, and as donor I will distribute to them of what sort God has given me." ' The textiles (Colgrave translates *oraria* as 'napkins') were presumably intended for use within the mass, as covers for the host, cloths with which to wipe the chalice, or similar. Incense played a key role within the service. Their donation to fellow priests was therefore particularly appropriate. That said we might take a moment to recall just how exotic pepper and incense were at this date. Pepper derives from a perennial climbing shrub, *Piper nigrum*, which is indigenous to southern India and can only have reached Anglo-Saxon England via a laborious set of trade routes through Arabia, Byzantium and, perhaps, Frankia, Germany or Scandinavia, all of which rendered it both exotic and extremely expensive, so presumably accessible only to a small social élite. Frankincense came via the same set of trade routes from Arabia and the Horn of Africa, where it was derived from trees of the genus *Boswellia*: again this was an exotic of extraordinarily high value. That Bede should have had both in his gift in quantities capable of being divided between several – perhaps even numerous – recipients goes some way to challenging the impression gained from archaeology that the monks of Wearmouth/Jarrow had few if any personal possessions and raises again the issue of the Rule he followed. At the same time, Bede's effects have the capacity to remind us that this was a richly endowed, royal house, which was fully engaged with the Northumbrian system of élite patronage, and probably had links too to Frankia.[66] Cuthbert seems to have included the incident in order to illustrate the appropriateness of his behaviour on his death bed, giving his possessions to his senior brethren for their use in return for prayer on his behalf, as opposed, for example, to leaving anything outside the community, to his blood relations or others. This was represented as engaging the whole community, and not just his pupils, in the sadness of his imminent death but the joy of his anticipated entry to everlasting life, but Bede's actions also resonate, of course, with Wearmouth/Jarrow's papal privilege of some thirty years earlier and the concern of Benedict Biscop, even earlier, to exclude his own family from inheritance of the monastery. That Bede had such exotic possessions does, however, underline his status within his own society as priest and author and as a senior figure inside a major monastic community, who was in friendly communication with many of the great and good across contemporary Anglo-Saxon society.

Cuthbert's letter is, therefore, less an objective account of Bede's death than a first salvo in the ensuing debate as to how he should be commemorated and remembered. It is Bede's reputation as blessed interpreter of the sacred that should be considered the cardinal message of this narrative, not the details deployed in its support. At the close Cuthbert stated his intention to write a fuller account at some later date, which suggests that he may have intended a full-blown hagiography. Whether or not he achieved this, no such work has survived or was certainly later referred to, but Cuthbert's correspondence when abbot (assuming that this was one and the same individual) does suggest that he was then promoting Bede's cult as a saint. The evidence comes in his letter as abbot to Lul, archbishop of Mainz, *c.*764, in which he refers to himself as 'a disciple of the priest Bede' and thanks his correspondent for receipt of the 'silk robe for the relics of Bede, our master of blessed memory, in remembrance and veneration of him'.[67] Thirty years later, therefore, the cult of St Bede was being promoted at Wearmouth/Jarrow,[68] and Abbot Cuthbert was in charge of this whole process. Of course, that does not mean that it was necessarily particularly successful: the Lorsch Calendar, which arguably derives from one which began its life at Wearmouth/ Jarrow, celebrates several insular figures, including St Cuthbert, Œthelwald (Cuthbert's successor as anchorite on Farne, with whom Bede opened *EH* V), and Benedict Biscop, but not Bede,[69] and he is likewise omitted from every surviving insular calendar prior to the 1020s, and several thereafter.[70]

Neither his own testimony nor that of his pupil, Cuthbert, should therefore be taken out of the cultural context within which each was conceived, as if capable of presenting an objective account of Bede to a modern audience. In both instances, the author's own purposes dominate the very limited detail which is offered. It is the overall impact on which they focused: the specifics were selected, edited and managed primarily in pursuit of their own particular agendas, which need to be recognised and evaluated before being adopted into ours. This does not mean that the details given were knowingly falsified – they probably were not on the whole, and then more by omission and/or selection than otherwise. However, it does mean that they cannot bear the weight which modern readers, in pursuit of their own very different purposes, are prone to place on these short passages.

Reputation and commemoration

Cuthbert is arguably best seen as the first in a long succession of authors seeking to develop and promote particular memories of Bede post-mortem, in a sequence which should be recognised as stretching right to the present day. Since these various commemorative strategies necessarily influence the ways in which we now view Bede and affect how we read meaning into his works, it is necessary to explore the cardinal points, at least, of this process, so as to make it explicit. As will become apparent, the purposes for which Bede has been memorialised have varied considerably across a period of almost 1300 years, with his name and work invoked in support of a wide variety of different causes. Yet in some respects his reputation has remained remarkably constant, characterised by a general, long-lived and recurring perception of him as both peculiarly gifted and particularly blessed – an image which was eventually to be encapsulated in the common currency of his 'venerability', which occurs repeatedly even in the titles of modern works. The excellence of his scholarship has been recognised at many different junctures and a high value attached to some, at least, of his works. Bede has been both described and judged primarily by his admirers, whose instincts have been to accentuate those aspects of his putative personality and/or output which they most admired or found most useful to their own purposes. Those who for their own reasons later found his work uncongenial in any way have generally been disinclined to challenge his formidable reputation directly but have tended either to work round him or to critique specific parts of his literary output while trenchantly defending others. There are very many variations in the way that Bede has been remembered, and several different senses in which he has been 'owned' by later writers, but there is comparatively little open discord overall, by comparison with treatments accorded numerous other historical figures.

Bedan texts were clearly valued by Anglo-Saxon missionaries in mid-eighth-century Germany, particular by St Boniface, his successors at Mainz and the monks of Fulda. Boniface wrote both to Archbishop Egbert at York and Abbot Hwætberht at Wearmouth/Jarrow in 746–7 asking for copies of his works, then again to Egbert in 747–51, having apparently received some texts, now asking for others by name.[71] Abbot Cuthbert later despatched both Bede's lives of St Cuthbert to Archbishop Lul, with a letter which suggests that, in severe wintry conditions, his *scriptorium* was struggling to keep up with demand. Further correspondence implies that continental requests thereafter continued unabated,[72] with specific pleas coming from Lul to the archbishop of York in the 760s or 770s.[73] Indeed, most of our earliest surviving manuscripts of the *Ecclesiastical History* found their way to Germany and were copied there, making the northern reaches of the Carolingian Empire by far the most important arena for the proliferation, then preservation, of Bedan texts across the eighth and ninth centuries. This seems to have been due to the significant number of Anglo-Saxons who engaged in mission there, who actively sought texts of relevance to themselves in their new role from 'back home', and who found in this work perspectives on mission, the life of the hermit and pilgrimage of particular relevance to themselves.[74] Readers – particularly Christian readers – of the *Ecclesiastical History* today sometimes comment on the 'feel good' factor which they experience, containing as it does tales about God-beloved men and women at English Christian centres or as missionaries overseas. This arguably had a far bigger effect among Anglo-Saxon missionaries, for whom it laid out a virtuous tradition of monastic and eremitic endeavour stretching right back to Gregory the Great, via a host of exemplary figures, both English and other, whose deeds they could emulate and against whom they could then measure themselves.

However, it is to another Northumbrian emigrant to Frankia, Alcuin, a teacher, writer and cultural impresario rather than a missionary, that we must turn for an extended treatment of Bede himself. Alcuin had been raised on Bede's works at the school at York, and was primarily responsible for their dissemination, reproduction and popularity among the Frankish monasteries of the early ninth century. He paid his respects to Bede in a lengthy poem, *On the Bishops, Kings, and Saints of the Church of York*, written for a readership primarily at York, probably in 781/2 or 792/3.[75] Bede's own *Concerning the Art of Metre* had almost certainly shaped Alcuin's approach to verse, so was fundamental to this his major poetic study: following notice of Bede's exegetical works, this was the first of his books that Alcuin praised (in line 1308). Two-thirds of this 1658-line work draws on the *Ecclesiastical History* or, to a lesser extent, Bede's two lives of St Cuthbert.[76] In a sense, Alcuin paid the *Ecclesiastical History* the same compliment that Bede had previously offered the anonymous *Life of St Cuthbert*: he rewrote a prose work which he valued and which was on a theme which he wished to develop, but in verse. That said, this rewriting was in conformity with his own very different purposes, which centred on York and its reputation as an archdiocese. Alcuin included an extended discussion of Bede and his monastic context which follows his treatment of Archbishop Egbert (that Egbert to whom Bede directed his letter in November 734) and his brother, King Eadberht of Northumbria. This sequence, which is slightly out of chronological order, serves to add his lustre to theirs, and this was apparently Alcuin's intention: Bede was *presbyter eximius meritis* ('a priest of exceptional merit') and *praeclarus doctor* ('a brilliant scholar'); his works were highly commendable and his life 'followed the footsteps of the ancient fathers in actions, spirit and faith'. Alcuin added a miracle: 'when a sick man was surrounded by relics of that blessed father he was completely cured from his illness', which is original to this work but perhaps suggests some debt to a posthumous healing cult of Bede at Wearmouth/Jarrow.

The principal source of his comments regarding Bede's person lies in Alcuin's own extensive acquaintance with his works, but most particularly the *Ecclesiastical History*, which had already been his primary quarry for those scenes from Northumbrian history which are featured to this point throughout his poem. Bede's admission to the monastery aged seven, his close associations with both Ceolfrith and Jarrow, his early love of learning and the breadth of his works all derive from *EH* V, 24 and, as his editor notes, the broad sequencing corresponds to that same passage.[77] Alcuin used the 'autobiographical' section of the *Ecclesiastical History*, therefore, as the basis for his appropriation of Bede as an ornament of Northumbrian Christianity capable of being positioned within the orbit of York, its churches and its archdiocese, to enhance the status, therefore, of his own alma mater. Among other things, Bede represented in this work Alcuin's vision of a cultural golden age in Northumbria in the early to mid-eighth century, out of which the school at York had emerged, contrasting, of course, with the picture of current ecclesiastical decline which Bede had himself invoked in his *Letter to Egbert*. He treated various other regional cult figures, such as Wilfrid, Cuthbert and Æthelthryth, in a similar fashion, mining their stories also for the greater glory of York, but it is primarily Bede's works that underpin Alcuin's – a debt that he frequently acknowledged as once again lending status to his poem.

Bede was actively commemorated, therefore, both in mid-eighth-century Northumbria and on the continent, where his texts were in demand. His admirer, Alcuin, developed his memory in a lengthy narrative poem based largely on Bede's own works, but explicitly as just one of several subsidiary hero-figures from within the archdiocese whom he used to underpin the greater story of York as a focus of ecclesiastical power, sanctity and learning. Combined, the missionary demand plus Alcuin's role within the Carolingian renaissance guaranteed Bede a receptive audience across Western Europe, and his works were arguably better known on the continent than in England by 800, where the *Ecclesiastical History*, at least, may quickly have lost much of

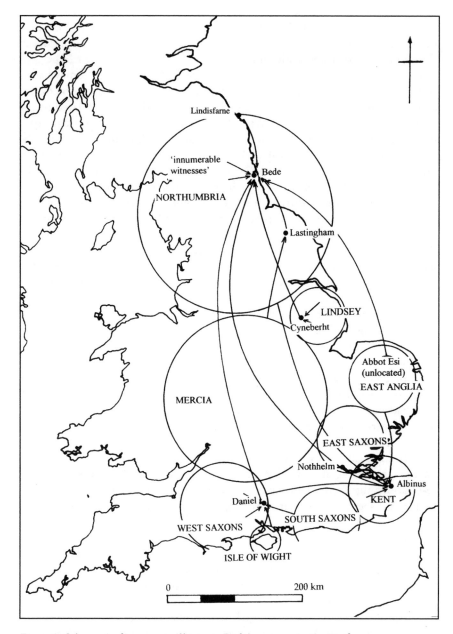

Figure 2 Schematic diagram to illustrate Bede's sources in the Preface

its appeal among the audience for which it was originally intended.[78] Many of Bede's works went on to become a staple of learning in the monasteries of Frankia and Italy thereafter, and his authority as author was recognised in the accounts of Church Councils in 816 and 836 (see above). These several strands came together at Fulda, *c.*819, when Hrabanus Maurus, in a poem on the dedication of the church of the Holy Saviour within the monastery, claimed his relics lay alongside those of several other Christian heroes of the period, in the crypt of his own monastic church.[79]

As regards his original domicile, our knowledge dissipates somewhat at this point. Bede is noticeably absent from the Lorsch Calendar (as above),[80] and also fails to appear in the only surviving northern calendar dated to the ninth century,[81] so his cult may not have sustained its early impetus. York lost Alcuin's copies of Bede's works, which followed him to France when he became abbot of Tours (in 796), and the community there seems to have been unable, or unwilling, to respond positively to requests for Bede's work in the mid-ninth century.[82] The cult may, therefore, already have been faltering. Its prospects were perhaps further damaged by Viking attacks, which began to affect the north-east coast in particular in the 790s, and ultimately by the Scandinavian settlement of parts of Northumbria in the 860s, which threw the archdiocese of York into disarray. Wearmouth/Jarrow lay in a region which, on the evidence of place-names, saw little direct Viking settlement, and it is perhaps simplistic to suppose that the monastery ended primarily on account of these traumas, but, for whatever reason, monasticism seems to have died away over this period. Archaeological research has revealed that a major fire engulfed Jarrow at some point between the late ninth and late eleventh centuries, leaving much of the complex severely damaged and roof-less. Like many other religious communities, Wearmouth and Jarrow prob-ably metamorphosed into parochial centres, with cure of souls over extensive territories but little left directly of the estates and other assets with which they had been endowed in the late seventh century. The cemetery at Jarrow was in near-continuous use into the eleventh century,[83] but the damaged buildings were neither repaired nor replaced. While the Lindisfarne com-munity famously removed their foremost saint, Cuthbert, and bore his remains on a lengthy peregrination of what remained of English Northumbria before re-establishing themselves successively at Chester-le-Street then Durham, Bede's cult seems to have remained *in situ* and his sanctity decayed along with the status of his house.

The utility of Bede's works, however, had the potential to sustain his reputation at a distance. A new reading of Bede's *Ecclesiastical History* came with its translation into Old English in southern England in the late ninth century. By the late tenth century, this version was believed to be the responsibility of King Alfred, but there is now some scepticism regarding the extent of his personal involvement.[84] It is probably safe to assume that this work formed part of the broader programme of translation and book produc-tion which is closely connected with the West Saxon king, but there is no nearer contemporary evidence of Alfred's active involvement, and the language suggests that it was undertaken by one of the king's Mercian clerics.[85] Within this broader context, Bede's history featured alongside works by St Augustine, Boethius, Gregory the Great, Orosius and the first fifty psalms – reputed at this date to be the work of King David. His was, however, the only 'English' work to feature in this great exercise in translation, emphasising his unique status as an authoritative Christian figure of insular extraction.

A court context certainly seems implicit in the way that the Old English Bede treats its royal patron in the Preface, which arguably mirrors Alfred's own current concerns. The new version reads: 'as God chose you out to be king, it behoves you to instruct your people'.[86] Such a shift away from the original text is not surprising in a work which was apparently translated within a small group of intellectuals gathered around a ruler who had both an advanced notion of his own royal status and an interest in promoting himself as the sponsor of Christian learning. The role of Abbot Albinus of Canterbury was also enhanced and both Theodore and Hadrian were introduced to the Preface, for contemporary purposes. Bede's own voice here is somewhat muted, therefore, but the 'autobiographical' passage in V, 24 plus the listing of his works are included virtually in full, despite abbreviation having occurred elsewhere.[87] This was a rendition of Bede which invested more heavily in southern cults and church sites (such as Winchester and Canterbury) than in Northumbrian examples and rid itself of virtually any material which was not central to the English conversion: so letters and documents were largely omitted, as were accounts of non-English saints such as Germanus, Columba, Ninian and Adamnan, most items relating to Roman history, aspects of Gregory's life which were not directly relevant to England, and the chapters concerning the Holy Land.[88] The translation sought to redeploy the *Ecclesiastical History* as an aid to the West Saxon king's promotion of vernacular literacy, combined with an appreciation of the wider story of the conversion of the English to Christianity and their membership of the broader community of God's peoples, which had a particular significance in a Christian England under attack from the Vikings. Bede's conception of a golden age of English learning under Archbishop Theodore and Abbot Hadrian had resonances with the efforts in this direction being made by Alfred and his associates. This was, therefore, a text which was translated, abbreviated and reissued in support of current government preoccupations in southern England in the late ninth century, so for immediate cultural-political purposes.

Contemporary with this translation came, of course, the construction of a new, 'national' chronicle in the vernacular, the *Anglo-Saxon Chronicle*. This made extensive use of Bede's *History*, to the extent that the chronological summary therein provided the skeleton of its treatment of events up to the early eighth century. Material was also taken from other parts of the work, particularly where a West Saxon interest was recoverable. The author had both an excellent working knowledge of the *Ecclesiastical History* and of chronology as a whole but was constructing a work for his own purposes, which perhaps best exemplified in the Preface, where the story of the West Saxon people and the centrality of its dynasty are very clearly foregrounded.[89]

Bede was himself commemorated in this work in its earliest iteration: his death was entered under the year 734, alongside and in the same breath as that of Tatwine, archbishop of Canterbury, in a year when 'the moon looked as if it were suffused with blood'.[90] To this point the deaths recorded reveal the king-centric nature of this text: including both Penda and his son Peada, who were not herein explicitly royal,[91] there were twenty-four kings' deaths out of the total of forty-five named individuals. Alongside these there were nine archbishops or archbishops-elect (including Wigheard in 667), two bishops (Aidan, whom Bede had championed, and the West Saxon scholar Aldhelm) and a mere twelve others of all ranks. Half of the latter were secular figures of high birth, such as Ælfwine and Ingild, brothers to kings Ecgfrith and Ine respectively, several others were described as æthelings (close members of royalty and potential heirs) and others again were the political and/or dynastic opponents of various kings (such as Eadberht among the South Saxons and both Cuthred and Cynewulf). The remainder were religious figures: apart from Bede, these included Gregory the Great, the so-called 'apostle of the English'; St Hild, a royal princess and abbess; St Æthelthryth, princess, virgin queen and abbess; St Egbert, who had converted Iona to the Catholic method of dating Easter; and finally St Guthlac. Of these, only the last was a figure whose reputation had not been developed by Bede, whose work in this respect as in others dominates this phase of the *Chronicle*. Bede's own commemoration presumably reflects the particular value of his work to this author, therefore, and his status and reputation as a figure central to perceptions of English ecclesiastical history and chronology in southern England in the late ninth century. His entry in tandem with Tatwine, whose obit does arguably belong in this year, perhaps reflects the high esteem in which both were held as scholars and as poets.[92] This is again august company for a mere monk and priest, albeit a celebrated author whom the chronicler had certainly read, and can only have promoted his reputation as a major figure of the Christian English past.

Bede was highly regarded, therefore, in the south of late Anglo-Saxon England and his *History* was utilised in the effort to revive both learning and monasticism across the period. Bedan works feature in seven of the surviving thirteen Anglo-Saxon book lists, with seven separate works represented (albeit the *EH* is the commonest, appearing four times), putting him behind both Augustine and Isidore but level in this respect with Jerome.[93] Whether the *Ecclesiastical History* was in Latin or the vernacular is not clear, but its occurrence twice in one list, possibly deriving from Worcester, may imply that both were present. The high profile of Bede's works should perhaps be associated with his inclusion in several West Saxon calendars across the eleventh century, most particularly from Winchester.[94] However, he was omitted from all surviving ninth- and tenth-century examples, and features in only a single example of the litanies surviving from Anglo-Saxon England, in the 'Portiforium of St Wulfstan' (of *c.*1065), and even here in a hand of the first half of the twelfth century over an erasure.[95] That said, Bishop Wulfstan of Worcester (1062–95) does seem to have been an enthusiast for the cult, having reputedly dedicated a church to Bede.[96]

At the same time, the major historical effort of the period went into the continuation of various versions of the *Anglo-Saxon Chronicle* rather than into a renewal of Latin learning. Bede's cult site at Jarrow was distant from the direct influence of English kings who might otherwise have patronised its revival, and his sanctity seems to have suffered accordingly. The shrine of St Cuthbert, at the heart of England's most northerly diocese, did attract occasional royal largess and was a significant presence in regional politics. Bede's cult, around 15 miles (24 km) away, can only have suffered from this competition. It was not until the early post-Conquest period that either his cult revived somewhat or the *Ecclesiastical History* recovered the centre ground in its original Latin.

This 'rediscovery' of the *EH* was very much a consequence of the Norman Conquest, which brought a wave of incomers to England's monasteries and access to a variety of texts which were perhaps commoner on the continent. Bede's *History* was championed by such scholars as William of Malmesbury in the second quarter of the twelfth century, who explicitly modelled his own approach to history on his reading of Bede, acknowledged his debt to this 'most learned and least proud of men' in the first lines of his Prologue,[97] and quoted verbatim from *EH* V, 24, where Bede had 'summarised his whole life in a sort of epilogue'.[98] There follows the text of a letter sent by Pope Sergius to Abbot Ceolfrith, which William seems to have adapted so as to make it request Bede's presence in Rome.[99] Although he held back from actually claiming that Bede had ventured there, he developed this inference for what were clearly contemporary purposes as a means to elevate his fellow country-man's reputation as a religious authority to levels unequalled among the 'proud Gauls' or in 'mighty Rome'. Thereafter he included an adapted form of Cuthbert's *Letter*, in chapter 60, to invest Bede's death with meaning for himself, for 'With Bede was buried almost all historical record down to our own day.'[100]

William was therefore portraying himself as Bede's heir in the role of historian of the English, bringing forward and updating the latter's work to his own era following a period which he characterised as one of cultural decline. Other monastic writers of the period treated Bede's work with, if anything, even greater respect, although Geoffrey of Monmouth is an exception: despite having absorbed the detail, his *History of the Kings of Britain* played fast and loose with Bede's portrayal of the past.[101] More typically, Henry of Huntingdon noted in the Prologue to his mid-twelfth-century *History of the English People* that: 'I have followed the venerable Bede's *Ecclesiastical History* where I could, selecting material also from other authors and borrowing from chronicles preserved in ancient libraries.'[102] Elsewhere he treated the work with reverence, almost as a sacred text. His most recent editor estimated that only eight of the 140 chapters of *EH* had not been used by Henry, of which six concern non-English saints.[103] Some twenty-five were used virtually complete, an equal number via substantial verbatim extracts and the remainder in abbreviated form. Bede himself was described in IV, 11 as 'holy and religious, the man of brilliant genius and the philosopher of Christ', and virtually the whole of books III and IV were taken by Henry from his eighth-century predecessor.

By the mid-twelfth century, therefore, Bede was well established in the role of the founding father of English History, mined comparatively indiscriminately for stories and 'facts' and widely subjected to the plagiarism by which intellectuals of the period showed their appreciation. He was sufficiently popular for a number of brief lives to be written across the central and later Middle Ages. However, the earliest consisted of little more than the addition of his own biographical piece in *EH* V, 24 to Cuthbert's letter, with minimal amounts of supporting text, while later versions were largely extracts from works at earliest of the twelfth century which had used the same materials.[104] None of these were developed much beyond a very narrow body of material, but they do reflect considerable interest in Bede as an exemplary figure.

The early post-Conquest period also witnessed the reawakening of more localised claims to Bede, his cult and his reputation. Monasticism had withered at Wearmouth/Jarrow during the ninth and tenth centuries, jeopardising Bede's continuing cultic association with his own monastery. William of Malmesbury noted that 'at that time [i.e. when he died] he was buried in his own monastery, but now, it is asserted, he lies at Durham with St. Cuthbert'.[105] This tradition, unsurprisingly, emanated from Durham itself. Bishop William of St Calais's wholesale replacement of the secular priests with monks in 1083 had stimulated a revival of interest in earlier Northumbrian monasticism in general, and the world described by Bede in particular. The monks now come to Durham were drawn from communities which had been established at the sites of Wearmouth and Jarrow as recently as the 1070s by English Benedictines from Evesham and other southern houses, escaping the 'Normanisation' of their houses and inspired by nostalgia for what they thought to have been a peculiarly English monastic golden age, of which they had apparently learned via their reading of Bede's *History*.[106] In the north, they found initial support among a local aristocracy which was seriously unsettled by the Conquest, so willing to invest in a project which offered some potential to revive divine support for themselves. The upsurge in historical research and writing at Durham around 1100 owes much to the influence of such men, and much too to the need for the reformed monastery there to reinforce its claim to the earlier monastic traditions associated with the cults of SS Aidan and Cuthbert and the lands and other assets which they had attracted.[107]

The body of St Cuthbert was translated into the massive new cathedral in 1104 and within a very few years the precentor, the monk Simeon, had completed a new history of the community, opening with a Bede-originated story of Oswald's patronage of Holy Island, *c.*635.[108] During the 1070s, the control of monasticism within the diocese seems to have been a central issue for Bishop Walcher, who sought to manage it to his own advantage,[109] and this theme now resurfaced in Simeon's work, but as if played out a generation or more earlier. The key figure is the priest Elfred, who was presented as a keen defender of the traditions of St Cuthbert in the first half of the eleventh century. This Elfred putatively travelled to various religious sites in the region, such as Hexham and Melrose, ostensibly so as to reinvigorate local cults by excavating and exhibiting the bones of the saints but more particularly in order to collect relics which he then brought back to Durham and deposited with the body of St Cuthbert. Simeon's narrative was apparently designed to reinforce a superiority claimed in the present by his own house over other cultic sites across the diocese, by positing the capture and translation of their relics most of a century earlier.[110]

Bede's grave in a portico on the northern side of the church at Jarrow was singled out for particular attention within this account as having been excavated by night under conditions of great secrecy and the entirety of the remains translated 'in a little linen bag' to the coffin of St Cuthbert. His separate treatment suggests that the acquisition of Bede's cult was of particular importance to the newly rebuilt monastic cathedral at Durham but the clandestine nature of the deed and the reported unwillingness of the perpetrator to disclose it can only detract from the credibility of this story. Bones were presumably acquired and redeposited, but it must be doubted whether or not these represent Bede's actual remains. For a while, at least, Jarrow's claim to Bede retained some credibility: a list of saints' burials included in Hugh Candidus's mid-twelfth-century chronicle includes the entry: 'And in Jarrow saint Bede the priest', while he noted both Cuthbert and Boisil at Durham,[111] although Hugh may, of course, have been working from an earlier source. Notwithstanding, Bede was commemorated effectively in Simeon's work, largely via extended quotation, once again, from his autobiographical account in the *EH* and Cuthbert's letter.

Whatever the reality of their claim, Durham's cultic colonialism was certainly effective. By the thirteenth century Jarrow and Wearmouth were firmly established as dependent cells, with staff appointed and managed by the priors and accounts rendered centrally at Durham.[112] Manuscripts of his works were kept and copied by the monks.[113] Bedan cult was securely centred within the cathedral, where it would henceforth be subordinated to that of Cuthbert. In 1370, his putative remains were reinterred in a splendid tomb in the Galilee Chapel, a large Lady Chapel added in the late twelfth century to the western end of the nave of the great Norman church. In this guise, Bede was being utilised very much as the community's second-string cult, at the extreme opposite end of the building from St Cuthbert's tomb and in the only part accessible to women, whose burials gradually accumulated around his.

Leland noted 'a tumble [tomb] of Bede the noble monke' in the Cathedral *c.*1540,[114] which was destroyed shortly thereafter in the Reformation, but Durham retained its exceptional claim to Bede. The first edition to use and compare several texts of his historical works formed the principal life work of

John Smith, a prebendary there and rector of Wearmouth (from 1704), under the inspiration of Thomas Gale, dean of York, and the first flowering of Anglo-Saxon scholarship which both had experienced as students at Cambridge University. This great project was only brought to completion after Smith's death and published in 1722 by his son, George, whose anti-papal views clearly coloured criticism therein of Bede's use of the *Book of Pontiffs*, for example, and led him to describe the author as 'an honest and holy man, but not of the most distinguishing and accurate judgement'.[115] George Smith was in his turn buried at St Oswald's, Durham, in 1756.

Durham's ownership of Bede's memory showed no sign of abating thereafter. Volumes describing the cathedral's antiquities which were published at Durham in the mid-eighteenth century gave detailed descriptions of the tomb which had been lost,[116] and a new monument was erected in 1831 above the burial site, re-emphasising his importance to the cathedral's history and traditions, with a massive tomb topped with a thick black marble slab into which was cut the legend: HAC SUNT IN FOSSÂ BÆDÆ VENERABILIS OSSA ('In this tomb are the bones of the Venerable Bede'). Much later, Bertram Colgrave took the principal role in providing modern editions and translations of early English Latin hagiography, including Bede's prose *Life of St Cuthbert*, from his tenure of a post in English at the University of Durham, remarking in 1940 that: 'To edit the two most important Lives of St Cuthbert is almost a pious duty for one who lives under the shadow of Durham Cathedral.'[117] This native of Bernicia eventually, of course, went on to provide the standard text and translation of the *Ecclesiastical History*. The *Essays* published in 1935 to commemorate Bede's death included papers by two Durham scholars, one of whom was Colgrave, and opened with an introduction by Herbert Dunelm, Lord Bishop of Durham, dated at Auckland Castle to 26 May, which was of course, as far as we can judge, the precise anniversary. Dunelm claimed for Bede features which he considered distinctive of English (i.e. Anglican) Christianity in the present, such as a particular devotion to biblical studies, sound learning and a hold on history, and patriotism, and directed particular attention to 'the moral beauty of Bede's life',[118] but the claim he left implicit was that on Bede's own person, whose epitaph was inscribed in his own cathedral. Alongside this somewhat highbrow, academic celebration, a pageant or play, written by the dean of Durham, Dr Cyril Alington, and reportedly 'largely compiled from Bede's own Chronicles',[119] was staged by students of the university in the cloister of Durham Cathedral to celebrate the 1200th anniversary of Bede's death, and close to 12,000 school children reputedly visited the Galilee Chapel.[120]

As the centenary of Bede's birth approached, a memorial to Cyril and Hester Alington was put up on the cathedral wall above Bede's tomb (in 1970) consisting of an extract, in Latin with English translation below, from Bede's *On the Apocalypse*. Then a new window in somewhat abstruse, modernist style, celebrating Bede, was added on the north side of the chapel in 1973. A conference was convened at Hatfield College, Durham, in the same year, the papers from which were published in 1976, edited by Gerald Bonner, then Reader in Church History at the university, and containing in addition an excellent précis of archaeological work at both Wearmouth and Jarrow which had been conducted by Rosemary Cramp, newly professor of archaeology there.[121] Most recently, a new lamp has been suspended over the tomb itself, dedicated on 11 June 2005, to commemorate the centenary of the Rotary International.

At Durham, Bede has, therefore, been memorialised in many different ways over a lengthy period, each of which has something to say about those commissioning the particular strategy. This was not, however, the sole location of efforts at commemoration in the modern period. A group of streets adjacent to Springwell Paper Mills, near Jarrow, in the later nineteenth century were given 'Bedan' names – Bede Terrace, Biscop Terrace, Ecgfrid Terrace and Ceolfrid Terrace. More monumentally, a massive cross set up at Whitby in 1898 in honour of Cædmon, whose memory the *EH* had promoted, stimulated a comparable effort on Bede's behalf. This was intended initially for Jarrow, but led ultimately to the erection of a massive cross, designed by Clement Hodges, the same architect as at Whitby, on the basis of motifs put together by a committee including R. H. Hodgkin, the historian, and the distinguished Anglo-Saxonists, Professors Skeat and Sweet, alongside several senior local clergy. The resultant monument, decorated with panels intended to tell the story of Bede's life was put up on Roker Point, Sunderland, and unveiled on 11 October 1904, to considerable acclaim and comment in the national press.[122] It stands beside Roker Terrace on the very edge of the cliffs, and on what was perhaps the first green space encountered on leaving the congested factories and terraces of Monkwearmouth. The principal inscription, on the landward side, features extracts (in translation) from Bede's Preface to his *Life of Cuthbert* followed by the opening lines of the *Ecclesiastical History*, apparently selected as exemplification of the author's deference towards his superiors in church and state. Such should be read, in part at least, as a message concerning the contemporary social order, aimed at instilling a comparable deference towards their social superiors among the holiday-making Edwardian mass of working folk from nearby industrial towns.

The 1200th anniversary of Bede's death was marked at Jarrow on 19 May 1935 by a service led by the archbishop of York, which was trailed by a eulogy in *The Times* based, unsurprisingly, in part on Cuthbert's letter, in part on Bede's own autobiographical comments in *EH* V, 24.[123] Then in 1958, the Revd George Beckwith, rector of the church at Jarrow, inaugurated the Jarrow Lectures, given each year in St Paul's on 23 April in commemoration of its original consecration, and thereafter published. While not specifically associated with Bede himself, these have, of course, done something to reclaim Bede's memory for his best-known place of domicile, as well as providing an important focus for early Anglo-Saxon studies across the later twentieth century and on into the twenty-first, which their subsequent collection and publication in two volumes (to date) has consolidated.[124] The rehabilitation of a favourite son on the banks of the Tyne has since been popularised by the aforesaid excavations and an exhibition of archaeological finds, initially at Jarrow Hall, which opened as the Bede Monastery Museum in 1974, and ultimately by the establishment of the lavish and multi-stranded 'Bede's World' beside the Hall, overlooking St Paul's, the central building of which was opened by Elizabeth II in December 2000, and which seeks to follow, interpret and illustrate the narrative of the *Ecclesiastical History* within its exhibition. Alongside is an Anglo-Saxon 'demonstration farm', experimentally reconstructed timber buildings, and the obligatory café and shop, within the Hall itself.

Other recent celebrations of Bede have broken entirely with the long-established, twofold tradition of place. A series of lectures and seminars at Cornell University between 1972 and 1974 began the trend,[125] to be followed by conferences held in 1990 at the University of Groningen in Holland,[126] and then early in this millennium at Villeneuve d'Ascq and Amiens, France,[127] all of which emphasise that Bede should not today be considered the exclusive preserve of either Jarrow or Durham. As we have seen, his memory was earlier contested by eighth-century York, and was then shared very widely via the dissemination and copying of manuscripts of his works during the Carolingian period and thereafter across Western Europe. His reputation was sufficiently well established in Italy *c.* 1300 for his name to be included with eleven other blessed spirits depicted within the fourth heaven in Dante's *Divine Comedy*, albeit with virtually no comment,[128] and he featured as a standard of veracity in Ranulph Higden's *Polychronicon* of *c.*1327, wherein his omission of any reference to King Arthur was thought significant.[129] C. W. Jones remarked that his works circulated across Western Europe for five centuries as widely as those of any western author excepting only Augustine and Jerome.[130] Many of Bede's writings, including the *Ecclesiastical History*, were certainly well-used, standard texts throughout the Middle Ages and surviving manuscripts are often in poor condition as a consequence of the heavy demand. They were still being copied in the fourteenth and fifteenth centuries and were rapidly then adopted as suitable materials for printing. *The Art of Metre*, for example, was first typeset in 1473 and had gone through eleven editions by 1600,[131] while the *EH* was first printed (at Strasbourg) around 1480, and his computistical works in 1537.

Bede's historical work was clearly in demand in the early sixteenth century, being used for example by Polydore Virgil in his reappraisal of English history under the patronage of Henry VII. However, the English Reformation had a considerable impact on Bede's memory and reputation. Leland's *Itinerary*, which he compiled across the Dissolution in the late 1530s and early 1540s, makes few references to his work, despite the fact that stray comments regarding Dunwich, Beverley and St Herbert's Isle on Derwent Water all imply a good working knowledge of the *Ecclesiastical History*.[132] Bede's monkishness and his clearly stated commitment to Rome and to Catholic doctrine made both his memory and his works problematic inside England under the Tudors, even while his work still remained fundamental to the construction of an English, national history.

Elizabeth's first archbishop of Canterbury, Matthew Parker, illustrates the problem. Parker knew his *Ecclesiastical History* well and had even marked up in his own copy the sections about Theodore and Hadrian, to whom he was misguidedly attributing any Greek or Arabic text then in his possession, even while writing his own *Concerning the Antiquity of the British Church* on a reformist agenda.[133] Bede was thereafter claimed for the Protestant cause in a variety of polemical texts, such as *The Protestants evidence taken out of good records* of 1635,[134] and he became a prophet-figure to be manipulated in support of social causes, as in the 1652 publication, *Sundry Strange Prophecies of Merline, Bede, Becket, And others*, wherein he was associated with a whole series of apocryphal sages and credited with generalised doom-laden messages, opening with: 'sinne shall cause great trouble in every Land, and right shall not raigne in his inheritance'.[135] Much of this was, of course, based on second-hand readings: Ranulph Higden's work, for example, proved extremely popular in the later Middle Ages, leaving over 100 manuscripts, and it was both translated into English (in particular by John Trevisa in 1387) and printed repeatedly, both in Latin and English, providing one of several vehicles by which Bede was taken to a widening audience, principally inside England.

At the same time, the opportunities Bede's views afforded were not lost on the Catholic intelligentsia: the second printed edition of the Latin *EH* was published at Antwerp in 1550 with the express purpose of opposing the spread of Protestantism in England,[136] and the first English translation, in 1556 and also at Antwerp, by the brilliant émigré Thomas Stapleton (thereafter author of the Catholic apologia, *Fortresse of the Faith*) was likewise undertaken in the Catholic cause.[137] A new insular edition had to wait for Abraham Whelock at Cambridge, who, in 1643, produced an impressive Latin text with the Old English version in parallel columns, thus implicitly emphasising its essential Englishness. Thereafter the continental output fell away and there were comparatively numerous English editions in Latin up to the nineteenth century, with others of his works also then appearing in insular volumes and even translations. Giles produced a collected works in twelve volumes in 1843–4, which remained the best available edition of most of them well into the twentieth century.

Protestant authors in the seventeenth century tended to view miraculous elements in the works of Bede and his contemporaries as symptomatic of that divergence from the primitive Church of the Apostles which had led the Middle Ages into error, while still recognising merit in his *History* as a source for their own. John Milton, the republican author of *Paradise Lost*, took time out on several occasions to write history, seeking parallels for the present in a distant, semi-mythical, British past which he laid out to contemporaries as *Britain under Trojan, Roman, Saxon Rule*. A large part of his book IV is little more than a version of the *Ecclesiastical History*, reorganised somewhat to a stricter chronological sequence and embellished on occasion. Milton was clearly not much impressed by Bede but he recognised his value as a source and rued his passing:[138]

> Thus representing the state of things in this island, Bede surceas'd to write. Out of whom chiefly hath been gather'd, since the Saxons arrival, such as hath been deliver'd, a scatter'd story picked out here and there, with some trouble and tedious work from among his many legends of visions and miracles . . . Yet, from hence to the Danish invasion it will be worse with us, destitute of Beda.

Degory Wheare took a more polemical stance,[139] arguing that 'in the times of our venerable *Bede*, the Ocean of Miracles and Wonders burst in upon the Church, and overflowed it', although he approved the comments of 'this diligent and pious Writer' on near-contemporary matters. Thomas Salmon expressed a similar ambivalence:

> Venerable *Bede* was indeed very devout, and apt to swallow the Fabulous Relations, which supported the Superstitions of his Time: But then he appears to be a very honest Man, that would not report what he thought to be false, out of Design to delude his Readers: Nor was the *Christian* sincerity so much forsaken in his Time, as it was soon after.[140]

Such writers generally viewed Bede's *History* far more favourably than his works of exegesis, which were thought, at best, 'not probably . . . very useful, but they are striking and curious examples of early learning and application, under great disadvantages'.[141] But such were not considered central to his memory: John Berkenhout, for example, considered the *Ecclesiastical History* 'a work of so much merit, notwithstanding the legendary tales it contains, that it were alone sufficient to immortalise the author'.[142]

Insular commentators writing in an increasingly 'Germanist' tradition dominated history-writing from the mid-eighteenth century well into the twentieth. David Hume's grand, national narrative, for example, was grounded on a comparatively literal and uncritical reading of Bede, quoting, paraphrasing and generally adapting the *EH* to his own purposes,[143] and this approach was developed thereafter by the early Anglo-Saxonist, Sharon Turner,[144] then by a whole string of nineteenth-century thinkers keen to demonstrate that both the contemporary British constitution, and the Anglicanism that they saw as its spiritual doppelgänger, could and should be traced back to the Anglo-Saxon period. For writers such as Freeman in 1869 or Green in 1881 and 1892, the history of the seventh century was essentially a matter of paraphrasing Bede's text with the more 'papist' elements excised and its 'Englishness' elaborated with additional – and generally apocryphal – detail and direct speech,[145] although Freeman, in particular, found Bede's

Northumbrian focus difficult to reconcile with a national story which he preferred to ground in the royal succession of later Anglo-Saxon Wessex.

Other authors found Bede more problematic. Lord Macaulay, the great Whig historian of the 1840s, saw both advantages and disadvantages in the Anglo-Saxon conversion to Christianity to his vision of overall improvement across time of the national human condition:

> At length the darkness begins to break; and the country which had been lost to view as Britain reappears as England. The conversion of the Saxon colonists to Christianity was the first of a long series of salutary revolutions. It is true that the Church had been deeply corrupted both by that superstition and by that philosophy against which she had long contended, and over which she had at last triumphed . . . Yet she retained enough of the sublime theology and benevolent morality of her earlier days to elevate many intellects, and to purify many hearts.[146]

On balance, therefore, he could promote the conversion as a beneficial step, marking the first stage of England's admission to civilisation, but the benefits had to be balanced against the evils of papism as those were conceived within the mid-nineteenth-century political establishment. Macaulay only acknowledged Bede in the briefest of passages and in terms of his deserving fame across Europe, treating him as a prelude to the 'last great migration of the northern barbarians' – the Vikings, whose contribution clearly impressed him somewhat more.[147]

Kemble, a few years later, found Bede even more difficult to reconcile with his German-centric conception of early England and was clearly disturbed by his miracle-stories, taking refuge in damnation by faint praise: 'Though not entirely free from the prejudices of his [Bede's] time, and yielding ready faith to tales which his frame of mind disposed him willingly to credit, he seems to have bestowed some pains and critical appreciation of the materials he collected.'[148] This early writer had, he felt, neglected 'our secular history' and in particular the 'pagan and barbarous chieftains' of early England, in favour of a story foregrounding conversion to Catholicism which he would rather not invoke.[149] Kemble's critique has something in common with the 'Introductory Sketch' of English History with which William Stubbs prefaced his *Select Charters* in 1870, which succeeds, quite extraordinarily, in omitting both notice of Bede and any reference to Rome in its brief treatment of pre-Viking England:

> We thus arrive at the point of time at which the conversion of the people to Christianity introduces a new bond of union, the influences of a higher civilization, and a greater realization of the place of the English in the commonwealth of nations. The reduction of the whole of the Church organization of the seven kingdoms into the National Church, was the work of Theodore of Tarsus.[150]

The future bishop (of Chester, 1884, then Oxford, 1888) preferred to seek the origins of the English nation in Germany's great forests, as described by Tacitus, than in Bede's *History*, with all the threat to his 'National' religion that that might imply, and depended heavily on recent German scholarship for his take on the Anglo-Saxon period, having himself specialised primarily in the twelfth century.

The 'scientific' approach to the past pioneered in Germany, with its focus on the critical editing of early texts (which Stubbs himself championed, of course) to establish the historical 'facts', necessarily encouraged a revival of Bedan studies. The *Ecclesiastical History* was the text *par excellence* available to English historians of the insular Middle Ages and, along with his *History of the Abbots* and *Letter to Egbert* – plus the anonymous *History of Abbot Ceolfrith* – it was re-edited in two volumes with full scholarly apparatus and voluminous notes by Charles Plummer in 1896, providing a text of quality surpassing even that of John Smith. This was to serve the academic community well, at least until the surprising discovery of an exceptionally early manuscript at Leningrad/St Petersburg in the 1920s,[151] then the decay in the modern teaching of Latin, which, combined, led eventually to the modern Oxford text with parallel translation published by Colgrave and Mynors in 1969. Plummer was the chaplain of Corpus Christi, Oxford, and he presented Bede as an exemplar of his own High Church Anglicanism within the Oxford Movement, as 'the very model of the saintly scholar-priest; a type in which the English Church has never, thank God, been deficient, and of which we have seen in our own day bright examples in the person of men like Richard William Church and Henry Parry Liddon'.[152]

Bede's reintegration to national history has been very much a feature of the twentieth century. Take Charles Oman's remarks in 1910, for example, who as a non-specialist in the period was reiterating the impression gained from reading a range of recent work. In his view, Bede should be seen as:

> a model to later ages for his admirable habit of citing his personal authority for each statement, and his anxiety to get his chronology correct. Here indeed was a real historian; and the wonder grows when we find that his *Ecclesiastical History of the English People* was only one among very many works of theology and scholarship which engrossed his busy life.[153]

Bede was valued, therefore, primarily as an historian of the English nation rather than as a biblical scholar – a role which English scholarship of the period generally dismissed as so heavily derivative of the early Church Fathers and sterile of new ideas as to be not worth reading.[154]

New historical approaches of the interwar period adopted a more inclusive narrative style, in which Irish, Scottish and British histories were increasingly acknowledged and integrated to the, admittedly still dominant, English story, to construct a more balanced, complex and multi-stranded national narrative than hitherto. Ambitious studies even attempted an interdisciplinary approach, as did R. H. Hodgkin in 1935, drawing not just on a variety of literary evidence but also on the work of archaeologists, anthropologists and art historians.[155] Still, however, discussion of the English conversion and of the seventh century in general relied very heavily on a reading of Bede and something close to 100 pages of volume I of *A History of the Anglo-Saxons* was little more than a cautiously balanced paraphrase of the *Ecclesiastical History*.[156] The emphasis remained firmly fixed, however, on his historical writings, stretching only to include those on chronology. Take, for example, the position adopted in 1943 by (later Sir) Frank Stenton on the relative merits of his output: 'Through this work Bede emerges at last from the atmosphere of ancient science and exegesis to prove himself the master of a living art [history].'[157] His *History* was, therefore, considered to be in a class of its own and the absolute pinnacle of Bede's own scholarship. To it all his other works should be subordinated, to be interrogated only to the extent that they have something to reveal regarding the history of the world in which he himself lived. Of it, Stenton wrote:

> its essential quality carries it into the small class of books which transcend all but the most fundamental conditions of time and space. Bede was a monk to whom the miraculous seemed a manifestation of the divine government of the world. But his critical faculty was always alert; his narrative never degenerates into a tissue of ill-attested wonders, and in regard to all the normal substance of history his work can be judged as strictly as any historical writing of any time.[158]

The major national histories of the mid-twentieth century displayed, therefore, a continuing anxiety regarding Bede's miracle-stories and a reluctance to explore his exegesis, combined with huge respect for the historicity of the *Ecclesiastical History*, which, credited with universal values, was deemed of a quality to be accepted even under the shifting definitions of the discipline appropriate to the modern era.

Over the second half of the twentieth century, however, an increasingly critical strand of historical enquiry has subjected the *EH* to ever more incisive interrogation, treating it more as an historical source to be read with close care and less as an authoritative canon. While many still revered Bede himself, both as historian and for his broader scholarly output,[159] a major effort was now underway to explore such aspects as the economic underpinning of contemporary England,[160] the kingships into which it was divided and their origins,[161] the Christian cult centres which were developing,[162] contemporary views on such issues as ethnicity and gender,[163] and the broader behaviours, beliefs and perceptions of its inhabitants. The *EH* was being viewed less as a text actively defining the history of the period and increasingly as a quarry of material capable of being submitted to a variety of interrogations, including attention to specific vocabulary,[164] its allusions to other literature (preeminently the Bible) and even quasi-statistical treatments.[165] Its author's

assumptions and his vision of his contemporaries' self-perceptions and purposes have been questioned in ever more disparate ways,[166] and his purposes in
writing reinterpreted against the secular and religious politics of the day.[167]

This Anglo-centric and essentially historical tradition of Bedan scholarship
has increasingly benefited in the later twentieth century from the attention
of scholars from a broad cross-section of religious perspectives, from Anglo-
Catholic and High Anglican through to secular, agnostic and atheistic.
Alongside, however, there has re-emerged a second, less nation-centred and
more fundamentally Catholic interest in Bede, his memory and his works,
with distant but still significant roots in the Counter-Reformation. A small
college had been founded at Rome in 1852 by Pope Pius IX to accommodate
English Catholics visiting Rome and students seeking ordination, and this
was effectively refounded and renamed in 1898 by Leo XIII, becoming
the *Pontificio Collegio Beda* – the Pontifical Beda College. In parallel, in the
following year, Bede was officially named a Doctor of the Church, the only
'Englishman' ever to be so named and a prestigious honour, which was taken
to its logical conclusion in the context of his centenary by his formal sanctification in 1935, alongside such martyrs of the English Reformation as
Sir Thomas More and Bishop John Fisher. At the same time as commemorations were underway in Durham and Jarrow, the twelfth centenary of Bede's
death was also being celebrated in the Beda College by Cardinal Lépicier, who
marked the occasion by opening a new library there on 21 May 1935, followed by an address on Bede himself by the Roman Catholic archbishop of
Liverpool, before an audience of almost 2000 which included the archbishop
of Westminster and the British Minister to the Holy See.[168]

As a consequence, the twentieth century witnessed a significant upsurge of
interest in Bede within Catholic communities. His name had already long
been attached to a small number of institutes of learning of various kinds,
primarily in the region of his birth, and this number had continued to grow,
particularly in the later nineteenth century, with, for example, the construction in 1880 of the Catholic St Bede's College a stone's throw from my own
university in leafy Whalley Range, Manchester, in an Italian renaissance style.
However, it was now invoked repeatedly in the drive to establish a sufficiency
of Catholic schools across the English-speaking world, so both in Britain and
the New World. Let just a handful suffice as examples: St Bede's at Kingston-
upon-Thames was founded by the De La Salle Brothers in 1938; on the
other side of the Atlantic, St Bede is a Calgary Roman Catholic school in
Alberta. In parallel, Bede's name has been attached to numerous comparatively recent religious establishments in the USA, for example St Bede's
Monastery of Benedictine sisters at Eau Claire, Wisconsin, and several
episcopalian churches, including examples at Atlanta, Santa Fe and Stanford.

This upsurge of interest in Bede as a saint particularly associated with
learning has had a profound impact on his memory and on the ways that his
works are viewed. Already, High Anglican clerics in the later nineteenth
century had on occasion claimed a special affinity with the author of the

Ecclesiastical History. Charles Plummer, for example, wrote: 'It is no light privilege to have been so long a time in constant communion with one of the saintliest characters ever produced by the Church of Christ in this island.'[169] But Bede's sanctification now attracted new attention from scholars with less interest in his role as historian than as Christian thinker.[170] Sister Carroll of the Sisters of Mercy, Pittsburgh, exemplifies the new direction, publishing her dissertation, *The Venerable Bede: His Spiritual Teachings*, in 1946 with the Catholic University of America Press. Carroll was quite clear where Bede stood within contemporary society: 'His critical acumen, objectivity, and attractive style have made the *Ecclesiastical History of the English Nation* a classic'; 'to the general reader he is a man of one book',[171] but it was her purpose to refocus more specifically on Bede's religious stance, so onto what she perceived as 'the ideal monk, priest, and Christian scholar of his age',[172] whom she effectively reimagined somewhat as if a regular within the early twentieth-century Catholic Church. It is this alternative perspective of Bede the religious thinker and theologian which has since been successively revisited by, among others, such notable Bedan enthusiasts and scholars as the great monastic historian Dom David Knowles,[173] Paul Meyvaert[174] and Sister Benedicta Ward.[175]

In part as a consequence of this refocusing on the religious persona of Bede has come an upsurge in scholarly interest in his exegesis. The poor quality of published editions has long been a major disincentive to pursue an academic interest in Bede's biblical commentaries: as Plummer long since remarked,[176] the several continental editions of his collected works published in the sixteenth and seventeenth centuries contained within them numerous pieces which were not Bede's, and Migne's reprintings in the *Patrologia Latina*, from the 1860s onwards, did not always distinguish these additions to the canon. The first edition of Bede's complete works by Johann Herwagen the Younger at Basel in 1563 had passed various other works off as his and it was essentially these editions that Migne used, although he took the *Ecclesiastical History* from that offered by Giles in 1843–4, which derived from John Smith's edition (above).[177] In consequence, Sister Carroll was still using at least one spurious work as if genuine in the 1930s. Twentieth-century scholars have frequently lamented the poor condition of their raw materials and this issue has only been given the attention it deserves in the post-war period, which has seen most of Bede's exegetical works published within the *Corpus Christianorum Series Latina* from 1962 onwards, with scholarly apparatus of increasing value across the period – although several scholars have since in their turn expressed dissatisfaction with some of the earlier editions. At the same time, a significant proportion have also been subjected to scholarly translation and interpretation, via Cistercian Publications in the USA since the 1980s but more systematically across the 1990s within the Translated Texts for Historians series published by Liverpool University Press. These volumes, equipped as they are with full introductory material and copious notes, make it possible for those without the necessarily high competence in Latin that these works require to acquire a level of familiarity with Bede's works which was hitherto simply not possible.

One consequence has been the gradual convergence of historical and patristic approaches to Bede, as exponents of particular traditions of scholarship have become increasingly familiar with and interactive with others. For a century or more, historians have recognised that their understandings of the *Ecclesiastical History* could benefit from some recognition of Bede's exegesis but few pursued this path with much vigour before the 1980s, leaving his commentaries on the whole to patristic scholarship. But in the late twentieth century, there was an increasing realisation that the *EH* is ultimately incomprehensible outside a broader understanding of Bede's work,[178] so not as just influenced by Bede's experience of biblical commentary but as a profoundly religious form of writing in its own right, 'a world history in miniature, in which they [the English] take their place among the people of God awaiting the "eighth age of the blessed Resurrection in which they shall reign forever with the Lord".'[179] We are witnessing, therefore, in the twenty-first century a reintegration of all Bede's works as a single area of study inclusive of his *Ecclesiastical History*, and a revival in consequence of his reputation as first and foremost a biblical scholar, for whom history was just one among several branches of Christian knowledge, and but one means alongside others of inculcating Christian values.

Bede and his audience

Turning from the ways in which Bede has been remembered over the centuries, we need also to make explicit other aspects of the relationship between ourselves as audience and Bede as author. Of one thing we can be sure: the very notion of ourselves as consumers of his works was unimaginable on his part, for Bede was not writing to be read in the twenty-first century. Rather, his works were aimed primarily at his own contemporaries, whose edification was a primary motive for much, at least, of his literary output.[180] He did not write for a distant posterity – hardly any of us do. Our present would be beyond the imagination of a monastic writer of the early eighth century in very many ways, and even the notion of a time so distant in the future was arguably beyond Bede's expectation. His magisterial *Concerning the Reckoning of Time*, which on this issue follows St Augustine, reveals Bede's hostility to the millenarianism which was popular in Late Antiquity, arguing that only God knew the ending of the present, sixth age of the earth. However, given that he adopted 1656, 292, 942, 473 and 589 years respectively as the lengths of the previous five ages, he is most unlikely to have imagined that the Lord would let the sixth age continue running in excess of 2000 years from the incarnation.[181] The later chapters of the *Ecclesiastical History* and also his *Letter to Egbert* convey the impression, as he approached and then entered his sixties and experienced deteriorating health, that he supposed that the sixth age was close to its end,[182] although he did still anticipate a future of indeterminate duration to which he left judgement of the deeds of his contemporaries.[183] So although Bede was far too humble before the Lord to second-guess the actuality of the event, he was probably under the impression that the day of judgement by which the sixth age was destined to end would arrive in the not too distant future, bringing history to its final close.

Nor should we suppose that he would have been entirely comfortable with a modern audience in other respects. His own exclusively male pupils, generally in their late teens or twenties, were expected to make use of his output as appropriate at different stages in their own education, and he may have ensured that a copy of the *Ecclesiastical History* was very quickly available to the monastic school of SS Peter and Paul, Canterbury, for similar purposes,[184] but their education was fundamentally different from our own schooling, being grounded in Latin via both grammar and the rote learning of sections of the Bible, beginning with the Psalms. The precise curriculum at Wearmouth/ Jarrow is nowhere specified but it clearly included chronological studies and singing, in both of which Bede had himself been trained from an early age. Gregory of Tours listed grammar, dialectic, rhetoric (including metrics), geometry, astrology (i.e. astronomy), arithmetic and harmony[185] as the curriculum necessary to a bishop's education in Gaul in the late sixth century, and Aldhelm's list of subjects which he learned at Canterbury differs little: 'Roman law, metrics, musical *modulamina* ['harmony', so 'chant']), *computus* [i.e. calculating time] and the zodiac'.[186] This probably approximates to Bede's curriculum, with perhaps some Greek added, to the extent that such was available. Charles Jones emphasised Bede's role as choirmaster as well as teacher, and described the process of education in which he was engaged very much in terms of master and apprentice, all turning to the development of competence in the conduct of the monastic office and way of life.[187]

This educational experience is so different from that of today, in both substance and purpose, that we should acknowledge quite explicitly the great gulf existing between Bede's immediate audience and ourselves, as regards both the mechanics of textual access – Latin in other words – and the presumptions and pre-existing knowledge brought by his readers to the task. Bede had every reason to expect that his readers would have a good working knowledge of Latin grammar and composition, of the Bible, of Virgil, of some exegesis at least, of *computus* and of sacred music, and his audience would have approached his works from a fundamentally religious perspective, and within a web of Christian meaning. Our fundamental divergences from this world mean that modern audiences are liable to take very different messages from the *Ecclesiastical History* from those which Bede intended, foregrounding, for example, the political and social content as opposed to messages about relationships between man and God which he was attempting to propagate.[188]

The *Ecclesiastical History* has often been assumed to have been intended for a rather different audience from the remainder of Bede's work, owing to its unique dedication to a secular figure, King Ceolwulf,[189] but we must be wary as to how to interpret this distinction. Was Bede really trying to communicate directly with the central figure of the secular élite? And, just supposing he was, was Ceolwulf, for his part, capable of engaging with Bede's *History* directly as consumer? Latin authors on occasion addressed ninth-century Frankish rulers as if they might be capable of both understanding their language and grasping the code of discourse which they commonly used,[190] but there is little to indicate that many English kings of the previous century were versed in comparable levels of literary culture. And Carolingian rulers, even after the great cultural reformation of the eighth century, were generally expected to hear rather than read such works, accompanied by a running commentary from a scholarly cleric. The common assumption that Ceolwulf was a learned man depends heavily on the logic that 'Bede dedicated his *EH* to Ceolwulf, ergo he was capable of reading and comprehending it', which is far from safe. Bede's *Letter to Egbert*, of 734, referred to Ceolwulf's 'love of religion' and suitability as an associate in the task of inculcating Christianity among the Northumbrians, but it was as much the close kinship between bishop and king that Bede expected to bring him on side, and there is no indication herein that he was literate. The earliest promotion of Ceolwulf's reputation as learned was part and parcel of the post-Conquest reorientation of Northumbrian Christianity around Cuthbert, at Durham, where the monastic community presumably preferred to view as cultured a king who was believed to have retired to Lindisfarne, but this seems devoid of any contemporary evidence beyond Bede's few and highly ambiguous comments, although it does provide notice of his later cult and the transfer of his relics to Norham.[191] Bede remarked King Aldfrith's expertise regarding the Scriptures but offered nothing comparable regarding Ceolwulf.

Given, as above, that a good knowledge of Latin, of the Gospels and of allegorical or metaphorical readings thereof was a prerequisite for accessing the lessons Bede was offering, it is far from clear how widely the necessary levels of education had spread within contemporary society outside an intellectual minority within the Church. Even many priests seem to have been deficient in Latin – hence Bede's translations into the vernacular – and some could not read. Comparable issues were raised at the Council of Clofesho just twelve years after Bede's death, and an attempt was made to rectify such weaknesses for the southern archdiocese.[192] Aldhelm's exceptionally erudite letters to kings Geraint of Dumnonia and Aldfrith of Northumbria, a generation earlier, might be thought to imply a level of Latin literacy within parts at least of the secular élite, but there are grounds herein for extreme caution: Geraint was Cornish, and patterns of education in the Celtic West need not have been directly comparable to those in Anglo-Saxon England, and in any case his clergy may well have interpreted this letter for him;[193] Aldfrith grew up in Ireland with little expectation of the Northumbrian succession and almost certainly had a clerical training, given his later reputation in Ireland for wisdom, so his literacy, and perhaps also his interest in collecting texts, was highly atypical. Ceolwulf himself eventually became a monk but need not have been a literate one,[194] given that other adult incomers who had earlier pursued secular careers did not necessarily involve themselves in reading and writing.[195] While Stephen's *Life* suggests that many young noblemen were fostered in Wilfrid's household,[196] this is no guarantee that they received more than the most elementary education, if any, and his example finds no support elsewhere, with even monastic schools apparently few and far between. The manuscripts necessary to support education of the secular élite are most unlikely to have been available in Northumbria in the early eighth century.

There is, therefore, very little reason to suppose that the Northumbrian court was generally literate. There are three illustrations which are apt. Stephen's *Life of Wilfrid* provides a rare insight to the issue in his account of a northern synod held *c.*706, where one Berhtfrith, described as 'a prince second only to the king', was represented as asking the archbishop for a translation of the written statement received from the papacy concerning Wilfrid's case.[197] Clearly, Berhtfrith was unable to understand Latin and it may well be that he could not read either,[198] since the translation would presumably have been given verbally. Secondly, in the *Ecclesiastical History*, Bede annotated Abbot Ceolfrith's *Letter to King Nechtan*, which he apparently quoted in full,[199] to underline the need for it to be translated into the king's own language – Pictish. He is most unlikely to have had much knowledge of the Latinity of the Pictish court some two decades earlier so was probably basing this assumption on his knowledge of contemporary Northumbria. Thirdly, in 746–7, Boniface sent a letter of admonishment addressed to King Æthelbald of the Mercians via a priest, Herefrith, with a note asking him to read it to the king along with 'your explanations', which could well have been delivered in the vernacular, again suggesting that the monarch may not have been up to the task of comprehending this communication.[200] Ceolwulf, like the vast majority of the secular nobility, was, therefore, very likely to have been dependent on clerical associates for expounding texts. In his Preface, Bede anticipated despatching the *EH* to Ceolwulf a second time in the expectation that it would be both 'copied' and 'meditated upon' (or 'studied'), which ties in well with a vision of clergy making manuscripts from which to be able to translate and read particular passages to members of the court. In book V, 15, he referred to King Aldfrith having Adamnan's work on the Holy Land disseminated, which presumably means that he resourced its copying and dispersal to favoured recipients, which apparently included Wearmouth/Jarrow.

Bede wrote exceptionally clearly, arguably with the expectation that his work would be accessed, even by most of his Latin-literate audience, by being read out loud.[201] In the Preface, he expected Ceolwulf to 'lend an attentive ear' to the Bible, not read it, and his focus was at least as much on an aural audience as on a readership. The king may well have heard sections of the *Ecclesiastical History* as a running translation in Old English. One can easily imagine a clerical aid showing him the opening page and picking out the highly honorific reference to himself as king at the start, but then explaining the text to him in the vernacular. Indeed, it may well have been with precisely that scene in mind that Bede placed the first of his mere three references to the king by name, which occur in just two passages, so prominently in the first line.

Without further evidence, it seems inadvisable to suppose that the *Ecclesiastical History* can have reached a very different primary audience from that of Bede's biblical commentaries without considerable mediation by the clergy in the form of translation and oral transmission. As he himself stressed, his literary output was generally intended for his 'own benefit and that of my brothers',[202] and others, perhaps, who shared his moral universe and the training which underpinned it.

The significance of King Ceolwulf as dedicatee is something to which we will return, but it does seem very improbable from all this that he would have been capable of actually reading the *Ecclesiastical History*, let alone of appreciating its less literal messages without considerable assistance. Assuming that those whose opinions and expertise Bede had requested for this work would have had an interest in reading the finished product, the target audience outside Wearmouth/Jarrow which is recoverable internally from the Preface consisted almost exclusively of middle-aged or elderly men of high or comparatively high rank within the religious hierarchy. Not surprisingly given the case made above, King Ceolwulf looks like the exception to this general rule: we cannot know his precise age but he had only recently become king at the time of writing, and although he was to retire to the monastic life only six years later he putatively lived for a considerable period, perhaps suggesting a man in his late twenties, thirties or at most forties in 731. However, others whom Bede named had already lived the bulk of their comparatively long lives: Albinus, abbot since *c.*710, would predecease Bede himself; Nothhelm was to die in 739 and Daniel had been bishop of the West Saxons ever since 705 so was presumably elderly by the 730s.

This seems consistent with his earlier output. All of Bede's surviving letters and all but one of his longer works which carry any sort of dedication or address were directed at adult males, in clerical and/or monastic orders – in particular his contemporary, colleague and latterly (post-716) abbot, Hwætberht,[203] and, most commonly, Acca, bishop of Hexham and Bede's own diocesan from 709 to 731.[204] The only piece to have been written expressly at the request of a woman was the single-book work *On the Canticle of Habakkuk*, which Bede noted that 'my dearly beloved sister in Christ' had 'requested to have expounded'.[205] He did not, however, name this nun – or abbess, perhaps – with whom he was on such apparently friendly terms, so we do not know her identity or the house in which she resided. This song was one which was a normal part of the Divine Office within monasteries at Lauds on a Friday, so the issue of interpretation would have been apparent to anyone taking part and not just advanced students of the Scriptures. This was virtually Bede's only commentary on any part of the monastic office,[206] and it may be significant that it was the only one addressed to a woman. That said, he certainly saw St Hild as a keen educator, although not necessarily herself particularly learned;[207] both Aldhelm's works on virginity were directed at nunneries, where these highly complex texts were presumably read and their Latinity appreciated, and several of Boniface's correspondents were literate, Anglo-Saxon women.[208] Collectively these examples suggest that there was an educated female intelligentsia capable of understanding Bede's works. While women do not seem to have figured prominently among his correspondents, they had the potential to form a minority group within Bede's contemporary audience.

Bede would, therefore, have observed that a present-day audience differs from that which he had anticipated when writing in terms of its educational and life experience, its awareness of God, its dominant age range, the social status of its members and its gender mix. It was in part, perhaps, this mismatch between Bede and his modern audience which led Kathleen Biddick to imagine a meeting within Stanford University between the Dean, a professor of Old English, Bede and 'a self-identified Chicana feminist theorist',[209] with whom she envisaged that he might have struck up an intellectually fruitful, if sometimes challenging and occasionally embarrassing, relationship. Biddick particularly focused on the various linguistic negotiations which she identified as implicit in the *Ecclesiastical History*, and on Bede's role as a 'go-between' active on the interfaces between 'power-charged', linguistically defined communities,[210] which leads us usefully into another fundamental aspect of the relationship between Bede and his several audiences, namely the issue of language.

Bede was an exceptionally gifted multi-lingual. He was a native speaker of Old English and enthusiast for poetry in that medium,[211] and enjoyed a seemingly effortless command of Latin by the time he was in his late twenties, if not before. In later life he taught himself sufficient Greek to study the Scriptures therein, and even learned a modicum of Hebrew from his study of the writings of Jerome. Yet even this flowering of linguistic expertise did not give Bede the ability to converse with every other inhabitant of Britain in their own vernacular – as Irish, Pictish and Britonnic – so he was probably dependent on English observers, Latin texts or Latin-speaking clerics for the comparatively little that he offered in his *Ecclesiastical History* regarding the affairs of 'non-English' neighbours. It is illuminating to note in which languages he chose to develop expertise – which were those central to Christian exegesis – and those which he preferred to neglect. Bede made numerous very positive comments concerning the Irish, at least, but never seems to have learned their language. Nor does he ever reveal knowledge of Old Welsh, which he may perhaps also have heard on occasion within Northumbria during his lifetime, particularly given that his knowledge of local Romano-British place-names must have derived, in some instances at least, from British communities,[212] albeit perhaps indirectly.

Bede was apparently skilled as a translator between the English vernacular and Latin. So, for example, he rendered Cædmon's Old English poem into Latin even while advising his readers why he had had to abandon the vernacular word-order and write 'with some loss of beauty and dignity',[213] and his dictation of a translation into the vernacular of the first part of *The Gospel according to St John* (now lost), during his final illness, speaks volumes for his fluency. On occasion his remarks regarding Old English have been judged inaccurate, but this is perhaps more a matter of mistaking his purpose than Bede's faulty linguistic skills. Take, for example, his rendering of the OE place-name *Streanæshalch* – which has traditionally been identified as the monastery at Whitby – as *Sinus Fari*, 'Bay of the Lighthouse'.[214] *Halc* is 'a cavity' in OE, commonly in place-names having the meaning 'a corner', 'nook' or 'angle', so translation as *sinus* (bay) seems to stretch the meaning somewhat. *Strean* (or *Streon*) is rare, perhaps a personal name, or referring to property rights or 'treasure'.[215] The combination of these two elements has been thought ill-suited to the location of Whitby, so Bede's interpretation of the term has been rejected as inaccurate, and the case has been put forward that the monastery should instead be located at Strenshall, near York,[216] even despite the current lack of any evidence for a monastic site there and even in apparent disregard of Bede's statement that *Hacones* – presumably Hackness with its surviving seventh/eighth-century carvings – was only 13 miles (20 km) distant.[217] This is not the place to be drawn into a debate about the location of *Streanæshalch*,[218] but it is important to realise that Bede was attempting something other than to provide a *bona fide* literal translation: the meaning of *interpretari* here is closer to 'paraphrase' than 'translate' and he is unlikely to have intended that this be read literally. Rather, this 'lighthouse' should be related to the 'signs' of Hild's saintliness, in particular the jewel worn by her mother which 'seemed to spread such a blaze of light that it filled all Britain', and the 'great light' which miraculously revealed her death simultaneously with the event to the nun Begu at Hackness.[219] This use of *Farus* should be read figuratively, therefore, and has no bearing on Bede's ability to translate between Old English and Latin, which was clearly fluent.[220]

As this anecdote would imply, Bede intended his works – including the *Ecclesiastical History* – for an audience which was highly competent in Latin but whose underlying mother tongue was Old English. The collapse of Latin as a subject central to British and American school curricula has left the majority of readers today without the ability to check received texts in translation against the original. This circumstance places a particularly heavy burden of responsibility on modern scholarship in terms of its role in mediating Bede's texts, and accurate translation is a major but often neglected issue, not just for the minority of Bede's current readers wishing to read his patristic works. Let us take as illustration a single sentence from two modern, English versions of the *Ecclesiastical History*. The selected passage is one in which Bede was quoting verbatim from Gregory I's letter to King Æthelberht of Kent in 601, first in the Penguin and secondly in the Oxford editions.[221] The Penguin edition reads:

Make their conversion [i.e. that of his people] your first concern; suppress the worship of idols, and destroy their shrines; raise the moral standards of your subjects by your own innocence of life, encouraging, warning, persuading, correcting, and showing them an example by your good deeds.

The Oxford edition reads:

Increase your righteous zeal for their conversion; suppress the worship of idols; overthrow their buildings and shrines; strengthen the morals of your subjects by outstanding purity of life, by exhorting them, terrifying, enticing, and correcting them, and by showing them an example of good works.

Comparison with the Latin original quickly reveals that the latter is the more literal and conveys Gregory's meaning more accurately. The point is a very real one, particularly for first-time readers of Bede today, who risk exposure to English texts which are necessarily some considerable distance removed from the one he actually conceived, with real consequences for their relationship with him as author. The issue of translation is, therefore, a significant one in terms of the relationship between a modern audience and Bede as writer.

There are, however, other equally cogent issues which distance Bede from a modern audience. The vast majority of modern readers are citizens of western-style, liberal democracies, each with a comparatively free press and a considerable breadth of political, social, philosophical and religious opinion on offer, from which individuals are more or less free to choose for themselves on the basis of reasoned debate or personal preference. Bede's works operate within a very different intellectual environment. Much of the historical literature written since venerates Bede as a saintly scholar, as a Christian thinker and as a moral being – one has only to recall the high incidence of the term 'venerable' in the titles of recent works.[222] Yet his was a teleological vision of the world and man's place within it, which is vastly different from that current among his modern readership. Bede supposed mankind to be at a particular stage in a system of time managed by the divine and destined to end at a pre-ordained but unknown, not too distant, end-point. To place this issue within current debates regarding education, he was very much a creationist, with a total belief in intelligent design within the Universe, as opposed to the evolutionist approach to the origins of life which is currently dominant (albeit increasingly under threat) in western schooling. He shared a contemporary, Christian perspective which derived from collective dependence on established readings of a central and prescribed body of sacred literature – the Bible – which he considered divinely inspired, virtually free of error or internal contradiction and of indubitable authority,[223] and which was properly interpreted for the remainder of society by an exclusive minority of elderly males, among whom Bede clearly positioned himself, to challenge whose judgement was not just foolish or erroneous but heretical. Around this select group of *doctores*, trained by them and in doctrinal terms dependent on them, was a wider priesthood, again composed primarily of middle-aged and elderly males, who exercised the exclusive right to both sacred knowledge and the power to mediate between God and His people via prescribed rites. Their behaviour and opinions were regulated by overseers of various kinds (such as abbots and bishops), synods and, overall, an archbishop, through whom instruction might reach the English clergy from superior authority on the continent. Those who did not share their collective view of the world were considered by Bede to be either heathen awaiting conversion to the truth, or heretics, whose interpretive system was in some recognisable but often obscure way at variance with this system of prescribed orthodoxy. And this was an élite culture, accessible to only a small minority of a total population which was supported by a large majority consisting of a rural proletariat plus household servants, most of whom were so short of either legal or economic freedoms that they would today be equated with slaves, in some sense of the term at least.

Bede's was not a system of knowledge which many of us today would wish to own or accept, and there are, in consequence, considerable dangers for a modern audience in the venerative approach to Bede which is adopted in many modern commentaries.[224] Rather, as historians we need to foreground Bede's humanity over and against his sanctity, the author and advocate rather than the truth-teller and his role as a spokesperson for his own epoch, as opposed to the eternal, with whom we can react from our own contemporary context. Claims on any specific culture shared between Bede and ourselves are little more than a chimera, and a dangerous one at that. Take for example, Dom David Knowles vision of Bede as: 'Simple, sane, loyal, trusting, warm-hearted, serious with that ready sense of pathos which has always been a mark of English literature'.[225] Such an 'English literature' does not exist in a universal setting and we can most certainly not share it with Bede, be he considered 'simple' or otherwise. Nor is it helpful to think of him as 'the father of English history': such makes it far too easy for those today who think of themselves as 'English' to welcome Bede as 'one of themselves' and a defining one at that, albeit one who happened to live a very long time ago.[226] It is far more constructive to read Bede as representative of a quite foreign community, distant and strange, whose thought world should be approached with caution, in anticipation that it will take a wide variety of scholarly skills to make any sense of it. Bede, we should recall at all times, is not and was not much like us. Nor was, or is, his thought world – his cosmos – ours. This is to urge not any sort of hostility but merely a distance appropriate to the 1300-year deficit which divides us, and a full critical apparatus when reading his works. Bede is best read at arm's length and not as if a fellow citizen of any particular community, real or imagined, to which we may suppose ourselves to belong.

We get a brief glimpse of Bede when his assumptions on such an issue as his own orthodoxy were challenged, from one of his few surviving letters. In 708 he wrote angrily to one Plegwin, a priest in Bishop Wilfrid's household, to contradict an accusation of heresy which had putatively been made in Wilfrid's presence and which his correspondent had thought fit to divulge to him just two days before.[227] The accusation apparently related to his earlier work *On Times* (*Liber de Temporibus*, written *c*.703), and he set about a lengthy and detailed defence of his opinions, which he asked Plegwin to pass on to a certain David (a priest whose powers of advocacy he clearly thought superior to Plegwin's), to rehearse before Bishop Wilfrid. But it is the energy and ire with which Bede responded, the fundamentals of his rebuttal, taking his stand as an orthodox believer and priest, and the temporary loss of his normal composure that collectively reveal the degree of his discomfort, resorting to language far removed from his norm to denounce his accusers – who were necessarily comparatively well-read priests to make such technical accusations – as 'lewd rustics in their cups', and in the singular as 'an unreasonable brother' suffering from 'a madness of spirit'. Within Bede's thought world, heresy was the most serious indictment conceivable. Although nothing very much seems to have come of the episode thereafter, this was an issue which resurfaced when he was writing *Concerning the Reckoning of Time*, so deeply did it disturb his equilibrium. This is a world-view comprehensible in some respects within the terms of twentieth-century communism, which likewise developed notions of orthodoxy and heresy, but not inside the boundaries of a liberal democracy: inhabitants of the latter would do well to recognise at all times that Bede was not much like themselves.

In conclusion

In this chapter, we have explored the gulf between Bede's perceptions of the cosmos and those of modern audiences, which has considerable repercussions for the current reception of his work and sense of ownership of a figure so distant in time and cultural affiliation. It is primarily by making these differences explicit that we can best hope to benefit from a study of Bede's output. We have reviewed, therefore, the evidence concerning Bede's own life as set down both in his own words and in those of his younger colleague, Cuthbert, who described his death, and recognised some of the dangers of reading these passages as if carrying some single, universal meaning. Bede and his immediate circle have, to an unusual extent, been allowed by later generations to mould his historical persona, but the cultural conditioning which permeates these brief texts needs to be approached with rather more caution than has necessarily been adopted.

Nor does Bede look to have been quite so isolated a figure as is on occasion imagined. We know both his abbots to have been cultured men and Bede seems to have been just one figure – albeit the principal one – within an intellectual circle among his brethren, on whose skills he is likely to have become increasingly dependent in later life, from which derive many of his more ambitious works. Behind most 'great men' are groups of less well recognised individuals and it seems likely that Bede was no exception.

We have then explored the cultivation of his memory successively at Wearmouth/Jarrow, at York, then at Durham, and finally in the national and international arenas, and the ways in which his works were utilised, interpreted and exploited by successive writers, during the Middle Ages and thereafter. That his sanctity long proved problematic is due very largely to a set of historical circumstances, beginning with the decline of Wearmouth/Jarrow as a cult centre, then his remains' putative transferral to Durham and subordination to one of the more vigorous cults of the Middle Ages, that of St Cuthbert, which was of course earlier promoted by Bede himself. Bede's reputation has rested primarily on his works, rather than hagiography, and this has, peculiarly, left Bede as 'The Venerable', as opposed to the far more widely used 'Saint'; even medieval pieces purporting to be brief hagiographies consist primarily of passages from the *Ecclesiastical History*, Cuthbert's letter or works derivative of both, which seem to have been put together as exemplars of the monk-scholar for contemplation by a contemporary audience.

Bede's works gained a wide European readership across the later eighth and ninth centuries, and in England the *Ecclesiastical History* was valued sufficiently to have been translated into the vernacular in Alfred's reign. The extent to which their consumption in their original Latin had fallen away during the later Anglo-Saxon period is unclear but Bedan texts were valued as essential ingredients of any self-respecting monastic *scriptorium* in their original language in the post-Conquest monastic boom, taking a prominent place in the new wave of historical, computistical and theological endeavours of the twelfth century. Many of his works remained central to learning across Western Europe right up to the invention and spread of printing, as did the *Ecclesiastical History*, which retained its role as the cornerstone of English historiography into the sixteenth century. They then suffered within the insular community as a consequence of the Reformation, but were valued by Catholics as vehicles of the Counter-Reformation. However, his *Ecclesiastical History* could not long be ignored in any age with an interest in reconstructing its own past, and this work, but much less so his exegesis, has been revisited repeatedly in the modern period, and was taken up particularly by members of the Oxford Movement in the second half of the nineteenth century.

At the close of that period, Charles Plummer considered the *Ecclesiastical History* Bede's most important work but he shied away from discussing its author's agenda as such, in favour of a listing of memorable scenes 'which will live as long as Englishmen have any care for their country and their Church, as long as the story of saintliness and self-sacrifice can awake an answering echo in human hearts'.[228] What he foregrounded was the continuing relevance of the work to a Christian community which felt a strong sense of fellowship with Bede for both spiritual and patriotic reasons. Bede was viewed, therefore, as the starting point for a High Anglican tradition of quintessentially

'English' Christian scholarship to which Plummer and his associates were laying claim in the present.[229]

In several respects, Plummer's identification with the person of Bede has had a powerful effect on how he has been seen by scholars since, detailing a particular vision of the early medieval author in terms of 'the scholar's uneventful life, spent in a round of religious service and of quiet study'.[230] Indeed, Plummer's remained the standard text of Bede's 'historical' works right up until the late 1960s, and has since been widely quoted, and only mildly critiqued, giving his views a pervasive influence. Most modern commentators remain keen admirers not just of Bede's works but of what they perceive as his historical person.

Yet, alongside, the discipline of history has broadened out exponentially since the start of the twentieth century as an area of academic enquiry, and its promotion has been embraced by ever wider sections of an increasingly secular society, whose interests have encouraged a multiplicity of approaches to ever broader definitions of the past. There is a significant dichotomy here, and a degree of tension between the broader subject and the particular niche which English conversion history continues to occupy. There have been new approaches to Bede's historical works, certainly, and a global upsurge in scholarly interest in his patristic works – the latter in particular has been stimulated in part, at least, by his re-emergence as a doctor of the Catholic Church (1899) and, ultimately, as a saint (1935). But Bede has remained strangely impervious to investigation in the secular mode. Chateaubriand wrote of his older contemporary, Napoleon: 'Bonaparte was such an absolute despot that, after enduring the tyranny of his person, we have to endure the tyranny of his memory.'[231] A long-lived historical tradition in England – and now to an extent in the New World – has similarly promoted culturally conditioned aspects of Bede's memory and understandings of his works, in which historical scholarship on the one hand, and religious veneration on the other, have remained entwined. And this has passed over in addition into the realm of public history: for example, a visitor to Bede's World at Jarrow may well pass by the Bede Industrial Estate on their way, and buy 'Venerable Bede Beer' brewed close by; or we can engage with the issue with which this work began: Should the plinth in Trafalgar Square have been appropriated for some form of commemoration of Bede?

There are other issues which are also worth raising regarding our relationship as a modern audience with Bede as an early medieval author. Fundamental differences of outlook and perspective divide this eighth-century writer and ourselves and are best made explicit, if only to develop our sensitivity towards his techniques, authorial position and purpose. All historians write within theories of history, be they implicit or explicit: while few now will share Bede's explicitly, far more have implicitly, or have simply omitted to explore the issue, feeling comfortable within an intellectual lineage which stretches from Bede himself via Alcuin to William of Malmesbury and finally Charles Plummer and High Victorian scholarship. Our own age is often characterised as one of moral relativism, in the West at least. In contrast, Bede's works were redolent with transcendent ethical and spiritual certainties. In important respects, we need to recall that Bede was not much like us: for that matter he may have been quite unlike all but a very few of his own contemporaries as well, but nor were they, in turn, much like us.

2   The *Ecclesiastical History*: Bede's purposes and ours

He [Bede] is credulous, and relates the foolish stories of an uncultivated age, as if they were true history.[1]

The *Ecclesiastical History* rapidly came to have a life of its own in other company and at other times, but it originated from Bede's fertile mind, and his purposes at the time necessarily determined both its style and content. What was Bede thinking as he was writing and then as he looked back over the work as he brought it to completion? These are important questions which should be born in mind when reading any section of the *EH*, but they are far from easy to resolve. Although he did discuss what he considered history to be and how he had pursued it herein, modern historians have understandably been loath to accept that his brief, introductory passage, added retrospectively, provides a sufficiently rounded vision of his purposes to pass unchallenged, or at least without considerable further development.[2] Additionally, this is a very substantial and multi-faceted work, which it is reasonable to suppose addresses complex purposes, so Bede's intentions need not be susceptible to simple definition, be that his or ours.

Initially this chapter will engage with recent discussions of Bede's purposes, centring on scholarship over the last twenty-five years or so, to explore the directions which this debate has taken. Thereafter we will move to the issue of how Bede himself viewed this work in the final stages of completion. We will home in, therefore, on the comments which Bede proffered his 'readers and hearers' in the Preface with which he opened the final version of his work, which was the one certain addition to the first draft once that had returned from perusal at court.[3] Then, finally, we will turn to that other somewhat anomalous addition, namely the concluding chapter of the work, V, 24, and in particular the first section in which Bede promised 'to recapitulate events already dealt with', to gain further insight to his stance as he brought the work to its conclusion.

Contemporary issues: alternative agendas

Bede's agenda for the *Ecclesiastical History* has traditionally been characterised by its intellectuality, its religiosity, its idealism and its concern to graft English Christianity onto the wider world of divine grace,[4] within the terms by which he understood that from his study of the Scriptures, of pre-existing histories and theology. Behind these purposes, however, scholars have striven to uncover other agendas with a more particular relevance to the decade or so within which the *EH* was conceived and executed. Should not Bede be seen in some respects as a man of his own political world, a writer reflective of particular visions of contemporary and primarily Northumbrian realities? Professor David Kirby has long since made the case for King Ceolwulf having influenced Bede's construction of the *Ecclesiastical History*,[5] since when the main arguments have grouped into two very different camps: on the one hand is the notion of Bede as a proactive religious reformer, whose agenda in writing his *Ecclesiastical History* was at least influenced, perhaps even dominated, by his desire to further both structural and moral reform of the Church; on the other is the view that Bede was pursuing a fundamentally political agenda in opposition to other clerical writers and in particular against Stephen, author of the *Life of Wilfrid* and spokesman for the influential Wilfridian party within the English – and particularly the Northumbrian – Church. We must explore both these important sets of arguments at some length.

Bede and reform

The vision of Bede in later years as a committed reformer was set out most clearly in a seminal article by Dr Alan Thacker, published in 1983.[6] Basing his case particularly but not exclusively on Bede's *Letter to Egbert* of November 734, Thacker interpreted Bede as very critical of poor practice and leadership within the contemporary Church. His remedy was based on Pope Gregory's advocacy of a monastic pastorate, an 'elite order of preachers who were to teach and more particularly embody the holy life',[7] and he developed St Cuthbert, in particular, as a role model of the ideal prior, hermit and bishop whose combination of the contemplative with the pastoral could be viewed as an English counterpart to Gregory's model in *Pastoral Care*. Indeed, Bede's desire to develop Cuthbert as an English exemplar of the ideal cleric as both represented and advocated by St Gregory can be seen as the principal reason for his belated provision of a prose life of the Bernician saint. At the core of Bede's model of a new society lay a muscular form of monastic Christianity, which would be capable of providing the teaching within a contemplative environment necessary to develop a well-educated, right-minded and motivated pastorate, whose role would be not just to preach but also to practise a Christian life, so teach by example. General reform of the body politic should engage all of monasteries, a well-instructed king and aristocracy, and a rejuvenated episcopacy based in model communities, all working in harmony towards a shared set of religious goals. Bede was not alone in urging reform: the Council of Clofesho in 747, just sixteen years later, advocated a somewhat similar programme for Southumbria, in part in response to the agenda being advocated by St Boniface,[8] on the continent.

This reading of Bede's *Letter to Egbert* is in general terms uncontroversial and Bede's redevelopment of Cuthbert in his prose *Life* certainly lends itself well to this interpretation. In addition, more recent scholarship has highlighted the reform motif in other of Bede's works. For example Scott DeGregorio has directed attention to the similarities of approach between the *Letter* and Bede's commentary *On Ezra and Nehemiah*, which should be read in terms of concerns regarding such issues as taxation of the poor and corrupt monasteries, which he proposed should be rectified by the combined attention of the priesthood and the king. Ezra represents, therefore, a type of the Northumbrian bishop in the present, with Nehemiah as an Anglo-Saxon king, although Bede seems less than confident that the latter, at least, was currently entirely onside.[9] Nor was this exclusively an issue for Bede in later life, since he made reference to his concerns regarding the poor quality of reading prevalent among his fellow countrymen in the letter to Hwætberht which prefaces his *On the Apocalypse*, apparently written before 716.[10]

If a reforming agenda was central to Bede's authorship of the *Ecclesiastical History*, how does it manifest itself? As Bede set out in his Preface, he intended to provide a gallery of local case studies of both good and bad behaviour for purposes of present, moral edification, and these can easily be construed in terms of his advocacy of a particular type of Christianity, and a particular relationship between Man and God, with very real meaning for his contemporary audience. So, for example, in a chapter of exceptional length, Gregory himself was portrayed as the ideal of the active-contemplative and monk-bishop, who had not 'lost any of his monastic perfection by reason of his pastoral cares', whose writings Bede particularly lauded and whom he held up as the archetypal, proactive, Christian leader – the apostle to the English, who 'snatched our race from the teeth of the ancient foe'.[11] Gregory was arguably developed as Bede's core model of Christian behaviour in the context of his *History*, against whom all others would be measured, and as a key authority on precisely this subject: his praise of *Pastoral Care* foregrounds Gregory as the source of his own reformist thinking. Augustine and the fellow monks of St Gregory who were his companions were described in a suitably Gregorian mould as imitators of the lives of the apostles, 'constantly engaged in prayers, in vigils and fasts', preaching to the English and living the faith even in expectation of martyrdom (I, 26), then Aidan, Cuthbert, Chad, Egbert and others were represented as insular types of the same model of selfless, modest, learned, monkish pastor. Indeed, variants of the Gregorian model of the Christian life, encompassing all of pastoral care, exceptional learning and scholarship, devotion to the Scriptures and exemplary patterns of behaviour, often reinforced by miracles as signs of divine approbation, run through the entire work, from Bede's depiction of St Germanus (I, 17–21) right up to his commemoration of Bishop Wilfrid (V, 19), Bishop Acca (V, 20) and, far more briefly, both Bishop Tobias and Archbishop Tatwine (V, 23). There seems no obstacle, therefore, should we choose to include the *Ecclesiastical History* under the wider umbrella of Bede's reformist agenda: indeed, that provides a valuable tool by which to read contemporary meaning into this text.

That said, it must be stressed that there is comparatively little which is explicitly and actively reformist in the *EH*, as regards the Church at least. There are, for example, very few complaints regarding secular or corrupt monasteries such as one finds in the *Letter to Egbert*, and no expression of dissatisfaction at the small number of Northumbrian dioceses. Bede noted Archbishop Theodore's enthusiasm for the subdivision of bishoprics, as expressed in the record of the Synod of Hertford which he quoted,[12] his subsequent division of the see of Bishop Wilfrid,[13] and the eventual creation of northern dioceses at both Hexham and Abercorn (which proved short-lived[14]), then Whithorn, making a total of four Northumbrian bishoprics in 731,[15] but he offered nothing of his own personal views on the issue and forbore to look forward to the possibility of new foundations to come. Regarding his notice of a current trend among Northumbrians to become monks, Bede's remarks are far less obviously critical, and far less clearly related to his comments on the subject in his *Letter to Egbert*, than recent editors have argued.[16] Indeed, if the later text be set aside for a moment, this passage could more easily be read in an affirmative context, with only a slight potential sting in the tail, but even that is drawn to a large extent by its proximity to Bede's final, very positive comments which close the chapter and, indeed, this whole exercise in ecclesiastical history.[17] Here is a literal translation of his specific remarks regarding the current trend into monasticism:

> In these favourable times of peace and serenity, many of the people of the Northumbrians, both noble and plebeian, have put down their weapons and accepted the tonsure, preferring that they and their descendants should take monastic vows rather than practise military skills. What the result will be in the end, a later age will see.

This is hardly an indictment as it stands and would not be read as such had we not got the *Letter to Egbert*, from three years later, from which to import a very different agenda by which to interpret this text. While Professor James Campbell was right to stress Bede's discretion,[18] the cryptic nature of many of his remarks means that it is often unclear from this work alone precisely where he stood on major issues.

While acknowledging that Bede had a reformist agenda, therefore, as expressed in several of the works of his later years, that agenda is comparatively low key and very largely implicit in the *Ecclesiastical History*, occurring primarily in a host of carefully constructed characterisations which are offered up in affirmative contexts as exemplars of appropriate behaviour to his audience. While cumulatively these should be recognised as extremely influential both in terms of the whole work and (even more so) in terms of role models for his readership (as he himself stressed of Gregory's *Dialogues*), it must be remembered that the 'Bede as advocate' whose voice is so powerful in the *Letter to Egbert* is generally absent from the *History*, the tone of which is far more muted and far less openly hortatory. Indeed, Bede rarely expressed his own views with any degree of openness, preferring generally to guide his interpretation of the past along particular pathways without overtly himself staging an appearance. In that respect he is far less vocal a presence within his *EH* than either Orosius, for example, in his *Seven Histories*, or Gregory of Tours in his *Ten Books of History*, preferring far more subtle means of persuasion than either of the latter.

As a supplement to this discussion we need to pause briefly to consider more hagiographical interpretations of the *Ecclesiastical History*. The earlier is to see the entire work as if a hagiography the hero of which is the English race *in toto*, as was proposed by Charles Jones in 1947,[19] but this is in large part an attempt to explain its structure (for which see below, pp. 101–8), rather than its agenda. While this view finds some echoes in later studies,[20] it has not evolved into a full-blown interpretation, appearing primarily as just one comparatively minor aspect of the work. The more recent is to think of Bede's *History* as focused primarily on mission and missionaries. Professor David Rollason suggested that Bede was 'working in an environment where the mission was important, not only to churchmen but perhaps also to the kings of Northumbria' and viewed the work, 'in effect, about mission, or at least about conversion'.[21] This is the approach adopted also by Professor Ian Wood:[22] 'Bede's *Ecclesiastical History* is, to a large extent, a history of mission, and although, strictly speaking, it is not a work of hagiography, it spends much time recounting the lives of saints, one after the other.' For Wood, Christianisation via the work of missionaries was the 'driving force of Bede's narrative' from the 'middle of Book One to the end of Book Three' and 'perhaps more than any historian since Luke . . . Bede set himself a task where the history that he wished to cover was, to a large extent, missionary history'.[23]

Of course, a work which was conceived for the purpose of writing the English into universal, providential history needed to make frequent reference to missionaries and necessarily had a high regard for their way of life, but this vision of the *Ecclesiastical History* is only partial: it neglects what Bede himself has told his audience concerning his purposes; it virtually ignores the shift in emphasis across the last two books, from the English as recipients of mission to their role as practitioners, which combined make up around 42 per cent of the entire work; even within the earlier chapters it disregards numerous passages of no direct relevance to mission, and only comparatively short sections do actually consist of a succession of hagiographical stories. In practice, Bede is extraordinarily reticent about the mechanics of missionary activity among the English, contenting himself in most instances with the simple equation: missionary presence + royal baptism = the conversion of a people, apparently on the assumption that the divine foreknowledge of the conversion to which he alluded as a prelude to the process provided sufficient explanation of its success on its own,[24] and he preferred to ignore the presence of numerous unbaptised Anglo-Saxons across his own lifetime, apparently for the sake of creating an illusion in the present of a fully Christianised people already included within the universal, Catholic whole. Somewhat more on this subject was written by Bede's correspondent, Bishop Daniel, at some point during the previous decade or so, in his letter to Boniface in Germany, which actually focuses on the dialectics of the process.[25] While I do not wish to ignore or play down Bede's interest in mission, therefore, I consider that this thesis does not offer us a viable explanation of Bede's authorship of the *Ecclesiastical History*.

Bede and Wilfrid

Bede certainly said less than he might have about Wilfrid,[26] and there has long been 'a recurring suspicion that Bede did not like' his diocesan bishop of the period *c.*705–9.[27] Charles Plummer listed in this context Bede's omission of almost all the miracles recounted by Eddi (Stephen), including only a vision of St Michael which Wilfrid had putatively shared with his then priest and ultimate successor, Acca,[28] his lack of criticism of those responsible for Wilfrid's several expulsions, contrasted with his praise for the kings involved, his complacency regarding Oswiu's appointment of Chad during Wilfrid's prolonged absence in Frankia, his failure to comment unfavourably on Theodore's division of his diocese and his approval of those who replaced Wilfrid, two of whom, Cuthbert and John of Beverley, are particular heroes of the *History*. In the background, of course, lies the accusation of heresy made against Bede in Wilfrid's presence and by members of his household, of which Plegwin warned him in 708 and which he took pains to refute in a lengthy reply,[29] although we have no knowledge of the eventual outcome of this affair.

This sense of unease regarding Bede's attitude towards a leading Northumbrian cleric, who had been his diocesan and was personally known to him at some point in the period 705–9, was developed by Professor Walter Goffart, in three complementary essays published in 1988, 1990 and 2005,[30] to propose an ingenious theory of Bede as advocate in the *Ecclesiastical History*, with its focus firmly on the immediate, Northumbrian, political context. Goffart took as his source material Bede's 'historical' works,[31] which he subjected to close reading alongside the anonymous but broadly contemporary *Life of Ceolfrith* and Stephen's *Life of Wilfrid*. He interpreted them all as highly interactive and viewed Bede's later authorship of the *EH* as both less detached and less idealistic than had hitherto often been supposed, but rather conditioned to a large extent by his desire to counteract the message offered by

Stephen's hagiographical essay. By these means Goffart proposed both to circumvent and to explain Bede's diplomatic silences concerning the recent past in the *EH* and to restore the work and its author to their immediate, regional context,[32] interpreting the *Ecclesiastical History* as a large-scale intervention in an ongoing contest for power within the Northumbrian Church which originated in a rancorous competition between Wilfrid and his political opponents in the 680s but now centred on the struggle for control of York as the recovery of its metropolitan status gradually became a reality (which it finally did in 735).

Goffart argued that, despite some appearances to the contrary, Bede's *History* was predominantly about Northumbria, reaching the region in the closing chapter of book I and remaining there very largely thereafter,[33] and he saw it as the culmination of the comparatively large-scale hagiographical effort which occurred there from the 690s onwards, stimulated very largely by Wilfrid: 'by dominating the horizon, generating hostility towards himself, and continuing to be an issue after his death, he incited the Northumbrian Church, alone in England, to provide itself with a written history'.[34] This highly interactive process began with a series of cultic ceremonies designed to promote particular church sites: these included the elevation of St Æthelthryth at Ely (*c.*695),[35] which Goffart considered 'dramatised and honoured Wilfrid's time as bishop of Northumbria';[36] the translation of Oswald's remains to Bardney, which he likewise interpreted as potentially associated with Wilfrid;[37] and the elevation of Cuthbert at Lindisfarne in 698, which was accompanied quite rapidly by the composition of an anonymous *Life of Cuthbert* at Lindisfarne.[38] Edwin's putative remains were also reburied at Whitby, and an anonymous *Life of Gregory* was written there,[39] which Goffart interprets as anti-Wilfridian acts by Abbess Hild in support of the erstwhile Whitby monks who had been appointed bishops in place of Wilfrid: Bosa at York (678–86, 691–706) and John of Beverley at Hexham, then York (687–706, 706–21).[40] For Goffart, Cuthbert's reputation as a miracle worker was developed by those opposed to Wilfrid during Aldfrith's reign (686–705) and the appearance of his first *Life* was associated with the last expulsion of Wilfrid following the Council of Austerfield in 703, with the *Life of Gregory* also produced at this time as an antidote to the centrality of Wilfrid to the Catholicism of Northumbria.[41] In opposition to Wilfrid's dominant position within Northumbrian Christianity across much of the late seventh century and the first decade of the eighth, Gregory was being promoted as 'the true fountainhead of Northumbrian Christianity' alongside Cuthbert as the 'singular patron of his land' by authors at Whitby and Lindisfarne who 'effectively solicited the past to redress the balance of the present'.[42]

The dynastic conflict which provides the backdrop to these events is interpreted by Goffart as a major influence on the ongoing literary conflict between Wilfrid's followers and his opponents. King Aldfrith's death in 705 without adult sons or other close kin provided an opportunity for other branches of the royal family to assert a claim to the throne. Wilfrid initially attempted to return to Northumbria by forging an alliance with a candidate named Eadwulf but was rebuffed, so instead threw his weight behind the supporters of Aldfrith's young son, Osred, who included his aunt, Oswiu's daughter Ælfflæd, abbess of Whitby. Osred's faction seized Bamburgh and achieved power, despite being besieged there.[43] A Synod of the Northumbrian Church was then staged under the presidency of Archbishop Berhtwold near the River Nidd,[44] to hammer out a settlement: Wilfrid was able to reoccupy Ripon and the diocese of Hexham when Ælfflæd's protégé, John of Beverley, the erstwhile bishop, was moved to York on the death of Bosa,[45] and Wilfrid's priest, Acca, eventually succeeded him on his death in 709. However, Osred was killed in 716, once again opening the door to rival factions and throwing the northern Church into disarray. Abbot Ceolfrith's departure for Rome coincided with the year of Osred's death, while a distant cousin of the king, Coenred, secured Northumbria from 716–18, followed by Osric, whom later annalists assumed to be Osred's brother. Osric, however, died in 729, immediately after having 'appointed Ceolwulf, brother of his predecessor Coenred, as his successor'.[46] Ceolwulf, therefore, represented a branch of the Northumbrian royal dynasty which had been attempting to establish itself on the throne for some time, and which had just succeeded in doing so when Bede was writing his *Ecclesiastical History*.

Bede's verse *Life of Cuthbert* was self-evidently written in Osred's reign,[47] but Goffart interpreted the king's death in 716 as coinciding with a spate of new works, including the anonymous *Life of Ceolfrith*, the *Life of Wilfrid*, and Bede's prose *Life of Cuthbert* (written by 721), plus his *Greater Chronicle* (c.725), *Martyrology* and *History of the Abbots*. Goffart suggests that Ceolfrith's sudden resignation was timed to secure the succession to the abbacy of Wearmouth/Jarrow before the new King Coenred could intervene,[48] but the latter's rapid replacement by Osric (718–29) revived Wilfridian influence, implying that the *Life of Ceolfrith*, with its reference to the Wilfridian connections of its hero, was written in this reign. The *Life of Wilfrid*, in contrast, was written by an associate of Wilfrid's later career, who quoted from the anonymous *Life of Cuthbert* in his Preface, chapter VI and elsewhere, and mirrored also that work's use of biblical parallels and perhaps even selected and adapted examples of its miracles.[49] This was despite his failure ever to mention Cuthbert or his *Life*, and Goffart felt that the Lindisfarne community would have reacted to this 'rather gross rivalry' by seeking a replacement from Bede of the existing prose life which they perhaps now viewed as 'soiled and devalued'.[50] Bede's new prose *Life*, which neglected to mention its predecessor but incorporated the somewhat discreditable appropriation of Ripon by Wilfrid, was therefore written because Stephen had 'befouled the original *Life of St. Cuthbert* by placing it in the service of the very different sanctity Wilfrid had embodied'.[51]

And why was the *Life of Wilfrid* commissioned by Bishop Acca and Abbot Tatberht? Goffart interpreted it as an 'obstinately Northumbrian narrative' which said remarkably little about his Mercian interests but, rather, highlighted the strong connections within Wilfrid's career between North-umbria and Rome, which might be read in terms of current interest in the issue of an archdiocese at York: therein Colman was presented as 'metro-politan bishop of York', then Wilfrid himself as 'metropolitan bishop of the city of York', suggesting that 'as the hero of a biography, he [Wilfrid] became the stalking-horse for the strivings of other men' seeking control of the impending archdiocese, namely Stephen's sponsors.[52]

For Goffart, therefore, Bede's prose *Life of Cuthbert* was a direct response to the writing of a *Life of Wilfrid* and the ambitions of the Wilfridians which that represented. The new work sought to match in Cuthbert's story Stephen's 'stately advance through Wilfrid's Life', incorporated Cuthbert's participation in the establishment of a monastic outpost of Melrose at Ripon, which had then been expelled on behalf of Wilfrid, and alluded to terrible times at Lindisfarne between Cuthbert's death and Bishop Eadberht's elec-tion, neither of which episodes appears in the earlier, anonymous *Life*: Wilfrid was never named by Bede but his malevolent influence is interpreted as bulking large.[53] Bede's new work, therefore, represents an institutional alli-ance between Wearmouth/Jarrow and Lindisfarne early in Osric's reign, dir-ected against the Wilfridians whom he favoured. In it Cuthbert was no longer just an eccentric worker of wonders but became the model monk-bishop of English provenance, capable of comparison with the apostles, Pope Gregory and St Augustine, and a very different figure from Bishop Wilfrid.[54] In his *History of the Abbots*, which Goffart dates to 725–31, Bede then refocused the foundation of his own house away from Abbot Ceolfrith, whose connections with Wilfrid the anonymous *Life of Ceolfrith* had admitted, back to Benedict Biscop, whose sixteen-year rule, travels and book-collecting dominate the first book, and whose death opens the second. For Goffart, 'that Bishop Wilfrid had helped Benedict Biscop by letting him have Ceolfrid as assistant . . . Bede blotted out'.[55]

With these interrelationships very much in mind, Goffart then turned to the *Ecclesiastical History*, and the shifting political arena against which it was written, with its completion in 731 coinciding approximately with Ceolwulf's temporary loss of the crown and Acca's of the see of Hexham, plus Wilfrid II's replacement by Egbert as bishop of York soon after.[56] Why did Bede write his *History*? Goffart rejected the solutions previously offered on the grounds that all presuppose that he was operating within a calm and scholarly atmosphere entirely outside the political world. Rather, 'Bede capped a series of fragmentary essays on local Church history, some of them his own, and summed them up in a grandiose but hardly dispassionate synthesis.'[57] The key issue for Bede was active co-operation in the present between the Northumbrian Church and Canterbury to revive or refound the archdiocese at York,[58] and Goffart saw this as the decisive factor in, for example, the prom-inence given to Albinus and Nothhelm in the Preface. The *Ecclesiastical His-tory* breaks down, however, into three unequal parts: the first Goffart sees as underpinned by the work of Gildas, the second by the Whitby *Life of Gregory* and the remainder by Stephen's *Life of Wilfrid*, with which Bede had a particularly 'adversarial relationship'.[59] So, for example, Goffart sees Bede's championing of the Irish mission to Northumbria in book III as designed to contradict Stephen's presentation of Wilfrid as the central hero of Romanisation versus 'an error-filled past',[60] his veneration of Chad as opposition to Stephen's condemnation of his Anglo-Irish faction within the Church as 'Quartodecimans', and Stephen's admiration for Wilfrid's missionary work in Frisia and Sussex as 'tarnished' by Bede in the *EH*.[61] Stephen's hostility towards Theodore then contrasts with Bede's vision of his presence as a 'golden age' for the English Church, with its roots firmly linked back to the work of the Gregorian mission, and the 'relationship of the two narratives can be traced in detail, as a succession of responses by Bede to Stephen's statements'.[62] So, for example, Bede's much longer description of the Synod of Whitby in 664 reduces Wilfrid's significance by stressing the survival to this date of Roman paschal dating in Northumbria, the priority of a Rome-trained Irishman's contradiction of Irish dating and the greater authority of Bishop Agilbert, even while providing Wilfrid himself with a lengthier speech, so it generally subverted Stephen's account and his foregrounding of Wilfrid.[63] For Goffart, 'Stephen's *Life* impelled Bede to seek information from elsewhere that would contradict, dilute, or reorient Stephen's claims for his hero', requiring us to see the *EH* as an 'active refutation' of the earlier work, which 'lurks behind the main narrative of the *Historia Ecclesiastica* as the rival to be rectified or contradicted, the mirror whose image must be meticulously reversed'.[64]

By this interpretation, the *Ecclesiastical History* should be read as a focused piece of advocacy written in the context of a continuing dialogue between the Wilfridians and their opponents within Northumbria, of whom Bede was a leading member, which was already some four decades old in 731 but which had a new vibrancy in terms of the imminence of archdiocesan status for York, which both sides wished to control. For Bede, as revealed in his *Letter to Egbert*, abuses within the Northumbrian Church began following King Aldfrith's death in 705, which coincided, of course, with Wilfrid's last restoration and the prominence of his principal acolyte, Bishop Acca, whose expulsion in 731 Bede could be expected to have viewed in a positive light. Bede's position in the *EH* built on his preference for the Irish and his hostility towards Wilfrid's memory, which were already apparent in his verse *Life of Cuthbert* (written by 716). In the intervening years he produced a prose *Life of Cuthbert*, from which the passages of the anonymous *Life* which Stephen had appropriated on behalf of Wilfrid were expunged, and his *History of the Abbots*, sanitised of links between Abbot Ceolfrith and Wilfrid. Bede's widespread praise for the Irish contrasts with Stephen's stigmatisation of them as 'poisonous weeds', and his closing image in the *EH* of the Ionan and Pictish churches as converted to Catholicism by champions of English orthodoxy should be read in the context of the pending northern archdiocese, which might hopefully extend to include all northern Britain.[65] Bede, therefore, wrote the

Ecclesiastical History using existing insular texts as models and offered it with the intention of superseding other pre-existing accounts of the conversion of the English to Christianity, for primarily political purposes.[66]

Goffart's interpretation is a highly developed and tightly argued one which is in some respects persuasive,[67] but overall fails to convince, largely because Bede simply does not display the required levels of hostility towards the Wilfridians across the first third of the eighth century. His numerous, effusive dedications of works of exegesis to Bishop Acca necessarily undermine any interpretation of Bede as the mouthpiece of a rival faction within the Northumbrian Church and there is no evidence that a rift had occurred more recently when the *Ecclesiastical History* was nearing completion.[68] On the contrary, therein Acca was invariably highly regarded and represented as an exemplary churchman of the very highest calibre. So he was *reverentissimus* ('most reverend') as the source of two miracle stories relating to King Oswald,[69] and Bede's witness to Wilfrid's miraculous vision concerning the archangel Michael's intervention in the timing of his own death.[70] Bede vouched for him in a much longer passage:[71] he was *strenuissimus et magnificus* ('most strenuous and noble'), an enthusiastic and successful embellisher of his diocesan church, a keen collector of relics, manuscripts and various religious paraphernalia, a dedicated patron of sacred music and a *peritissimus* ('most skilful') chorister, *doctissimus* ('most learned') in the Scriptures, *castissimus* ('entirely spotless') in his Catholicism and *sollertissimus* ('very knowledgeable') as regards his grasp of ecclesiastical rules. Rarely did Bede deploy so many superlatives on behalf of a single individual and never did he express such confidence in any character's future virtues: 'he [Acca] will not cease to be so until he gains the reward of his piety and devotion [i.e. goes to heaven]'. Bede's admiration of Acca is so marked and his treatment so exceptional that to suppose them to have been in rival camps of the Northumbrian Church is simply not a sustainable thesis.[72] Nor was he hostile to others of Wilfrid's erstwhile connections: his treatment of Willibrord, the missionary bishop of the Frisians in the 690s who had spent a lengthy period in Ireland but was in origin a member of Wilfrid's Ripon community, was entirely supportive both in the *Greater Chronicle*, in which he was singled out for especial treatment, and in the *EH*.[73]

Goffart's thesis also requires Acca to have been a political opponent of King Ceolwulf. This is just one aspect of a general over-confidence in his ability to reconstruct Northumbrian politics in these decades, on the basis of very little evidence, often of quite ambivalent kinds. Again, this view is far from proven, although it is perhaps plausible. Bede wrote in his prologue to *On the Temple* regarding Acca's 'present worries of temporal affairs', but this is in such general terms that it cannot be used as evidence of any difficulty vis-à-vis the king, whether Ceolwulf or his predecessor.[74] It might simply mean that Acca was weighed down by the affairs of his office. It is his appearance in the first year of the continuation to the Moore manuscript that is the key piece of evidence. This reads: 'King Ceolwulf was captured and tonsured and given back to the kingdom; Bishop Acca fled from his see.' Colgrave perhaps over-interpreted this passage when he translated *fugatus* as 'was driven',[75] but Acca's unusual behaviour is at least very likely to have been connected with the dynastic crisis which had just been mentioned.[76] We do not, however, know whether he fled when Ceolwulf was tonsured or when he returned to power, nor if he returned. Even if his absence was just a matter of weeks or months, it might well have been felt of sufficient significance to be noted by an author at Wearmouth/Jarrow, where he was the diocesan bishop.[77]

The second and much longer continuation of Bede's recapitulation in the *EH*, which was probably written in 766, had Acca replaced only in 735, which suggests either that there was an interregnum or that he did return to Hexham and resume his duties under Ceolwulf. This chronicle fails to record Acca's death, although those of Bishop Cyneberht (732), Archbishop Tatwine (734), Bede (735), Archbishop Nothhelm (739) and Bishop Æthelwold (740) were all included. The *Anglo-Saxon Chronicle* similarly makes no reference: the much later *History of the Kings* (*Historia Regum*) dates his obit to 740, describes him in highly laudatory terms (to a large extent taken from Bede), and has him entombed at Hexham, with a cult developing there and healing miracles performed.[78] This is non-contemporary and should not be accepted uncritically but it does open up the possibility that Acca returned to his see and then perhaps retired to the contemplative life at a date nearer 735, still within the community,[79] but there can be no certainty: Acca was certainly among the saints venerated at Hexham in the twelfth century but on precisely what authority is unclear.[80]

Retirement – if that was what was involved – need not, however, necessarily imply political reasons. Acca had been a bishop since 709 and several Northumbrian Church leaders did retire to the ascetic or monastic life before they died, as had John of Beverley, Bishop of York, for example, *c*.714, long before his death in 721.[81] His successor, Wilfrid II, likewise retired in 732 but lived on until the mid-740s and, again, we need not think the reason was necessarily political, although such is often assumed. That Acca was a political opponent of Ceolwulf is, therefore, unproven, although it does remain the simplest explanation of the few snippets of information available to us. It is quite possible that his departure from Hexham in 731 was temporary, and that he both returned and retired there, eventually being buried in his own church. He was, however, a figure who was widely connected, having been an associate of both Wilfrid and, earlier, Bishop Bosa of York, whom Bede lauded and who had been trained at Whitby in the school founded by Abbess Hild, an adherent before 664 of the Ionan method of dating Easter. The division of the early eighth-century Northumbrian Church into two hostile camps, with Bede in one and Acca in the other, lacks the clear boundaries that would make it credible.

Nor does Bede, in fact, offer an 'abasement' of Wilfrid himself,[82] rather treating him throughout with considerable respect. Wilfrid occurs by name in no less than eighteen chapters of the *Ecclesiastical History*,[83] but references to him are to be found particularly in book IV, in which he features in eleven separate chapters.

Like Acca but in a less concentrated fashion, Wilfrid's appearances were conditioned by superlatives: any difference owes more to the greater spread of his presence across the text than to any failure of its author to laud his character or achievements. Two of the superlatives he used of Acca were also applied to Wilfrid (*doctissimus* and *reverentissimus*). The fact that he was dead by 731 led to his otherwise being commemmorated in a slightly different way: 'of blessed memory' (*beatae memoriae*) occurs twice of Wilfrid but obviously not of Acca. It is worth noting that Bede massively extended Stephen's treatment of Wilfrid's contribution to the Synod of Whitby,[84] placing in his mouth a systematic rendition of what were apparently his own views on the subject of paschal dating. While this provides little indication of what Wilfrid actually said, Bede's identification with him can hardly be read as other than supportive of his role. Certainly, Bede was very discrete – even cryptic at times – concerning Wilfrid, perhaps in large part because he was uncomfortable regarding the confrontational positions he at times seems to have adopted,[85] but there is not the slightest explicit criticism in what he wrote. Rather, Wilfrid's primacy as an English Catholic was particularly remarked and promoted, representing him as the harbinger of the eventual inclusion of the Anglo-Saxons within that Universal Christendom towards which Bede was steering the Anglo-Saxons in this work. His relationships with various members of the Northumbrian royal family were mentioned, most particularly in terms of his close connection with Queen Æthelthryth, who was, of course, a particular heroine of Bede's. He made no attempt to explain the rift between King Ecgfrith and Bishop Wilfrid, which he could hardly ignore, but he made clear where his sympathies lay by terming Wilfrid *reverentissimus* ('most reverent') at this point, while failing to balance the passage by any comparable praise of the king, despite his being the primary lay patron of his own house.

His record of Wilfrid's death in V, 19 was Bede's opportunity to provide a coherent summary of his career, which offered a vision of the exemplary monk and bishop, resting on, so to an extent legitimising, both the *Life of Wilfrid* and, more particularly, his verse epitaph at Ripon, which Bede quoted in full and in apparent approval.[86] This passage stands comparison with Bede's provision of summaries of the careers of other of his clerical heroes in association with notice of their deaths,[87] but it must be significant that his treatment of Wilfrid is almost as long as that of the major excursus with which he dealt with the death of Gregory, and longer by far than any other English character dealt with in a single chapter. In addition, Wilfrid features in the earliest substrate of the calendar of Lorsch, generally thought to derive from a Jarrow original,[88] which suggests that he was commemorated not just by Bede but by his whole community.

Neither Acca nor Wilfrid is the object of any explicitly adverse comment, therefore, let alone open hostility, in the *Ecclesiastical History*. Rather, both are treated consistently as significant and honourable participants in the unfolding story of the English en route to becoming full members of God's family of peoples. Nor does Goffart's thesis command complete respect as an explanation of the several earlier works. Bede had noted his intention to write a prose *Life of Cuthbert* when he produced his metrical *Life*, so it is unsurprising that one eventually emerged. It is not safe to interpret this notice as a late addition to the text. The earlier anonymous work depicted Cuthbert as a wonder worker in the tradition of the Irish Church and as an early architect of a Northumbrian Church in the Catholic tradition.[89] The latter was no longer really an issue by *c.*720, when Bede was apparently more interested in promoting the Northumbrian saint as a model monk-bishop and pastor along Gregorian lines, so as an exemplar in the context of his own reform agenda, and it is in this guise that Cuthbert recurs so powerfully in the *Ecclesiastical History*. There were, therefore, plausible reasons for Bede writing a new prose *Life*, without recourse to the arguments offered by Goffart, and the replication of works in both prose and verse was in any case an accepted and much-admired mode of the time, which we see in the works of Aldhelm, for example, and later Alcuin. There is, for that matter, no particular reason to suppose that the Lindisfarne community would have taken exception to Stephen's use of passages from the anonymous *Life of Cuthbert* in his *Life of Wilfrid*. After all, the anonymous author of the former had himself incorporated material from earlier works, including the *Life of Martin* by Sulpicius Severus,[90] which he presumably expected his readers and hearers both to recognise and to appreciate in the new context. That the *Life of Wilfrid* made more limited but in some senses comparable use of an insular text devoted to Cuthbert is more likely to have been viewed as a compliment than an insult. And while Stephen clearly had had a copy of the first *Life of Cuthbert*, there is no evidence that his *Life of Wilfrid* was thereafter actually known to the monks at Lindisfarne, who may even have been entirely ignorant of his use of their own *vita*, although Bede, of course, had both.

Nor is it safe to argue that Bede necessarily sought to expunge the memory of the earlier anonymous *Life* by the production of his own prose version. Although he failed to mention the earlier work therein, even while naming numerous informants, his use of it would have been blatantly obvious to the target audience at Lindisfarne, and he did name it as a source in his Preface to the *Ecclesiastical History*, directed towards a wider audience for whom the connection would perhaps have been less obvious, which seems inconsistent were his motive in writing the prose *Life*, as Goffart described, to replace entirely the anonymous version, as if that had never existed.

That Bede's *History of the Abbots* should have focused primarily on Benedict Biscop as opposed to Ceolfrith need not be read as a response to the *Life of Wilfrid*, which also, of course, made honourable mention of the former but not the latter.[91] Benedict was, after all, the initial founder of Wearmouth and had some role also in establishing Jarrow, so could well have been thought the primary subject of this work, given that the unity of the two houses was central to Bede's agenda. But the connection with Wilfrid was hardly critical to the anonymous *Life of Ceolfrith*, which claimed that Ceolfrith first became a monk at Gilling, where his brother, Cynefrith, had been abbot before retiring to study in Ireland, but when he and others were carried off by the plague, the new abbot, Tunberht, with Ceolfrith and others at the monastery, took up Bishop Wilfrid's invitation to join the monks at Ripon. As bishop, it was naturally Wilfrid who ordained Ceolfrith to the priesthood.[92] Benedict Biscop then sought and obtained Ceolfrith's aid in establishing Wearmouth, apparently recruiting him from Ripon, but when he departed once more for the continent, leaving Ceolfrith in charge, 'he suffered from the jealousies and most violent attacks of certain nobles, who could not endure his regular discipline', and returned 'to his own monastery', only to be re-recruited by Benedict on his return.[93] That Bede should have omitted from his *History of the Abbots* a sequence of events which reflected vacillation on Ceolfrith's part, and even divergent foundation histories for the two sites, is not surprising, given the role he was expected to play therein as the steadfast father of the double community over the long years separating Benedict's death in 689 from his own departure for Rome in 716.[94] Nor was his decision to leave in that year necessarily sudden, although it does seem to have caught Bede somewhat by surprise. Rather, the copying of three great bibles, one of which he was to take with him as a presentation copy for the papacy, surely implies a long drawn out and planned process, albeit one which was not necessarily widely understood by his brethren. Ceolfrith's death en route suggests that he had left the journey rather too late for his plans to be fulfilled, rather than that he had set off precipitously and earlier than intended.

Nor is the relationship between the *Life of Ceolfrith* and Bede's *History of the Abbots* necessarily as Goffart presented it. There has been considerable sympathy for the view that Bede was himself the author of the *Life of Ceolfrith*,[95] but the arguments remain indecisive and it could easily have been written by any one of several of his contemporaries at Wearmouth/Jarrow. There is also the issue of the respective dates of these two works. Although the anonymous piece is generally supposed to have been written soon after Ceolfrith's death in 716, its Preface is clearly post-735 since it treats Bede as already deceased. Elsewhere within it the use of dating from the incarnation also seems suspicious at such an early date, if Bede should really be viewed as the prime insular champion of this dating mechanism as late as 731, having not adopted it for his *Greater Chronicle* c.725. Again, reference to those companions of Ceolfrith who returned to Wearmouth/Jarrow as narrating the miracles attending his tomb exclusively in the imperfect tense implies that this practice was no longer current at the time of writing but was being recalled by the author, suggesting that some years separated the events from their recording, and perhaps even that those responsible were now dead.[96] If it be accepted that Bede used it in his brief treatment of Ceolfrith's departure and death in *Concerning the Reckoning of Time*, then the *Life of Ceolfrith* has to have been written before 725,[97] but it would be entirely possible to reverse this relationship, given that Bede can be expected at that date to have had recall himself of the details of his old abbot's decease nine years earlier and the bare statistics of his life as referred to here. This is not to suggest that the anonymous *Life of Ceolfrith* is necessarily either later than Bede's *History of the Abbots* or *Concerning the Reckoning of Time*, or written by Bede himself: there is just insufficient evidence to make either case that strongly. It is to suggest, however, that the relationship between these texts that is required by Goffart's thesis is far from being the only one which is permissible by the evidence.

The last issue which we need to confront is the centrality of York's forthcoming elevation to Bede's decision to write his *Ecclesiastical History*. While it may be safe to assume that this was something which was known to be in process by 731, and could conceivably have underlain Bede's familiarity with such figures as Nothhelm, representing Canterbury in discussions taking place with the Northumbrian élite, the absence of the entire subject from the *EH* is difficult to reconcile with the view that it was his overriding interest therein. Rather, York was somewhat neglected by Bede following the departure of Paulinus in 633, and he seems to have been far more interested in, and familiar with, the Bernician sees which were nearer to hand, at Hexham and Lindisfarne, than with this Deiran diocese. While the basic succession of the York diocese is recorded, Bede's willingness to tell miracle stories connected with York are limited to those which relate to John of Beverley, who had earlier been his own diocesan. To view the *EH* as dominated by the coming elevation of York[98] seems to go beyond the evidence.

There are several reasons, therefore, to lay aside Goffart's thesis regarding Bede's purposes in composing the *Ecclesiastical History*. Bede certainly used Stephen's *Life* when writing the *EH* but to nothing like the extent that Goffart supposed: it is central only to book V, 19.[99] Stephen's *Life* was a work of deliberate advocacy concerning a single individual but Bede's purpose was very different. While the earlier writer sought to portray Wilfrid as a great bishop acting out the roles variously of apostle, prophet, confessor, martyr, patron and protector,[100] Bede had little sympathy for the confrontational approach towards both royal and ecclesiastical authority which his older contemporary had regularly adopted, in Stephen's version at least. Rather, Bede admired and wished to perpetuate the Gregorian model of the monk-bishop following an apostolic life of simplicity and humility, and portrayed this as replicated in an insular context by Augustine, then by Aidan and Cuthbert. His attempt in the *Ecclesiastical History* to press Wilfrid into the same mould required that he shift attention away from his prolonged disagreements with the Northumbrian kings and Archbishop Theodore in favour of his portrayal both as the advocate of orthodoxy at Whitby and later as a Northumbrian missionary spreading the Word of God among the heathen in Frisia and then Sussex. Both of these Bede achieved, but there remains, perhaps, some embarrassment implicit in his handling of Wilfrid's stormy career, which seems less a matter of personal antagonism (for which there is absolutely no evidence) than of deep-rooted differences between Stephen and Bede, and perhaps also

Wilfrid and Bede, concerning the style of life and the conduct of affairs appropriate to the episcopate.[101] He seems to have been unwilling in the *EH* to offer open criticism of even a bad priest, and Bede's attitude towards Wilfrid was always far more ambivalent than that. Indeed, he did on occasion praise the type of churchman whom Wilfrid represents in Stephen's *Life* – his whole-hearted approval of Acca's embellishment of the church at Hexham is a case in point, and Bede knew several such models of episcopal behaviour from his reading of the *Book of Pontiffs*. But his treatment of Wilfrid is redolent of an unwillingness to portray, so in some sense condone, the more abrasive aspects of his diocesan experience as a model appropriate to the Northumbrian Church in the present. The Wilfrid whom Bede offered his audience was, therefore, far removed from the contentious, self-righteous, persecuted but justified and ultimately triumphant hero of Stephen's work. He was woven back in as far as possible to the warp and weft of Bede's vision of the Northumbrian Church as a focus of apostolic humility, pastoral excellence, Christian orthodoxy and missionary zeal, alongside such other of his heroes as Egbert, who took Catholic practices back to Iona, and Chad, who ministered to the heathen Mercians.

Bede did not, therefore, conceive the *Ecclesiastical History* as his retort to Stephen's *Life of Wilfrid*. His Wilfrid was to be different from Stephen's, certainly, and they were pursuing variant agendas, but there is far more evidence of his friendship with Stephen's dedicatees than of hostility towards them and he treated both Wilfrid and Acca with due honour.

Bede's agenda: the Preface

So, what did Bede claim that he was setting out to achieve? He turned to this issue right at the opening of his Preface, within the first few sentences:

> I am pleased to acknowledge the unfeigned enthusiasm with which, not content to just lend an attentive ear to the words of Holy Scripture, you [King Ceolwulf] commit yourself to learn the sayings and deeds of the men of olden times, and more especially the renowned men of our own race. Should history tell of good men and their good estate, the thoughtful listener is spurred on to imitate the good; should it record the wicked ends of evil men, no less effectually the devout and earnest listener or reader is motivated to rebut what is harmful and perverse, and himself with a great deal more care pursue those things which he has learned to be good and pleasing in the sight of God.

As in several of his earlier works, in which prefaces are in the form of letters written to an extent at least separate from the main work, the Preface of the *EH* was self-evidently written after the return to Bede of his first draft of this work. It may well always have been his intention to add a preface but this reads as if in response to comments made, orally or perhaps by letter, in

Ceolwulf's name. Ostensibly, at least, Bede was here reinforcing a message which he believed already to have been implicit in his work, namely that he was offering his work primarily as a vehicle for the transmission of stories about past human behaviour, and particularly of Anglo-Saxon and/or Northumbrian hero figures of the past, to facilitate his audience's search for patterns of behaviour likely to gain divine approval. Bede was voicing his assumption that a narrative constructed of stories with a local provenance would have a greater relevance to the Anglo-Saxon élite for whom Bede was writing than those derived from peoples distant in either or both of space or time, including examples culled from the Bible.[102] Examples of past behaviour – both good and bad[103] – were to be understood by his audience in terms of their capacity to present cautionary tales in an insular context, to persuade them to reorder their own behaviour into closer conformity with a divinely sanctioned model of human life. Ceolwulf – as the audience personified – was being presented as a type of the virtuous Christian king who would both fully grasp and entirely share this vision, and could be expected to be delighted to take the opportunity, through his 'zeal for the spiritual well-being of us all', to lend his authority to the dissemination of the *Ecclesiastical History*, in pursuit of Bede's expressed goals. His spelling out of his expectations of the king perhaps implies that Ceolwulf had so far fallen short of Bede's expectations. There is a defensive quality, therefore, to the Preface, to which we shall return.

Lets us focus on this exemplary king-figure for a moment. Ceolwulf threatens to emerge from the Preface as if an exceptionally Christian king, and this view is if anything enhanced both by Bede's recommendation of him in 734 as a willing supporter to Bishop Egbert,[104] and by his ultimate retirement to a monastery in 737.[105] However, it is probably safer to read this portrayal by Bede primarily as rhetorical. There were several reasons why kings might take the tonsure at this date, only some of which were likely to be spiritual, and it is virtually impossible to choose between potential motives at this remove.[106] If Bede felt that both his *Ecclesiastical History* and his *Letter to Egbert* needed royal support to further their respective aims, he could do little more than put the best gloss available on the ruler of the day in the hope that he could be induced to adopt the role of proactive, virtuous Christian king. That Ceolwulf was Egbert's cousin, and presumably responsible for his elevation to diocesan status, arguably necessitated sympathetic treatment in the *Letter*, and Bede's own purposes apparently required a diplomatic form of address in the *EH*. In practice, Bede may even have been increasingly unsure as the year 731 progressed just which king he should address, given Ceolwulf's forcible tonsure then recovery of power within the year, as reported by the continuator of his recapitulation in the Moore manuscript.[107]

Bede's portrayal of Ceolwulf as *gloriosissimus* ('most glorious') has already been noted,[108] but does nothing to suggest a particularly erudite, Christian figure. This is a superlative which he used infrequently, and on only four occasions in this work.[109] The two instances which are Bede's own constructs are first of Ceolwulf in the Preface and then of Pippin, 'duke of the Franks'.[110] Otherwise these occur within documents which Bede had incorporated: first Pope Gregory's letter to Æthelberht, then the letter of Abbot Ceolfrith to King Nechtan of the Picts.[111] Neither recipient is likely to have been literate. Both these instances are, in fact, more fulsome than Bede's proem. Gregory addressed Æthelberht as his *Domino gloriosissimo atque praecellentissimo filio* ('most glorious lord and most excellent son') while Ceolfrith wrote: *Domino excellentissimo et gloriosissimo regi Naitano Ceolfrid . . .* ('To the most excellent and glorious Lord King Nechtan . . .'). That said Gregory and Ceolfrith were both addressing distant rulers whose support they were seeking, while Bede was penning a dedication to his own king, so the contexts were somewhat different. His address is certainly not excessive, particularly given the greater scale of the *Ecclesiastical History* compared to these letters. It is not difficult to find parallels for Bede's terminology: so, for example, Isidore singled out King Sisebut of the Visigoths for honourable mention in the preliminaries of both his chronicles, then termed him *gloriosissimus princeps* and *religiosissimus* in his first *Chronicle* but omitted both in his second, which conferred only the second superlative on the later king Suinthila.[112] Isidore clearly felt it appropriate for his own purposes to glorify whichever rulers of Visigothic Spain were contemporary with his own works and Bede's position was arguably comparable. It is fair to see his language as proportionate, therefore, but there is no reason to think him particularly enthusiastic in addressing Ceolwulf: any less would have been niggardly indeed.

Equally, in such circumstances, Ceolwulf might be forgiven if his priorities were very much elsewhere across most of the year in question. As already discussed (pp. 41–4), he is unlikely to have had the skills to have read Bede's work for himself, and is therefore likely to have had the first draft read for him by clerics. We have no material derivative from his close circle capable of reflecting how the *Ecclesiastical History* was received initially, only Bede's response. As so often, we are dependent on Bede himself for the context in which he wrote and there is a real danger of circularity. The assumption that Ceolwulf's purposes were, therefore, virtually identical to Bede's own is best read primarily as a rhetorical strategy on the part of the author, rather than an objective reflection of the king's predisposition.

In the context of Ceolwulf, however, one thing that we need to keep in mind is Bede's vision of the body politic as expressed within the *Ecclesiastical History*, in which kings play a major role, effectively personifying their peoples vis-à-vis the divine and with responsibility for moral leadership as well as physical protection. Such comes out very clearly from his treatment of successive conversion episodes, which were envisioned primarily in terms of exchanges between missionaries and kings. Bede prefaced each of his five books with a brief contents list, apparently drawn up after each book was written, which provide a useful entrée to what he considered central to each chapter. If we analyse the personnel named in these lists, most are clerical figures of one kind or another, including archbishops, bishops, abbots and abbesses, plus a small number of other religious, who total seventy-four individuals and account for a hundred instances of naming,[113] although the latter would be increased if we were to take account of the several successive contents listed in which the principal subject is referred to only by use of a pronoun.[114] However, a substantial minority of named individuals are secular leaders, with forty-one names in fifty-one instances. In some cases these occur primarily for dating purposes but most are active agents within the chapter and the majority are English kings. It is, therefore, reasonable to view the *Ecclesiastical History* as focused on élite personnel, with a ratio of approximately two-to-one clerical to royal, but with other groups seriously under-represented. The behaviour of past kings was, therefore, expected to carry an important share of the lessons which Bede felt to be appropriate to his present audience, and they were on occasion presented as indicative of the relationship between their entire people and the Christian God. This is nothing new, of course. The Old Testament offered a set of exemplars built around the interactions of prophets and kings with Jehovah, and this biblical vision of kingship as the moral and sacral pivot of society had also been reinforced by the focus on emperors to be found in Late Antique histories. Although in his commentaries Bede made few allusions to contemporary political issues and generally avoided discussion of bad kingship,[115] he still wished to address Ceolwulf, in ways influenced by the Old Testament, as king of the Northumbrians and as responsible for leading his people in the ways of the Lord. It was in this context that he provided examples from the past of the behaviour of various royals and how their careers had interacted with God,[116] then sought royal support for the dissemination of his work. It was rational, therefore, to make Ceolwulf the audience personified for this work, so the dedicatee in the Preface. By treating the English past as a gallery of examples, both good and bad, Bede was attempting to set out how kings (and others) should behave as protectors of a Christian people, observers of the Church's teachings and both defenders of, and spiritual guides to, their peoples.[117]

Bede was therefore positioning his new work alongside and as an addendum to the Bible as a source of exemplars capable of offering guidance of a kind more accessible to his own people regarding how Christians in the present should behave. He had already drawn this same analogy elsewhere in the work,[118] so clearly had it in view while writing. See, for example, his justification for inclusion of a hymn on the subject of virginity which he had written years earlier in honour of St Æthelthryth, 'imitating the method of sacred scripture, in which very many songs are inserted into history'.[119]

Bede had spent the previous thirty years or so teaching his younger brethren to read the Scriptures and had obviously thought long and hard about how this could best be achieved. The exposition of his methodology underlay several of his works of exegesis and he set it out quite explicitly in the letter to Bishop Acca that prefaces his commentary, *The First Book of Samuel*.[120] It may be fair to assume that he intended the *Ecclesiastical History* to be read in similar ways, particularly given recent argument in favour of typological interpretations of the *Life of Wilfrid*.[121] That view is sustained by detailed attention to the text, which offers a plethora of past behaviours offered within a moral nexus and carrying a variety of metaphorical meanings.

At its most developed, this interpretive scheme breaks down into four categories, namely the literal or historical, allegorical, tropological and ana-gogical. At the simplest level, Bede expected the Bible to be read literally and accepted as a factual, historical account of what had actually occurred. So, for example, the Israelites left Egypt under the leadership of Moses, and John the Baptist baptised Jesus. Similarly, he expected his audience to accept the *Ecclesiastical History* as a factual account of the history of the English as a people foreknown to God to join the ranks of the Universal Church. At the same time he expected his brethren to identify references to Christ or to his Church and its sacraments via allegorical interpretation of 'mystical' language or events. He interpreted the building of the Temple, for example, by a combination of Jewish and Gentile workers, as an extended allegory prefigur-ing the foundation of the Church.[122] He arguably expected the *EH* to be read in similar vein, in particular as regards events recounted in early sections, before the arrival of Augustine, prefiguring the ultimate English absorption into the Universal Catholic Church. Tropological understandings encompass the moral sense of sacred text, either in terms of direct instruction by authori-tative figures such as prophets, kings, Christ or the apostles, or in terms of metaphorical interpretations of their sayings. Moral instruction was Bede's avowed intention in the Preface to the *Ecclesiastical History* and is liberally to be found therein. The anagogical approach pertains to the spiritual sense of the Bible, in particular the future life in heaven, either literally or meta-phorically. There are frequent references in the *EH* to the Christian expec-tation of the afterlife, in terms both of the failure of that expectation, for example among the fifth-century Britons,[123] and of its triumphant fulfilment, for example in the case of Gregory the Great.[124]

Bede attributed a very similar system of biblical interpretation in the *Ecclesiastical History* to Gregory himself, but this time threefold: the first was again the literal; the second was bearing on the mysteries of Christ and the Church (i.e. the allegorical) and the third was in the sense which applies personally to each of the faithful (so combining the remaining two categor-ies).[125] A comparable, threefold schema was attributed to Rufinus by Gennadius, claiming that 'he wrote in a threefold sense, that is the historical, moral and mystical sense'.[126] In practice, the boundaries between allegorical, tropo-logical and anagogical readings were often blurred and Bede elsewhere contented himself with a twofold system, distinguishing only between the historical and the figurative or allegorical, with the latter encompassing all non-literal meanings.[127]

Bede was, therefore, accustomed to teasing out an overtly moral and spiritual agenda and he arguably expected his audience to bring to this 'his-torical' text all the skills of reading and interpretation appropriate to the

Scriptures.[128] But this was not an entirely new departure, for he was well read in literature which mirrored these aims, in part at least. Bede found in Josephus's Preface to *Judean Antiquities* the notion of history as something from which readers were expected to learn by consideration of the past deeds of others.[129] Orosius's *Seven Books of History against the Pagans*, written *c.*416–17,[130] offered an historical apologia for the sack of Rome in 410, arguing that, in contrast to a pagan past, the Christian present (*c.*417) was remarkable for its unity, peace and stability. Bede adopted a similar end point, referring in V, 23 to 'these favourable times of peace and prosperity' and concluding with quotations from Psalms 96 (97) and 29 (30). The latter was particularly appropriate to Britain's geography but, as Benedicta Ward has stressed, this peace should be read as much between man and God, as between man and man.[131] Bede's stated concern to affect present behaviours did, therefore, have precedents in earlier works.

Bede described his work in the opening lines of the Preface as a *Historia gentis Anglorum ecclesiastica* (an 'ecclesiastical history of the people/race of the Angles/English') and repeated use thereafter of the term *historia* reinforces his own positioning of this volume within a wider framework.[132] Unlike the remainder of his literary output, this was to be a 'history', as he understood the term. Bede had read examples of classical 'history', as a fundamentally secular account of the imperial state through time: Eutropius's *Breviarium* provides an example which generally avoided discussion of religious cult but focused on selected reigns and the deeds of individual rulers across a long time period stretching from the legendary Romulus to the near-present – the mid-fourth century.[133] Bede took much from his reading of such works, including dating by regnal years, structuring by reign, and the construction of a meta-history of a people which transcends the deeds of any one individual, group or generation. The concept of 'ecclesiastical history', however, was rather different, primarily in the sense that history was being interpreted in terms of the unfolding of divine will powering forward the development of a Christian society. Bede had experience of the genre primarily from his familiarity with the work of Eusebius of Caesarea, which he knew in the Latin version and continuation of Rufinus of Aquileia.[134] Eusebius's provided the standard text of universal Christian history available across the early Middle Ages, which revealed a wide breadth of interests, reliance upon numerous communications from acquaintances and an impulse to glorify martyrdom. Rufinus's expressed purpose was clear: he addressed Chromatius, bishop of Aquileia, offering a work which was intended to provide relief to its audience by encouraging them to focus on higher things at a time when the Gothic invasion of Italy was causing much distress. The time period is likewise comparable: following a brief survey of ancient authors used, Christ was the starting point appropriate to history. All that had been commemorated previously, including such Old Testament figures as Abraham, signified only to the extent that they foreknew and prefigured Christ. This was, therefore, the story of the Roman Empire in the sixth age, of the Christian Church and its apostolic succession, its suffering under persecution and its ultimate triumph under God's protection. Central was the relationship between Church and state, and their final integration once the state accepted Christ. For Eusebius, and Rufinus too, the secular authorities mattered, and substantial passages are given over to a Christian take on the policies of Constantine, for example, within a greater meta-history of man's relationship through time with God.

Bede seems to have written with this opus as his principal exemplar:[135] he likewise offered a history which rested on whatever 'official' documents suited his purposes and were accessible, augmented by his own knowledge and both written and oral contributions of several named and numerous unnamed individuals; he stated his intentions and, like Eusebius and then Rufinus, conceived of his work as a specifically 'ecclesiastical' history;[136] like his predecessors again, he was very concerned with apostolic succession within the Church,[137] with the struggle for orthodox Catholicism and with martyrs and other Christian heroes; he was likewise conscious of Christianity serving as a new beginning for his people, which rendered inconsequential much of the story of their non-Christian past, which he therefore very largely neglected, even to the extent that he knew it. In his *Lesser Chronicle*, Bede had edited out pagan references which occurred in his principal source, Isidore's *Chronicle*,[138] so his studied neglect of the pagan past was nothing new in 731. As Wilhelm Levison aptly remarked, Bede was providing a kind of 'British and Anglo-Saxon supplement' to the historical works of Eusebius and Rufinus.[139] Bede, like Eusebius, intended to produce an authoritative story of the foundation, organisation and development of the Church and a record of salvation history,[140] but in an insular rather than a universal context, formatted and directed in such a way as to deliver particular Christian lessons to his audience in the present. For both, as well as for Gildas, whose work Bede also of course used, Christian conversion played a gate-keeping role at the entrance of history, before which there was little point in either enquiry or record.[141]

This last point is brought out quite forcibly in Bede's *Concerning the Reckoning of Time*, completed only a few years before he undertook the *EH*, in which he offered just one chapter referring to pre-Christian English customs. This occurs in his iteration of the nature and naming of the months, in which he first set out their calculation and structure thematically, then described particular systems as used by the several nations of the world. This whole section was designed to explain the evolution of the Julian calendar, as used by the western Church, beginning with the Egyptians, then going on to Romulus's putative regulation of the year for his new Roman state, and then the Greeks.[142] Bede last and with least detail offered an antique English version, explaining this unusual lapse into vernacular Anglo-Saxon culture on grounds that 'it did not seem fitting to me that I should speak of other nations' observance of the year and yet be silent about my own'.[143] Following his exposition of the name *Blodmonath* (November) in terms of the unsavoury, pagan sacrifice of cattle to the gods, he closed this passage with a heartfelt expression of thanks to Jesus for the conversion and cessation of such practices.

He had positioned the pre-Christian English successfully alongside the prestigious peoples of the ancient world, therefore, so staked a claim for their inclusion in this élite fraternity, but he did it with brevity and a distaste for their errors, apparently in the expectation that his audience would share his reaction, to the benefit of their faith. This is less commemoration of the pagan past than a slightly more explicit example than was his norm of Bede's extirpation of English heathenism to the forgotten margins of history, much to the irritation of some modern scholars.

Returning to the Preface of the *Ecclesiastical History*, Bede concluded the first section with a sentence which borrows from Gregory's *Dialogues*,[144] in which he expressed his concern to address doubts regarding his work by establishing the names and reputations of his principal collaborators, so implying, perhaps, that such doubts had in fact been voiced. In what might be read, therefore, as a defensive response, he claimed the 'very learned' and 'most reverent Abbot Albinus' as his 'foremost authority and helper', from whom he had obtained, via the London-based priest Nothhelm as go-between, both documents and oral accounts relating to the missionary efforts of Gregory's disciples, particularly in Kent but also to an extent among the East and West Saxons, and in East Anglia and Northumbria. Bede's attention to Albinus dwarfs that accorded the other helpers he would go on to name and even purports to hand over responsibility not just for the veracity of particular historical facts but also, in part at least, for the very act of authorship: 'Lastly I was encouraged by the especial exhortation of Albinus himself, so that I dared to undertake this work.' His surviving letter to Albinus makes somewhat similar claims,[145] suggesting that the Kentish abbot had been heavily involved, albeit at a distance, in the very inception of the project.

But just how dependent Bede had been on Albinus's encouragement is difficult to assess.[146] Certainly, his relationship with Nothhelm was far less reliant on that with Albinus than this passage would suggest, for by the time he completed the *Ecclesiastical History* he had already long since addressed his *Thirty Questions on the Book of Kings* to him, as 'my most beloved brother'.[147] Nor was Nothhelm a minor figure, a mere messenger. That he was consecrated as archbishop of Canterbury in 735 implies that he was already a prominent figure in 731. He and Bede seem to have known each other comparatively well and enjoyed a relationship which was independent of Albinus, to an extent at least, and Nothhelm's questions suggest that he, also, had scholarly interests.[148] By *c*.725 Bede had at least begun to acquire the Gregorian letters which he would ultimately copy into his *History*, since he made an unambiguous reference to one in *Concerning the Reckoning of Time*, which he completed in or about that year.[149] If these reached him from Albinus, who presumably had access to the originals of some at least in Canterbury, then contact between them had already occurred long before 731. Gregory II had been pope since 715, so Nothhelm's visit to Rome under his papacy, as noted in his Preface, was not necessarily very recent in 731, which was the year in which he died. Notice of Tatwine's consecration to the archdiocese in June 731 could be read to imply new information reaching Jarrow at that date, but representatives of the Northumbrian sees may well have attended, providing a second potential source of information. It may be that Bede had received a tranche of material from Rome and Canterbury quite recently,[150] but the case depends heavily on the authenticity of his surviving letter to Albinus, which is not entirely certain.

What of the significance of Albinus's material? Bede certainly viewed Gregory's role as 'the apostle of the English' and the consequential foundation of Canterbury as the single most significant episode in England's shift from paganism to Christianity – the acorn, if you like, from which the oak of English Catholicism had sprung – and he depended heavily on Albinus for material about the early days of Christianity in Kent and the south, but it is difficult to view this as the fulcrum of a *History* which pays far greater attention to the conversion of Northumbria and England north of the Thames across the seventh century and rarely discusses, let alone centres on, Kentish affairs once book II has progressed beyond the opening few chapters. While it is probably fair to say, therefore, that Albinus provided the largest single body of written and oral material to Bede of any individual informant, and was perhaps involved in the initial inception of the project, so deserved special attention in the Preface, it is difficult to view his encouragement as critical to the overall design, which was in practice inclined to shift away from this material to the portrayal of characters of greater interest to the author and his immediate, regional audience, and of comparatively little significance at Canterbury. Indeed, it is quite possible that Albinus would have been very hostile indeed to Bede's portrayal of the Scottish Church across central sections of this work.

Bede mentioned Albinus by name only once more, very close to the end of his work and in the context of his account of the death of Abbot Hadrian:

> It is one testimony among many to his [Hadrian's] learning and to that of Theodore, that his disciple Albinus, who succeeded to the government of his monastery, was so well trained in the study of the scriptures that he had no small knowledge of the Greek language, and of Latin no less than the English which was his native tongue.[151]

This is obviously high praise of his correspondent but Albinus's learning was actually here being redeployed rhetorically to sustain the memory of Abbot Hadrian as teacher, and his reputation was otherwise entirely overshadowed by that of Bishop Acca, Bede's diocesan, whose succession to Hexham, career as bishop and many outstanding virtues form the subject matter of the remaining three-quarters of this chapter. There is an uncanny parallel here between Albinus and King Ceolwulf, who likewise appears prominently in the Preface but then only in a single chapter (V, 23), very briefly, at the close. Both underline the sense in which the Preface should be viewed as a composition somewhat separate from the main text, written in a different context and to a subtly shifting agenda.

On the face of it, then, there seems a mismatch between Albinus's prominence in the Preface, where he was named four times in all, and his comparative obscurity in the main text, where he occurs only once. One can certainly point to similar cases in other historical works which Bede had read: so, for example, there are parallels between Albinus's role within the *Ecclesiastical History* and the figure of Epaphroditus in Josephus's *Judean Antiquities*,[152] who was similarly introduced in the Preface as one who had exhorted the author to carry it through, was praised for exceptional learning, but only appears just once in passing at the close of the *Life* with which Josephus ended this work. It is the separateness of the Preface from the main text which is striking here, as if it were written in somewhat different circumstances and to a new agenda. It is tempting to view the especial treatment of Albinus here as an attempt by Bede to dress his work in the prestige of England's oldest Rome-founded cult centre at Canterbury as a defence for his own authorial voice, rather than as strictly warranted by his actual contribution.

The treatment of Albinus and Bede's other named sources has parallels with Pope Gregory's defence of the truthfulness of the stories which he was about to recount in the Preface to his *Dialogues*. Peter, the author's priest and collocutor, was given to remark that Gregory was justified in interrupting his normal exegetical study of the Bible for the purpose of relating equally edifying miracles, the authority of which was sustained by their attribution to 'reverent men of great seniority'. Gregory allegedly used correspondents to supply some of the miracle stories which he wished to include, and, like Bede again, he regularly named witnesses, so, for example, identifying the priest Gaudentius as his source for a story concerning Bishop Boniface of Ferenti, who 'since he was brought up by him there can be no question that he can recount everything the more truly'.[153] There are significant parallels here, which Bede stressed: 'by describing the miracles of the saints' in the *Dialogues*, Gregory set out 'what virtues men ought to strive for',[154] and quotations from every book of this work are scattered across the *EH*. Bede was similarly interrupting his more normal practice of commentary on the Scriptures in order to write a history which was intended to provide local case studies for the edification of his own people. His treatment of Albinus, and indeed his entire practice of naming witnesses, to miracle stories in particular, arguably owes much to his sharing with Gregory the need to substantiate such stories by reference to the stature as truth-tellers of his informants. Again, therefore, the exposition of his putative authorities in the Preface reads as if a defensive strategy, intended to outface criticism.

Bede went on to include further witnesses, to an annotated list of subjects organised so as to move steadily nearer home, who collectively tend to confirm this view: 'Daniel the most reverend bishop of the West Saxons, who even now survives', whose correspondence related to his own people, plus Sussex and the Isle of Wight; the monks of Lastingham (collectively but not by name) concerning the conversion of the Mercians and recovery of the East

Saxons for Christianity, as bound up with the lives of their founders Cedd and Chad, 'highly religious priests of Christ'; 'the most reverend Abbot Esi' (who is otherwise unknown) providing material relating to East Anglia; and a letter from 'the most reverend Bishop Cyneberht' passing on knowledge of Christianity in Lindsey.[155] Innumerable unnamed witnesses had contributed regarding Northumbria, but Bede singled out the anonymous *Life of Cuthbert* and the monks of Lastingham for especial mention. Like Gregory, therefore, he was claiming that he had written and/or spoken to various churchmen to request information and, again like Gregory, he was keen to stress that the reliability of his material rested quite explicitly on the venerability of these individuals or groups as witnesses, rather than just himself as sole author. However, if his work had returned to him accompanied by comments under the name of the Northumbrian king, it may be significant that his named witnesses are all southern churchmen, so adding external validation to his own authority as author. Bede was clearly being selective. That he also appealed to the memory of Cuthbert may imply that he considered this to have value in addressing Ceolwulf, who was later believed to have retired to Lindisfarne when he became a monk in 737 (see below, p. 198), and it is interesting to note that the only other Northumbrian institution which he named, the monastery of Lastingham, had been founded by Oswald's son, Œthelwald. Bede was, therefore, emphasising in his Preface his claim on the authority of a string of venerable figures from southern England for aspects of his history, particularly concerning the 'disciples of St. Gregory', but there is no comparable listing of his sources for the Scottish mission, or overt mention of it.

Bede closed this part of his Preface with something of a disclaimer:

> And I humbly entreat the reader that, if he shall come across anything other than the truth in this which we have written, not to impute it to us, who, according to the true law of history [*vera lex historiae*], have simply collected that which is generally known [*quae fama vulgante*] [and] have sought to commit to writing for the instruction of posterity.[156]

While it was recognised by the end of the nineteenth century that Bede had earlier used the phrase *vera lex historiae* in his commentary on Luke, this concern for 'the true law of history' was generally read in terms of good historical technique and his awareness of the dangers inherent in using popular stories passed on orally.[157] In 1947, however, Charles Jones noted that Bede was here adopting a phrase derived from the writings of Jerome concerning the virginity of Mary,[158] the meaning of which was rather different. Jones explained that: '*Vera lex historiae* . . . is not a plea for literal truth, but for a truth which denies the literal statement or uses the literal statement to achieve an image in which the literal statement is itself incongruous',[159] suggesting that Bede may have felt entirely justified in using stories which he considered untrue when they fitted his overriding authorial agenda. This contention has since, in turn, been challenged by an in-depth examination of the issue by Roger Ray,[160] who pointed out that Bede would have appreciated the highly rhetorical style of Jerome's riposte to the views of Helvidius, in which he coined the phrase, and had such a sound grasp of classical rhetoric and the theory of history implicit in scriptural writings that he would not have read this as 'the true law of history' but rather as 'a seldom practised and altogether minor principle of . . . history'.[161] Given Bede's explicit and oft-noted care in stating his sources, this phrase reflects rather, Ray suggested, concern at his inability to check or verify the oral testimony on which he was reliant, enabling him 'to embrace unverifiable popular information without calling into question his own respect for the ideal of truth'.[162] Rather than reading this as Jones suggested, therefore, Ray argued that it was more likely that Bede was indirectly confronting Isidore's *Etymologies*,[163] as he did with some persistence in later life, since therein the Spanish bishop had described history primarily as a narration of events by eyewitnesses (rather in the manner of Thucydides and Herodotus). There was a clear conflict between such a theory of history and Bede's express purpose in telling of the deeds of his own people from the comparatively distant past as a vehicle through which to convey good advice to his own audience.

Bede's adoption of this particular phrase seems, therefore, indicative of his determination to utilise numerous stories which fell outside Isidore's definition of the materials appropriate to a 'history', and implies a certain disregard for the historicity of specific passages,[164] even while he was clearly committed to the veracity of his work on the broader level, for example in terms of the arrival of his own people within the Universal, Catholic communities of the world. Bede used a very similar phrase (*verax historicus*: 'truthful historian') of himself in his treatment of Bishop Aidan (in *EH* III, 17), and this context is one where it is an easier matter to establish his meaning. He was offering his audience access to a popular tradition of Aidan's deeds and 'preserving their memory for the benefit of my readers', while at the same time reserving his opinion of the latter's position on the Paschal question.[165] The first Irish bishop of the Northumbrians had died two decades before Bede's birth, and Bede is unlikely ever to have spoken in later life, when he was collecting material for this work, with any individual who had first-hand knowledge of the bishop, so orally transmitted stories were all that he could offer, collected perhaps primarily from Lindisfarne and its satellites, where Aidan's memory was presumably still cultivated. Even more was this the case when dealing with Gregory's first encounter with English slaves in the Roman market-place prior to 590, which Bede ascribed to *traditione maiorum* ('the tradition of our forefathers') and recalled lastly as 'a vision which we have received from antiquity'.[166] Bede elsewhere exhibited a cautious approach to the veracity of popular stories: when he revisited his commentary on the Acts of the Apostles, for example, he used the phrase *opinio vulgi* ('common opinion') as a convenient explanation of error in Stephen's oratory before the Sanhedrin, on the grounds that the proto-martyr would have rather quoted misinformation knowingly than have challenged the existing knowledge-base of his audience on a minor issue when that might divert their attention away from far more important matters.[167] For Bede, therefore, part of the function of history as a genre was the setting down of traditions and stories from the past of a kind capable of providing the kind of lessons of moral value in the present to which he had referred in his opening lines. While he was conscious of the desirability that such stories be factual rather than purely fictional, their value lay as much in terms of this pastoral utility as in any specific historical reality, which he presumably recognised to be ultimately untestable. Bede was probably aware that a great deal of what he had managed to collect was neither more nor less than opinion formed and passed on within monastic or clerical circles in order to construct particular pasts which were ever evolving, as appropriate to their respective presents. Bede's self-appointed task was to systematise and convey such material on to his own audience, but marshalled, developed and interpreted in such a way as to provide an edifying experience for the reader or hearer in the present.[168] Such stories would not be excluded simply because there was no reliable witness able to verify them.

This placed Bede very much at the mercy of his informants and the *Ecclesiastical History* should be read with the historicity of many of his stories at issue. Our inability to locate alternative and nearer contemporary sources for many of his earlier tales, in particular, necessarily distinguishes the kind of history we can write of England in the late sixth and seventh centuries from that capable of being written, for example, concerning the eighteenth. So, while Bede *c.*731 is our only source for King Æthelberht's initial reception of Augustine in 597 (I, 25), leaving us with a somewhat picturesque story of pagan naivety which we can query but which we have ultimately either to take or to leave,[169] it is quite possible to test the authenticity of a century-old story about, for example, the highwayman Dick Turpin (executed 1739), as written by William Harrison Ainsworth in 1834, and establish the extent to which historical events were being recast a century later.[170]

In his Preface, therefore, Bede spelled out to his audience how he expected them to profit from his work of history. Primarily, he anticipated that the work would contribute to their well-being by providing examples of good and bad behaviour from which a Christian audience could learn and take moral guidance. Ceolwulf, in particular, was being addressed by name in the expectation that he would adjust his behaviour to be 'good and pleasing in the sight of God' and, enlightened by Bede's stories about the past, lead his people on the paths of righteousness. This was a fundamentally 'Gregorian' agenda, but heavily weighted to just one part of his overall reform programme, and neglectful of numerous aspects which he would later address in the *Letter to Egbert*. It was also very much an *ecclesiastical* type of history, with its emphasis on the arrival and spread of redemption and salvation among the English people, and far less a political, social, economic, cultural, ethnic or military history. It offered, for example, a defence of Roman orthodoxy on such issues as the Paschal question, very much in line with the hostility towards heresy which characterised Eusebius's earlier work, and highlighted several of the insular cults which served to validate and legitimise the young Church of the English. In many respects, this was 'as much a theology as a history'.[171] Nor is his claim on factual truth quite as sound as was suggested by Charles Plummer.[172] Much of his material was quite incapable of any sort of critique and Bede's decisions regarding its inclusion or exclusion, and just how inclusion might be achieved, owed as much to his underlying agenda as to any specific standard of historical criticism. At the extreme, several narrative episodes seem to have derived from pre-existing texts written in entirely different contexts, and were simply adopted to sustain Bede's agenda, from the writings of such as Gregory.[173] His overriding theory of history therefore seems to have placed emphasis not just on the literal, but also on the figurative or allegorical.

It should be stressed, however, that the Preface was a somewhat defensive addition to the main text. As already noted, Bede positioned his own name as author to maximum effect by juxtaposition with both Ceolwulf and Christ, and sought to portray the king in the best possible light. By then paying tribute to the aid of a string of high-status churchmen he enlisted their collective authority for his work. When naming Abbot Albinus, in particular, as 'principal authority and helper', he took the opportunity to invoke memories of Archbishop Theodore, Abbot Hadrian and St Gregory, whose prestige, likewise, was thereby captured in support of the *Ecclesiastical History*, but there was no comparable claim on the heroes of the Scottish mission. It is quite possible that Bede elected to name these specific individuals as much for their rhetorical value as for their actual input, including as they did two southern diocesans but also, and perhaps more importantly, a senior representative of the church at Canterbury. With four references by name to Albinus and three additionally to Nothhelm, who fails to appear elsewhere in the text, Bede loaded his Preface with figures of unimpeachable authority. Bede seems almost to be saying, 'Now challenge my version of events if you dare!' Such strategies, combined with his autobiographical passage and then the list of his works, in V, 24, seem designed to place this work beyond criticism. Where Bede referred to 'instances of doubt concerning those things [which] I have written, either in your mind or in the minds of any others who listen to or read this history', it is a reasonable surmise that precisely such doubts had indeed been expressed by those who had read his first draft. While Bede may well have always intended to add a preface, the one that he eventually wrote seems somewhat preoccupied with reinforcing his own authorial voice in order to face down criticism, following despatch of his primary text to the king.

The recapitulation

It is a peculiarity of the *Ecclesiastical History* that the last narrative passage, which describes the state of Britain up to the present, is not in fact the final chapter. Excluding only the single sentence pertaining to Saracen activity in Gaul, which either is an interpolation (see pp. 183, 192) or has been misinterpreted,[174] book V, 23 covers the six years up to the present, 731. It details the deaths of Wihtred, king of Kent (725) and Tobias, bishop of Rochester (726), and describes the arrival of two comets in 729, which are interpreted as harbingers of the deaths of Egbert and Osric and as introducing Ceolwulf's reign. Berhtwold's death in 731 and the consecration of Tatwine to Canterbury close the historical narrative, giving way to a summary of the bishoprics of the English in first Southumbria then Northumbria, in the present. There are then brief passages descriptive of relations between the several peoples currently inhabiting Britain and God (very much to the detriment of those who had not adopted Catholic practices), comment on the popularity of monasticism among the Northumbrians and a final valedictory conclusion, which, as already mentioned, incorporates quotations from the Psalms:

> This is the state of the whole of Britain in the present, around 285 years after the arrival of the English in Britain, in the year 731 since the Lord's incarnation. In whose perpetual kingdom let the earth rejoice, and let Britain rejoice in His faith and let the multitude of isles be glad and give thanks at the remembrance of His holiness.

This reads so like a passage intended to close the *Ecclesiastical History* that it is arguable that it did at some stage serve precisely this purpose.

If that be accepted, then we need to account for Bede having then added a new, 'last' chapter comprising a recapitulation of events, the brief autobiographical passage that we have already considered (pp. 6–16) and a list of his own works, all offered sequentially to form a section which lacks internal cohesion, or much real connection with what has gone immediately before. While there are precedents for the inclusion at this point of both an autobiographical section and list of works completed (see pp. 10–11), the presentation of all three elements in a single chapter is exceptional. The view that this final chapter was a comparatively late addition to the work is sustained by the presence of the *Ecclesiastical History* in the list of works within it, which likewise implies that Bede wrote it after the main text was complete. Such observations emphasise the lateness of its creation. Of the three disparate passages making up V, 24, however, it is the recapitulation which offers our best means of assessing both what Bede was attempting to achieve by this addition, and at what stage it was appended.

It has long been recognised that the recapitulation is not literally what it says, since it does not merely 'recapitulate events already dealt with', as Bede claimed, containing as it does material which had not previously been included. It has been suggested that what we have here is an early 'working summary', which Bede had written as a preliminary to compilation of the main work and which had then been tacked on to approximate to the purpose described.[175] This is not, however, a satisfactory explanation of the particular features which we encounter, in three main areas. First, it seems a remarkably clumsy process. Did Bede really append to an extended narrative of such subtlety and literary merit a piece of rough, preparatory work, without even rendering it fit for the purpose? Given his high standards as an author, this seems improbable, and it is no solution to suppose that it was the work of his associates. Second, the most potent single objection to the recapitulation having derived from the main text, namely that it contains entries which are absent therefrom, also applies in reverse but on a far greater scale. Taken together, the presence of information which did not find its way into the main text, added to the vast quantity of detailed, dated information in the main text but which is absent from the recapitulation, renders this solution implausible. Third, reference in the recapitulation to Tatwine's consecration in June 731 cannot have formed part of a preliminary piece written before work on the main text had begun, but has to have been written at the close. If Bede felt it worth updating the recapitulation to this extent, why not undertake more extensive reworking to bring it closer into line with the main text, and so justify it as a recapitulation?

Taking these several objections together, we should arguably abandon the notion of the recapitulation as a set of annals written preparatory to the main text. Its position at the end of the work and closure with contemporary events requires that it was completed, at least, no earlier than the latest events narrated in chapter V, 23, so very late indeed in the process of composition. The simplest solution is to suppose that this entire chapter was added following return of the manuscript of the first draft from court, so at the same stage which saw the Preface written. As already noted (pp. 10–16), the brief autobiographical section and list of his own works share something of the same train of thought to be found in the Preface: all these passages bear the imprint of efforts to sustain Bede's own authority as author. In addition, it is worth noting that the brief prayer which ends the Preface in the Moore manuscript is found at the end of V, 24 in the manuscripts of *c*-type, which may have been slightly earlier, which again sustains the view that we should envisage these particular passages being finalised together, after the remainder of the work was completed. Viewed in this context, there is a case for supposing that the brief entries making up the recapitulation provide an entrée to what Bede felt it most necessary to emphasise as he reviewed his narrative, so perhaps indirect evidence of the nature of the comments made by those who had read his first draft. It is instructive, therefore, when considering Bede's purposes as he brought his work to a conclusion, to consider this annalistic summary in some detail.

Let us first consider the places named. Excluding kingdoms, provinces and groups of islands, only nine places are specified in the recapitulation. Not surprisingly, given that it is named most often in the main text, Rome is the commonest named place, in five separate entries (167, 409, 680, 688, 709), plus occuring as a collective noun, 'the Romans' (60 BC, AD 46) and in adjectival form (46). Otherwise, only Iona occurs more than once

(565, 716: it was named in seven passages in the main text). Excepting only a synod of the English church at Hertford (673), and both Rochester (644) and Canterbury (731), in Kent, all other places are either certainly or quite possibly Northumbrian: the latter include the lost *Degsastan* (603)[176] and 'the plain of Hatfield' (680);[177] certain examples are York (644) and *Streanæshalch* (?Whitby: 680). In contrast with something like ninety-four insular places (including rivers) named in the main text, therefore, those in the recapitulation seem tightly focused on a small and exclusive group.

The numerical dominance of Rome among places named in the recapitulation suggests a writer who was particularly keen to emphasise the Catholicism of the Northumbrian Church and the strength of its connections with the papacy. In contrast, Lindisfarne was the third most commonly named place in the main text (after Rome and York) but does not occur in the recapitulation. Several even of the insular sites which were included were closely associated with bishops sent from Rome (as Canterbury, Rochester, York, Hatfield and Hertford), or with the cult of Gregory (?Whitby), all of which serve to emphasise the point made above.

This inference is reinforced by attention to the personnel named. This is a sparsely inhabited framework, with a mere fifty-one entries spread across 791 years, although some detail more than a single event. A small number name no one, referring rather to specific happenings, such as the arrival of Roman missionaries (597) or the battle of *Degsastan* (603), albeit the personnel were most probably known to Bede's audience. Only fifty-nine individuals are named, in total, of whom all but eleven occur only once.

In the first part of the recapitulation, pre-547, eleven names occur, all male, of whom ten were Romans, in some sense of the word, including two popes, one papal deacon and seven imperial figures (to include Caesar). Thereafter, of forty-eight named individuals, just three were women, Abbess Hild, Princess Eanflæd and Queen Osthryth, all of whom were Northumbrian royals. Twenty-nine were secular figures, of whom, excepting the women, all but five were kings (provided we include Penda, whose kingship Bede did not here acknowledge, although he had previously, and Peada whom he termed *princeps*), the remainder being Northumbrian royals or ealdormen. Fourteen Northumbrian seculars occur in all eighteen times, followed in declining numerical order by ten references to seven Mercian kings and six to Kentish kings, all of whom were named just once. By far the commonest event reported was the death of an individual, accounting for twenty-one entries.

The remaining nineteen individuals mentioned were churchmen: three were Irish but seven were Italian or despatched from Rome (to include Archbishop Theodore), leaving just nine insular figures, all of whom were probably Northumbrians (the only query concerns Egbert) except only the most recent and current archbishops of Canterbury, Berhtwold and Tatwine. Some nine consecrations were recalled: those of Augustine (against the year 601, although this arguably marks his receipt of the pallium rather than his consecration), Paulinus (625), Chad and Wilfrid (664), Wilfrid's several replacements, Bosa, Eata and Eadhæd (678), Theodore (668) and Tatwine (731).

Of these churchmen, Paulinus, Northumbria's Gregorian bishop, stands out with four references by name, a total which was equalled otherwise only by Archbishop Theodore. The chasing pack is led by Gregory himself with three entries, then Augustine, Wilfrid and Egbert, with two. All were, of course, peculiarly 'Romanist' figures. Consecration as bishop was comparatively well reported, so it is not surprising to find Wilfrid's entered here, but, given their prominence in the text, there are several noticeable omissions, including all of bishops Aidan (although his death is noted), Finan, Colman, Cedd, Cuthbert, Acca and John of Beverley. Excepting only Tatwine of Canterbury, the consecration of no current bishop was recorded. Bede was being very rigorous in his decisions concerning whom to include in this brief, annalistic synopsis, and whom to exclude, and in this sense the recapitulation is far from being a true likeness of the main text of the *Ecclesiastical History*, which offered a far higher visibility to the Ionan missionaries and their associates.

The second entry regarding Wilfrid is perhaps the more revealing of Bede's valuation of his career. It reads: '678 a comet appeared; Bishop Wilfrid was beaten off from his see by King Ecgfrith; and Bosa, Eata and Eadhaed were consecrated bishops in his place'. The language used mirrors that in the main text and again emphasises Bede's lack of sympathy with Ecgfrith's treatment of his bishop.[178] Inclusion of the comet enabled Bede to contextualise the event within the language of celestial 'signs', as he had Wilfrid's consecration. Such otherwise occur in the recapitulation in the entry for 729, when comets, plural, were associated with the deaths of St Egbert and King Osric. The fuller reference to their appearance, a few pages earlier, specified both that there were two and that they struck 'great terror into all beholders'.[179] The arrival of a comet in 678 was highlighted with considerable and fiery detail in IV, 12, and should be read as indicative of Bede's disquiet. Wilfrid's expulsion was therefore established rhetorically in both literary contexts in very negative terms via the language of 'signs'. That Bede opted to include this item in his brief recapitulation emphasises its continuing importance. Whatever else it may have been, the recapitulation was certainly not 'anti-Wilfridian'.

The first ten entries provide a summary of what Bede considered important prior to the mid-sixth century. He initially established Britain as part of the Roman Empire, and the third, for 167, notes the conversion of the Britons to Christianity by Pope Eleutherius at the request of the (apocryphal) British King Lucius. The inclusion of Britain in the Christian Empire was thereby established but this was then brought to nought, first via Maximus, who was created emperor in Britain but then killed Gratian in Gaul (381), and then by the sack of Rome (409), following which 'the Romans ceased to rule in Britain'. Across the period between 409 and 538, Bede then singled out just two items from the many that he had included in his account in book I: the dispatch of Palladius by Pope Celestinus as bishop to the Christians in Ireland

(430) and the coming of the Angles to Britain (449×56). Two eclipses follow (538, 540), completing this primary phase of the annals.

What was Bede trying to achieve here? He clearly wished to emphasise the primacy of Roman engagement with Britain, first in a secular capacity but then more particularly as the origin of a Christianity which the Britons had specifically requested. He also wished to establish British responsibility for the closure of that phase. The statement that Roman rule in Britain had ended in 409 made it quite clear that there had been no clash between the Anglo-Saxons and the Romans. Rather the new incomers arrived 'on the summons of the Britons' and had neither implicit nor explicit responsibility for the closure of Roman rule in Britain almost half a century earlier. The dire state of affairs in the first half of the sixth century was treated allegorically via inclusion of two eclipses, neither of which appear in the main text but which he offered here apparently as metaphors for the heretical and immoral behaviours of the Britons, which are such powerful messages of the middle chapters of book I.[180] Neither St Germanus nor many of the numerous episodes derived from Gildas occur here (excepting only the arrival by invitation of the 'English'), perhaps because of difficulties with dating, but, alongside notice of the terrible state of affairs in Britain, Bede did include the arrival in Ireland of a bishop despatched from the papacy. The effect is both to give Rome the ultimate credit for Irish Christianity and to provide evidence of the papacy's continuing concern for the spiritual well-being of the British Isles. This early phase is, therefore, developed by Bede in ways supportive of the long-continuing interest of Rome in the Christianising of the far west and prefigures the mission despatched by Pope Gregory. The nadir regarding affairs in Britain which the two eclipses denote was a necessary precondition of an insular history characterised by complete disconnection of the Christianity of the Britons from that of the English. Rather, mid-sixth-century Britain was being presented as a Godless place, where the sunlight of Christian faith had been eclipsed as a consequence of the Britons' disobedience to the Lord.

A resolution of this parlous situation was then offered across the next half-century or so, via just four entries. The first gives notice of King Ida, 'from whom the royal family of the Northumbrians trace their descent', inserted against the year 547 but with reference to a twelve-year reign.[181] There follows the mission of Columba from Ireland to the Picts in 565, leading to the establishment of Iona, and then Gregory's despatch in 596 of Augustine and his fellow monks to Britain 'who were to preach the word of God to the people of the English', whose arrival he noted in 597, 'more or less 150 years after the arrival of the English in Britain'.

Several core themes are introduced here. One is the primacy of the Northumbrian royal dynasty to this vision of salvation history, from whom Ceolwulf, of course, claimed descent in the present. The virtue of Ida's reign is signalled by use of the apostolic number, which reappears thereafter in the context of the first Northumbrian royal baptism, of princess Eanflæd in 626, then the companions of the short-lived king Eanfrith when he was slain, in

633, conjuring up images of Christ in support of the status of all three. The Northumbrians were the first named of any English *gens* here, to be followed an entire half-century later by the East Saxons (604), Kent (as a place rather than specifically a people, 633), the Middle Angles (653) and finally the Mercians over a century later (655). This foregrounding of the Northumbrians is reinforced thereafter by repetition, in 625, 664, 685, 698, 705 and 716, making them the most frequently named of the English peoples with seven entries, followed very belatedly by six for the Mercians. The presentation of early members of the Northumbrian dynasty via Christian number symbolism and then this broader preferential treatment of the Northumbrians as a people were both perhaps calculated to appeal to Ceolwulf and his associates in the present.

Another feature here is Bede's prefiguring of the Irish as members of the Universal Church, which he had already signposted via the despatch to them of a bishop by the papacy in 430. The Irish were now, 135 years later, fully fledged Christians. Like the main text, the recapitulation would obtain its final rhetorical climax from Egbert's conversion of the last bastions of Irish idiosyncrasy in 716, but the Irish input to English conversion is only a matter of inference in the recapitulation, via the death of Aidan (651) and retirement of Colman in 664. Rather, it is the Roman mission which is foregrounded, as if solely responsible for Christianising the English. Alongside and overall, therefore, is the third of these core themes, that is the role of the papacy in despatching a mission into Britain, but not to the Picts (as the Irish) but to the English, so embracing the English in the Catholic world. Fourth is the sense of co-operation between these several agencies: Bede was placing the Northumbrian dynasty in a lead position within Anglo-Saxon England, ready to provide secular support to missionaries from Rome, while leaving the activities of Irish missionaries very largely a matter of inference. It was primarily the partnership between Northumbrian kings and Roman missionaries, therefore, which was set to take forward the Christianising agenda in Britain.

To this point, Bede's entries had been few: the first ten span the period from 60 BC to AD 540, so occur on average only once every sixty years, providing the most skeletal framework of insular history up to and including the moral and religious dereliction in which that period putatively culminated. Thereafter the frequency of entries begins to rise, with four from 541 to 600, so a rate of one every fifteen years, then a veritable spate from 601 to 633, with nine entries. This period of plenty opens with a group of Canterbury-centric events which stem naturally from Gregory's mission. Augustine's receipt of the pallium appropriate to his new archdiocesan status in 601 is followed by the conversion of the East Saxons (604) and King Æthelberht's death (616). The inclusion of Gregory's death in 605 reflects the extended treatment within the main narrative.[182] The 'southern' focus then gives way to a set of entries of particular relevance to northern England from 625, beginning with Paulinus's consecration as bishop for the Northumbrians.

Paulinus's significance had already been signalled by his naming alone of the party despatched by Gregory in 601, despite mention in other entries of both Mellitus (604) and Justus (625). A single 'Northumbrian' event (in 603) had also been included alongside the entries related to the Kentish mission, albeit in an anonymous form, namely King Æthelfrith's victory over the Scots at *Degsastan*.[183] This is the only battle named and, assuming Bede's audience would have been aware of the protagonists, it establishes the Northumbrians as particularly responsible for the protection of the English against their neighbours.

The 'northern' group of early seventh-century entries is particularly dense. The eleven entries of the period 596–633 comprise two 'Roman' events (the departure of the mission and Gregory's death), three Canterbury-centric examples (above), and the 'northern' battle of *Degsastan*, all before 625, then four entries in just nine years which are exclusively 'northern', including material offered against three consecutive years from 625 to 627, dealing with the conversion of King Edwin, his relatives and his people. This is not the sole group of consecutive entries, three having occurred in 603–5, but these were disparate in subject matter and not tightly focused like the 'northern' group. These four entries include two references by name to Paulinus and three, consecutively, to King Edwin. The relative explosion of Northumbrian content coincident with Paulinus's mission to Edwin's court should be viewed as the first rhetorical climax of the recapitulation. It is the densest group of material in these annals and the most uniform sequence regarding both subject and location. At this point, therefore, Bede was investing very heavily indeed in the story of the Gregorian mission and the Christianisation of the Northumbrian people at the hands of the Italian Paulinus and under the protection and leadership of King Edwin, whose foundation of a diocesan church at York for his bishop is recalled at the notice of the latter's death in 644. It may be that York's claim to archdiocesan status under the dispensation drawn up by Gregory the Great was in Bede's mind when writing the recapitulation,[184] but if so it is not explicit here, particularly given the lack of reference to the city thereafter. What is present is the foregrounding of the Gregorian mission as responsible for conversion, and of the Northumbrian kings as having established leadership of the first wave of English peoples to be converted, following Æthelberht's death in 616, and as having been central to the success of Christianisation over the decades which followed.

Following Edwin's death and Paulinus's return to Kent, Bede neglected the crisis of Northumbrian Christianity, which is such a feature of the early chapters of book III. Were we today reliant on this text alone, then Edwin's conversion would stand as the cusp event in the process of the Christianisation of the north of England, without notice of either Oswald or Aidan, on whom he had dwelt at such length in the main text.

The regional focus remains, although it is no longer exclusive. Of the nine entries from 640 to 670, two explicitly name the Northumbrians and a further two note the deaths of Northumbrian kings (Oswald, killed 642;

Oswine, murdered 651). While several others do not refer directly to the Northumbrians or their leaders, their presence is generally implicit. So the Northumbrians would presumably have been understood by Bede's audience as the unnamed agents who had engineered the conversion of Prince Peada and the Middle Angles in 653, and Penda's death and the Christianisation of the Mercians in 655.[185] That Aidan's death in 651, and then the departure of Colman and the Irish in 664, occurred in a Northumbrian context depends on Bede's audience having additional information. There is, also, a distinct strand of Kentish material, beginning with notice of King Eadbald's death in 640, which encourages the reader to view Northumbria and Kent as combined seamlessly to push forward the Christian agenda, so obscuring the whole issue of differences between the Scottish and Roman churches.

The entry for 664 is by far the longest, including six potentially separate events: a solar eclipse, the death of Eorcenberht of Kent, Colman's return to Ireland, a plague and the consecration of both Chad and Wilfrid. Bede took the opportunity to weave together events in his two lead, Christian kingdoms in this entry, but notably failed to mention the synod of Whitby in that year, which had been such a significant feature of the main text (III, 25), so obviating the need to tell the story of Irish missionary activity among the Northumbrians to that date. This phase of the recapitulation then closes with the consecration of Theodore as bishop (668: Bede might have specified archbishop but did not) and the death of King Oswiu of the Northumbrians (670).

The same two kingdoms then recur across the last phase, with the death of Egbert of Kent recorded in 673 alongside notice of King Ecgfrith and Archbishop Theodore co-operating successfully to manage a synod (at Hertford), which Bede lauded as *utillimus* ('most useful'). The close personal co-operation between Northumbrian king and Rome's choice as archbishop marks what might be termed the second rhetorical highlight of the recapitulation, but it also marks the point from which events then began to unravel: Æthelred secured the Mercian kingship following Wulfhere's death in 675, then 'devastated Kent' in 676, following which a comet appeared in 678 and Wilfrid was driven out by Ecgfrith. The death of Ecgfrith's brother, Ælfwine, was noted in the next year, Abbess Hild died in 680, Ecgfrith was killed and Hlothhere, king of Kent, died in 685 and Theodore followed in 690. Despite Theodore's successful presidency of a second synod in 680, the general trend from 676 onwards for a generation is towards dissension and violence, with the crucial accord and mutual co-operation between Church and kings slipping away and Northumbrian leadership undermined. The Mercians were partially responsible, having ravaged Kent and then faithlessly murdered the Northumbrian-born Queen Osthryth in 697, but the Picts were also involved, being responsible for Berhtred's death in 698.

That said, Bede's later material is less traumatic. There are more positive events reported and less attention is given to deaths, and particularly violent ones. The spate of Northumbrian travails which characterise the later reign of Ecgfrith and then that of Aldfrith give way to notice of Berhtfrith's campaign against the Picts in 711, the outcome of which is unstated but was at least less obviously dire than Ecgfrith's violent death in 685 or Berhtred's in 698. Gone are the signs of divine disapproval and there is a sense of the beginnings of reconciliation here between the Northumbrian dynasty and God, leading towards a more hopeful present. Bede added further evidence of English engagement with Rome by including Cædwalla's departure for that destination in 688 and then Coenred of Mercia's in 709, plus emphasised the triumph of Egbert, 'the man of God' and ultimately 'Saint',[186] in correcting 'the monks of Iona to the Catholic Easter and ecclesiastical tonsure'. Egbert's success at Iona provides the final rhetorical climax of the recapitulation. His achievement establishes the English as full members of the Universal Church and active within its apostolic traditions, by carrying Roman orthodoxy to the further reaches of the British Isles. This connects once again, therefore, with the alliance of the Northumbrian dynasty with the papacy which Bede had highlighted a century and a half earlier, as the key players in his historical saga.

Bede acknowledged Mercian power at the close, noting Tatwine's consecration as the ninth archbishop of Canterbury in the fifteenth year of the *imperium* of Æthelbald, king of the Mercians. *Imperium* was a term used by Bede to denote 'overkingship' and wide authority in both the Roman and Anglo-Saxon contexts,[187] and this stands out as his sole use of the term in the entire work of a Mercian ruler. His attitude to the Mercians changes across the recapitulation, as it does across the main text, but it is important to note his apparent acquiescence in Mercian control of both Church and state – in southern Britain at least – in the closing lines.

The language used to denote death provides an indicator of his attitude towards particular individuals. In all, twenty-eight deaths were noted but the terminology varied considerably. The commonest terms by far were *obiit* and *defunctus est*, which combined account for fifteen instances, with *obiit* favoured for the deaths of religious figures (as Gregory, Hild, Theodore and Berhtwold). Two events were picked out by the use of euphemisms, Paulinus *migravit ad Dominum* and St Egbert *transit*, in each case underlining their particular significance as Christian heroes within the recapitulation. Several violent deaths were noted by *interfectus* (Gratian, Berhtred, King Osred) and *occisus* (King Oswald, King Oswine, Ælfwine and King Ecgfrith), but two such were singled out as particularly heinous: King Edwin was *peremtus* and Queen Osthryth *interemta*, which carry the implication of murder. Indeed, it is difficult to see any other reason for the latter's inclusion than as evidence of Mercian perfidy, unless unbeknown to us she was in some way related to Ceolwulf or one of his henchmen. One individual was treated very differently: the Mercian Penda *periit* ('perished') in 655, with implications not only for his body but also for his soul as the only non-Christian whose death was recorded. In addition, Penda's royal status and people went unnoticed here, although both were presumably well known to Bede's audience and were widely acknowledged elsewhere in the text.[188] This is in contrast to his normal practice in this section of naming rulers as 'king of the – ans'.[189] The only exceptions were Penda, who was here being presented, implicitly at least, as destined for hell, and Osric in 729, the king of the Northumbrians named by Bede in V, 23, but whose affinity was here omitted, perhaps for fear of causing offence. That said, King Ceolwulf is not even named in the recapitulation and his tenure of the throne since 729 passes without mention.

Treatment of the Mercians therefore begins over a century later than reference to the Northumbrians (via Ida in 547) with the death of the pagan Penda (655), several of whose crimes had already been included, albeit anonymously (as the deaths of Edwin, 633, and Oswald, 642). The death of Penda's Christian son, Wulfhere, was dealt with in language comparable to others of the faith (675), but Æthelred, his brother and successor, devastated Kent (676),[190] and in 697 Queen Osthryth was murdered 'by her own household men, that is Mercians'. Æthelred's eventual retirement to become a monk in 704, then Coenred's departure for Rome, mark the end of this phase and the Mercian atrocities which characterised it, which their behaviours apparently atoned for, enabling Bede to accommodate current Mercian *imperium* across southern Britain under King Æthelbald. The present was being treated here, therefore, much as in the main text,[191] as a time of Christian peace among the English, under divine approbation. Egbert's successful mission to Iona marked a fulfilment of the destiny of the English people as a whole in accommodating the apostolic agenda of the Universal Church. If he was known to be Northumbrian, then this marks the final reconciliation between that people and God, but Bede never actually reveals Egbert's origins, leaving us unable to be sure of that connection.[192] However, the Church was administered in Britain by an already long-established archdiocese of Canterbury. The succession of its ninth primate, under the protection of the Mercian king of the day, ends the recapitulation and arguably the final section of the *EH*.

It is worth exploring the overall relationship between the recapitulation and the remainder of the text in two respects: one is the extent to which it fulfils the proposal with which it begins that it would literally 'recapitulate events', and the second is the faithfulness with which it represents the remainder of the work.

First, as already noted, the recapitulation does contain new information, in six different places, which is appreciable within an annalistic framework of only fifty-one entries.[193] This includes the two comets of 538 and 540, which it is suggested (above) Bede used primarily as spiritual scene-setting prior to the English conversion, plus the next entry, for 547, relating to Ida and the foundations of the Northumbrian dynasty, which opens his introduction of several virtuous agents of change. Ceolwulf and most other eighth-century aspirants to the Northumbrian throne based their claims on descent from Ida. From the perspective of current dynastic politics, that Bede had omitted from his first draft such a key player in Northumbrian history, at least, perhaps exposes his comparative lack of interest in the various royal hopefuls of the day and the strengths and weaknesses of their individual claims. The omission perhaps drew criticism, however, from those to whom Ceolwulf had deputed the task of reading it, hence Ida's belated appearance here.

There are then another three 'new' entries in the last phase of the annals: Osthryth's murder in 697;[194] Berhtred's death at Pictish hands in 698;[195] and Berhtfrith's campaign against the Picts in 711. These collectively confirm the view that Bede's agenda was not here exclusively bound by the need to summarise his narrative, and perhaps also reflect his reaction to comments received. The problem, however, is that we now lack the web of knowledge shared by Bede's audience in 731, leaving their relevance obscure. All three clearly have a bearing on relations between the Northumbrians and their neighbours, but without better understanding of possible interconnections between these three and members of the court in the present, it is unclear why these particular individuals were singled out for comment.

Reverting to the issue of coverage, it is useful to consider this first of all in mechanistic terms. Entries in the recapitulation do reflect material contained in all five books but do so far from evenly. The densest coverage is of book II, the shortest book, which deals with the Roman conversion of Northumbria, to which eight entries relate, at a ratio of one entry per two and a half chapters, followed by book I with 1:2.8 and book IV with 1:3. Book V has only seven entries compared with twenty-three chapters (excluding this final one) at a ratio of 1:3.3, but the addition of the three further entries which belong to this time period but contain new information would reduce this ratio (to 1:2.4). The least coverage is of book III, with a mere seven entries relating to thirty chapters and with no additional information. The poverty of treatment accorded this section of the *EH*, which focuses primarily on the reigns of kings Oswald and Oswiu and the Irish mission, reflects a fundamental shift on Bede's part from his stance in the main text, which placed Oswald and Aidan at the very core of the work. Had we only the recapitulation and not the *Ecclesiastical History*, we would be led to the view that Northumbrian Christianity derived almost exclusively from the Gregorian mission, via Paulinus, with Theodore later working in close collaboration with Ecgfrith to push the agenda forward. Irish or Scottish participation would be barely acknowledged and impossible to evaluate. This was, as we shall see (below, pp. 126–7), a position midway between that adopted in the main text of the *EH* and that which appears in Bede's *Greater Chronicle*, written *c.*725 (see below, pp. 117–22), so something of a compromise on Bede's part and a significant shift away from the overall balance of the *Ecclesiastical History*.

What can we take away from these observations? While the whole question must remain beyond final solution, the proposal that we view the recapitulation as a text written in preparation for the *EH*, but then appended to it, clearly fails to convince. The Preface was certainly appended to the work after the first draft had been read and commented upon by those to whom Ceolwulf had deputed the task, supposing that his own probable illiteracy and other responsibilities had prevented his undertaking the task for himself.

Within his new Preface, Bede arguably made an effort to respond to comments made, in particular by shoring up the authority of his text. There is a case for the final chapter, V, 24, having been written at the same time. First, chapter V, 23 reads as if it had been intended to be the final section of the work, which implies that it had initially served precisely that function. Second, V, 24 is made up of three disparate sections, all of which look rather like afterthoughts. Third, the list of works, which makes up the final section of V, 24, actually includes the *Ecclesiastical History*, as if that had already been completed. Fourth, there are significant connections between the autobiographical section and the Preface, which might suggest that they were written in parallel, and the final prayer seems to have migrated between the Preface and the close of V, 24 in different manuscripts. Lastly, the recapitulation, which makes up the first part of V, 24, was written according to a somewhat different agenda to the main text, as regards both the individual entries included and the overall balance of history which emerges.

Two features seem particularly significant, albeit that may be to an extent a product of the time which has elapsed, which has obscured the meaning of other changes made. One is honourable mention of Ida, whose omission from the main text may well have seemed unhelpful to readers interested in dynastic claims to the throne in the present. The other is the cultural amnesia which Bede was here exhibiting regarding the Irish contribution to English, and particularly Northumbrian, Christianity. If these and other changes reflect adverse comments from those who had first read the *Ecclesiastical History* in draft, then those remarks presumably consisted both of items to be included – to which Bede responded by adding new material – and of criticism of his comparatively liberal treatment of the Scottish mission. The latter was the more major issue and Bede seems to have responded in two ways. One was to defend what he was attempting to do, in his new Preface, by both emphasising the role of his many stories as exemplary narratives for present consumption and invoking external authorities to reinforce the status of his own authorship. The second was to tone down the Irish contribution in the recapitulation, but without making much, if any, effort to redress this issue in the bulk of the work. The defensiveness which has here been identified seems peculiar to just these passages which it has been suggested belong exclusively to the second draft. The story which emerges from the recapitulation is simpler than in the *EH* as a whole, as one might have expected of an annalistic summary, but it is also profoundly different, even to the point where it serves as a partial recantation of the vision of history already offered. The recapitulation is purposeful and clearly authored, not a mere preparatory list but an independent version of the past. In a sense, it could even be termed apologetic. Certainly, Bede was not being entirely honest when he attempted to pass off his annalistic summary as if it was merely 'recapitulating' what had gone before. Such subterfuge again implies that it formed part of a wider defensive strategy.

Supposing this rebalancing of the insular past to have been a consequence of adverse comment, then that is likely to have derived not from any part of the Northumbrian Church which owed its origins to the Scots, but rather from individuals associated with those cult sites which viewed themselves as descended in some sense from the Gregorian mission. That both York and Whitby are named in the recapitulation, in the absence of such 'Scottish' foundations as Lindisfarne or Melrose, just might hint at those responsible.

In conclusion

Considerable efforts have been made in recent years to explore the immediate social, cultural and political contexts of the *Ecclesiastical History*. The problem is, of course, that we have a very poor conception of those contexts, particularly if the *Ecclesiastical History* itself be set aside as ineligible as evidence through which that contextualisation should be attempted. While there are several narratives capable of aiding this endeavour which derive from Northumbria in the first quarter of the eighth century, there is a serious shortage of similar material from the second quarter, within which Bede's principal historical work was almost certainly conceived and certainly written, leaving the *EH* as the principal tool by which it has itself to be contextualised. There have, in consequence, been several comparatively disparate theories regarding the immediate circumstances in which Bede wrote, and therefore what he was setting out to achieve. These stretch from the neo-Plummerian view, at one extreme, of a cloistered author writing a primarily meditative work, fired by idealism and with very little contact with the world of contemporary politics,[196] through the *Ecclesiastical History* as a specimen of reformist literature, written by an enthusiast for moral renewal in the present,[197] to a vision of a more politically engaged author, writing on behalf of a particular faction within the Northumbrian Church in the contest for the coming archdiocese of York (which actually came to fruition in 735, the year of Bede's own death).[198]

The strength of the first of these theories lies in its appreciation of the highly contemplative nature of so much of Bede's discourse, but his connection with the world of contemporary politics seems clear from his decision to despatch the completed work to the Northumbrian king of the day, to whose oversight he had already submitted a preliminary draft before writing the Preface. Bede was certainly idealistic in many respects and writing as a committed Christian from deep conviction and for largely spiritual purposes, but this and other evidence of engagement must be allowed to set aside the vision of a writer whose world was entirely bounded by his own monastic house and the Mediterranean-centric literature with which he was there engaged,[199] in favour of one who, while himself a biblical scholar by training and inclination, was also an integral member of the Northumbrian élite of the day, and seeking to voice his own thoughts to an audience which was in part at least outside the handful of prominent religious houses to which he normally addressed his work.

Nor should the *Ecclesiastical History* be viewed as conventional reformist literature. While there can be little doubt that Bede was pursuing a reformist agenda in the closing years of his life and this was certainly a work written around moral renewal, with a past 'golden age' set out as an implicit – and occasionally explicit – critique of the present, there is very little criticism of the current state of affairs within the Church. This was not about the number of sees or the quality of the priesthood, therefore, but offered an agenda aimed primarily at senior members of secular society. The *EH* is reformist in the broadest, Gregorian sense, but it needs to be viewed as written for somewhat different purposes than the views being expressed so forcibly in the *Letter to Egbert*, in 734: it was primarily aimed at changing the behaviour of the Northumbrian establishment, and in particular the secular establishment.

The opportunity has also been taken in chapter 2 to reconsider the most elaborate and influential attempt to establish the *Ecclesiastical History* within a contemporary dialogue – that which Walter Goffart has presented in three essays published in 1988, 1990 and 2005 – but the view that Bede wrote primarily to confront the vision of history offered by Stephen's *Life of Wilfrid* proves ultimately unsustainable. This does not mean that Bede failed to challenge Stephen on particular issues, for of course he did on such matters as the condemnation of the Irish-Northumbrian church as Quartodeciman, much in the same way that he 'corrected' other authors such as Isidore when he believed them to be wrong. But while some 'corrections' of Stephen's work occur in the *Ecclesiastical History*, these are generally implicit and Bede never singled out Stephen or his work by name as erroneous. Even taken together, the differences are not sufficient to imagine this to be an important motive for Bede's composition, and it is far from clear that many of his own audience will in any case have known the *Life of Wilfrid*, the circulation of which was probably always very limited.[200] In very general terms, Bede showed considerable cordiality towards both Wilfrid and Acca and some disquiet at King Ecgfrith's expulsion of his bishop, which he seems to have viewed as a critical moment as regards divine support for the Northumbrian kings. That said, he explained Ecgfrith's eventual death in battle as a consequence not of his treatment of Wilfrid in 678 but of divine anger at his despatch of an army to raid Ireland, in 684.[201] While it is fair to argue that Wilfrid had had some committed opponents and had been a factional figure, his reconciliation with the Northumbrian establishment *c*.705 and death a few years later does seem to have been the end of the matter. There is no evidence that such tensions were still dominant within the Northumbrian church by 731 and no such divide between Wilfridians and their opponents can safely be deduced from this work or other of Bede's output. Rather, Bede was a close associate of Wilfrid's friend and ultimate successor, Acca, and simply cannot be imagined as a spokesman for his opponents. Bede admittedly attempted to recast Wilfrid into his own preferred mould of the monkish bishop, humble missionary and learned ascetic, over and against Stephen's more righteous and princely prelate astride the world stage, and the transformation was not always easy. However, it is the roles which Wilfrid's character and career were designed to perform that differ in these two works, rather than any innate difference of opinion regarding his position as a hero of insular Catholicism. In answer to the view that the *Ecclesiastical History* should be read as a salvo in an ongoing contest to control the archdiocese of York, when that should actually become sanctioned, one can only say that York receives scant attention over the previous half-century and there is no explicit reference herein to the effort being made – or perhaps about to be made – to resurrect its status, let alone any view on who might be installed when the current incumbent, Wilfrid II, should leave it vacant (as he did in 732).

We have, therefore, explored a variety of potential agendas underlying Bede's authorship of the *Ecclesiastical History* and suggested that his purpose should be framed in terms of his wish to set before his audience a series of exemplary relationships between God and His peoples in an insular context. The principal focus is on the Northumbrians and Bede wrote for an élite, northern English audience, in terms designed to inculcate appropriate behaviour among his fellow countrymen in the present. Gregory the Great had earlier written extensively about the relationship between social, religious and political authority and Christian morality,[202] and Bede used his *EH* to explore and set out views which are to an extent comparable.

After review of recent discussion of Bede's agenda, two sections of the work in particular have been under the spotlight in this chapter, the Preface and the recapitulation, which were arguably the last substantial passages to have been written. What has been investigated here is just what Bede was using these two separate passages to achieve, as he completed the work.

The Preface was self-evidently written after his first draft had been despatched to Ceolwulf, then returned with comments. Given the improbability of the king having himself the time and education necessary to critique the *Ecclesiastical History*, such comments were presumably provided by churchmen to whom the king had delegated the task. In the Preface Bede took the opportunity to spell out his purpose in terms of lessons provided by examples of both good and bad behaviour, from which he expected his immediate audience to learn; as Professor James Campbell put it: he intended to 'use it [the past] to teach lessons to the present, mainly by treating seventh-century England as a gallery of good examples'.[203] That he belatedly felt it necessary to make this agenda explicit may imply that the comments he had received had suggested that this aspect of the work had not been sufficiently appreciated. He singled out the Northumbrian king of the day as the personification of this present audience, signifying that his message related not only to individuals seeking salvation but also to the body politic as represented by the king, so the collective interaction between the Northumbrians as a people and the one Christian God. It was the role of the king to lead his people in ways of righteousness and support well-educated and pious clergy in their efforts to spread the word and reap the harvest. Bede was seeking to guide the king in this endeavour via a whole set of complex allegories, masquerading as a history of the insular past.

The *Ecclesiastical History* carried messages, therefore, which were quite specific to the present political élite and Bede's treatment of the king needs to be viewed very much in the context of the role he was expected to fulfil. This is, in a sense, a contemporary, political agenda, in terms of Bede's understanding of history as the unravelling of the interaction between mankind and divine providence: he was writing both as a biblical scholar and as a Northumbrian, with a preference for the re-establishment of his own immediate *gens* ('people') within the full force of divine approbation. Bede's agenda as he concluded the *Ecclesiastical History* fits naturally alongside his works of exegesis to the point where it is valid to see it as in some sense a work of pastoral theology. It was never intended to provide the type of analytical survey of the past from a secular standpoint that is central to the writing of history today. Its style connects with existing narratives of various kinds, stretching from the Scriptures via the ecclesiastical histories of Eusebius and Rufinus to Gregory's *Dialogues*. Bede apparently meant the same analytical tools to be applied to his *History* as he himself used when approaching biblical texts. He expected it therefore to be read, appreciated and understood on the literal, historical level but also as allegory and as a vehicle by which to teach and put over moral truths. The *Ecclesiastical History* seems a comparatively easy work to read on first acquaintance but this is an illusion. It is, in fact, also a pastoral work which is as complex and multi-layered as Bede believed Scripture to be.

Bede's method depended heavily on his ability to derive useful information from a variety of sources, both written and oral, with a particular emphasis on letters and documents provided by southern correspondents whom he named. The historicity of his account necessarily rested heavily on the reliability of his many informants, which is now beyond testing and is defended primarily, even solely in many instances, by his insistence on their status as truth-tellers. Some of his material was arguably apocryphal and he was inclined to include unsubstantiated stories about the past, largely for the sake of the moral lessons which they enabled him to develop. In very general terms, decisions regarding what should be included and what excluded, and the way in which material was presented, depended at least as much on Bede's underlying agenda as on any judgement of the historicity of the actual story, although he was often prepared to divulge his sources, so allow his immediate audience to determine how credible a particular story might be on the basis of the reputation of his informant. He was as interested in the exposition of particular higher truths, moral exemplars and fundamental Christian lessons as in the recording accurately of the nuts and bolts of specific past actions. That does not mean that the *Ecclesiastical History* should be read as fiction: it does arguably contain as accurate a record as Bede could contrive of diocesan succession and royal chronology, in particular, but its two-dimensional and stereotypical characterisations, numerous miracle stories and providential system of causation all betray Bede's intention to write something other than what would today be termed history. This work should therefore be treated very much as source material and deconstructed very critically indeed, to explore the message(s) underlying each passage. A history written for early eighth-century purposes should not be allowed to masquerade as one written for the twenty-first century.

There is also a degree of defensiveness in the Preface which needs to be acknowledged. In the first few lines Bede paid tribute to the religiosity of the king in ways apparently designed to ensure his co-operation. Thereafter he deployed the reputations of several leading churchmen as responsible for numerous passages, if not the whole work, and invoked in addition the memories of all of Gregory, Theodore and Hadrian. By so doing, Bede was arguably seeking to underpin his new history with their authorities, so place it above criticism. Such implies that it had, in fact, been received with less than total enthusiasm by those who had read it on Ceolwulf's behalf. Indeed, Bede refers to what he termed 'doubts' at the close of his first paragraph. We have the sense, therefore, of a text which, on first acquaintance, was considered somewhat contentious, and Bede reacted to face down his critics.

Finally, the recapitulation with which Bede closed his narrative was reviewed in order to explore its potential as another indicator of Bede's purposes in the ultimate stages of its completion. That this was not, literally, a 'recapitulation' of the earlier text has been long recognised, but previous suggestions that it originated as a preparatory text are less than convincing. Instead, we have here explored the possibility that this too, alongside the Preface, was written after Bede had received the first draft back from the court, in part, at least, to provide him with a means of responding to criticisms. Bede used his recapitulation to incorporate individuals and/or events who had earlier been omitted and readjusted the balance of the historical narrative which he had previously offered. In a truncated, annalistic form, the recapitulation foregrounds the Northumbrian kings and highlights their early achievements as lead advocates and patrons of Christianity in England, but this is a specifically 'Romanist' story, foregrounding Rome itself, Gregory, Edwin and Paulinus, then Theodore. In contrast with the main text, the Irish mission is seriously neglected, despite inclusion of the foundation of Iona. So there is, for example, no mention of Lindisfarne or the arrival of Aidan, and the reigns of Oswald and Oswiu are predominantly a list of deaths. Colman is noted only for his departure. Cuthbert does not appear, despite his prominence in the later chapters of book IV, and nor does John of Beverley, despite his dominance of the early chapters of book V. The Northumbrian focus gives way somewhat after Wilfrid's expulsion, which is followed by a rash of adverse events which Bede seems to have portrayed as 'signs' that the long-established accord between the Northumbrian dynasty and the Christian God had faltered. In the recent past, calamities had abated but Bede picked out the virtues of several southern kings, and particularly Mercian kings, on whom he envisaged that divine favour had fallen since the early years of the eighth century and whose *imperium* finally contextualised the succession of a ninth – and Mercian – primate at Canterbury in 731. There is a strong connection here between types of behaviour on the part of kings that Bede considered had been particularly valued by God – such as retirement into a monastery or to Rome – and the recent political and military successes of West Saxon and Mercian kings, which his predominantly Northumbrian audience was presumably expected to embrace.

The shift in emphasis from an 'Oswaldian' past to an 'Edwinian' one, plus the addition of six events unmentioned in the main text, arguably reveal an author struggling to amend the text he had written without taking on the enormous task of a complete rewrite. The most plausible interpretation would be that Bede only decided to add this final chapter after he had received back his first draft. If his change of emphasis in the recapitulation accurately reflects the comments attached thereto, then this final response may imply that his original manuscript had been read by clerics closer to the traditions of history which Bede had himself earlier espoused, and which we might envisage as popular at this date at Whitby or York, rather than Lindisfarne.

Whether or not this explanation be accepted – and it has to be admitted that there can be no firm conclusions – it is established that Bede did make significant adjustments to his story in this final chapter, in ways which to an extent conflict with the remainder of the work. What is revealed here, therefore, is the *Ecclesiastical History* as a rather more fluid, and indeed contested, version of the past than it has hitherto seemed. Differences between the main text and the recapitulation reveal narratives which were just two of numerous possible representations of history in 731. The past was arguably then being quarried by many different individuals for their own purposes, and different glosses were being placed thereon to accord with a mass of contemporary agendas. That Bede's historical *magnum opus* should have failed to satisfy the needs of various parties is hardly surprising, but their failure to write alternatives has left us with just Bede's voice in the main text, along with the merest shadow of those of his critics, discernible only via his reaction thereto in the recapitulation.

It is important to note that Bede had himself earlier offered a brief version of insular history, in his *Greater Chronicle*, which had important similarities with the recapitulation but less in common with the main text of the *Ecclesiastical History*. In pursuit of Bede's shifting agendas, chapter 3 will look in far greater detail at the *EH* itself in terms of its structure and organisation, and focus too on the precursors to its historical content within Bede's previous output, to explore this sense of a work breaking away from accepted history as that was apparently perceived within sections of the clerical establishment in Northumbria in the first third of the eighth century.

3 Structure, organisation and context

The British, it is said, are made up of four races, the best of these are the Derby and the Oaks.[1]

In chapter 2, we focused on two different parts of the *EH*, in particular the Preface and recapitulation, which were arguably the last major sections which Bede wrote, in order to explore how he perceived his agenda and how he responded to the comments of his first readers as he brought the work to a conclusion. This third chapter will look at evidence for his purposes at an earlier stage in the process, when setting out to write the *Ecclesiastical History*, first by exploring his structuring of the work overall, and secondly by comparing the core messages conveyed by the *Ecclesiastical History* with those offered by his earlier and much briefer excursion into English history in the *Greater Chronicle*. This latter will lead us in turn into a discussion of the role of book III, and the Irish and Ionan connections which it highlights, within the overall structure of the work. Throughout, this exploration has some potential to provide insights into the author's overall agenda as he undertook and developed this, his major 'historical' work, in the particular circumstances pertaining around 729–31.

Structure

Excluding only the Preface, Bede organised his *Ecclesiastical History* into five books of somewhat unequal lengths.[2] This organisation was necessarily subject to a series of decisions and choices on the part of the author, who presumably considered how many books would be appropriate to his overall design, how long they should be, where each should begin and end and how many chapters each should contain. It is possible that Bede set out from the beginning with a clear vision of his intended structure, but some signs that he may have felt it necessary to reorganise the work, to an extent at least, at a late stage have long been recognised.

Bede's *On the Apocalypse* opens with a prefatory letter to 'Eusebius' (Hwæt-berht, his abbot post 716), in which he explains the division of this new work into three short books, 'in order to relieve the mind'.[3] He very properly attributed this reasoning to St Augustine, who had earlier compared a reader completing a sub-section of some major work with a traveller refreshed by resting at an inn.[4] Bede felt that this advice was particularly appropriate to his own audience, remarking somewhat dismissively that he considered that 'the indolence of our nation, I mean of the English, ought to be taken into account'. His comments betray a poor opinion of both the Latinity and the powers of concentration of his own fellow monks. Alongside his use of comparatively simple sentence construction, clear and frequent subdivision of his works seems to have been something which Bede consciously adopted in order to make them easier for an audience whose stamina when confronted by a long Latin text he had reason to doubt.[5] By dividing the task into a subset of smaller but perhaps more attainable challenges, he hoped to make his works more accessible to a primarily local reader- and hearership, whose first language was not Latin.

The organisation of such works as the *Ecclesiastical History* into both books and chapters was founded, in part, on the Bible, which was Bede's ultimate exemplar for the writing of history. Books and chapters divide the Scriptures into coherent, short passages and provide a means of both referencing and locating particular sections, without which biblical scholarship would have been extraordinarily difficult. However, Bede's immediate exemplar was arguably Eusebius's *Ecclesiastical History*, which was similarly divided into books and chapters plus provided with a contents list at the beginning of each book, very like Bede's. That said, his reading of pre-Christian literature had also acquainted him with works which were similarly divided, to an extent at least, such as Virgil's *Aeneid*, for example, which was in twelve books, although these were not organised internally into chapters. While far from universal, the subdivision of long texts into books and/or chapters was, therefore, widely used in Late Antiquity, particularly in historical writing.

Bede had already on occasion subdivided his lengthier writings but his adoption of this strategy had been quite variable. At one extreme, the twenty-eight-book structure of his *On the Acts of the Apostles* (which he adopted once more when he revisited the subject in his *Retractatio*) merely replicated the division of the biblical text into chapters. At the other, the single-book formats in which he cast his two versions of the *Life of Cuthbert* were each divided into forty-six chapters, either following the chapterisation of Constantius's *Life of St Germanus*, which Bede used extensively in book I of the *EH*, or the years of the rebuilding of the Temple.[6] That said, most of his major works are divided into comparatively small numbers of books, varying from two in the case of *On the Building of the Temple* and *The History of the Abbots* up to six in *On the Gospel of Luke* and *On the Song of Songs*. Although it is fair to say that only his longer works were generally subdivided into books, there is no simple equation between the length of any particular text and the number of books allocated to it. For the sake of establishing a single standard unit of length applicable equally to all Bede's works, I will here adopt the number of page-length columns that the Latin text occupies in the *Patrologia Latina*. This provides a very rough and ready degree of comparability which enables us to see just how variable book length could be.[7] Taking only multi-book works, the six-book *On the Gospel of Luke* lies at one end of the spectrum with an average of 55.5 columns per book, while the two-book *History of the Abbots* marks the opposite end, averaging only 8.5 columns. In practice, the latter looks exceptional and Bede perhaps had particular reasons for dividing his *History of the Abbots* as he did.[8] Excluding his *On the Seven Catholic Epistles*, which was naturally divided into seven books (averaging only 17.3 columns per book), Bede's other multi-book works all fall within a range of 28.5 to 55.5 columns per book. While this is a comparatively broad band, it does contain eight works which do seem to cluster, to an extent at least, as regards their subdivision. The *Ecclesiastical History* occupies 269 page-length columns in the *Patrologia Latina* and is divided into five books. In the context of Bede's other multi-book works, its average of 53.8 columns per book does not look exceptional, being almost identical to his commentary *On the First Book of Samuel* (53.75) and very close to his *On the Gospel of Luke* (55.5). The *Ecclesiastical History* lies, therefore, close to the top end of Bede's range as regards average book length, but comfortably within it. It is also among his longest works, being exceeded only by the commentary *On the Gospel of Luke* (with 333 columns to the 269 of the *EH*).

The particular organisation of the *Ecclesiastical History* also invites discussion, in that it is the only work which Bede divided into five books. Numbers mattered to Bede and his contemporaries, being used extensively as 'signs' capable of either suggesting or sustaining particular readings of his text. Three had hitherto been the commonest number of books in his works, as befits the number of the Trinity, followed by four. Given the comparatively weak correlation between length and number of books across his works as a whole, the division into five is more likely to have been premeditated than to have arisen merely as a convenience in the process of subdivision after the work had been sketched out. Five may well have been the minimum number Bede will have entertained for a work of this length, since division into four would have made the average length of his books markedly longer than any other of his multi-book works (at 67 columns). However, division into either six or seven books would have kept comfortably within his existing range (44.8 and 38.4 respectively) and even ten or twelve books might not have been out of the question (26.9 and 22.4 respectively). Bede would have been aware of Orosius's adoption of seven books for his historical work, given his frequent use of it in book I, and was also conscious of Rufinus's reorganisation of Eusebius's *Ecclesiastical History* into eleven (Eusebius's original had ten). None of the pre-existing works of history which he used in writing his own was divided into five books, so there was no obvious precedent, although he was familiar with several texts which were so divided: all of Hegesippus' *Ecclesiastical History*, which despite its title is a précis of Josephus's *Judean Antiquities*, Ambrose's *On Faith*, Primasius's *Exposition of the Apocalypse* and

Vegetius's *Concerning Military Things* had five, but Bede only certainly consulted the last of these when writing the *EH*,[9] and it is difficult to imagine
that he will have judged any of these particularly appropriate as models for
his work of history, even though *On Faith* was dedicated to the emperor of the
day. He did know of the *Ecclesiastical History* of Theodoret, bishop of Cyrrhus,
which was divided into five books, but it is not particularly likely that he had
access to it, being aware of it primarily from Gennadius's continuation of
Jerome's *Concerning Illustrious Men*.[10] Similarly he may have been aware that
Hegesippus had written a five-book *Ecclesiastical History*, given Jerome's
notice of it in the same volume and reference to it additionally in Eusebius's
Ecclesiastical History (IV, 8), but he had probably never seen a copy. He certainly knew that Isidore had placed his brief chronicle within book V of his
Etymologies,[11] but it is not clear whether or not this will have weighed heavily
with our author. In numbering his books, Bede may, therefore, have been
influenced by the organisational style of pre-existing works of history but
there is at least as strong a case for his following his own internal logic.

He did introduce the number 'five' into the first chapter of his own book
I, at the point where he shifted his attention away from what one might
very loosely describe as background, and geographical and topographical
information, to a discussion of the present inhabitants:

> Here at the present time just as divine law is written in five books, there
> are five languages of peoples devoted to seeking out and confessing one
> and the same knowledge of the highest truth and of true sublimity,
> namely English, British, Scots, Pictish and Latin, which is common
> among all through meditation of the Scriptures.

The comparison is, of course, with the Pentateuch, the first five books of the
Old Testament, termed the five books of Moses,[12] on which he remarked, in
V, 24, that he had previously written in summary terms. However, Bede
made few other connections in this work with this section of the Bible: he
did quote from the Pentateuch in the *EH* but not with any frequency in
sections which he had authored himself (as opposed to his transcription of
Gregory's letters to England, and Abbot Ceolfrith's letter to Nechtan, both
of which quote from these books with some frequency). In fact, Bede's only
two original references to them come in the very last chapter of book I, in
which he compared King Æthelfrith of the Northumbrians to the biblical
Benjamin,[13] and in his treatment of the poet Cædmon,[14] each of which could,
of course, have derived from a written source by another hand. So only this
brief aside in the first chapter alerts the reader to Bede's interest in the
number five in this work. It is perhaps worth noting that there is a degree of
artificiality about its appearance in this context, for he is unlikely to have
intended that his audience should imagine that the British language was
regularly used across the seventh and into the eighth centuries to discover or
to bear witness to 'knowledge of the highest truth and of true sublimity',

given that he considered many of its users in the present to be in a state of doctrinal error, so excluded from the Universal Church and 'opposed by the power of God and man alike'.[15] This disjunction in his message, therefore, suggests that we should read this sentence primarily for its figurative meaning, in terms of its capacity to explain his internal organisation of this work into five books, rather than as a literal statement regarding how he viewed these several languages.

It may be that this is of itself sufficient explanation of Bede's five books. When writing his *Greater Chronicle*, Bede had included a reference to 'the five books of Moses' taken directly from Jerome's *Chronicle*,[16] and elsewhere in his exegesis he regularly related other occurrences of the number 'five' in the Bible to the books of Law, for example in *On the Tabernacle*,[17] *On the Temple*,[18] and his studies of the first part of Samuel[19] and of Luke's Gospel.[20] There are some meaningful parallels to be drawn between his *EH* and the Pentateuch, which could have attracted Bede to this biblical number. So, for example, both offer a starting point for the history of a particular people, both involve 'Fall' narratives,[21] both include significant journeys into the 'Promised Land' (literal and metaphorical), and both feature major religious leaders of a people foreknown to, and under the active protection of, the Lord. The end point of Deuteronomy, which closes with the death of Moses and with the Israelites poised to enter Canaan, bears some comparison with Bede's closure of his narrative in book V with the deaths of two key Church leaders, the saintly missionary Egbert and Berhtwold, archbishop of Canterbury, alongside a state of general peace and well-being within the relationship between the English as a whole and the One Christian God which he remarked on in part via brief quotations from the Psalms.[22] It might be that Bede was attracted in particular by the prospect of a closure of this his major historical work which could be represented metaphorically by a moment in Scripture when God was perhaps more actively protective of His own people than at any other. In this sense, the passage of the Israelites through the desert from Egypt to the Promised Land can be read as a 'sign' of, or metaphor for, the passing of the English via conversion out of paganism and into the Universal Church. However, such a view seems difficult to equate with the dissatisfaction with the current state of the Northumbrian Church in particular, which is an essential prerequisite of the reform agenda which Bede prioritised in his last years and which is evidenced in works completed at around the same time as the *Ecclesiastical History*,[23] as well as therein. There seems little point offering a whole series of good and bad examples to his contemporaries if their behaviour was already exemplary: rather, we are back to the sense in which Bede judged that his audience faced a choice, whether to seek the Lord's approval, as the Irish had done, and so gain the Promised Land, or fall away into sin like the Britons.[24] In addition, there is little correlation between the respective chapterisations of these works either in detail or in total: the 138 chapters of the *EH* compare with 187 of the Pentateuch,[25] and although the number of chapters in book I equates with that of Deuteronomy, such a correlation between Bede's first book and the last in the Pentateuch is as likely to be fortuitous as intentional or meaningful.

Bede did organise several of his exegetical works in ways that reflected either the questions which he had received or that section of the Bible on which he was commenting. His failure to reinforce the comparison with the Pentateuch in similar ways via his internal structure can only weaken the connection. On these several grounds, the argument that Bede was so attracted by the parallels offered by the Pentateuch that he decided to adopt a five-book format is far from proven, but it should be stressed that his comparison of Britain's languages with the Pentateuch is an explicit simile, not a metaphor. The mode of delivery, therefore, does add some weight to the possibility that he was deliberately modelling the structure of this work on the books of Moses.

Several authors have sought alternative explanations. So, for example, Wilhelm Levison was impressed by the general symmetry of the *Ecclesiastical History*,[26] and looked to other works of history which Bede had read for clues as to the numbering of his books. He noted that Gregory of Tours had organised his historical opus into ten books, and Bede's work had in common with Gregory's a preliminary sketch which positions the main story, an auto-biographical section and a list of his own works. That said, while this connection would be comparatively convincing had Bede opted for ten books, his choice of half that number is less obviously explicable via this comparison.

A more sustained and nuanced case was put forward by Benedicta Ward,[27] who related the five books of the *Ecclesiastical History* back to Bede's construction of universal history itself, which he, like other early medieval writers, divided up into six ages, each approximating figuratively to the six days of creation in Genesis, to which he added 'the six ages of man who is the microcosm of creation'.[28] In *Concerning the Reckoning of Time*, Bede explained the first age of the world in terms of the infancy of mankind, the second as childhood, the third as adolescence, the fourth as youth, the fifth as senility, 'wearied by heavy age', and the sixth awaiting death, alongside which exists the seventh age of 'perennial sabbath', all to be followed by the eighth 'of the blessed Resurrection'.[29] As Ward recognised, Bede's *Ecclesiastical History* was located almost entirely within his sixth age of the world,[30] which convention-ally began with Christ's birth, but she suggested that it might be appropriate to imagine Bede positioning himself as author in the sixth age and looking back across five subordinate ages of English history exhibiting the same basic characteristics as those of the past ages of universal history, so adopting a specially adapted version of the latter for his own local needs. Ward therefore saw Bede as portraying the infancy of the English Church in his first book, its childhood in the second, with James the Deacon's bringing of music, 'the full articulation of words, to York in the conversion of the north',[31] and its ado-lescence in the third, which focuses on the 'fruitful life of the Church in Northumbria'. The fourth age, which opens with the biblical kings, was then developed in terms of 'firm leadership for the Church under its "princes",

Theodore and Hadrian', while the fifth, when 'the Hebrew people were shattered by frequent misfortune as though weary with the weight of age', replicated Bede's treatment of the near past of Northumbria.[32] Ward portrayed the English past, therefore, as 'a world history in miniature, in which they take their place among the people of God awaiting the "eighth age of the blessed Resurrection in which they shall reign forever with the Lord" '.[33]

This is arguably the most persuasive theory so far offered to account for Bede's adoption of a fivefold division of his *Ecclesiastical History*, but it is far from certain that it is really appropriate, given the difficulties of penetrating his thought processes. In favour of this type of solution is its strong interconnection with another of his comparatively recent works and with theories of time that Bede clearly had considered deeply and on which he was an authority. As is noted at greater length below, the chronicle included by Bede in his *Concerning the Reckoning of Time* occupies book V thereof, then book VI, on time still to come, is offered in just five chapters. The parallels are interesting, if not obviously compelling, and it may well be that his adoption of five books stems in part at least from this arrangement. There are, however, several factors militating against the logic of Ward's case. One is the comparative artificiality of five ages when all else – the Creation story in Genesis, the ages of universal history and Augustine's construct of the ages of man[34] – is subdivided into six. This is not adequately explained, particularly given the sense in which book V clearly encompasses Bede's own present in its two final chapters, and it is difficult to accept the notion of the sixth age in which Bede was writing as somehow separate from the endpoint of this work. All bar the sixth age were, in Bede's vision of universal history, pre-Christian ages, which might be a problematic metaphor by which to structure an ecclesiastical history of his own people. When, in his mature years, he discussed chronology at length in *Concerning the Reckoning of Time*, he arranged his study in six books, not five, although here the chapters were numbered consistently across the work rather than starting afresh at the beginning of each individual book. Another difficulty is the selectivity among stories within the work to establish the characteristics of any one book which is necessary for Ward's thesis to stand. So, for example, it is difficult to justify treating James the Deacon's role as a teacher of chant as the central characteristic of book II, despite its closure on precisely this point, when Paulinus and Edwin play so much greater roles herein. That said, thinking of this kind is likely to have been one factor in Bede's organisation of his *Ecclesiastical History* into five books.

There are, in addition, other possibilities which need to be borne in mind. That part of the Scriptures which encompassed the sixth age is conventionally today divided into five, being the four Gospels and the Acts of the Apostles, followed by Revelation, which closes this age by looking forward in time and ushers in Bede's eighth age. There may, therefore, be a superficial resemblance between the structure of the New Testament, which is also a history of the sixth age, and Bede's *EH*, which is perhaps strengthened by observation that the 139 chapters in the New Testament as a whole approximate to Bede's

138 in his *Ecclesiastical History* (to which one might add the Preface): within the latter there is a far greater profusion of allusion to and quotation from the New Testament than from the Pentateuch, but this observation is much weakened by observation that the *Codex Amiatinus*, which was presumably identical to the most authoritative bible at Jarrow, was divided into not five but seven parts.[35] This does not, therefore, constitute a case for arguing that Bede consciously modelled his own historical work directly on the New Testament, but he may have been interested in, or at least aware of, such similarities. Alternatively, one might foreground Bede's preference for five books in either of his other two commonly encountered uses of the number, in reference to the five human senses of sight, hearing, taste, smell and touch,[36] or five divisions of the world, which he particularly set out in *Concerning the Reckoning of Time*,[37] but had already addressed in *On the Nature of Things*.[38] There are additionally several other allegorical readings of 'five' by Bede in his exegesis which may be significant, including in particular his explanation of the comparative narrowness at five cubits of the top storey of the Temple in Jerusalem, in terms of a gradation of human virtue to an apex at which a minority 'who have renounced the bond of marriage and consecrated their virginity to the Lord ought to give evidence of behaviour consonant with virginity . . . and earnestly give themselves instead to holy vigils, prayer, divine readings and psalms'.[39] This has a relevance to Bede's promotion of a reformist agenda in his later years and has numerous parallels in his modelling of the virtuous monk/cleric and scholar in the *Ecclesiastical History*.

The last possibility to be considered here is almost mechanistic, in that it may be that Bede simply had five major areas which he wished to include in this work and these virtually obliged a division into five books. Certainly, there is a case for this view, as a brief survey reveals. Book I is in part introductory – setting out Britain's earlier relationship with both Rome and God, the descent of its inhabitants from virtue into error and divine punishment thereof via the English settlement – in part (chapters 23–33) the story of the Gregorian mission to this benighted people which was foreknown by God as His own. Book II is the story of the comparative failure of this mission in Kent but its glorious success under the patronage of King Edwin, the new, *imperium*-wielding king of the Northumbrians, his promotion of conversion via mass baptisms across his own realm and among subordinate kings and peoples, but ending with the trauma of his death at the hands of the Welsh and Mercians in 633 and the flight south of Bishop Paulinus and his surviving family members. Book III focuses on the glorious redemption of Northumbria and its allies (including Wessex) for Christianity by Oswald as a new *imperium*-wielding king, alongside his clerical associates from Iona led by Bishop Aidan, the subsequent story of Christianity in the time of King Oswiu, his brother, and the working out of differences regarding (primarily) the dating of Easter between Lindisfarne and Canterbury/Rome in favour of the latter. Book IV centres on Archbishop Theodore's tenure of the see of Canterbury, which Bede looked back to as a golden age of Christian learning and portrayed as ornamented by the lives of several insular saints (as Æthel-thryth and Cuthbert) and miracles, and which saw the concluding processes of conversion of the Anglo-Saxons, among the South Saxons and on the Isle of Wight, at the hands of the émigré Northumbrian bishop Wilfrid. The final book sets out the case, albeit implicitly, for the Anglo-Saxons in the present to be considered among the peoples of the Lord within His Universal Church. So it relates several miracles associated with recent (Northumbrian) church-men (such as the hermit Œthelwald, and John, bishop of Hexham, then York), and the role of his countrymen as apostles to the northern Irish, Scots, Picts and continental Germanic pagans, and offers various warnings (visions, out-of-body experiences, etc.) to the English, urging them to aspire to higher norms of Christian behaviour, all alongside narration of both episcopal and royal succession to the present. That said, it would not be particularly dif-ficult to propose a rather different framework, so, for example, closing a purely introductory book I at the end of *EH* I, 22, then telling the story of the Canterbury mission in a new, second book, to include chapters 23–33 of *EH* I, plus, perhaps, II, 1–8. Such would place the seminal introduction of Gregory in I, 23 at the opening of a book, as might have been considered appropriate, which could have then closed either with his extended obituary, which currently opens *EH* II, or with the unfortunate sequel thereof (II, 2–8).

This brief exploration of Bede's structuring of the *Ecclesiastical History* therefore comes to no very firm conclusions as regards its division into books. The case for his modelling this work on the Pentateuch remains the best evidenced, but taken on its own it is less than overwhelming and at the last we can do little more than recognise that Bede had previously made several complex interpretations of the number 'five' and was, in his organisation of the *EH*, making use of both literal and allegorical readings with which he was already familiar to construct a framework which he felt was apt to the task. At this point it is perhaps appropriate to consider the internal organisation of Bede's five books, so as to explore his thinking as to the sub-sections of his new work.

Chapterisation

As already established, the five books of Bede's *Ecclesiastical History* were initially subdivided into some 138 chapters, to which the addition of book IV, 15 and consequent division of the previous chapter later added two more to bring the total to 140. These are distributed somewhat unevenly across the five books, with the number of chapters per book varying from twenty to thirty-four, but such variations are slight in comparison with those in Eusebius's *Ecclesiastical History*, the original Greek text of which had ten books with the complement of chapters varying far more widely from nine (book X) to forty-six (book VI). By such standards, Bede looks to have been structuring his work comparatively evenly. If we turn from the actual chap-ters to length overall, then this impression of a balanced work divided into five approximately equal sections is enhanced: including the Preface and the later additions (above), the total work comprises some 80,000–85,000 words making up some 9058 lines of text in the modern edition,[40] averaging 1794 lines per book. Exclusion of the Preface (as being outside the book structure) and IV, 15 (as a probable late addition) makes little overall difference, reducing the total length by a mere 102 lines. The shortest book, II, with 1378 lines, comprises 77 per cent of this notional average, while the longest (in terms of lines but not chapters), IV, is only 114 per cent, demonstrating that the degree of variability between books was in fact comparatively small (see table 1).

Chapter length was, however, extraordinarily variable, from a low of a mere nine lines in I, 4 to a high of 410 lines in I, 27. To an extent, however, this variability was inescapable. In total, there were twenty-nine chapters with fewer than thirty lines in the completed work, but these do not seem to reflect Bede's preferred format: they are very largely concentrated in book I, where he was generally confined to brief exposition on any one subject owing to the scarcity of available evidence at his disposal, most of which derived from very short textual references. Not surprisingly, thirteen of these come in the first twenty-two chapters of the work, so prior to the arrival of the English, and seventeen in all occur in book I, where these short chapters comprise half of the total, leaving a mere twelve spread across the remainder. Bede's preferred length of chapter seems to have been between about thirty lines and ninety-nine, of which there are ninety-three in this work, comprising 65 per cent of the total. Passages of this length enabled him to tell a story effectively, so recount a particular miracle or narrative sequence, with or without subordinate information thrown in for good measure as broadly contemporary or otherwise relevant. Bede invariably preferred to include the whole of any passage from which he was quoting verbatim within a single chapter,[41] and the same tended to apply even to passages derived from single existing texts but substantially rewritten by the author, as, for example, his treatment of Alban (I, 7) and Fursa (III, 19). It did not, however, apply to his own works: the passages from his abridgement of Adamnan's *On the Holy Places* were divided between two comparatively short chapters (V, 16, 17), which might easily have been combined into one, and he included six miracles associated with Cuthbert at the end of book IV, giving each a separate chapter (IV, 27 (25) to 32 (30)), the longest of which is only seventy-six lines. Such runs of chapters on a particular theme and with very similar subject matter are comparatively rare, occurring primarily in the context of particular clerical hero figures, including Aidan (III, 15–17), Cuthbert (above) and John of Beverley (V, 2–6), but we also find similar glorifying of such secular figures as Oswald (III, 9–13). On the whole, Bede used the chapter as a vehicle for containing any of subject matter, theme or period, and the breaks between chapters as opportunities to shift his attention from one individual, location, subject or time period to another. That said, the needs of his narrative to range in time frequently overcame his attempts to provide a broadly

Table 1 The structure of the *Ecclesiastical History*: books, chapters and numbers of lines (figures in brackets denote the group to which each chapter has been assigned in table 2, below)

Chapter	Preface	Book I	Book II	Book III	Book IV	Book V
	89					
1		107 [4]	217 [5]	35 [2]	75 [3]	41 [2]
2		37 [2]	102 [4]	60 [3]	50 [2]	53 [2]
3		25 [1]	40 [2]	49 [2]	173 [4]	46 [2]
4		9 [1]	59 [2]	63 [3]	31 [2]	27 [1]
5		19 [1]	85 [3]	62 [3]	100 [4]	26 [1]
6		22 [1]	36 [2]	32 [1]	30 [2]	79 [3]
7		108 [4]	40 [2]	74 [3]	32 [2]	57 [2]
8		21 [1]	48 [2]	70 [3]	26 [1]	39 [2]
9		17 [1]	86 [3]	52 [2]	59 [2]	69 [3]
10		18 [1]	90 [3]	25 [1]	31 [2]	70 [3]
11		24 [1]	70 [3]	74 [3]	55 [2]	56 [2]
12		77 [3]	115 [4]	34 [2]	56 [2]	193 [4]
13		23 [1]	66 [3]	48 [2]	72 [3]	71 [3]
14		34 [2]	47 [2]	88 [3]	81 [3]	40 [2]
15		60 [3]	35 [2]	29 [1]	13 [1]	49 [2]
16		14 [1]	37 [2]	22 [1]	44 [2]	42 [2]
17		64 [3]	39 [2]	73 [3]	52 [2]	39 [2]
18		27 [1]	52 [2]	29 [1]	57 [2]	43 [2]
19		26 [1]	50 [2]	143 [4]	110 [4]	250 [5]
20		45 [2]	64 [3]	14 [1]	60 [3]	41 [2]
21		45 [2]		47 [2]	13 [1]	390 [5]
22		17 [1]		79 [3]	73 [3]	45 [2]
23		38 [2]		71 [3]	167 [4]	87 [3]
24		21 [1]		93 [3]	103 [4]	185 [4]
25		53 [2]		227 [5]	101 [4]	
26		30 [2]		65 [3]	58 [2]	
27		410 [5]		68 [3]	76 [3]	
28		22 [1]		36 [2]	76 [3]	
29		46 [2]		81 [3]	56 [2]	
30		39 [2]		24 [1]	46 [2]	
31		30 [2]			36 [2]	
32		68 [3]			35 [2]	
33		21 [1]				
34		21 [1]				
Total		1638	1378	1874	2041	2038
Average		48	69	62	64	85

sequenced and chronologically ordered work. To take a single example of unexceptional length, book III, 4 contextualises the mission of Aidan to Northumbria in terms which were important to Bede and in so doing begins with an historical narrative concerning the foundation of Iona in 565, then reaches back in time to Bishop Ninian's undated missionary activity among the southern Picts in or very soon after the Roman period before jumping forward to Egbert's persuasion of the Ionan community to adopt Roman practices in 716. This is an extreme case but far from unique and Bede frequently adopted the strategy of narrating the significant elements of a particular issue or an individual's life at a single juncture in his meta-narrative, most commonly inserting such in conjunction with notice of their death.

This practice resulted in several of the small number of very long chapters. Admittedly, the longest two, I, 27 and V, 21, consist almost entirely of documents quoted verbatim, being Gregory's famous *Libellus Responsionum* and Ceolfrith's *Letter to King Nechtan* respectively. Bede had apparently decided that these were of such value to his work that they should be included virtually *in toto* and undivided (although he arguably edited out reference to the cult of St Sixtus from the *Libellus*), despite their exceptional length. Other chapters in excess of 200 lines (group 5 in table 2) were his own compositions, however, comprising a retrospective appreciation of Pope Gregory inserted at his death (II, 1), his portrayal of the synod of Whitby (III, 25) and his extended treatment of Bishop Wilfrid (V, 19), to which we might add a further four chapters in excess of 150 lines: IV, 3, being his appreciation of Bishop Chad; IV, 23 (21), concerning Abbess Hild; V, 12, Dryhthelm's dream or vision (which he apparently wrote from oral testimony); and V, 24, which contains the recapitulation, his autobiographical summary and a list of his own works. Clearly there were several reasons to write lengthier chapters than the norm but, setting aside causes unique to individual passages, it is notice-able that Bede was particularly prepared to offer extended chapters when providing retrospective appreciations of exemplary hero figures: all of his treatments of Gregory, Wilfrid, Chad and Hild fit this category. Although these longer chapters are comparatively few in number, their length makes them of rather greater consequence within the overall balance of the work than their number might suggest. Taking just the four chapters here singled out, these total over 800 lines and comprise just short of 10 per cent of the total work. Combined, such chapters dedicated to clerical heroes combined with the runs of shorter chapters which serve the same purpose, as identified above, make up some 16 per cent of the whole.

Table 2 Distribution of chapters by size across the *Ecclesiastical History*. The number of lines in each category is listed in brackets in the left-hand column.

Group	Book I	Book II	Book III	Book IV	Book V	Total
1 [1–29]	17	–	7	3	2	29
2 [30–59]	10	11	7	16	13	57
3 [60–99]	4	6	14	7	5	36
4 [100–199]	2	2	1	6	2	13
5 [200+]	1	1	1	–	2	5
Total	34	20	30	32	24	140

Within the overall structure of the *Ecclesiastical History*, lengthy appreciations of particular figures are, therefore, of considerable importance and were arguably developed and weighted quite consciously. Bede's stated intention in the Preface was to offer his audience examples of both good and wicked men drawn from an English past. Given the exceptional length of chapters focused quite specifically on the qualities and deeds of particular individuals, all of whom he wrote up approvingly, the presumption must be that the author was offering them as particularly significant religious heroes within his overall reconstruction of the past, on whom his readers were being invited to model their own behaviours. Consideration of chapter length and content therefore enables us to begin to explore how Bede proposed to take forward the agenda which he had set himself and to which he later referred in his Preface. However, Bede had already had some practice in this regard when he came to write the *EH*, since he had earlier made two excursions into universal history, the last just six or so years before the *EH* was completed, and established therein a particular suit of English figures as his preferred exemplars. Comparison of the individuals established in his earlier works with those identified via attention to the use of particularly honorific language and/or extended chapters in the *EH* provides an important means by which to explore his thinking further as he set out to compose and organise the *Ecclesiastical History*. It is opportune at this point to consider how his depiction of English history carried over from his earlier works to the later.

Bede's chronicles and the *Ecclesiastical History*

Bede wrote two chronicles, each attached to a work about time. The earlier and by far the briefer, generally known as his *Lesser Chronicle (Chronica Minora)*, is attached to his *Book on Times (De Temporibus)*,[42] completed in 703, and forming chapters 16–22 thereof. The Empire of the Romans, which was to dominate the sixth age, was prefigured at the close of chapter 21, then opens with the equation of the rule of Octavius with Christ's birth at the start of 22. There follows a staccato summary structured by imperial reigns, into which are inserted a variety of individuals (including the apostles Peter, Paul, John, and several martyrs, translators, bishops, ascetics and theologians) and events of Christian significance (including persecutions, heresies, discoveries, translations of relics and conversions). The latter part of this brief summary of history, into which Bede wrote notice of the key events of his own people, reads as follows:[43]

> Marcian [ruled] for 7 years. The Council of Chalcedon is held [451]. The race of the Angles comes to Britain.
> Leo the Elder [ruled] for 17 years. Egypt barks with the error of Dioscorus.
> Leo the Younger [ruled] for one year. King Theodoric occupied Rome.
> Zeno [ruled] for 17 years. The corpse of Barnabas the Apostle is discovered.

Anastasius [ruled] for 27 years. Bishop Fulgentius is praised.

Justin [ruled] for 8 years. The Acephalite heresy is rejected. Abbot Benedict won renown.

Justinian [ruled] for 39 years. In whose 6th year the first cycle of Dionysius begins.

Justin the Younger [ruled] for 11 years. The Armenians receive the faith of Christ.

Tiberius [ruled] for 7 years. Herminigild, king of the Goths, is crowned with martyrdom.

Maurice [ruled] for 21 years. Gregory, bishop of Rome, flourished.

Phocas [ruled] for 8 years. The Saxons in Britain receive the faith of Christ.

Heraclius [ruled] for 26 years. The Jews in Spain are made into Christians.

Heraclenos with his mother, Martina, [ruled] for 1 year. In these times the Acephalite heresy is repeated.

Constantine [i.e. Constans], son of Constantine, [ruled] for 28 years. An eclipse of the sun took place in the 7th indiction, 5th of the Nones of May [i.e. 2 May].[44]

Constantine, son of the last Constantine, [ruled] for 17 years. He convened the sixth synod.

Justinian, son of Constantine, [ruled] for 10 years. He, on account of a crime of treachery, was deprived and exiled from the glory of his kingdom. Africa was restored to the empire of the Romans.

Leo [ruled] for 3 years.

After that, Tiberius is spending his 5th year, in the first indiction. The rest of the sixth age is known only to God.[45]

As becomes clear from this extract, most imperial reigns were used to frame just one 'fact' of significance to the annalist.[46] This might be the floruit of a key Christian individual, or a particular event of Christian significance. So, across the fifth and sixth centuries, Bede noted several prominent clerics with approval, including Augustine of Hippo, Abbot Benedict and Pope Gregory, successful confrontation with several heresies (for example, Pelagius condemned at the Council of Carthage, Nestorius at the Synod of Ephesus) and several conversion triumphs. It is a generally positivist story of expanding Catholicism, which omits much reference to the collapse of Roman authority in the West and, Theodoric's occupation of Rome excepted, selects only such 'barbarian' entries as redound to the credit of Catholicism, including, for example, the martyrdom of the Gothic king Herminigild, which Isidore had omitted. Bede's audience was primarily his own brethren, and this was an attempt to place into a chronological framework some of the key figures and events of Christendom for their benefit. Their own inclusion in the Christian world was necessarily one aspect of this orientation and Bede made just two references to his own people, adding to Marcian's reign (450–7) an unusual, second event, to incorporate notice of the English arrival in Britain,[47] then made their conversion the single, cardinal 'fact' contextualised by the reign of Phocas (602–10). These two events constitute the very barest inclusion of the English into universal history but this is an extraordinarily sparsely populated chronicle, so the paucity of such references is not, perhaps, remarkable. The scantiness of his format means, however, that there is very little opportunity here to map Bede's annalistic comments onto the *Ecclesiastical History*: the arrival of the English was dealt with in the latter in book I, 15, and the conversion initially in book I, 26, although the period post-602 which features in the *Chronicle* is primarily covered at the start of book II. Bede seems at this stage to have been aware only of the second group of missionaries despatched by Gregory in 601, among whom Paulinus, first bishop of York, was of course included, which should probably be interpreted in terms of his lack of contact with Canterbury to this point, or access to *The Book of Pontiffs*. Following the reign of Phocas, Bede reverted to universal history and entirely neglected the local stage throughout the remainder of this highly sketchy account.

A far more elaborate summary of history was offered by Bede in his second and much fuller work on chronology, *Concerning the Reckoning of Time*, which he completed over twenty years later, *c*.725.[48] The World-Chronicle occupies book V, with only a single chapter (66), while book VI comprises his commentary on the remainder of time still to come, in five chapters: cautionary words concerning the remaining length of the sixth age (67),[49] supportive quotations from the Fathers of the Church (68), the time of the Antichrist (69), the Day of Judgement (70) and the seventh and eighth ages (71). The Chronicle is structured according to years since the Creation (known as AM reckoning),[50] with an absolute date set against each of the regnal periods into which the work was organised, combined with the length of each reign, with events therein either bundled together or, on occasion, individually dated, most commonly by regnal year, but several other systems do occur. In illustration, Christ's birth, which heralded in the sixth age, was dated to the year 3952 of world history since the Creation, being also Octavius's 42nd regnal year, twenty-seven years since the deaths of Anthony and Cleopatra (with which Egyptian regnal years close), the 3rd year of the 193rd Olympiad and the 752nd from the foundation of Rome.

Bede wove far more insular material into this, his *Greater Chronicle* (*Chronica Maiora*), than he had into his earlier and far shorter version, including subjects which he would, some six years later, marshal in the later books of the *Ecclesiastical History*, as well as the first. The expansion of his first work on time was the avowed intention behind the second, as spelt out in its Preface, and the chronicle-section certainly sustains this purpose. That said, there remains a heavy preponderance of individual items in the *Greater Chronicle* which later appear in the first book of *EH*: of something like thirty-two individual entries referring to matters within the British Isles,[51] twenty relate to events covered in book I, leaving a mere dozen spread across the remaining four books. Given the much longer period of time covered by book I (60 BC to AD 604) compared with the other four books (605–731), however, this distribution is not disproportionate: entries paralleled by book I of the *EH* have one event on average every thirty-two years while the remainder of the work has one every eleven years. Furthermore, the bulk of the early entries consist of snippets of information culled from his reading in pre-existing chronicles which were not making any attempt to prioritise 'British' material. For example, inclusion under his description of the reign of Diocletian of the fact that 'Constantius, a man singularly mild and unpretentious, died in Britain, at York'[52] might be judged less a part of insular history *per se* than of pre-existing universal history but which happened to have occurred in this particular part of the empire. The same can be said of entries connected with Julius Caesar, Claudius, Severus, and other rulers of the Roman world. Bede was mindful of the need to write Britain into universal history, therefore, and gave local colour where it seemed appropriate to wider issues,[53] but made sure to sustain his overall meta-story of the development of the Catholic Church and the Christian world.

In the *Greater Chronicle*, Bede again introduced the Angles to Britain in the reign of Marcian (although here joint with Valentinian), but the event was now contextualised in terms of problems confronting the Britons and Vortigern's invitation to them in the previous reign (of Theodosius the Younger), on the basis of his reading of Gildas,[54] to which he then added material from Constantius's *Life of St Germanus*, to include the 'Alleluia' victory. Unsurprisingly, this much-extended treatment of the English settlement and the creation of Anglo-Saxon England approximates to a truncated version of comparable passages in the *Ecclesiastical History*.[55] There is, however, no attempt even in this extended chronicle format to include an 'English' note in every subsequent reign: since first notice of the Angles, Bede returned to them in eleven out of the twenty-three regnal periods remaining to him and there was a particularly long gap in the sixth century (four reigns totalling eighty-five years), which is replicated, by omission at least, in the *EH*, presumably owing to the scarcity of appropriate written information between notice of warfare between Saxon incomers and the Britons (following Gildas and Constantius) and the arrival of Gregory's missionaries in the final years of the century.

This, the second 'English' entry in the *Lesser Chronicle*, likewise appears much extended, and corrected, in the *Greater Chronicle*:

> He [Gregory] sent to Britain Augustine, Mellitus and John, and many others, with God-fearing monks with them, to convert the English to Christ. Æthelberht was soon converted to the grace of Christ, together with the people of the *Cantuarii* over whom he ruled, and those of neighbouring kingdoms. [Gregory] gave him Augustine to be his bishop and teacher, as well as other holy priests to become bishops.[56]

This entry, placed firmly within the reign of Maurice (582–602), reflects Bede's new understanding of the Gregorian mission and its dating, which was now positioned somewhat earlier than he had offered in the *Lesser Chronicle*, following new information reaching him from Canterbury via Nothhelm and from *The Book of Pontiffs*, a very recent version of which he had obtained by the mid-720s.[57] Indeed, excluding only the first four words of this translation, the opening sentence is in its entirety quoted from that work. He did not, however, intend that his brethren should equate the conversion of their own communities with this event, for he added: 'However, the people of the Angles north of the river Humber, under Kings Aelle and Aethelfrith, did not at this time hear the Word of life.'[58] While his earlier, much briefer annal had effectively conflated the English conversion in its entirety into the reign of Phocas (602–10), he now proposed to unravel that event into two separate but interrelated stories. This is his earliest notice of an especial interest in the Northumbrians. By remarking their exclusion from the initial conversion story of the English, Bede was encouraging his audience to anticipate the Christianisation of their own forebears which was still to come, so, by implication at least, his strategy focuses attention on the deeds of the first Northumbrian Christians, to which he would shortly turn. Bede reinforced this prolepsis by reference at the close of Maurice's reign to Gregory's letter conferring metropolitan status on the bishops of both London and York, which he would later include as I, 29 of the *Ecclesiastical History*. This was of central relevance to York's aspirations to metropolitan status, which may have been on the agenda by the mid-720s. Notice of York's archdiocesan aspirations at a stage of this *Chronicle* preceding even the arrival of a ministry or construction of a church there again serves to raise suspense and anticipate what was to come.

Material which Bede would later cover in his first book closes with this reference to Gregory's letter, but it is worth noting that he chose to introduce both the Northumbrian kings *c.*600 as well as the issue of York's metropolitan status at this point, which are central to the later chapters of book I of the *Ecclesiastical History* (I, 34; 29, respectively).[59] Only three events were recorded in the *Greater Chronicle* which were taken up in the second book of the *EH*, namely Gregory's death, to which he would later affix a fulsome eulogy (II, 1), the conversion of the Northumbrians under King Edwin, and letters from Pope Honorius, then John as pope-elect (in 640), to the Irish, concerning the dating of Easter and the imputation of heresy (II, 19). The brevity of this list threatens to mask, however, the emphasis which he here placed on the conversion of Edwin:[60]

In the sixteenth year of Heraclius' reign and in the fifteenth indiction, Edwin the most excellent king of the transhumbrian people of the English to the north in Britain, through the preaching of bishop Paulinus, whom the venerable archbishop Iustus sent from Kent, received the Word of Salvation more or less 180 years following the coming of the English to Britain and he gave York to Paulinus as his Episcopal see. As an omen of the arrival of the faith and of the heavenly kingdom, the power of the king's earthly power grew, so that he received under his authority even the very limits of Britain, wherever either the people of the English or the Britons live, which no one of the English before him [had achieved].

The multiple dating of the event and its association with 'signs' or 'omens' draws attention to it and emphasises its presentation as if the crucial moment from which his readers were expected to assume that both the Christianisation of the English and their insular dominance were firmly established. Dating in relation to the English Settlement in particular bears comparison with Bede's use elsewhere both of years since the foundation of Rome and of years since the expulsion of man from the Garden of Eden, again emphasising the significance of this event in terms of the history of the English: while the *adventus* recalled their arrival in Britain, so the opening move in their formation as a people, Edwin's baptism at the head of the English was being used by Bede to mark their arrival within the community of Christian nations. Bede made very little use of superlatives in the *Greater Chronicle*, but Edwin was here *excellentissimus*,[61] and the account of his kingdom and the expansion of his 'overkingship' was developed as a 'sign' of the exceptional role with which he was being credited within providential history. Again, York's significance as Paulinus's see is emphasised. *Venerabilis* occurs in the *Greater Chronicle* only of Iustus (here), Willibrord (see below) and Pope Gregory II (715–31), who was pope at the time of writing. It is Edwin's conversion which is here elevated rhetorically, not that of Æthelberht, which by comparison is presented as a comparatively localised event and offered devoid of rhetorical support. There is much here which Bede would include and develop further in book II of the *EH*, within which it is the central story (encompassing chapters 9–20), around which all else is massed.

Edwin's conversion occurred in the 620s. Thereafter, English affairs were neglected by Bede in his *Greater Chronicle*, which only reconnects with Bede's later work with the arrival of Theodore and Hadrian in May 669, with which he later opened book IV of the *EH*, marking an end to a lengthy hiatus concerning 'English' affairs since Edwin's death, which Bede later dated to 633.[62] There then follow two substantial entries concerning individuals whom Bede would also cover in book IV, Æthelthryth, virgin queen and abbess, and Bishop Cuthbert.[63] Again, as in his treatment of Edwin, Bede gave prominence to both these figures as revered members of the Northumbrian Church. Æthelthryth is represented as the archetypal female saint of high status:

The saint (*sancta*) and perpetual virgin of Christ Æthelthryth was daughter to Anna a king of the English and first wife to another very great man (*viro permagnifico*) and after to King Ecgfrith. After she had kept the marital bed incorrupt for 12 years, she abandoned the role of queen becoming a consecrated virgin by taking the holy veil. Immediately thereafter, she also became a mother to virgins and the pious foster-mother of holy women, accepting a place called Ely to build a monastery. Of her enduring merits even her dead body attests, which was discovered incorrupt along with the clothes in which she was wrapped after 16 years entombed.

Æthelthryth was here being developed as a unique exemplar of English, Christian womanhood (in the context of this work at least) for Bede's primarily monastic audience, which is fitting, perhaps, given her role as the wife of the first patron of his own monastery, King Ecgfrith. Excluding references to culted saints and the dedications of churches, *sanctus* was used sparingly in this work of individuals prior to their death, only otherwise of the distant Abgarus, ruler of Edessa, and the English Egbert (see below). The incorrupt state of her body when recovered from the tomb was offered as a demonstration of her sanctity. Bede's treatment of Cuthbert was similar:

> The most reverend Cuthbert, who progressed from anchorite to bishop of the church of Lindisfarne in Britain, even from infancy up to old age, led a life justly celebrated for miraculous signs. When his body had remained buried but incorrupt for 11 years, it was discovered after this just as if it was the same hour he had died, with the clothes in which he was covered, just as we have stated in the books of his life and virtues, recently written in prose and in hexameter verse some few years earlier.

Once again Bede was dipping into his rarely opened store of superlatives (in this work at least) with which to clad Cuthbert with a particular holiness: *reverentissimus* is otherwise used in the *Greater Chronicle* only of the emperor Constantine,[64] and Bede's old friend and abbot, Ceolfrith (see below); once again he was commemorating an English Christian hero in terms of the incorrupt state of his body as a 'sign' of his sanctity, and of other 'signs' which had characterised his entire life. Parallels between these last two entries are transparent.

Between his treatments of these two religious heroes, Bede also paid tribute to Willibrord, the English missionary to the continent, whom he dealt with somewhat later in the *Ecclesiastical History*, primarily in book V, 11:[65]

> The same Pope Sergius ordained the venerable man Willibrord, given the family name Clement, as bishop of the people of the Frisians, where even today he is a *peregrinus* for the eternal homeland (for he derives from the English people in Britain), achieving innumerable daily losses for the devil and gains for the Christian faith.

Again, this represents a highly honourable mention of another Northumbrian churchman,[66] whose connection with the papacy is foregrounded and who was being presented here as an ideal English missionary to the heathen. *Peregrinus* was used in this work only in reference to Willibrord and Egbert, to whom he turned for a second example of the missionary life following his treatment of Cuthbert:

> Egbert, a saintly man of the people of the English and a priest in monastic life, even training himself for the celestial homeland as a *peregrinus*, converted many of the provinces of the Scottish [Irish] people to canonical observance of the dating of Easter, from which they had long diverged, by pious preaching, in the year from the Incarnation of the Lord 716.

Bede's last English hero was his own abbot, Ceolfrith, who had departed for Rome in 716 and whom he had already written up extensively in his *History of the Abbots*:

> In this period many of the peoples of the English, both nobles and commoners, men and women, leaders and people in private life, were accustomed to journey from Britain to Rome, inspired by divine love. Among them was my most reverend abbot, Ceolfrith, 74 years old, who had been a priest for 47 years and abbot for 35, who died when he reached Langres and was buried there in the church of the blessed twin martyrs. Among other gifts which he had arranged to bear with him, he sent on to the church of St. Peter a complete Bible (*pandect*) translated by the blessed Jerome into Latin from Hebrew and Greek originals.

Ceolfrith closes the succession of English figures that Bede included and Bede ended his *Greater Chronicle* just a few lines further on. Bede provided his readers, therefore, with a series of English figures woven into universal history. Excluding only the comparatively prosaic appearances of Augustine and Æthelberht, which map onto book I, they stretch through time across the period of Northumbria's Christianity, from King Edwin (died 633) right through to Egbert (who was still alive in 725), and he would later re-engage with them all to some degree in books II, IV and V of his *Ecclesiastical History*. Apart from three kings who were contemporaries of Augustine, namely Æthelberht of Kent, Æthelfrith of Bernicia and Ælle of Deira, these were the only English figures named. There were just six figures picked out: Edwin, Æthelthryth, Willibrord, Cuthbert, Egbert and Ceolfrith. Each seems to have had a particular niche to fill: Edwin was offered as an exemplar of Catholic kingship, Æthelthryth as an exemplary virgin queen, bride of Christ and abbess; Willibrord was the *peregrinus* who returned to the continent – whence the Anglo-Saxons had putatively come – to convert the heathen, and was ordained there by the papacy, with Egbert another devoted to the spread of Catholic orthodoxy nearer home, in the British Isles, among the Scottish monks who had earlier preached among his own people; Cuthbert was the saintly monk-bishop of Lindisfarne, whose lives, in verse and prose respectively, Bede had already composed, and Ceolfrith his learned and venerable abbot, who had undertaken a last pilgrimage, bearing gifts to Rome. Each, therefore, fulfilled a different role, beginning with the secular leadership and working through the religious. All were presented as exceptional, Christian hero figures by use of superlatives (*excellentissimus, reverentissimus*), biblical number (in one instance) and/or the language of veneration (as *sanctus, venerabilis*), by reference to connections with the papacy or its agents and by the recall of stories concerning their incorrupt remains in the tomb (two instances). By comparison with Bede's treatment of other Christian heroes in this work, these are exceptional episodes marked by unusual language and images. Collectively, it seems reasonable to interpret them as figures whom Bede had selected to act as exemplars of different kinds of Christian life for the benefit of his abbot, Hwætberht, to whom this work was dedicated, and his brethren, whose exceptional treatment overall was intended to confirm the English race as full members of the family of Christian nations. This is a purpose which resonates, of course, with Bede's stated agenda in his Preface to the *Ecclesiastical History*: 'Should history tell of good men and their good estate, the thoughtful listener is spurred on to imitate the good.' Within the strict bounds of even an expanded chronicle format, Bede was apparently here offering the stereotypical examples of good men (and one woman), drawn from several walks of life and selected to provide exemplars of ideal Christian behaviours applicable across the span of his intended readership, within élite and, more particularly, monastic society.

Bede was writing here for a Northumbrian audience, primarily for the abbot and inmates of his own royal Northumbrian monastery, and it must be significant that all these figures were either Northumbrians by birth and/or childhood or at least had strong Northumbrian associations. Edwin was of the Deiran royal house, and a near antecedent of King Ecgfrith,[67] the first lay patron of Wearmouth/Jarrow. His head had putatively been deposited at York and his body had supposedly been recovered and reburied with honour by his daughter, Abbess Eanflæd, at *Streanæshealh* (?Whitby), in association with the veneration there of St Gregory, through whose missionaries he had been converted. There is a case for claiming this as the central royal cult being promoted by King Aldfrith and his heirs. Æthelthryth, although of royal East Anglian birth, had been Ecgfrith's first queen and Bishop Wilfrid's patron, providing him with the land on which Hexham had been established before retiring south to Ely *c.*673, around the time Wearmouth was founded. Cuthbert and Ceolfrith were certainly both members of the Northumbrian land-holding classes by birth, who had pursued highly successful, monastic careers within the region, Ceolfrith at Wearmouth/Jarrow itself. Willibrord trained at Ripon and Alcuin claimed him for the same noble lineage as himself,[68] and he spent time in Ireland before arriving on the continent,[69] while Egbert was probably Northumbrian and certainly had strong Northumbrian connections,[70] although in the last resort his origins are obscure.[71]

There are strong parallels here, therefore, with Bede's presentation of a succession of exemplars in the *Ecclesiastical History*, the majority of whom were likewise Northumbrian or closely associated with Northumbria. While the development of particular insular exemplars was clearly not the sole purpose of the *Greater Chronicle*, it does seem to have been a consistent feature of Bede's overall design to which he was committed throughout the latter part, at least, of this work.

There are, however, significant differences between the presentation of exemplary Englishmen and -women in the *Greater Chronicle* and the *Ecclesiastical History*, which have some potential to shed light on the organisation and perhaps even the context of the latter. Of the four figures concerning whom Bede offered particularly lengthy chapter-length appreciations in the *EH*, only Gregory received honourable mention in the *Chronicle*, with all of Chad, Hild and Wilfrid entirely omitted. Furthermore, Bede closed his account of King Edwin's conversion in the *Greater Chronicle*, with which his succession of English exemplars therein properly opens, with a brief description of papal letters to the Irish variously condemning their 'Quartodeciman error concerning the dating of Easter' and 'the Pelagian heresy, which was reviving amongst them',[72] which not only completes this separately dated passage but also terminates his treatment of the reign of Heraclius (610–41) as a whole. Inclusion of papal condemnation of the Irish implies Bede's approval and serves to emphasise the orthodoxy of Edwin's Rome-derived Christianity, as delivered, of course, by the Italian Paulinus, and that seems, to an extent at least, Bede's intention here, given that he could easily have excluded these letters, or at least ameliorated their impact, were he to have found them in any sense in conflict with his overall message. These papal condemnations were, of course, later repeated to the advantage of his hero-figure by Stephen in his *Life of Wilfrid*,[73] who pictured Wilfrid as the embattled champion of Roman orthodoxy confronting Anglo-Irish Quartodecimans in Northumbria. Aldhelm quite separately threw his weight against studying in Ireland, comparing Irish scholars of the day very unfavourably with Theodore and Hadrian (his own teachers, of course) and urging his fellow countrymen against peregrination there, while also making clear his sympathy for Wilfrid's cause in his fall-out with King Ecgfrith by urging the abbots of his monasteries to share their leader's exile.[74] This 'Romanist' stance is consistent with the viewpoint of Bede at an earlier date: his Homily for the feast of Benedict Biscop prioritises the links between Wearmouth/Jarrow's founding father and the continent, and in particular Rome, remarking particularly on his connections with the Holy City itself, his bringing of relics, manuscripts and pictures to his new monasteries, his obedience to the papacy and his role in bringing both Theodore and John the Precentor to England, positioning his audience collectively, therefore, as a peculiarly 'Roman' colony in the far north-west of the world.[75] In the *Ecclesiastical History*, however, Bede took care to distance himself from a narrowly 'Romanist' stance, repeatedly facing down the substance of the charge of Quartodeciman heresy among the Irish and even editing John's letter when he included that in the later work so as to omit the central section and with it all direct reference to the Quartodeciman heresy as if then current in Ireland.[76] This represents a very different approach to the issue of Irish Christianity, which suggests that Bede had considerably altered his position on the subject in the short space of years which separate authorship of these two 'historical' works, moving away from a stance which seems to have had much in common with those of Aldhelm and Stephen towards one which is both far more apologetic regarding the Scottish missions and determined to foreground their apostolic fervour and spiritual values.

In the *Ecclesiastical History*, Bede went out of his way to deny that the Irish were heretical, explaining that just one of their provinces – that based on Iona – was so far distant from the remainder of Catholic Europe, on the very edge of the inhabited world, that it was unsurprisingly in error as regards the dating of Easter and the tonsure, and treating their eventual convergence with Roman practice under Egbert's guidance as a fitting point at which to conclude his account, with the whole process of conversion then having gone full circle, so to speak.

This is not, however, the sole difference between Bede's treatment of the Irish in his *Greater Chronicle* and the *Ecclesiastical History*, for while the latter attaches considerable value to the successes of the Irish mission to Northumbria in the reigns of Oswald and Oswiu across the bulk of book III, the entire subject is omitted from the *Greater Chronicle*, once the accusation of heresy had been made in the reign of Heraclius (610–41), leaving a distinct lacuna regarding 'English' affairs. Of all the material in book III of the *Ecclesiastical History*, only the solar eclipse of 664 was included in the earlier work, which was, of course, an event of significance far beyond England and entirely appropriate to a work of universal history.[77] In fact, the next 'English' event included in the *Greater Chronicle* after the story of Edwin's conversion was the despatch by Pope Vitalian of Archbishop Theodore and the most learned (*doctissimus*) Abbot Hadrian to Britain, who 'made many of the churches of the English fertile with the fruit of ecclesiastical teachings',[78] which anticipates Bede's lengthier treatment of the same events in the opening chapters of book IV. Although Cuthbert had initially been trained in the Ionan tradition at Melrose, he and all the remainder of Bede's exemplary English figures in the *Greater Chronicle* could reasonably be presented as Roman Christians. By contrast, a whole series of hero figures in book III of the *Ecclesiastical History* were entirely omitted from the *Greater Chronicle*, including King Oswald, whom Bede treated as a King David figure, developed as a particular focus of miracles and described, *inter alia*, as 'most Christian king of the Northumbrians' (*Christianissimus rex Nordanhymbrorum*),[79] Bishop Aidan, likewise the hero of several miracles and developed in the *EH* as a model monk-bishop,[80] the Irishman Fursa in East Anglia,[81] King Oswiu, who defeated and killed Penda and sponsored several missionary efforts,[82] and such idealised figures as bishops Cedd and Chad.[83] These omissions from the *Greater Chronicle* are far too consistent to be explicable by mere accident. Collectively they imply that it was Bede's intention in the mid-720s to exclude the Irish missions to Northumbria from his survey of world history,[84] but very much to include them in his *Ecclesiastical History*, just six or so years later.

Despite the disjunction between his treatments of the Christianisation of Northumbria in these two works, the position that Bede adopted in the *Greater Chronicle* seems generally consistent with his other writings and his position within the Northumbrian establishment. All of his Northumbrian hero-figures belong to the Roman tradition of Christianity, rather than the Irish, although Cuthbert, of course, could have been included for his capacity, implicitly at least, to bridge the divide. The anonymous author, whose work Bede used extensively in writing both his own, had modelled his *Life of Cuthbert* on that of St Martin in Gaul, whose orthodoxy as a Catholic was undoubted. While he had honoured Bishop Aidan as 'our holy bishop' (*sancti episcopi nostri*),[85] this was exclusively in terms of a vision of his death experienced by Cuthbert, the nature of which he compared with the patriarch Jacob, who met with God in Bethel.[86] Although the scene is reminiscent of the shepherds who were among those who were present at the annunciation,[87] this is very much an Old Testament characterisation of Aidan as Israelite rather than Christian, so as one loved and protected by God but under the old dispensation rather than the new. In his metrical *Life*,[88] Bede made the link explicit between Aidan's ascension and the shepherds of the annunciation,[89] and developed a novel miracle connected with Aidan as prophet predicting a storm and providing oil by which to calm it, which he had not found in the pre-existing anonymous *Life*, but he omitted this from his prose life, only to reintroduce it into the *Ecclesiastical History* (III, 15). Otherwise Bede made little attempt to advertise the Irish roots of Cuthbert's Christianity in either of his two *Lives*, building up the specific comparisons, for example between Cuthbert and St Benedict, which had already appeared in the anonymous *Life*, in his prose version,[90] and never mentioning the Synod of Whitby, so the deficiencies of the Christianity of Cuthbert's youth, in either. As founder of Lindisfarne, Aidan did receive honourable mention in Bede's works on Cuthbert, as was virtually *de rigueur* for pieces aimed either implicitly (the metrical *Life*) or explicitly (the prose *Life*) at the community on Holy Island, but Bede took care to develop the responsibility for Cuthbert's vision as Christ's and interpret it in terms of his hero's decision to enter a monastery.[91] Bede later deferred to Gregory's authority when approving the monastic nature of Cuthbert's see, so blending him into his own reformist model of monk-bishops, which depended heavily, of course, on Gregory's own vision of the priesthood,[92] which the anonymous *Life* entirely lacked. On the whole, therefore, Cuthbert was being presented as an orthodox, saintly focus for the loyalty and cohesion of the Northumbrians post-664 and the rupture with the Ionan Church, so to an extent at least as replacement to the earlier Irish saints as the especial protector of both the royal dynasty and the whole people in obedience to Rome.[93] Alcuin would later follow in the same vein, promoting

Cuthbert as a major saint of the Northumbrians in a Catholic context, as relevant to York as to Bernicia and Holy Island, while Aidan was honoured in more distant retrospect as a great holy man of Old Testament type rather than New.

The impression of Bede's conception of the English past gained from his *Major Chronicle* is confirmed by attention to his *Martyrology*, which is conventionally dated c.725–31,[94] so lies chronologically in between his two major historical works. This was a highly innovatory work, which took the well-established concept of the calendar of saints' days as festivals and grafted onto it a novel historical or narrative element, so that the nature of the martyrdom of each individual listed was briefly expounded, on the basis of hagiographical works or other information which Bede had to hand. While there are very real difficulties in distinguishing Bede's text from later additions, a core group of narratives has been identified, centred on 115 individuals, 104 of which are descriptions of martyrdom. As, in a sense, stories supportive of the universality of the Church, these are necessarily widely dispersed, drawing on Persia and the Near East as well as Western Europe, but three factors are comparatively clear: first the preponderance of Italian and Gaulish martyrs, second the virtual absence of British individuals, and finally the total absence of Irish or Anglo-Irish examples. Two Gaulish individuals reappear in the *Ecclesiastical History* (I, 17), namely bishops Lupus (29 July) and Germanus (1 August), having combated Pelagianism in Britain, but the sole 'British' presence is afforded by St Alban, who appeared, of course, as a subject of veneration in Constantius's *Life of Germanus*, which Bede had to hand, alongside a separate description of his martyrdom. Otherwise, Bede included only the two Ewalds, whose martyrdom in Saxony he later described in considerable detail (*EH* V, 10), and both Æthelthryth and Paulinus,[95] who occur in both the *Greater Chronicle* and the *Ecclesiastical History*. There was, of course, a distinct lack of martyrs to be reported from the Anglo-Saxon conversion story, but Gregory's writings had conveniently provided asceticism as an alternative route to a comparable status. The absence of every Irish or Scottish option sustains the view that Bede was still at this point taking a far from inclusive stance in his approach to the Ionan contribution to England's Christianisation, albeit this is entirely negative evidence.

Several popes feature in the *Martyrology* and the papacy was never far from Bede's presentation of Northumbrian Christianity in the *Greater Chronicle*. Pope Gregory's reputation had revived during the second half of the seventh century. This revival may have begun at Rome but was perhaps then developed in England primarily by Archbishop Theodore, who had good reason to commemorate the Gregorian missions as central to the foundation of his own archdiocesan see at Canterbury. St Augustine was a valuable antecedent to his own position as archbishop of all those obedient to Rome across Britain, to be exploited for current effect. It was perhaps Theodore who first endowed Gregory with the soubriquet 'apostle of the English', which

Bede later took up.[96] Gregory's reputation was then arguably furthered by Theodore's pupils, including Aldhelm in Wessex (died 709), Oftfor, who was still bishop of the Hwicce in 731,[97] and Bede's particular favourite, John of Beverley, bishop of Hexham then York (died 721),[98] and found support at both Canterbury and *Streanæshealh* (?Whitby), where an altar was dedicated to him and an early *Life* composed, which emphasised Gregory's apostolic stature and his responsibility for the conversion of an entire people.[99]

Bede was presumably much influenced by this tradition. He was a member of a monastic community founded in the first generation of revived Roman Catholicism within the Northumbrian establishment, under Theodore's distant oversight and by a king eager to ensure divine support for his own royal power, following his father's disengagement from Iona. Wearmouth and Jarrow were exceptionally rich endowments on Ecgfrith's part, established in conjunction with an ex-retainer of his father's who had considerable experience of continental monasticism and was very closely associated with Theodore, having travelled back to England with him and served as abbot at Canterbury until Hadrian's arrival. Part of the function of Wearmouth/Jarrow was arguably to replace Lindisfarne as the central powerhouse of Christianity within Northumbria with a completely new, royal centre unambiguously aligned with Rome and orthodox continental Catholicism, but not controlled by Bishop Wilfrid, whom Ecgfrith apparently distrusted, in part for dynastic reasons,[100] in part perhaps for his acquisitiveness, and in part owing to his connections with the leaders of contemporary Mercia. Bede's own work as a Christian scholar repeatedly emphasised the centrality of the papacy to his vision of the Universal Church, as was appropriate to an acolyte of both Benedict Biscop, who had travelled to Rome on five separate occasions, and Ceolfrith, who died in the attempt to reach the eternal city for the second time. Bede's *Greater Chronicle*, which was written for internal consumption, is entirely consistent with membership of a house within this tradition, blending in 'English' material to a universal framework and telling an episodic story of the English conversion (more particularly the Northumbrian conversion) which focuses initially on the Gregorian missionaries responsible for both Canterbury and York, then skips almost forty years to the revival of the connection with Rome represented by Theodore and Hadrian, while in between noting papal concerns regarding Irish heresy and effectively suppressing the memory of an Irish contribution to the Christianisation of England. This was a Rome-centric vision of English Christianity, therefore, which was entirely in accord with the institutional positioning of Wearmouth/Jarrow, from its foundation in the 670s/680s through to the 720s, and which we see reasserted in the recapitulation which was appended to the *Ecclesiastical History*.

Exploration of Bede's earlier discussion of English conversion history, primarily in the context of his *Greater Chronicle*, therefore highlights his shift away, in the main text of the *Ecclesiastical History*, from the manner in which he had recently constructed the past. Whereas his earlier account had foregrounded the Roman conversion of Northumbria, and highlighted 'Romanist' individuals to the exclusion of all others, in tandem with notice of papal accusations of the Irish as heretics, Bede's new and far more detailed excursion into the English past in the main narrative of the *EH* would tone down those accusations and give considerable weight to a new suit of hero-figures and to the Irish contribution to the English conversion.[101]

Bede had already demonstrated in his two lives of St Cuthbert and his *Concerning the Reckoning of Time* a willingness to write about the insular past for particular audiences and tailor his material accordingly. The *Ecclesiastical History* is another such essay but this time embracing a much bigger, insular scene and covering that past with far greater detail, particularly concerning the connections between Christianity and the role of kings. This new past was retold in novel ways and rebalanced to give weight to the traditions of Lindisfarne and the Ionan contribution to Northumbria's Christianity. The six exemplars around whom Bede structured his treatment of the English conversion in his *Greater Chronicle* survived into the *EH* to appear once again as significant figures around whom edifying stories were constructed, but a comparative casualty was Ceolfrith, Hwætberht's predecessor as abbot at Wearmouth/Jarrow, who appears therein only in asides, as Benedict Biscop's companion,[102] and Bede's own teacher,[103] excepting only his despatch of a lengthy letter to the Pictish king concerning the dating of Easter, along with masons to build him a stone church.[104] What each of both Benedict Biscop and Ceolfrith lacks in the *Ecclesastical History* is a narrative passage setting out their individual claims to venerability, or association with miracles, such as other hero-figures received. York also featured in the *Greater Chronicle* as the crucial northern cult site but surprisingly little elaboration of this central role is to be found in the *EH*. Given the far greater length of the latter, these look like deliberate changes by Bede, which were perhaps intended to tone down the overall positioning of both York and Wearmouth/Jarrow within the *Ecclesiastical History*. As one might expect, Lindisfarne, as monastic community and see, and several of its daughter-houses, such as Melrose, were significant beneficiaries of Bede's rebalancing, with Oswald, Aidan, Chad and Hild all developed as major saints, having been entirely omitted from the *Greater Chronicle*.

Several of the substantive differences between Bede's presentations of the 'English' past in his *Greater Chronicle* and the *Ecclesiastical History* centre on book III of the latter, the materials in which were almost entirely omitted from the former, although they are not all contained within that book. We now need, therefore, to assess the role of book III more generally within the overall context of Bede's *Ecclesiastical History*, to consider what it was intended to achieve, and in what ways, if any, it stands as separate from the remainder of the work.

Book III of the *Ecclesiastical History*

As we have already established, the contents of book III are almost entirely absent from the *Greater Chronicle*, which otherwise seems to replicate the core, at least, of the material included in the *EH*, centred on particular exemplary individuals. We have also seen that book III stands out as under-represented by comparison with the remainder in terms of its coverage in the recapitulation of book V, 24, which additionally offers none of the additional information regarding timescales covered by other books.[105] Likewise, the recapitulation offers a comparatively muted treatment of the Irish role in the English conversion (p. 99), which, while it is less extreme than the total omission of the *Greater Chronicle*, also marks this down as a problematic area in Bede's treatment of the past, at least as he reconsidered his positioning at the close.

These are substantive differences but they are not the only ones. To assess the positioning of book III within the overall structure, we need to explore its relationship with the *Ecclesiastical History in toto*, to come to a view concerning the level of its integration to the whole. To this purpose, we will first consider what evidence exists for significant alterations to the *EH* which might have impacted on this book in particular, and how effectively this book is integrated within the work in terms of Bede's use of prolepsis – that is the sense in which its contents are anticipated elsewhere or in turn anticipate other sections of the work, in terms of his use of different types of source material and of his use of language.

It has long been recognised that the *Ecclesiastical History* contains a small number of what seem to be minor inconsistencies,[106] which Wilhelm Levison interpreted as 'vestiges of an earlier plan' rather than mere 'slips of memory'.[107] Given the scale of the work, this is hardly surprising and we should perhaps expect to be able to detect a degree of rewriting and insertion of new material at a late stage in its development. Such are not peculiar to this work: Levison likewise noted Bede's reference in chapter 2 of his *History of the Abbots* to Vitalian's papacy as if he had already mentioned it, when in fact no such reference is to be found.[108] A comparable example in the *EH* occurs in the context of the first appearance of Benedict Biscop in IV, 18, as guide to John the Precentor, travelling from Rome to Northumbria: Bede here referred back to a previous mention of Benedict, while none in fact exists.[109] Benedict had begun his career as a thegn in the service of King Oswiu, by whom he was granted land, then executed a career change and travelled overseas *c.*653 with the young Wilfrid, setting out together from Canterbury.[110] We might, therefore, reasonably have expected him to have been introduced within book III, wherein Oswiu's career was discussed and Wilfrid's part in this very same journey was mentioned as a prelude to his role at the Synod of Whitby.[111] He might equally have been the subject of some comment in book IV, 1, in the context of the arrival of Theodore and then Hadrian: in his *History of the Abbots*, Bede had earlier noted that Benedict had accompanied the new archbishop and was Theodore's first appointee as abbot of SS Peter and Paul at

Canterbury, which he fulfilled for two years,[112] but in the *EH* he had Theodore appoint Hadrian 'immediately he came to him', so omitting reference to his temporary replacement. Instead, we are left to wait for Benedict's appearance until a surprisingly late date in his career, several years after his foundation of Wearmouth and in the context of his fifth visit to Rome.

It is tempting to view the omission or removal of earlier reference to Benedict's activities as part and parcel of the eclipse of his – and Bede's – close associate, Abbot Ceolfrith, in this work, despite the especial prominence which Bede had given him in the *Greater Chronicle* (above): as already noted, Ceolfrith occurs in the *Ecclesiastical History* only in a passing reference in this same chapter as companion to Benedict, as the author of the long letter to Nechtan, king of the Picts (V, 21), and in Bede's summary of his own life at the close of V, 24. Given its diplomatic and political dimensions, Ceolfrith's letter to the Pictish king does imply that he should be viewed as the religious mouthpiece of King Osred's regime at the time when this was written (*c.*706×16), so greater prominence might have seemed appropriate, particularly to a monk within his own house and in part trained by him. Instead, alternative English leaders travelling or intending to travel to retire in the proximity of St Peter's are offered, from Oswiu's failure so to do (IV, 5) to Cædwalla's successful journey (V, 7), which was later emulated by King Coenred of the Mercians and Offa of the East Saxons (V, 19). So, too, does Benedict's role seem under-represented, given Bede's motives for including a figure he considered to be central to the foundation of his own house. But, like Ceolfrith, Benedict was denied more than passing reference herein, appearing in IV, 18 as guide (albeit with an aside regarding the foundation of Wearmouth), in IV, 19 (which is his chapter-length biopic of Wilfrid) as Wilfrid's companion on his first visit to the continent, in V, 21 as Ceolfrith's predecessor as abbot of Wearmouth/Jarrow and in V, 24 in the context of Bede's own education. Both figures were notable omissions from the recapitulation.

Although it is obviously dangerous to extrapolate to the entire book from this particular instance, it seems appropriate to consider the possibility that book III had been rewritten after the initial draft of the *Ecclesiastical History* had been completed, in ways that reduced the attention paid to some of Bede's particular heroes, including the founding fathers of his own monastery, abbots Benedict Biscop and Ceolfrith. There are other differences as well between book III and the remainder which might sustain the view that this book had a rather different conception. For example, following the lead given in this respect by Eusebius's great *Ecclesiastical History*, Bede included in this work significant numbers of substantial passages from extant documents which he considered particularly relevant to his story and of especial authority. In some instances, entire chapters consist of such extracts, and letters and other documents are quoted in their totality; elsewhere documents are edited and/or only quoted in part. In total, these extracts make up something like 14 per cent of the entire work. Large-scale quotations occur in seven chapters of book I,[113] again seven chapters of the much shorter book II,[114] five chapters of book IV,[115] and six chapters of book V.[116] In contrast, book III has only a single chapter containing a substantial and incontrovertible quotation, chapter 29, into which Bede copied Pope Vitalian's letter to King Oswiu in its entirety. It might be argued that Bede was here attempting to write history with little of the stock of written sources on which he could rely elsewhere,[117] but the difference does seem quite marked, and again it is book III that is singled out as different within the overall work.

Another way of approaching the organisation and structure of the *Ecclesiastical History* is via the internal cross-referencing. The commonest term signifying a back-reference is *supra* ('above'), in such phrases as *supra dictum est, cuius supra meminimus, ut supra docuimus* and *supra diximus*. *Supra* occurs, in all, sixty-eight times across the work, but some instances refer to spatial relationships rather than textual ones, which are here omitted as irrelevant to the issue of structure and organisation. Phrases containing *sequentibus* (such as *ut in sequentibus dicemus*: 'as we shall discuss later') predominate in forward-referencing, although this is, not surprisingly, less common than back-referencing. Taking both together, with a small number of other means of cross-reference in addition,[118] but omitting references backwards or forwards within a single chapter, the following pattern emerges: in book I, all cross-references are internal to the book, but four in book II refer back to passages in book I, compared with five (certainly) or six which are internal to book II. In book III, twenty-two cross-references occur, of which fifteen are bounded by the book while one refers back to book I and one to book II (albeit the last chapter thereof), two look forward to book IV and one to book V; in book IV, sixteen cross-references were identified, of which single examples refer to books I and II and two to V, while six make reference back to book III, five are internal to the book and one is to a non-existent earlier notice of Benedict Biscop (as above), which should arguably have been located either in book III or at the very beginning of book IV. Of the eleven cross-references in book V, three are to book III, four to book IV and five to book V, while one (in V, 22) is to Egbert, whose activities span all three of these books (III, 4, 27; IV, 3; V, 9).

Collectively, such internal references serve to bind the whole work together and provide a test, of sorts, of the consistency or homogeneity of the whole and the extent to which book III is embedded within the overall work, which it passes comparatively well. Out of a total of around sixty cross-references identified, some twenty-four (40 per cent) are to book III, which exceeds the combination of any other two books (the next highest totals are book IV: eleven and book II: eight). Obviously, this is a very crude measure of the internal homogeneity of the *Ecclesiastical History* but it seems clear that book III must be considered fully integrated within the overall text. While it seems fair to suppose that Bede's missing back-reference to Benedict Biscop could have been edited out at a late stage, the exceptional incidence of accurate cross-referencing to that book mitigates against any theory that it was substantially rewritten after the remainder was effectively complete. The alternative option remains, of course, namely that we are seeing here an oversight on Bede's part, who referred back to what he may have planned to include but in fact had not before this point, but was about to in the following chapter within his summary of Wilfrid's career. In a work of this scale, which was arguably being dictated, such need not surprise us, although one might question how likely such a mistake would have been regarding a figure so central to Bede's own particular vision of the past.

If, however, we pursue the issue of internal referencing one stage further, it is noticeable that the numerous references elsewhere to passages in book III generally exclude the key figures around whom the book seems to have been constructed, namely King Oswald and Bishop Aidan. In book IV, for example, references back to passages in book III relate to Egbert,[119] the hero-figure of Bede's *Greater Chronicle*, the obscure Kentish Bishop Boniface of the East Angles,[120] Kings Sebbi and Sighere of the East Saxons,[121] Hild as abbess,[122] Ælfflæd, her successor,[123] Eanflæd, ex-queen and the latter's mother and co-abbess,[124] and Eata, abbot and later bishop.[125] All of these could be presented as Catholic and in communion with Rome, at least by the ends of their lives, even despite Hild's long preference for the Ionan dating of Easter, to which Eata and, presumably, the young Ælfflæd would also have adhered prior to 664.[126] That said, there is no apparent hesitancy in referring to either Oswald or Aidan elsewhere in the work. Oswald receives honourable mention outside book III in Bede's list of *imperium*-wielding kings in II, 5, in a forward-reference to his completion of the church at York begun by Paulinus,[127] and in terms of the regnal period within which Penda of the Mercians killed Edwin's son Eadfrith,[128] and finally his death was recorded in the recapitulation. Aidan occurs in reference to Abbess Hild,[129] as founder of Lindisfarne,[130] and in the context of Egbert's conversion of Iona to the Roman dating of Easter,[131] and, likewise, his death-date was entered into the recapitulation. One might additionally note that a miracle attributed to the intercession of 'the religious and God-beloved King Oswald' seems to have been interpolated at a late stage into the foundation story of a monastery at Selsey among the South Saxons, given that it is absent from the *c*-type of manuscript,[132] which may, therefore, have been copied from a version completed prior to this addition.

Given that the *Ecclesiastical History* was dedicated to a king, it seems appropriate to home in on Bede's treatment of exemplary kingship therein. Without doubt, it was Oswald who was developed within this text as the central exemplar of Christian English kingship, taking over in that role from Edwin's solo performance in the *Greater Chronicle*. Although Edwin's 'empire' had been extended as a sign that he would accept conversion, it was Oswald whom Bede depicted as gaining (in *EH* III, 6) 'from the same one God who made heaven and earth greater realms than any of his ancestors; then he received under [his] rule all the nations and provinces of Britain, divided among the speakers of four different languages, that is of British, Pictish,

Scottish and English'. Bede's revival of the theme of the different tongues spoken in Britain, this time apparently in order of their putative arrival, places Oswald at the centre of his association of this work with the Pentateuch, as established in I, 1. He is the only figure to be treated in this way.

A comparison of the adjectives used of his earlier hero-figure, Edwin, and Oswald herein demonstrates his shift in emphasis: while Edwin's treatment in the *Greater Chronicle* was exceptional in this respect, his abnormal power was recognised in the list of *imperium*-wielding kings which Bede constructed in *EH* II, 5 but without any distinguishing claims for his personal virtues, which contrasts with Oswald's appearance therein as *rex Christianissimus* ('most Christian king'). Thereafter, he was reintroduced in II, 9, in closely comparable terms, with his increasing power interpreted as an omen of his conversion, and his reign was recalled as proverbial for the peace and security it afforded (II, 16), but Edwin was not personally conditioned by superlatives or extravagant praise of any sort. The closest Bede came to actively praising Edwin was the somewhat curious phrase *Tantum vero in regno excellentiae* . . . ('So great was [his] merit in the realm . . .'), and in conditioning his rule by use of the adverb *gloriosissime* (II, 20: 'most gloriously') at the opening of the chapter in which he described his death, and this despite inclusion of letters from popes Boniface and Honorius, which addressed him respectively as *Viro glorioso Eduino regi Anglorum* ('To the glorious Edwin, king of the English') and *Domino excellentissimo atque praecellentissimo filio* ('To [my] most excellent lord and most distinguished son'). Bede's earlier depiction of Edwin as *excellentissimus* parallels, therefore, earlier papal usage, whether he knew that or not *c.*725, but he declined to go down that road in the *EH*, preferring a positioning of this royal exemplar which was significantly less effusive. In contrast, Oswald, to whom no pope is known to have addressed a single letter, was introduced in book III, 1 as *viri Deo dilecti* ('a man beloved of/chosen by God'), and was depicted quite transparently as a David-figure confronting Cædwallon's Goliath, then a Christ-figure associated with the cross (III, 2), and a culted saint, whose personal qualities mirrored those of Aidan (III, 6): 'it is marvellous to say that he was always humble, benign and charitable to the poor and strangers', despite an earthly power which was represented as transcending even that of Edwin before him. Elsewhere he was described as *sanctissimum ac victoriosissimum regem Nordanhymbrorum* ('most saintly and most victorious king of the Northumbrians'),[133] and *Christianissimus rex* ('most Christian king'),[134] and Bede recounted a string of miracle stories (III, 9–13) before finally referring to the hero-king as *religiosus ac Deo dilectus* ('religious and God-beloved') in book IV, 14. Oswald and Aidan were, therefore, firmly embedded in the *Ecclesiastical History*, with no effort made to conceal their unorthodox Christianity, and not just within book III where they are a particular focus of sanctity and virtue. And (as has already been postulated) Bede may have been actively seeking to expand that presence by incorporating at least one fresh story pertaining to Oswald at a very late stage in the production of this work, even after copies had begun to be made and circulated outside Wearmouth/Jarrow. Bede clearly did not originate the cult of Oswald, since that was already a force to be reckoned with before he wrote,[135] but he did place it at the very epicentre of this history of his own people.

If we broaden our perspective still further, the vision of an author who was actively cultivating a view of the Irish mission to Northumbria in positive terms is impossible to ignore. Despite his careful and repeated distancing of himself from Iona on the Paschal question, Bede was using Aidan and his associates quite explicitly to contrast the putative excellence of the pastorate in the past with a less virtuous present, in expectation that his lesson would encourage his immediate audience to emulate their forebears, very much as he set out in his Preface. Take, for example, book III, 5, where Aidan is presented as an ideal in the Gregorian mould of the active-contemplative and model monk-bishop, both teaching his clergy how to conduct their lives and providing them with an example of personal abstinence, self-control, asceticism, generosity to the poor, accessibility to all and a penchant for pastoral care, in marked contrast with the present:

> His life was far distant from the sluggishness of our time, so that all who travelled with him, either tonsured or lay, were expected to meditate, that is to spend time either reading the scriptures or running through the psalms. Such was the daily task of [Aidan] himself and all those who were with him, wherever they came to.

The comparison with the present conduct of clerical leaders was further developed thereafter, albeit implicitly, with Aidan represented as unwilling to make more than a nominal appearance at royal feasts and encouraging his associates to emulate his own practice of extended fasting, his refusal to cultivate the rich and powerful by gift-giving, his alms-giving and his redemption of those sold unjustly into slavery.

Oswald and Aidan were, therefore, being introduced as potent exemplars of idealised Christian behaviour into the *Ecclesiastical History*, the one at the apex of secular society, the other as the bishop heading his church, rather like a paired Old Testament king and prophet. Oswald was developed here by Bede as a replacement to Edwin in the *Greater Chronicle*, who although he certainly appears to good effect in book II of the *EH* simply fails to attract the praise-vocabulary by which Oswald was repeatedly conditioned. Similarly, Aidan was developed as an alternative to his earlier portrayal of Bishop Paulinus. Together, Oswald and Aidan overshadow Bede's portrayal in the *EH* of Edwin and Paulinus. They were presented very much as figures of reconstruction, following catastrophe for the Northumbrians at the hands of the Britons and Mercians, so Bede perhaps intended that they be read in terms of Ezra and Nehemiah – so as leaders heading the process of renewal of God's people following the Babylonian captivity. No later secular figures were accorded comparable treatment by Bede in the *EH*, who was particularly grudging regarding any praise due to Oswiu, despite his quite spectacular achievements.[136] Oswald was, therefore, Bede's premier secular role model herein as the archetypal, Christian king constructed around Old Testament models, with Aidan presented as a type of the ideal monk-bishop, who was explicitly compared to his advantage with the Church leaders of the present.

The centrality of Oswald and Aidan to the moral perspective embedded in the *Ecclesiastical History* again marks a significant shift away from the vision of the English past as enshrined in the *Greater Chronicle* and should alert us to a major upheaval in Bede's own positioning since writing that work. Instead, therefore, of seeing those factors which differentiate book III from the remainder of the work as evidence of its comparative detachment from the remainder, we should perhaps view his decision to write it and even to refocus the conversion story on it despite the poor quality of his source materials as reason to emphasise Bede's determination to write up the Irish mission at the very centre of his new historical narrative.

Another way of approaching the issue of structure lies in Bede's cast of characters and where these were first introduced into his narrative. In total, he introduced something like 247 separate English individuals into the *Ecclesiastical History*.[137] If the Preface be excluded on the grounds that it was arguably written last, rather than first, and contains only two names not mentioned elsewhere (Nothhelm and Abbot Esi), the breakdown is as follows: Book I has five named individuals; book II, forty-two; book III, seventy-six; book IV, seventy-three; book V, forty-nine.

This highlights the scarcity of English individuals in book I and to an extent also in book II. Despite its opening almost a century before the present and despite Bede's dependence particularly in this book on oral testimony, it is book III which has the most references to individuals, followed closely by book IV. This is consistent with the sense of an 'Oswaldian' reconstruction of the entire project of the English conversion, following the wholesale destruction of Edwin's Christian kingship on the cusp of books II and III.

The centrality of this second, Anglo-Irish start to the entire work is emphasised in addition by attention to the content of Bede's various sub-sections of the *EH*. Of particular significance are the first and last chapters which bracket the several books, which presumably influenced (and perhaps still influence) both how Bede's audience initially engaged with, and the impression they then bore away from exposure to, each in turn, so it is to these that we will now turn as a measure of the author's approval of the Irish and/or Scottish, and their Northumbrian associates, across the entire work.

Bede on Irish and Scottish Christianity

Book I, of course, opens with a geographical, topographical and ethnographic perspective on Britain, culled from various sources, but it is important to note just how efficacious is Ireland and its inhabitants therein: understandably, they were presented as central to the whole story of Pictish and Irish

settlement in Britain but there is also a lengthy, concluding excursus concerning the absence of snakes from Ireland, which should be read figuratively
in the context of the impact of Irish missionaries on the English in Britain, so
for its veiled references back to the Garden of Eden in Genesis, from which a
serpent was instrumental in having Adam and Eve expelled.[138] By emphasising the inherent virtues of the Irish and their manuscripts (scrapings from
which supposedly even cured snake-bite), Bede was perhaps encouraging his
audience to anticipate the Irish contribution to Northumbria's Christianity,
long before his narration of the Irish mission in book III, and before he had
introduced the papal mission to the English (I, 23 but foreknown at the very
close of I, 22), or even introduced the Roman Conquest of Britain. Book I, 1,
therefore, can be read as prefiguring that part of the English conversion story
which pertains to the Irish, the main gist of which we can assume was familiar
to Bede's audience. At the very least, his treatment left his audience at the
close of this introductory chapter with the impression that Ireland and all
things Irish were infused with peculiar, God-given virtues.

Thereafter, the Irish occur in book I as raiders who tormented the
Britons,[139] so, like the Saxons, presented as divine agents sent to scourge them
for their obstinacy, then as the recipients of a papal mission (I, 13), again like
the English. However, the closing chapter of the first book reintroduced them
in a new guise, as the opponents of King Æthelfrith of the Bernicians at the
battle of *Degsastan*. The abrupt shift of arena from Kent (in I, 33) and the
contrived nature of this 'northern' chapter, inserted at the close of an extended
treatment of the Augustinian conversion, has often been remarked, with
issues raised even as to its authenticity,[140] but it was arguably Bede's purpose
here in introducing a Bernician king whom he compared to Saul and Benjamin,
both figures with military reputations,[141] to anticipate the conversion of the
Northumbrians which was to follow. Like Saul, Æthelfrith was a great warrior-king but a flawed character, in part in terms of his paganism, in part
because of his hostility towards the virtuous Edwin,[142] his much younger
brother-in-law and dynastic opponent, who fled south to escape him, ultimately to East Anglia. It was by Edwin that he was succeeded following his
death in battle, much as Saul was succeeded by David, whom he had similarly
persecuted but who then married his daughter. The sequence and the comparable family connections make this parallel a strong one, but Oswald was
also presented, albeit implicitly, as a David-figure at the opening of book III
in opposition to the Goliath-like Cædwallon, and it was his reign which solved
the central problem behind the battle of *Degsastan*, namely the conflicting
pretensions to power of kings of the Northumbrians and Scots, opening a new
chapter of co-operation between the two peoples under his patronage which
was characterised by Irish missionaries converting his people. The closure of
book I introduces Æthelfrith as an effective warrior king who then reappears
in book II, 2 to defeat the Welsh at Chester and slaughter their clerics. In this
context, Bede was making connections between Augustine, whose prophecy
he was here supposedly fulfilling, and a contemporary warrior-king as divinely

appointed agent for the punishment of the Britons, which was a role peculiar in this work to Northumbrian kings.[143]

Book II opens with Bede's long and highly venerative exposition of the life and works of Pope Gregory, whom he held in the highest regard and whom he specifically here termed 'the apostle' of the English. To this point, the bulk of Bede's narrative of the Augustinian mission had centred on Canterbury but he took the opportunity at the close of this chapter to include a traditional story which shifted the focus to Northumbria, or more specifically to Deira – southern Northumbria – and the kingship of Ælle, Edwin's father and Oswald's maternal grandfather. This was, of course, the (probably apocryphal) story of Gregory's meeting with English slaves at Rome,[144] which had earlier been recorded in the Whitby *Life of Gregory*, although Bede need not have obtained the story from this source. He had specifically excepted the Northumbrian realms of kings Æthelfrith and Ælle from his discussion of the Augustinian mission in the *Greater Chronicle*, but he took care to position Oswald as heir to both their lineages (at the close of III, 6) and as the effective unifier of their two realms. Allusions to Æthelfrith at the close of book I, then again in II, 2, and to Ælle in the opening chapter of book II, therefore provide significant internal connections between Oswald in book III and the earlier two books, between which internal cross-referencing is virtually non-existent, and look forward to the resolution of numerous issues within his reign, including Northumbrian unity, her military supremacy and *imperium* throughout Britain, and his reinvigoration of the faltering English conversion.

Book II then tells the story of the increasing difficulties facing the Canterbury mission, its failure to gain control of British Christianity and its near collapse following Æthelberht's death. This narrative of decline was partially remedied by the list of *imperium*-wielding kings in II, 5, stories of miracles in Kent and the conversion of Æthelberht's heir, Eadbald (II, 6), but more markedly by the story of Edwin's conversion and his Christian overkingship, which encompasses all of the book from chapter 9 onwards and provides a new and triumphant moral focus for the work to this point, replacing in this role the arrival of Augustine and his establishment at Canterbury (I, 23–5). This, however, came to naught in the closing chapter, which reads as a story of almost unremitting disaster: British and Mercian rebellion against Edwin in his role of a 'soldier in the kingdom of Christ' led to his death and those of his adult sons – an end which paralleled Saul's, of course,[145] followed by the ravaging of Northumbria, and the flight south of Paulinus and the Kentish queen and her surviving children and grandson. That catastrophe was emphasised still further in the opening words of book III: *At interfecto in pugna Eduino* . . . ('Moreover Edwin having been killed in battle . . .'). The work of conversion was, therefore, virtually undone, as was entirely unrepresented in the *Greater Chronicle*, along with the union of Bernicia and Deira, the first chapter of book III describing apostates briefly on both thrones. But Bede finally closed book II in his final paragraph on a milder note, looking forward to the time of peace which was to come, under Oswald one presumes, within which James the Deacon would continue Paulinus's mission and, in particular, teach sacred music – something which was particularly close to the heart of Bede himself. While insisting that a catastrophe had occurred, therefore, Bede was making some connections between an Edwinian past and the Oswaldian future, at the close of book II, which would be to an extent cemented by virtue of James the Deacon's presence at the Synod of Whitby some thirty years later and via the matter of York's church, which he had already noted that Oswald had had finished following its partial construction up to 633.

The entry in the contents list for book III for its first chapter encapsulates quite neatly Bede's positioning of Oswald:

> How the first successors of King Edwin abandoned the faith of his people and Oswald the most Christian king (*Christianissimus rex*) restored both kingdoms.

This is one of only two uses of a superlative attached to an individual in any of his contents lists, the other being his reference to Tobias, bishop of Rochester, as 'a most learned man' (*vir doctissimus*), in the entry for book V, 8. Even praise-adjectives are comparatively rare in this setting, occurring otherwise attached to only seven individuals: two relate to St Gregory, who was termed *sanctus papa* ('saintly pope') in the contents summary for I, 23 and *beatus papa* ('blessed pope') in that for II, 1; another two are associated with Bede's hero of the *Greater Chronicle*, the missionary Egbert, who was *vir sanctus* ('saintly man') in both III, 27 and V, 9; otherwise King Sigeberht of the East Angles was termed *religiosus rex* ('religious king') in III, 18, and Swithberht and Willibrord (another of Bede's heroes in the *Greater Chronicle*) were *viri venerabiles* ('venerable men') in V, 11.

The first chapter of book III then fills out this awful story of apostasy by representatives of both Northumbrian dynasties following Edwin's death and the brutality and terrible ravaging of the land by Cædwallon, by which Oswald's first entry to the stage was contextualised. In passing, honourable reference was made to the role of the Scots, whose success in converting Æthelfrith's sons and their followers was recognised in the first paragraph, but it was Oswald who was the central hero-figure of the chapter, being brought on late to remedy the ills which had been highlighted and whose virtues were emphasised by a series of rhetorical strategies which included the moral demolition of Cædwallon as *infandus* ('abominable') and boastful,[146] damnation of the reigns of both apostate kings, highlighting of the numerical disproportion of the two armies,[147] and his portrayal as *vir Deo dilectus* ('a man beloved/chosen by God').

Bede's championing of the role of Oswald, and the Scottish Church which he patronised, is sustained across the chapters which follow, with emphasis on the miraculous qualities of his wooden cross (central to III, 3), his responsibility for and championship of the Scottish mission in III, 4 (which was contextualised in terms of the foundations of Iona and Whithorn in the following chapter), Oswald's supreme power and correspondingly supreme virtues in III, 6, his role in the conversion of the West Saxons in III, 7, his death and associated miracles in book III, 9, and further confirmatory miracles associated with his relics in III, 10–13. Bede was careful to make a plethora of connections with his own audience: he recounted a miracle story putatively told him by Bothelm, a monk currently of Hexham (III, 2); he closed his account of the foundation of Iona with Egbert's recent conversion of that community to the Roman dating of Easter – to which he would finally return in book V, 22, then in summary in V, 24; he compared Aidan's virtues with the putatively lacklustre performance of clerics in the present (III, 5); he recalled the story of Oswald's hand and arm, which 'have remained incorrupt until this present time' in the church at Bamburgh (III, 6); he followed through the story of West Saxon Christianity to the time of Theodore; he told the story of the translation of Oswald's body to Bardney in the reign of the Mercian King Æthelred (675–704) and paid tribute to Bishop Acca's testimony, in the present tense, as illustration of Oswald's reputation on the continent. His treatment of Oswald and the Scottish mission was, therefore, a highly contemporary one, anchored firmly in the here and now and presented as relevant to his own audience and shared not just by the heirs of the Ionan mission but even by such comparatively unrelated and 'Romanist' figures as Wilfrid, Acca and Willibrord (III, 13). There seems nothing artificial about this, since the community at Hexham clearly had an active interest in Oswald's cult, as the guardians of Heavenfield, and it was their advocacy that seems to have initially encouraged the spread of Oswald's cult to both Sussex and the continent. The interest of Willibrord, who had been one of Wilfrid's acolytes, in Oswald's cult is confirmed by his appearance as the sole king to have been included in the original version of his calendar.[148]

Bede finally abandoned his unique exemplification of Oswald at the close of III, 13 – within which he was *rex mirandae sanctitatis* ('a king of admirable sanctity'), 'to whose excellence of faith and virtue, frequent post-mortem miracles bear witness' – before turning to the morally devalued reign of Oswiu, who 'cruelly' slew his rival, Oswine (who was eventually culted at Tynemouth and whom Bede apparently preferred in moral terms to Oswiu[149]). From that point he centred on Aidan and commemorated him by another set of miracles, revealed by 'the internal judge' (i.e. God: III, 15–18), only once again distancing himself from his Scottish hero over the issue of Paschal dating at the close of this sequence. He then turned to southern England, to weave in the story of Christianity in East Anglia and Kent and the arrival and temporary settlement at Burgh Castle of the Irishman Fursa (III, 19), whose sanctity Bede fully defended, before narrating the conversion of Peada of the Middle Angles (III, 21) and Sigeberht of the East Saxons (III, 22) and the foundation story of Lastingham (III, 23), whence this material had apparently reached him, then the victory of Oswiu over Penda (III, 24) and the Synod of Whitby (III, 25). It was in the context of this last meeting that Bede set out his own vision of the relevant arguments regarding the Paschal question, making this one of the longer chapters in the *Ecclesiastical History*, but even thereafter he paid fulsome tribute to the Irish missionaries (III, 26), praising their frugality and austerity, as exemplified in the site at Lindisfarne when they left, their charity to the poor and their lack of interest in overly sumptuous hospitality, such that contemporary houses, implicitly at least, provided to the great and good, 'for the whole concern of those teachers was the service of God, not the world'. Bede was offering Aidan and his successors, therefore, as exemplars of Christian behaviour to be culled from the story of Northumbrian Christianity in a distant past but central to his current concern with reform and the relationship in the present between God and His people, while the harmonious relationship between king and bishop, which he presented particularly in book III, 3, 6, was likewise offered as a model to be emulated in the present.

Reverential treatment of the Scottish mission and its converts continued even thereafter, with reference to Irish hospitality towards English *peregrini* in search of religious education or asceticism, and in particular the story of the saintly Egbert, whose asceticism Bede rooted in Irish practices.[150] Bishop Tuda's debt to the Irish was acknowledged,[151] and the saintly Bishop Chad was represented quite explicitly as replicating the apostolic style of Aidan (III, 28). Bede incorporated sections of Pope Vitalian's letter to Oswiu as his penultimate chapter in book III, edited to exclude comment on the Paschal question,[152] which he might have considered an appropriate point at which to close the book, referring forward as he did to book IV in the closing lines, but instead he added one last chapter, 30, which focuses on the apostasy of King Sighere of the East Saxons and many of his people in the face of the plague (of 664 and immediately subsequent years) and the success of Jaruman, bishop of the Mercians, in his efforts to regain them for Christianity. Bede presented this as based on the testimony of one of Jaruman's companions, who putatively portrayed the bishop as 'a religious and good man' whose preaching itinerary was successful, thereby retrieving a missionary enterprise first begun under Augustine and Mellitus,[153] then rekindled under Oswiu by the Irish-trained Cedd and his companions (III, 22–3). Jaruman had been appointed before the Synod of Whitby, presumably in collaboration with the Scottish Church, and his name may imply that he was himself Scottish, enabling Bede to close this his central book of the *Ecclesiastical History* with affirmation of the righteousness of an Irish clergyman active in proselytising and combating apostasy among the English, even as the impetus given by Oswald to Irish conversion of the English slowly unwound over the third quarter of the seventh century.

The story of the rebuttal of the Ionan mission had been told by Bede alongside references to the plague (explicitly in III, 27, 30), which might indicate divine dissatisfaction at this turn of affairs. The departure of Bishop Colman from Northumbria then opens book IV, despite the fact that the first chapter is primarily about the appointment of Theodore and Hadrian by Pope Vitalian to lead the English Church, and their passage to Canterbury across Frankia. Colman's appearance here was almost gratuitous, so was perhaps Bede's way of emphasising the value which he was attaching to the Irish mission even as he celebrated the unification of the English Church under Theodore's leadership (IV, 2), and the injection of learning which he and his companions brought to Canterbury and the English Church at large. By emphasising the moral qualities of the Irish missionaries, primarily in book III, then recalling the high reputation of the next generation of clergy whom they had trained, Bede was, to an extent at least, balancing the 'Romanist' traditions of Canterbury with a second weighty source of Christianity of high moral value, centred ultimately on Lindisfarne and descending from the epis-copacy of Aidan. So, for example, Chad's tenure of the see of the Mercians at Lichfield was presented by Bede as modelled on Aidan's at Holy Island: Aidan's habit of conducting his ministry on foot was particularly remarked upon as replicated by 'the very reverend Chad' (albeit it was countermanded by Theodore as impractical (IV, 3 referring back to III, 5, 14)); Chad, like Aidan, liked to retire to pray and meditate in a small building set apart. Likewise Hild's commemoration (IV, 21 (23)) recalled the particular qualities and virtues of Aidan and the Irish mission more generally. It must be relevant that Bede condemned Ecgfrith's despatch of forces into Ireland in 684 (IV, 26 (24)), then viewed his death in 685 as divinely ordained on account of the earlier campaign against an innocent and God-beloved people. However, the key witness to the ongoing potency of the Irish mission within this text was Cuthbert, with whom Bede chose to conclude book IV, to whose commemor-ation he committed six chapters. Bede had, of course, already narrated the life of Cuthbert at considerable length on two occasions, with comparatively little notice of his connection to Aidan (see above, p. 124). However, here he fore-grounded Cuthbert's ascetic habits (IV, 28), which paralleled Aidan's, and his training at the Scottish-founded Melrose by Eata. Eata had been one of Aidan's earliest disciples, recruited in childhood, and would later be the cru-cial figure on Holy Island providing continuity across the events of 664 (III, 26). Bede's narrative of Cuthbert's ministry when prior of Melrose (IV, 27) is reminiscent of his description of Aidan's episcopacy (III, 5) as well as the more generalised vision of the Irish Church offered in III, 26, and many will have been conscious of his occupation of the same island hermitage that Aidan had earlier used. Closure with the achievements and death of Cuthbert, and mir-acles posthumously associated with his tomb, therefore serves to confirm the tenor of the whole book: despite the ending of the Easter controversy and the arrival, learning and overall authority of Theodore, it was Bede's purpose to bear witness to such virtues as asceticism, charity, poverty and a commitment to proselytising, which he preferred to associate most closely with those who had been trained in the Scottish Church set up by Oswald and Aidan.

Even book V was opened by a miracle story associated with Cuthbert's successor as hermit, Œthelwald, which Bede presumably had from Lindisfarne but which reads as a variant of the sea-calming miracle already attributed to Aidan in III, 15. It serves to foreground the moral authority of Farne Island and its resident ascetic in the Aidan tradition well into Bede's own adult lifetime, if not to the present. The final book then offers a series of miracle stories associated with John of Beverley, one time bishop of Hexham then of York (V, 2–7), who had been trained by Hild, whose position within the Anglo-Scottish hierarchy Bede had already established. John can be viewed, therefore, as yet another figure through whom continuity with the Irish mission was being advertised. These miracles, which Bede mostly had from Abbot Berhthun at Beverley, are health centred: both the third and fourth, concerning the healing of the wife and servant of two *comites*, respectively, are reminiscent of miracle stories which he had already told of Cuthbert.[154] John's sanctity was again a matter which resonated in the present: John had in person ordained Bede first as deacon, then as priest, and had only retired as bishop in 721, while Berhthun was 'now abbot' of Beverley (V, 2), where John's cult was apparently being promoted in 731, so this impressive array of miracles carry forward the legacy of Aidan into the present and confirm once more that the Irish mission was part of the divine plan for His English people.

Bede then turned in his final book to new exemplars of royal behaviour. In V, 7, he recounted at considerable length the story of Cædwalla's departure from England to receive baptism at Rome where he then died, to be followed in due course by Coenred of the Mercians and Offa of the East Saxons, both of whom retired to monasteries in the Holy City (V, 19: see below). Otherwise, book V is an amalgam of out-of-body or visionary experiences told to sustain Bede's reform agenda (as V, 12, 13, 14), notice of recent succession in various dioceses, two chapters about the topography of the Holy Land (16, 17), which derived from Bede's précis of the Scottish Adamnan's version of a Gaulish oral source, and a group of anecdotes told so as to project a vision of the Anglo-Saxons, in the present, as fully involved with the evangelical project to take Christianity to the very ends of the earth, which was, for Bede, a *sine qua non* of their full membership of the Lord's Church. A series of interconnected strands were offered by Bede in illustration, which start with Egbert's unfulfilled intention to go as a missionary to Germany (in V, 9) and close with this same individual's triumph in converting Iona to the Roman system of dating Easter, in V, 22. That the central message of the latter part of book V should be framed by Egbert's story is significant. Bede had already repeatedly made reference to him as an English pilgrim in Ireland, but now presented him in V, 9 as if under the particular guidance of a God ever mindful of His people, whose wish it was that he direct his missionary zeal not to the pagans of Old Germany, who might be considered the biological progenitors of the Northumbrians, but to the Columban monasteries, so their spiritual parents. Egbert's prominence in this section of the text, combined with the plethora of earlier references, often in tandem with discussion of the Irish mission to Northumbria,[155] suggest that his achievement was being presented as funda-mental to Bede's entire historical project, which it virtually concludes: while this triumph narrated in V, 22 was not used to close the book – and hence the work – the story of Egbert's death at Iona in 729 does effectively terminate Bede's treatment of the past, giving way to a portrayal of the present (i.e. 725–31) in the penultimate chapter, and then the recapitulation and summary of the author's own life and works in the last.

Egbert's success was not Bede's sole exemplar of the English as missionaries, of course: he introduced Wihtberht as an evangelist among the Frisians in tandem with his treatment of Egbert in V, 9, then moved on to Willibrord, who had also spent a long period in Ireland, in the following chapter, and both Willibrord and Swithberht in V, 11. Adamnan's conversion of other Irish dioceses to the Roman method of calculating Easter in V, 15 is also relevant, in addition to empowering Bede to incorporate excerpts from his reworking of the latter's description of the Holy Land in the next two chapters, before reminding his audience of Wilfrid's successes as a missionary both to the Frisians and the South Saxons in V, 19 and incorporating the entirety of Ceolfrith's letter to the Picts in V, 21. Yet Egbert's role as an evangelist stands out as fundamental to Bede's narration: it was used to frame all other of this group of anecdotes; it was anticipated extensively across books III–V; as has repeatedly been remarked, it was used to close the *Ecclesiastical History*, and it was represented as quite peculiarly divinely inspired, with Bede quoting from the Book of Jonah in the context of his initial attempts to ignore God's message,[156] and then from Paul's letter to the Romans so as to establish the symbolic meaning of his achievement.[157] His audience was left in no doubt that Egbert was being singled out by Bede as God's particular servant and a major figure in his narrative, through whose achievements the *Ecclesiastical History of the People of the English* could be brought to a triumphant close.

In conclusion

Exploration of its organisation seems to suggest that the *EH* was structured into five books quite deliberately. The thinking behind this pattern of subdivision remains somewhat opaque but arguably has connections with Bede's earlier treatment of the past in his *Greater Chronicle* and his interest in the number-symbolism of the Pentateuch in particular, but perhaps also the five senses of man and five divisions of the world. A review of the chapterisation of the *Ecclesiastical History* offers new ways to explore Bede's agenda, identifying, for example, the individuals around whom he crafted exceptionally lengthy passages or strings of multiple chapters as of particular significance.

As a starting point for an exploration of the balance of Bede's overall presentation of the past in the *Ecclesiastical History*, we have then discussed his treatment of the English past in his *Greater Chronicle*, completed *c.*725, which provides by far the nearest parallel: following a comparatively neutral treatment of the Gregorian mission in Kent, Bede there offered a series of figures drawn from Northumbrian history and illustrative of the English transition from paganism to full membership of the family of Christian nations, using King Edwin, Queen Æthelthryth, Bishop Cuthbert, Bishop Willibrord, ?Bishop Egbert and Abbot Ceolfrith as exemplars, all of whom were distinguished rhetorically from other characterisations in this text. Through these six individuals, Bede sought in this work to establish his own people as full participants in the Apostolic Church.

There are, however, significant differences between Bede's visions of the past as presented in the *Greater Chronicle* and the *Ecclesiastical History*, as regards both his willingness to condemn the Irish and his commitment to the traditions of the Scottish mission to Northumbria. While the key figures associated with the Scottish mission (and others, such as Bishop Wilfrid) were entirely excluded from the earlier work, and also from his *Martyrology*, which was perhaps written in the intervening years, they not only appear in the later study but therein take centre stage and occupy much of the moral high ground, even despite Bede's repeated condemnation of the Scottish dating of Easter and traditions of tonsure. To a marked extent, book III of the *Ecclesiastical History* was developed as if a new beginning for English Christianity, following the catastrophe which had closed book II, with Oswald and Aidan represented as key figures of renewal. Apart from Gregory, Wilfrid and Acca, hero-figures in the *EH* were predominantly members of, or trained by, the Scottish Church: Bishop Chad and Abbess Hild were each the subject of an extended chapter and both Cuthbert and John of Beverley of groups of chapters recounting miracles. The omission of the Scottish mission from the *Greater Chronicle* reveals a lacuna as regards English affairs between 633 and 669. Such might perhaps be expected of a work written by one of its inmates for the particularly 'Roman' foundation of Wearmouth/Jarrow as audience, since this community developed in consequence, in part at least, of the volte-face by the Northumbrian royal house in 664, when the dating of Easter was a principal bone of contention. It is the *EH* which stands out as different in this respect, not the *Greater Chronicle.*

Of the six exemplary figures in the latter work, the biggest casualty in the *Ecclesiastical History* was Bede's own abbot Ceolfrith, who appears only in a supporting role, or as author of the long letter to the Pictish king, ownership of which was not particularly critical to its message.[158] He might have been expected to have featured more heavily and even been allotted a chapter centred on an appreciation of his life, to mark his death in transit to Rome.

At the centre of Bede's intellectual journey from his position in the *Greater Chronicle* to that which he adopted in 731 lies book III of the *Ecclesiastical History*, the content of which had, excepting only the eclipse of 664, been entirely omitted from the earlier work. While there are slight signs that rewriting may have occurred within book III (and/or the beginning of book IV), leading perhaps to a loss of early references to Benedict Biscop, overall a review of the cross-referencing suggests that this section was not massively overhauled after the remainder had been completed but was fully embedded in the greater narrative. It was actually the most extensively referenced of any book. That said, it is rather different from the remainder, for example as regards the sparsity of pre-existing textual material replicated in it. However, rather than viewing book III as somehow marginal to the meta-narrative or even as a late addition, perhaps even rewritten after the remainder had been completed, it is proposed here that it should be seen as the moral focus of the entire work and at the very heart of his endeavour, to achieve which Bede overcame a scarcity of written evidence and paucity of eyewitnesses. In other words, in the particular context of this work, book III mattered a great deal to an author who struggled with the deficiencies of his material and with his own discomfort regarding the Paschal issue to write it at all, let alone make it central.

In support of this contention, characters who featured heavily in the early part of the book do seem to have been developed as key exemplars for consumption by Bede's immediate audience. In particular, Oswald was presented as the central model of insular kingship, replacing the earlier development in this role of Edwin, whose presence in the *EH* was overshadowed in terms of the much greater praise-vocabulary attached to his successor. Despite emphatic repudiation of their position on the Paschal question, Bede made extensive use of Aidan, his successors and English trainees within that tradition as exemplars, whose reputations should, in the present, stimulate both veneration and imitation. The treatment of Aidan *et al.* seems to have been central to Bede's promotion of his reforming agenda. Yet, although they were conveniently located in a comparatively distant past, so capable of being re-envisioned in an idealised setting, it has to be stressed that these were highly problematic figures from the perspective of the Northumbrian Church in the early eighth century, in terms of differences between Scottish and Roman customs which could be construed in terms of heresy.

Book III does, therefore, seem to have been at the very heart of Bede's 'historical' project. A brief survey of the 'Irish', 'Scottish', 'Ionan' and 'Oswaldian' elements across the *EH* suggests that he had taken care to embed the theme of a benevolent Irish or Scottish Christianity contributing to English traditions across much of the work, on occasion even going out of his way both to remark on related matters and to confer exceptional moral status on Ireland and/or Iona, its inhabitants and their asceticism. References to the Irish both open and close the whole work, occurring prominently at the end of the introductory chapter (I, 1) and in V, 22, in which Egbert's achievements in converting Iona to Catholic practices attracts one of the most valedictory commentaries in the entire *EH*. Divine anger at an attack on the Irish also explains the disaster which brought down King Ecgfrith, whose reputation, as the initial patron of his own monastery, Bede might otherwise have been expected to have furthered.

On the face of it, the special status of the *peregrinus* Egbert in Bede's narrative is bizarre. If we piece together the little we know of his career, he was an English figure of high status but of unknown origin, albeit probably Northumbrian, who spent the bulk of his life in exile among the Irish, failed to follow through his putative intention to evangelise in Germany, although some around him did go, but did eventually persuade the Ionan family of monasteries to adhere to the Petrine tonsure and Roman method of dating Easter, before eventually dying there in 729, probably with the status of bishop. As English figures go, it would be difficult to find a cleric who had less direct impact on Anglo-Saxon Christianity than this long-term exile. That said, Egbert had already featured as one of two English missionaries whose achievements had been highlighted by Bede in his *Greater Chronicle*, so the emphasis he now received was nothing new in 731. Reference to him in the recapitulation as if a saint may imply that he had already been culted, which implies rapid developments given his death as recently as 729. It had been apparent to Bede *c.*725 that he needed to present the English as full participants in the apostolic tradition of Christendom as part of his depiction of them as a people of the Lord, and Egbert's role enabled him to complete the virtuous circle of the conversion process, by which those converted (primarily the Northumbrians) were themselves enabled to correct the discrepant practices of those who had earlier converted them (the Iona community).

There was a certain logic to foregrounding English responsibility for Iona's adherence to Roman customs: many of the cult centres of the current Northumbrian church had been founded by members of the Scottish mission and/or their associates, and Bede's focus on Egbert's achievement had a real value in terms of legitimising local foundation stories and defending the moral status of such houses as Melrose and Lindisfarne; so, too, many of the senior clergy of early eighth-century Northumbria had personal experience of the Scottish missionaries or the first generation of their English acolytes, by whom most had been trained, including such figures as bishops John of Beverley and Wilfrid II. In fact, it could be envisaged that the entire status of Northumbrian Christianity was at issue were the Ionan mission to Oswald's realm excluded from his *History* as tainted by error, leaving Bede's story seriously compromised by the death of Edwin and the near collapse of Paulinus's mission in the 630s.

That Bede proposed to place his own Northumbrian people at the very core of English Christianity is self-evident.[159] It was perhaps in support of their special status that he chose to exclude such English missionaries abroad as the West Saxon Boniface, who was elevated to episcopal status by Pope Gregory II in 722, a fact of which Bede may have been aware given acknowledgement in his Preface of information from Bishop Daniel at Winchester, who was himself both Boniface's earlier diocesan and one of his correspondents.[160] To omit honourable mention of the Irish missionary effort might have been tantamount to surrendering the centrality of Northumbria to the wider story of English conversion, even risking presenting such figures as Oswald, Aidan, Cedd and Chad as agents opposed to the broader story of the English conversion by the true agents of Christ, in the Roman tradition. Focus on such figures as Paulinus, James the Deacon and Wilfrid to the exclusion of the hero-figures of the Scottish/Northumbrian church might have been thought by Bede to have been unsustainable as a thesis capable of delivering the Bernicia-centred narrative which he apparently intended.

To return to Egbert, therefore, this 'Mother Teresa' figure in long-term exile was perhaps being developed by Bede to construct a latter-day, insular type of St Gregory through whom to lay claim to full membership of the Apostolic Church for the English people. He was an individual who was clearly 'owned' in some sense by the Northumbrians and who was eventually culted at Ripon (although whether in the eighth century or later is unclear), as well as being included in Wearmouth/Jarrow's own calendar.[161] Like Gregory, Egbert had proposed to go as a missionary to convert the heathen but had putatively been held back by the Lord, through no fault of his own, for higher deeds; again, as Gregory, Egbert's followers had undertaken mission in his place; and like Gregory, again, Egbert was successful in spreading Catholic practices to the furthest reaches of the inhabited world. Other than his lack of notice of written works, Bede's treatment of their respective qualities was in important respects quite similar, both being offered as exemplars of the type of monk-bishop.

This exploration of the conception of the *Ecclesiastical History* has enabled us, therefore, to contrast Bede's differing visions of the past *c.*725 and *c.*731, and so identify the changing nature of his agenda. That he celebrated the Ionan contribution to English Christianity solely in the later work is a matter of some significance. Even more is the extent to which he allowed 'Oswaldian' history to overshadow the 'Edwinian' past which he had highlighted in the *Greater Chronicle.* Oswald's role then seems to have become less pressing by the time he wrote the recapitulation, since that seems to represent a shift in sentiment in some respects closer towards his stance in the *Greater Chronicle.* Yet Bede, or perhaps one of his close associates, later seems to have added an additional 'Oswaldian' chapter (IV, 14), even after the whole work had been completed, suggesting that he had once again shifted his ground. Why Bede's conception of the past should have been so fluid is yet to be explored but we still need to examine other aspects of his approach before we have a sharper vision of his purposes in writing.

4   Message and discourse

I have related only what Bede the master laid down with unquestionable
accuracy in his historical account of the English peoples and their deeds from
their first beginnings.[1]

Bede was a highly experienced and very accomplished writer who apparently
had a specific brief in mind when setting out to write his *Ecclesiastical History*,
although we can today only reconstruct his purposes haltingly from the
somewhat paradoxical evidence internal to it. As Alcuin makes clear in the
extract from his work quoted above, commentators only a generation or
so removed from the work particularly stressed Bede's historical accuracy.
Unsurprisingly, historians in the modern period have tended to trawl the
Ecclesiastical History with their attention fixed on the affairs of men (and
women of course, albeit they are a minority representation therein), seeking
out 'unwitting' as much as 'witting' testimony – that is, what the author
included to provide context and of necessity to make sense of other materials,
besides what he particularly purposed to write. By so doing they – we – seek
to extract insights through which to maximise the little that can safely be
surmised concerning the seventh and early eighth centuries,[2] and so build up
an historical narrative for the period, but this is only one approach and others
may be at least as valid.

Fifty years ago, in a seminal work of literary theory,[3] Meyer Abrams offered
an illustration of the basic tenets of textual criticism, with the work itself at
the centre. Around it and equally spaced were the three satellite concepts
of 'universe' (so the general nature of existing things reflected in the work),
'artist' (in our case the author, Bede) and 'audience' (in the immediate,
Ceolwulf and Co., but this ultimately embraces ourselves). Within the con-
fines of this model, the Anglo-Saxon historian approaching the *EH* has
generally privileged 'universe', largely because s/he is so far removed in time
from the work and its context that it is now valued primarily as a mirror
through which a distant past can be observed and interpreted. Since the
1950s, however, the separateness and objectivity of the several entities in this
model have been re-evaluated by literary critics, who have challenged both

the stability and meaning of Abrams's model, proposing other approaches instead, including both the 'New Historicism' of the 1980s – the proposition that all literature should be view primarily as cultural artefact within a chronological context defined first by authorship – and the proposal that the beholder's perspective is paramount and should be considered the key to reading any text.[4]

Given that Bede was writing for an immediate, contemporary audience, and that he was himself steeped in the skills of exegesis, which privileged metaphorical alongside literal interpretations, we can safely assume that he never intended his work to be read primarily as an historical 'source' by later generations, privileging the factual 'universe'.[5] While he was certainly bringing together material from a variety of informants and/or existing narratives into a single text, and while his work was rooted in an historical past, it seems fair to suggest that he was at least as interested in communicating particular lessons to his readers as in the relaying of specific past events: let us remind ourselves that Bede claimed that he was writing primarily so as to provide examples of both good and bad behaviour in an insular context capable of guiding the behaviours of his immediate audience.[6] In this sense it was less the precise events relayed which mattered to Bede, than the underlying message which particular narrative passages were intended to convey. If, therefore, we are to understand what Bede was attempting, we need to focus less on the 'universe' as revealed in his work – so his great work of history as a store of 'facts' defining the past[7] – but rather tease out what we can concerning the deeper messages which he was seeking to communicate, putting aside our 'historical' heads, in a sense, and focusing instead on the *Ecclesiastical History* as an organised and purposeful collection of apologues, or moral fables – parables if you will – containing moral exemplars capable of engaging, and being emulated by, his intended audience.

Perhaps I need to preface such a discussion by assuring fellow historians that it is not my intention by so doing either to denigrate or to underestimate Bede as a source of 'historical' information about the seventh and early eighth centuries. But for now I propose to shift the spotlight away from the issue of Bede as truth-teller to the equally pressing matter of the type of society which he, as author, sought to privilege, and so his take on such issues as the nature of authority and its moral use, and the relationships appropriate to kings and clergy, who are, of course, the dominant social groups in this work. Central to such an exploration is the role of the Lord in the *EH*, so it is with God's relationships with those groups that this discussion will open.

The divine, kingship and the Church

A central component of the *Ecclesiastical History*, which modern readers generally filter out, either consciously or unconsciously, in their quest for 'historical' material, is the presence of a muscular and active Christian God, deeply involved in the affairs of man in general and Englishman in particular, whose thoughtful potency substitutes for the sense of causation to be found in modern historical narratives.[8] Indeed, it would be fair to describe God and Christ in this work as the nearest to omnipresent of any of Bede's vast cast of characters. Christ appears in the opening line of the Preface as Bede's master in the context of authorship, so is in some sense given responsibility even for composition, if we allow masters in this society a degree at least of oversight of the actions of their servants.[9] God follows midway through the first paragraph as the arbiter of good behaviour, as Bede expected Ceolwulf to recognise. Thereafter, it was 'divine authority' which had appointed Ceolwulf himself to rule, and Bede's discussion of his sources makes it clear that he viewed a principal focus of this history to be the spread of the 'faith of Christ' across the various English kingdoms. At the close, Bede asked his readers to seek God's mercy for himself as author for the weaknesses of his work. He positioned himself as author as a key player on the great stage of life, along-side the characters whose deeds he described, but God was allotted the roles of instigator and editor, stage-manager and director, combined. Ceolwulf's own presence in the Preface as dedicatee is, therefore, overshadowed by the authority of the divine, with Bede, implicitly but quite profoundly, himself retaining the key role as interpreter of God's plan for His English people. From the very opening of the finished work (including the Preface as an integral part), Bede was therefore placing Ceolwulf's rule and his authority as king within and beneath the over-arching context of his own vision of the divine plan, and consequently less on his own factional leadership than on his acquisition, then retention, of divine favour, as interpreted and mediated by himself as author. If the kingship of the Northumbrians was effectively in the gift of the Lord, then the onus which Bede was placing in his Preface on its present incumbent to behave in ways which he interpreted as pleasing to God was necessarily a central tenet of the political and moral philosophy running through the work. Bede's appropriation of the divine as a participant in his own judgements concerning individuals and their deeds was perhaps the single most powerful rhetorical strategy within his entire history, making his recon-struction of the past at the same time both compelling and exceptionally difficult to contest.

Nor is the divine specific to the Preface: *Deus* ('God') occurs in some 313 passages spread across ninety-eight of the (eventual) 140 chapters,[10] and Christ in 172 passages spread across sixty-five chapters,[11] as Bede developed his type of Christian history in an insular context.[12] Bede was himself the narrator but the story he told was presented consistently in terms of the unfolding of divine providence.

At the start of the work, a particular issue was the violence of the arrival of the Anglo-Saxons in a Christian Britain, which, Bede apparently felt, required accommodation within the Lord's plan. So, for example, developing what Gildas had written, it was (I, 14) 'the will of God' that the sinful Britons should invite in Saxons as mercenaries, and he depicted the Saxon revolt (I, 15) in terms of 'the just vengeance of God on the people for its crimes' and their great raid across Britain as ordained by the 'just Judge'. Thereafter, the Anglo-Saxons were foreknown as His own by God (I, 22) and Gregory was divinely prompted to send Augustine to Britain (I, 23), at the head of a group of monks whom he described as servants of 'the living and true God' bearing an image of 'our Lord and Saviour on a panel' (I, 25).[13] Those of Gregory's letters which Bede included in his work have numerous references to God and/or Christ, with the result that seventeen consecutive chapters in book I, closing with I, 33, include reference to divine agency, with only the deeds of a pre-Christian Northumbrian king – as if a pagan Augustus-type figure – in I, 34, recounted devoid of explicit references. A notion of the English arrival and subsequent conversion as central to providential history in Britain and of God as an active agent therein is, therefore, a powerful message of the opening sections of the work.

The Lord's will was similarly central to the conversion of the Northumbrians. The expansion of Edwin's temporal power (II, 9) was depicted as a divinely given 'sign' of his impending conversion, with Paulinus, 'a man beloved by God', beside him as a type of St Paul. It was God who had revealed a vision to Edwin (II, 12), and God again who prompted Edwin's advisers (II, 13) to give counsel in favour of conversion when they met with the king and his bishop in conference. At the close of his life, Edwin was depicted as 'a soldier in the kingdom of Christ'. This king's acceptance of Christ, patronage of Paulinus and establishment of cult had been rewarded, therefore, by both spectacular success in this world and triumphant access to the eternal kingdom of heaven. His reign was depicted as beginning the great (if somewhat episodic) golden age of English Christendom which is such a feature of the *Ecclesiastical History*, enshrined in Bede's eulogy for his reign which he incorporated in book II, 16:

> At that time there was so great a peace in Britain, wherever the *imperium* of king Edwin reached, that, just as is still proverbial to this day, even one woman bearing a new-born child might walk the whole island from sea to sea and suffer no harm. So much did this same king care for the good of the people that in various places, where he had seen clear springs near to public crossing places, here he ordered stakes to be set up and bronze cups to be suspended from them for the refreshment of travellers: nor did any dare to lay hands on them other than for their necessary use for they feared him greatly, nor did they wish to for they loved him well. So great indeed was his kingliness in the realm that not only were standards born before him in battle, but even in times of peace, riding between towns, or estates or provinces with his court he would always be preceded by a standard-bearer.

This proverbial peace contrasts with the past ravaging of Britain 'even from the eastern to the western sea' by the heathen Saxons of book I, 15, which Bede had from Gildas. His provision of clear spring water for the use of travellers should surely be read as an extended metaphor for the waters of baptism, and the putative Romanity of his kingliness is surely again a metaphor for the conjunction in an English, insular setting of Roman style *imperium* and Roman Christianity.

Use of *gloriosissime* ('most gloriously') of Edwin's rule (II, 20) invites comparison between this exemplary but much earlier king and Ceolwulf himself, whom Bede termed *gloriosissimus* in the opening line of his Preface, and it is worth pausing for a moment to consider what the present king might have been expected to have taken away from this description of his predecessor. At the core lie messages concerning the furthering of Christianity via active co-operation between king, bishop and papacy, with royal authority harnessed to provide the necessary secular support to drive forward a Christianising agenda. Edwin's case was used to suggest that royal power might be enhanced in order to make it fit for such a purpose and/or sustained as a reward for appropriate levels of commitment. There is a rewards culture, therefore, implicit in these messages. Just as Ceolwulf's own authority was depicted as in God's gift in the Preface, so was Edwin's in book II, with his survival at Rædwald's court (II, 12), in particular, developed as part of a miraculous prelude to his kingship and conversion. It was through Edwin that Bede first developed in this work his type of the royal exile eventually triumphing to achieve exceptional power under God, which may have had some real significance for Ceolwulf (see below, pp. 202–3). Bede was certainly conscious of the political unrest current in Northumbria in 729–31 (V, 23) and, as the above quotation makes clear, it was in the context of Edwin's reign that he first depicted the ideal of a peaceful realm united by fear of, as well as love for, a Christian king. By presenting Edwin's rule as a manifestation of divine benevolence, therefore, with which Edwin was himself complicit, Bede was providing the king of the day with a lesson as to how he in turn should both exercise kingship in accordance with the Lord's commands and then engage with the rewards to be expected from a benevolent God.

Bede's next assay in this same direction, regarding King Oswald, has already been identified as his central royal exemplar, but, again, it is the presence of God in these early chapters of book III which allows him to press home his message regarding types of kingly behaviour particularly pleasing to the Lord. Oswald was introduced as 'a man beloved of God' and his triumphant army was 'strengthened by faith in Christ' (III, 1), all together praying to 'the all-powerful, ever-living and true God' for aid against 'the proud and ferocious enemy' (Cædwallon's army, of course, masquerading as Philistines: III, 2).[14] Oswald was, therefore, depicted as reinstating English Christianity following a sudden assault by the enemies of the Lord, and his relationship with God was developed by Bede in far more overt ways even than Edwin's had been. Much like the cross of Calvary, wood from that which he had erected on the eve of battle had healing qualities which God might manifest to worthy recipients, such as the monk Bothelm (III, 2).[15] Oswald was depicted as both single-minded and determined in his pursuit of Christian

conversion for his people from the very start, in contrast to the long pro-
crastination of Edwin, and he was rewarded by 'the one God who made
heaven and earth' with 'greater earthly realms than any of his predecessors
had possessed' (III, 6). His eventual death at the hands of the heathen was
hallowed by a series of healing miracles, via which God provided signs of his
sanctity and proof that he was now 'reigning with the Lord' (III, 12), as well
as still protecting his people even post-mortem. And Oswald's deeds, like
Edwin's, had become proverbial:

> It is also a common-place, however, which has become proverbial, that he
> even ended his life with words of prayer; for when he was surrounded by
> the weapons of his enemies and saw that he was about to perish, he
> prayed for the souls of his army. So the proverb runs: 'May God have
> mercy on their souls, as Oswald said as he fell to the ground.'

What was Ceolwulf expected to take away from this highly eulogistic but
somewhat stereotypical portrayal of Oswald (about whom this author in reality seems to have known comparatively little)? Bede generally had a less than
enthusiastic attitude towards warfare but here Oswald was portrayed as the
exemplary Christian warrior, turning his weapons triumphantly against the
iniquitous Britons only at the last to be slain in a ferocious battle by English
pagans, so martyred, implicitly, although Bede never actually pursued this
form of commemoration.[16] In both guises, as warrior king and tutelary saint,
he was seen as legitimately defending his own Christian, Northumbrian
people. Oswald was, therefore, being depicted as God's soldier-king *par excellence*, protective of his people and the champion of even the poorest among
them, and this portrayal comes over strongly via the story centring on his
hand and arm, which had 'remained incorrupt until this present time' as core
relics of his sanctity housed at Bamburgh, in recognition of his charity.[17]
Aside from his martial qualities, Oswald was developed by Bede as a unifying
figure within Northumbria, whose connections with both Æthelfrith and
Edwin enabled him to be portrayed as the rightful ruler of both Deira and
Bernicia (III, 6), so as the legitimate king of a peaceful and united land. Given
the divisions within the kingdom in 731, such acceptance across the whole
political community in the past may have had considerable appeal in what
seems to have been a faction-ridden present. Oswald was also developed as an
imperium-wielding king to whom all southern Britain was subordinate, over
and against the Mercian supremacy in the south at the time of writing, which
Bede acknowledged but for which Ceolwulf's court in particular, and the
Northumbrian élite in general, probably felt little enthusiasm. Oswald likewise comes over as a champion of Christian conversion, which offered an
example that Bede may well have intended Ceolwulf to emulate: he was
depicted as proactively supporting the efforts of his bishop and clergy to
harvest a rich crop for the Lord – even participating in the guise of Aidan's
interpreter, converting his Irish into the local vernacular so as to render

his preaching comprehensible. The close and mutual co-operation between Oswald and Aidan is clearly offered as an ideal of the king–bishop relationship and Bede later, in his *Letter to Egbert*, anticipated that active support might be expected from Ceolwulf in furthering Bede's own vision of the interests of the Church, in suppressing unfit monasteries, for example, and founding new, monastery-centred bishoprics. The Lindisfarne connection is also potentially of considerable significance in the construction of parallels between the 630s and 730s, given Ceolwulf's putative eventual retirement into the monastery which Oswald had helped Aidan found as a virtual clone of Iona.[18]

In his personal behaviour, Oswald was depicted as 'always wonderfully humble, kind, generous to the poor and to strangers', offering Ceolwulf a model which Bede presumably intended he should emulate. Oswald comes close in book III, 12, to being portrayed as if an idealised type of monkish king through the frequency of his prayers and the physical posture which Bede claimed that he adopted when seated. Indeed, one might argue that Bede was presenting Oswald as a secular type of the 'good ruler' as depicted in Gregory's *Pastoral Care*,[19] portraying him in terms which were closely comparable to his ideal pastor, so as one who was pure in thought, chief in action, discreet in keeping silent, profitable in speech, sympathetic, exalted above all in contemplation, a friend of good-livers and enemy of evil-doers, and who balanced effectively his own spiritual needs against the outward affairs of the world.[20] Oswald was therefore being presented by Bede as an idealised, Christian king, who exhibited all of wholehearted and enthusiastic support for his bishop, protection for his people, humility, charity and extreme personal piety, who was rewarded by a benevolent God, in life with victory and widespread *imperium* and in death with sanctity. All these messages had considerable potential in terms of Ceolwulf as audience in the present, who Bede apparently anticipated – for whatever reason – might be susceptible to the portrayal of Oswald as an exemplar of particular relevance to himself. Oswald was, therefore, an aspirational figure in the context of this work, offered as the central example of kingship, whose behaviour Ceolwulf was being invited to emulate.

As a saint, Oswald crosses the secular/religious divide posthumously in ways which offer a unique model of kingship within the *Ecclesiastical History*. So, for example, a column of light putatively marked the cart containing his corporal remains through the night after the monks of Bardney hesitated to accept them into their house (III, 11). Such direct indicators of divine favour were generally centred in this work on religious figures, such as the story of Breguswith's necklace and the twin pillars of light associated with Hild's ascent to heaven witnessed at Hackness and *Streanæshalch* (?Whitby: IV, 23), as they were in works known to Bede: so, for example, in his *Dialogues*, Gregory depicted St Benedict as witnessing the soul of Bishop Germanus of Capua carried to heaven in a fiery ball.[21] Such images involving brightness as a symbol of sanctity or God derive ultimately from the Bible, wherein virtuous kings, such as David, were on occasion associated with light,[22] and the connection between luminosity and all three members of the Holy Trinity in the New Testament is recurrent.[23] So too were healing miracles herein most commonly associated with religious figures, but several were offered in connection with Oswald's cross, earth from the place of his death and his tomb at Bardney,[24] which Bede paralleled elsewhere by miracles associated with John of Beverley, for example, and, more closely, Bishop Hædde of the West Saxons.[25] Such signs of Oswald's sanctity provide an important extra dimension to Bede's royal exemplars, developing his vision of the potential role of English kingship into a very different and far more potent model than a purely secular version would allow, and this, too, has important resonances for Ceolwulf in the present, whose own eventual retirement to the monastic life parallels that of Æthelred of the Mercians – who likewise seems to have been an enthusiast for St Oswald – and may even betray some interest in the type of royal cult which Bede otherwise described in favour of Æthelthryth and Hild.

Bede's treatment of Oswald therefore carries a powerful set of messages concerning the lifestyle and personal mores he considered best fitting a king concerned to gain and then retain divine support. Similar messages are also implicit in Bede's treatment of several more recent monarchs, particularly those who had resigned their kingships and retired to monasteries, either in England or at Rome, none of whom were Northumbrian. Cædwalla of the West Saxons was the earliest such figure, whom Bede presented as a comparatively brutal but successful war-leader whose eventual departure for Rome, baptism there by Pope Sergius, death very soon after and commemoration he included at some length (V, 7), including the full text of the epitaph on his tomb.[26] Cædwalla's struggle to gain power in the south may even have displayed similarities with Ceolwulf's in Northumbria in 729–31. It is characteristic of Bede's care not to offend his dedicatee that we should have more information about the more distant example than the nearer. For Bede, the connection with Rome was arguably of particular significance: certainly, he paid far less attention to Æthelred of Mercia's retirement to Bardney, to which he made only a passing reference in V, 19 and then echoed in the recapitulation of V, 24, despite the involvement of a Northumbrian princess and Mercian queen – Osthryth – in the translation of Oswald's putative body there some years earlier (III, 11). Bede's attitude can perhaps be interpreted most easily from his version of the departure to Rome of Coenred of the Mercians and Offa of the East Saxons, *c.*722 (V, 19):

> Coenred, who had ruled the Mercians very nobly for some time, even more nobly relinquished the sceptre of his kingdom. For he went to Rome, and was there tonsured, while Constantine was pope, and was made a monk at the threshold of the apostles, remaining there until the end of his days occupied in prayer, fasting and almsgiving . . . There came with him also a son of Sighere, king of the East Saxons, to whom we have referred above, called Offa, a young man very much loved and of

great beauty, whom his whole people very much desired should hold the sceptre of the kingdom. He too, led by a comparable devotion, relinquished wife, lands, kinsmen and fatherland for Christ and for the gospel, that he might receive in this life a hundred-fold, and in the world to come life everlasting.

Bede was clearly here privileging the monastic life over the secular and promoting the case for leading figures of the secular world to retire and take the tonsure, even including kings and/or their sons, and Ceolwulf actually seems eventually to have put this particular piece of advice into practice, whether or not Bede was in any sense responsible. Both Coenred and Offa may well have had their own reasons for retiring in general, and removing themselves to Rome in particular, but for Bede these could be offered as examples of royals putting aside the affairs of man and rewards of high status for the higher calling to follow Christ.[27] As anonymous 'kings of the Saxons', both appear in *The Book of Pontiffs*, which has them dead soon after arrival,[28] and Bede was presumably aware of this. An earlier example of a king whom Bede portrayed (IV, 11) in highly moral terms and as eventually retiring to the monastic life was Sebbi of the East Saxons, whom he described as 'devoted much to God' and 'given to religious acts, constant prayers, and the pious fruits of much alms-giving'. This picks up once more several of the characteristics with which Bede had invested Oswald. His earliest example, however, was Sigeberht of the East Angles, 'a good and religious man' (III, 18), who eventually, 'from love of the kingdom of heaven', gave his own earthly kingdom into the keeping of a kinsman and retired to a monastery which he had himself founded. When the Mercians attacked, however, the East Angles dragged Sigeberht into the battle, where he was slain in the general defeat, armed as he was with only his staff. The tale is told against the East Angles for having failed to respect Sigeberht's renunciation of the world and the moral of the story was presumably that such behaviours were doomed to fail, owing to divine disapproval of the involvement of the religious in secular affairs.[29]

Bede was also careful to provide examples of flawed kingship, as he had hinted he would in his Preface, but these were generally less overt than his treatment of either Edwin or Oswald, excepting only the extreme example of the British leader, Cædwallon (II, 20; III, 1). Book III offers an account of Northumbrian history following Oswald's death and by so doing presents two very different kings through whom Bede arguably had specific messages which he sought to impart. Oswiu's kingship was introduced in book III, 14 via a heavily ironic contrast between the 'heavenly kingdom' (*caelestia regnum*) attained by his brother and the 'terrestrial kingdom' (*regnum terrestre*) which the new king held for 'twenty-eight most laboured years', during which he was attacked variously by the heathen Mercians, his own son and his nephew. His first act recounted by Bede, in this same chapter, was the brutal murder of King Oswine, for which he later founded Gilling monastery as an act of atonement. God goes almost unmentioned in the narrative in this passage surrounding Oswiu,[30] being included only in the brief aside which detailed the death of Paulinus, plus the longer section which narrated a conversation between Oswine and Aidan shortly before his death, by which Bede emphasised that king's humility and the love existing between them, and enabled Aidan to both prophesy and lament his friend's imminent destruction. Oswine was presented by Bede in most respects as a veritable stereotype of kingliness:

> However king Oswine was both beautiful of aspect and tall of stature, delightful in speech, courteous in manner, and generous to all, that is both nobles and commoners alike; whence it came about that he was loved by everyone on account of the royal dignity which was revealed in his spirit, his appearance and his actions; and noblemen from almost every province flocked to serve him. Among all the other manifestations of virtue and modesty with which, if I may say, he was blessed in particular glory, humility is said to have been the greatest.

The qualities vouchsafed Oswine here map on to Bede's somewhat briefer description of the East Saxon prince, Offa, as quoted above, and, by offering an idealised stereotype of the 'good king', have the effect of accentuating the evil done by Oswiu in encompassing his murder. However his exemplary humility also had its downside, for Bede placed in Aidan's mouth the words: 'I know the king will not prevail for long, for I have never before seen a humble king.' This has some similarities with another royal death which Bede recounted (III, 22), wherein King Sigeberht of the East Saxons was slain by his own men at the instigation of the devil because 'he was too ready to pardon his enemies, calmly forgiving them for wrongs done to him as soon as they asked his pardon'. The emphasis on martial qualities with which Bede had invested both Edwin and Oswald, was, therefore, a necessary part of his vision of kingship, and he did expect rulers to retain and exercise authority in political matters: in the last resort, Bede believed that kings should be scary. Without bravery and the power to induce fear in others, as well as love, all the kingly virtues in the world – as exhibited via this presentation of Oswine – might be insufficient to sustain the task of ruling a kingdom. Treachery, as here, was a risk for any king and none more than he who was insufficiently feared. These were further lessons of some political value offered by Bede to his audience.

The problems inherent in Oswiu's reign were rarely spelled out by Bede, who forbore to recount the details of his struggle with his son Alhfrith, for example, but there was an implicit connection throughout his treatment between his difficulties and the moral failings of his early kingship, which included marriage within the prohibited bounds of consanguinity (although that was never openly acknowledged), internecine conflict and murder within his own kin group. With this moral vacuum at the centre of his kingship, it was Aidan whose prayers Bede depicted as bringing divine relief to Bamburgh under siege by Penda and the Mercians (III, 16), not Oswiu's, and there is a stark difference in moral characterisation between Oswald and Oswiu. Following his repentance for his responsibility for Oswine's death, however, Oswiu's behaviour was depicted as improving dramatically. He was recognised as a prominent supporter of Christian mission among the Middle Angles and East Saxons (III, 21, 22), then when he was *in extremis* in the course of his struggle against Penda, whom he had already attempted to buy-off, he was depicted by Bede as having 'turned to God's mercy for help seeing that nothing else could save them from this barbarous and impious enemy'. The bargain struck by Oswiu with the Lord (III, 24), promising to found twelve monasteries plus dedicate his daughter as a nun, facilitated his presentation in the battle hand-in-hand with Christ, so as if a veritable King David overcoming the Philistine hosts. In the aftermath, Bede was prepared to recognise the tangible successes of Oswiu in liberating his own people from attacks and converting the Mercians, but he took the opportunity to remind his audience even at this juncture of Oswine's murder and the purpose served by Gilling monastery to expiate this crime, so deliberately detracting from Oswiu's moral capital. Oswiu was, therefore, presented by Bede as morally flawed, despite his great victory over the heathen and his furtherance of Christian mission. He failed to condemn the Mercian revolt just three years later, apparently considering that the newly converted people had a right to self-determination. So, Bede was implying, military success, however impressive, does not compensate for a lack of personal virtues in a king, crimes against God's law will always bring adverse consequences upon the heads of those involved, and problems in the secular arena necessarily follow moral failings. In Oswiu's case, his putative wish to retire to Rome (IV, 5) should he recover sufficiently from his final illness was not vouchsafed by the Lord and he died with this aim unfulfilled, in February 670, after a long rule, certainly, and one which showed an upward trajectory in moral terms, but one also which was depicted as difficult, unhappy and riven by dynastic as well as external strife.

As case studies, therefore, Oswiu and Oswine were developed by Bede for his audience as different types of flawed kingship: both exhibited certain strengths but also particular weaknesses which in each case detracted from the potential relationship between king and God.[31] The lessons herein for Ceolwulf were transparent.

Central to the messages that Bede was developing for his audience was the nature of relationships between kings and bishops, or other senior churchmen. Somewhat hesitantly, Edwin was depicted as having placed his influence behind Paulinus's preaching effort, which had hitherto failed to bear fruit (II, 9), resulting in a glorious transformation of the entire process. Oswald was by far the more proactive of the two: Bede presented him as having urged his friends on Iona to provide him with a bishop and then as having involved himself very closely in the Christianising process, restarting it successfully and laying new and better-lasting foundations, in close co-operation with Aidan. Oswine was on excellent terms with his bishop and readily prepared to listen to his advice; Oswiu was less so and suffered accordingly. Bede was promoting, therefore, the ideal of kings living in harmony with their bishops, listening to them on matters to do with the Church or their own spiritual welfare, supporting them by gift and deed, and respecting their authority in matters appropriate to their office. Difficulties between king and bishop were narrated in terms which make it clear that Bede believed that misfortune would generally result: so, for example, the murder of Sigeberht of the East Saxons (above) was interpreted as a consequence of his ignoring Bishop Cedd's excommunication of one of his followers, whose house he subsequently visited despite this prohibition, even despite his innocence of the charges laid against him by the actual perpetrators. In this respect, Bede's narration of the events centred on Archbishop Theodore's time in England provides perhaps the most apt set of examples, including as it does his treatment of dissension between King Ecgfrith and Bishop Wilfrid.

Although book IV actually opens with Colman's departure, it very quickly turns instead to the appointment and arrival of Theodore at Canterbury in May 669, instigating a new wave of learning among the English and resurrecting Bede's lengthy but somewhat episodic 'golden age' of English Christianity into a late flush of glory:

> Never at all, from when the Angles arrived in Britain, had there been such happy times, having such very brave and Christian kings to be a terror to all the barbarian nations, and the desires of all were set on the joys of the heavenly kingdom of which they had lately heard, and all those who desired instruction in sacred lessons had at hand masters who could teach [them].

We have here, therefore, Bede's celebration of a Rome-appointed and learned archbishop travelling to Britain to take over leadership of the Church of the English and actively engaging with his new province to stimulate Christian culture, in collaboration with the over-arching prowess of the English kings as emperor-like figures protecting their peoples against their 'barbarian' neighbours: the parallels that Bede was drawing here between England and Rome were powerful. Chad's consecration as bishop of the Mercians was offered as the first fruits of this new beginning, and Chad encapsulates in his own person much of Bede's agenda in this work. His appointment was depicted as consequential on a three-way process of co-operation between King Wulfhere, who requested the new appointment, Archbishop Theodore, who consecrated his preferred candidate, and King Oswiu, who allowed Chad, a Northumbrian cleric and ex-bishop then resident at 'his own monastery of Lastingham' (III, 3), to be advanced. Bede dwelt at considerable length on Chad's exceptional qualities as a churchman in the mould of Aidan, in whose tradition he had been trained, and on the miraculous nature of his death. Chad's bishopric was, therefore, idealised as regards all of its inception, its (brief) actuality and its closure, enabling Bede to offer his audience an exemplary case study in the way of life and personal conduct appropriate to a bishop and in the interaction between kings and the leaders of the Church.

The central relationships between kings and bishops on which Bede drew for his own moral purposes were, however, those centred on King Ecgfrith, who, like his father, was portrayed morally in this work as a highly ambivalent figure. He first appears as a hostage in Mercia in the context of Oswiu's great victory over Penda, which circumstance provides the necessary explanation of his failure to aid his father in his hour of need (III, 24), then as Oswiu's heir and successor (IV, 5), whose regnal years were used by Bede to contextualise the Synod of Hertford.[32] His expulsion of Wilfrid was introduced in a chapter (IV, 12) which was characterised by large-scale and disturbing upheavals across England: first Bede briefly contextualised the succession of the West Saxon diocese in terms of the rule of sub-kings who were overthrown by Cædwalla, but his rule only then lasted two years before he retired to Rome; then there came a terrible Mercian attack on Kent (in 676), which devastated the see of Rochester so severely that the bishop, Putta, withdrew in the face of the consequent levels of poverty and ruin; then Bede introduced a comet, which he dated to August 678,[33] as a divine portent of the dire events which occurred in Northumbria in that year, namely 'the dissension between King Ecgfrith himself and the most reverend Bishop Wilfrid', following which 'the same bishop was expelled from his see'. As already noted above, Bede took the opportunity to stress the moral status of the bishop, whom he termed *reverentissimus*, and he reinforced this by emphasis on his station, not just as *antistes* ('bishop') but as *antistes episcopatus* (the addition is virtually untranslatable but enhances Wilfrid's 'bishop-ness'). Juxtaposition of comet and expulsion clearly positioned God as concerned observer of these events, very much in parallel with Bede's similar treatment of the pair of comets which putatively appeared in 729, with which he introduced his narration of the immediate present in book V, 23. This was an invitation, therefore, to Ceolwulf to take heed of Ecgfrith's deeds, to recognise the reality of divine oversight and to learn from his mistakes.

Although he made no comment here on the issue, his *Letter to Egbert* of 734 makes it clear that Bede favoured the division of large sees and he had nothing personally against Wilfrid's several successors as bishops of the Northumbrians,[34] whom he named and referred to in neutral, matter-of-fact terms throughout the remainder of this chapter. He listed Bosa, promoted to York, and Eata, to Hexham/Lindisfarne, plus Eadhæd, to Lindsey, as all having been monks of good standing who were consecrated at York quite properly by Theodore, to whose number Tunberht and Trumwine were added some three years later, as bishops of Hexham and 'the Picts' (at Abercorn), respectively. Elsewhere in this work Bede particularly praised three of these individuals: Bosa would later be included as one of five bishops emanating from *Streanæshalch*, 'all men of singular merit and sanctity' (IV, 23); Eata had already (III, 26) been termed *reverentissimus ac mansuetissimus* ('most reverend and mild'), and Trumwine was *reverentissimus vir Domini* ('a most reverend man of the Lord': IV, 26). Eadhæd, as bishop of Lindsey then Ripon, hardly occurs outside this passage,[35] and Tunberht was later deposed and replaced with Cuthbert by Theodore in 685 (before he transferred to Lindisfarne: IV, 28 (26)), which presumably explains Bede's reticence regarding his character. What we have here is a bland exposition of diocesan succession across 'greater' Northumbria: indeed, Bede took the opportunity to rehearse the tangled history of the diocese of Lindsey, which depended very much on the shifting fortunes of Northumbrian and Mercian kings. He was not here providing a detailed account of Ecgfrith's kingship but focusing on the bishoprics subject to him. So although he did not entirely avoid the subject of Ecgfrith's victory over Wulfhere of the Mercians early in his reign, this was offered not as a matter to be narrated for its own sake but solely as political backdrop to the shifting affiliations of the see of Lindsey. The later inclusion of this victory in the very brief chronological notes included within the Moore Memoranda[36] suggests that it was a Northumbrian triumph of some significance that was long remembered at Wearmouth/Jarrow. This impression is confirmed by Stephen of Ripon's graphic allusion to it in his *Life of Wilfrid*, in parallel with a victory by Ecgfrith over the Picts apparently slightly earlier,[37] which Bede never mentions. This can be read as having given Ecgfrith temporary 'overkingship' in the mid-670s, which in turn presumably contextualised his expulsion of Wilfrid.[38]

Stephen's message to his 'Wilfridian' audience was that Ecgfrith triumphed over his enemies when obedient 'in all things' to his bishop, but suffered reverses and eventually death after the king had succumbed to the advice of the 'wicked Jezebel', his second wife Iurminburg, and first humiliated then expelled the bishop, but Stephen was not writing for a royal audience. Bede was far less keen than Stephen to make direct and explicit connections between Ecgfrith's dispute with Wilfrid and his eventual political and military failure, preferring to avoid the moral caricaturing of the earlier writer in favour of a more nuanced portrayal of the king, even while sustaining the moral status of the bishop whom he had wronged. He used the following chapter (IV, 13), therefore, to emphasise the apostolic status of Wilfrid, describing at considerable length his missionary work among the South Saxons, so portraying him as triumphant as an agent of the Lord even in adversity,[39] to which he later added a miracle story connecting Wilfrid's foundation of Selsey with the cult of St Oswald (IV, 14). By such means, Bede was reinforcing his moral support for Wilfrid in his dispute with Ecgfrith and establishing him as an exemplary churchman, but without explicitly contesting the status of the king who had excluded him. Rather, Ecgfrith's position was left in a state of ambiguity, as Bede may well have felt constrained to do in writing of a recent ruler in a work dedicated to a king in the present, albeit not one of his lineage. Presumably Bede would not have wished to risk writing in a manner which could have been construed as anti-monarchical, or in any sense socially subversive.

Thereafter, Bede's treatment of the king remained comparatively neutral: Ecgfrith occurs in the passage transcribed by Bede from the 'synodal book' in which Theodore provided an account of the Synod of Hatfield (IV, 17 (15)), in which he was the first mentioned of four *domini piissimi* ('most pious lords'), then as the patron of Wearmouth and an approving party to Benedict Biscop's acquisition of a letter of privileges from Pope Agatho (IV, 18 (16)). His marriage to the East Anglian Æthelthryth opens book IV, 19 (17), in a passage which underlines Bede's caution regarding his characterisation by emphasising the exceptional qualities of first his deceased father-in-law, King Anna, whom he here termed 'a very religious man and wholly noble in both mind and deed', then Æthelthryth herself, who, despite her two husbands, 'retained the glorious state of perpetual virginity' throughout the twelve years of their marriage.[40] It was perhaps no accident that Bishop Wilfrid 'of blessed memory' was here reintroduced as his witness to the queen's virginity, which he vouched for in part by virtue of Ecgfrith's offer of lands and precious gifts should the bishop persuade her to consummate her marriage. Wilfrid's involvement here as expert witness appears somewhat ironic, given the dissension between king and bishop which Bede had already described. Proofs of Æthelthryth's sanctity and her retirement to become a nun and later an abbess then dominate the remainder of this chapter, with the one that follows given over by Bede to a hymn on the subject of virginity, which he had earlier composed in her honour.[41]

From this hymn in praise of Æthelthryth, Bede passed directly to one of his shortest chapters (IV, 21),[42] which centred on the death in a battle fought between Ecgfrith and Æthelred of the Mercians by the River Trent of Ecgfrith's brother, King Ælfwine.[43] Although Bede forbore to make the outcome explicit, perhaps for reasons of Northumbrian pride, it becomes clear in the following chapter that this was a Mercian victory, given that it was the Mercian army which retained control of the field of battle – his audience will have known the outcome in any case. His moral contextualisation of the event is complex, but significant: the ambiguous figure of Ecgfrith had in previous chapters been associated with several individuals whom Bede held in high regard, including Bishop Wilfrid, Archbishop Theodore, King Anna and Queen/Abbess Æthelthryth, but he had now expelled the first and relinquished marriage to the last – and, through her, kinship with Anna's family as well. Ælfwine comes over as another of Bede's exemplary young royals, out of the same mould that had already produced Oswine and would later provide the East Saxons with Prince Offa, but his promise and popularity were lost to Ecgfrith at this point, leaving Theodore to preside over peace negotiations between the Northumbrian and Mercian kings and secure his brother nominal compensation for this death. Ecgfrith was being presented by Bede, therefore, as suffering his first defeat in battle in the late 670s and by then increasingly bereft of the counsel of the great and the good with whom he had earlier been associated.

Bede included at this point a small group of passages designed to sustain and reinforce the authority of Northumbrian Christianity and its special place in God's affection, prior to his narration of the final defeat and death of Ecgfrith, which he presented as a cusp point in his overall story in IV, 26 (24). First (IV, 22 (20)) comes an apparently well-known miracle story associated with one of Ælfwine's Northumbrian warriors named Imma, who, having been left for dead on the field of battle by the River Trent, was captured by the Mercians and sold into slavery, only for his fetters to fall off miraculously every time his brother, the priest and abbot Tunna, said masses for his soul. Bede was telling this story ostensibly at least because it had inspired many to 'greater faith and devotion, prayer and the giving of alms, and to the offering of sacrifices to God in the holy oblation' for the sake of their near departed. He claimed to have heard it from those who had had it from Imma himself, so from some of the numerous unnamed Northumbrian informants whom he mentioned in the Preface, but the topos of the prisoner whose chains fell off whenever a family member had masses said for his soul is to be found in Gregory's *Dialogues*,[44] and has connections also with Stephen's description of Wilfrid's imprisonment in Northumbria,[45] so may well be apocryphal. Bede may also have been conscious of Jerome's use of *vinctus* (literally 'a binding') to denote St Paul's role as 'prisoner of the Lord' on behalf of the gentiles.[46] The underlying purpose of this passage seems to be to substantiate the efficacy of masses said by a member of the Northumbrian élite on behalf of his brother and so establish God as accessible via ritual to the priests of His chosen people. It was not the Northumbrians, therefore, whose position vis-à-vis the Lord was becoming critical but Ecgfrith alone, whose defeat this was and who had lost his own brother in a battle in which God had given judgement against him.

Hild's death and a retrospective review of her life provide the second of this group (IV, 23 (21)). Hild is depicted in highly favourable terms, as beloved of the Lord and as a figure through whom the conversion history of the Northumbrians was bound together across much of the seventh century: she had, Bede informs us, been baptised in company with King Edwin back in the 620s through Paulinus, and then during the next reign had thought to journey to Frankia to join her sister, Hereswith, as a nun, but had been recalled to Northumbria by Bishop Aidan and had become abbess first of Hartlepool, then of *Kælcacæstir* and finally of *Streanæshalch* (?Whitby), where, of course, Oswiu presided over the meeting at which the adoption of the Roman method of dating Easter was agreed in 664. Hild is presented as the counsellor of kings (albeit they are unnamed) and as one who required her inmates to study the Scriptures so as to attain the learning necessary for high office in the church, producing five bishops, whose careers Bede here summarised as a complement to her achievements. Thence he turned to her exemplary personal qualities, to the 'signs' vouchsafed her mother that her daughter's achievements were to be veritable 'works of light', then to her exemplary death, to which the Lord likewise attached the *signa* of heavenly light, and of a vision of her ascent to heaven. In one of the longest chapters in this work,[47] Bede was here adopting a range of hagiographical techniques to present Hild, a long-lived and extremely well-connected member of the Northumbrian royal house, as saint. Hild's career has the effect at this point of reminding Bede's audience of Northumbria's deep roots in the conversion stories surrounding Edwin and Paulinus, in the first instance, and then Oswald and Aidan, and the reconciliation between the northern kings and Rome at the synod of 664, so rendering the subsequent loss of divine support by Ecgfrith the more dramatic.

The next chapter (IV, 24 (22)) then adds to this picture through the story of Cædmon, a poor servant of Hild's house whom God singled out to compose 'religious and pious songs', whom the abbess in consequence made a choir monk, had educated in the Scriptures and encouraged in his song-writing, and whom Bede finally describes as having died a 'good' death. Although there is a great deal in this chapter of interest to modern scholarship,[48] it seems to have been included here by Bede as an addendum to his treatment of Hild to provide further evidence of the exceptional sanctity and spiritual wealth of the community over which she ruled, as well as mark a cusp moment in Northumbrian Christianity's translation into a vernacular context. *Deus* ('God') occurs herein nine times as well as in several other guises – so as 'Maker', 'Creator', 'Father', 'Author' and 'Guardian', and *Dominus* (as Christ) three times – and there are two references to the Scriptures in general, and others to specific parts thereof. These two chapters should probably be read together, since they were arguably composed as a doublet concerning the special relationship which Bede wished to portray between God and Hild, in person, and the monastery over which she presided.[49]

It is noteworthy that Bede should have deployed two exemplary royal women in this section of his work interspersed with the deeds and career of Ecgfrith, first his wife Æthelthryth and then his cousin Hild. These are by far his longest and most reverential portrayals of women in this work. Both occur in paired chapters. In both instances the first offers a summary of the heroine's life, leading to a 'good' death. In both a second chapter was added with the general theme of verse: in Æthelthryth's case this is a piece of Bede's own writing, in Hild's it is a celebration of her poet, Cædmon. This patterning is unlikely to have been coincidental and the overall result is to leave the audience uplifted by the wonderful stories surrounding these royal heroines, whose deeds conjure once more the sense of a golden age of divine favour still capable of celebration in the years up to 680.

The last of this group of chapters (IV, 25 (23)) is a stark reminder that the benign God who had been cultivated so effectively by Æthelthryth and Hild was also a vengeful God, impatient of wickedness. This is the story of the burning of Coldingham nunnery, which was offered by Bede as a case study in divine retribution, but the emphasis is on one inmate, Adamnan, an Irish penitent, whose vision of impending disaster acted as a warning of divine vengeance that was carried to the abbess, Æbbe, who was, of course, Ecgfrith's aunt. Bede used here extensive direct speech to bring the whole scene to life for his own audience and elaborated the sins of the brethren in some detail:

> For the cells, which were constructed for prayer or reading, now are dens
> of feasting, of drinking, of story telling, and other delights; even the
> virgins dedicated to God put aside respect for their profession and, when-
> ever they have free time, spend it in weaving elaborate clothes with
> which they adorn themselves as if brides, so placing at risk their virgin-
> ity, or to make friends with men from outside. Therefore it is only right
> that a heavy vengeance from heaven is preparing on this place and its
> inhabitants in the form of raging fire.

Such presumably had considerable generic value to a monastic writer and
Bede ostensibly included this morality tale about crime and punishment as a
general warning to his audience concerning God's wrath, but its positioning
in the work is hardly accidental. It follows the paired chapters dedicated to
honouring Hild and her community and immediately precedes his description of Ecgfrith's destruction. Its focus on warning messages which, in the
last resort, went unheeded has an important role as precursor to the far greater
calamity about to occur, with the killing of Ecgfrith in far-off Pictland as a
direct consequence of his sin in ravaging Ireland: Adamnan's role as the Irish
prophet-figure here is telling. This was provided, therefore, as a prelude to
Ecgfrith's fate, and as an exposition on the dangers of ignoring the warnings
of those favoured by the Lord, but instead rousing Him to anger by continued
wickedness.

It is in chapter 26 (24) that this warning then comes to fruition, in a
passage which has powerful connections with what has gone before. It opens
with notice of Ecgfrith's despatch of forces to invade Ireland, under his
ealdorman Berht, which Bede abhors as having 'wretchedly ravaged a people
who were both harmless and always very friendly towards the nation of the
English' and spared neither church nor monastery. The Irish resisted and
called down divine vengeance on their attackers, and Bede made it clear that
he purposed to link this to Ecgfrith's subsequent fate. The king then 'heed-
lessly' led an army to ravage the Picts, ignoring the urgings of unnamed
friends and particularly St Cuthbert. Bede recounted his death, taken in by a
feigned retreat by the Picts into the hill-country of eastern Scotland, but then
immediately reverted to his theme of good advice ignored, stressing again
that he had been forewarned against the expedition by his friends, and likewise even by the *reverentissimus pater* ('most reverend father') Egbert, against
his attack on the Irish the year before: 'the punishment handed down to him
for this sin was that he would never hear those who wished to save him from
ruin'. This is, therefore, primarily a morality tale told against Ecgfrith, whom
Bede represented as set on a wicked course of action despite the warnings of
friends and senior churchmen, which led inexorably to divine punishment of
the king himself, his army, and the Northumbrians as a people, who had
never since enjoyed so successful a period as had occurred under Oswiu and
then his son and successor.

Ecgfrith was depicted by Bede, therefore, as having become detached from the advice of the God-fearing and wise: he had himself expelled the good bishop Wilfrid from his kingdom and divorced the saintly Æthelthryth; his kinswoman Hild, who was a renowned counsellor of kings and reverend abbess, had died in 680, and his aunt, the abbess Æbbe, was also deceased before 685; although he had worked closely in the past with the venerable Theodore, the last contact between them noted by Bede was in *c.*670, when the archbishop undertook to reconcile him with his enemies. His brother, Ælfwine, who was popular and might have had some potential to give him good advice was cut down as a consequence of his warfare. Egbert, one of Bede's exemplary Englishmen in his *Greater Chronicle* and a figure of exceptional moral status in this work as well, had warned against the Irish expedition of 684 but had been ignored. Although Ecgfrith had played a major role in persuading Cuthbert to accept a bishopric – albeit Bede did not refer to the matter until the following chapter – in 685 he ignored his advice, as well as that of other, unnamed friends, but pursued the course of action destined to lead to his own downfall. To this point Ecgfrith had been a morally ambivalent figure but in this chapter the picture clarifies and he is depicted as if rushing towards destruction, bringing down divine vengeance on his own head as a result of his unjust and ill-judged behaviours.

Cuthbert's connection with Ecgfrith's final battle already had a lengthy literary history by 731. The anonymous *Life of Cuthbert* had told the story of a conversation between Cuthbert and Abbess Ælfflæd, which had the solitary prophesying his imminent death and Aldfrith's succession, albeit somewhat abstrusely, then an account of Cuthbert at Carlisle having knowledge of the battle as it occurred, with the venerable bishop portrayed as witnessing at a distance this unfolding of the judgement of God.[50] Bede had followed this lead in both of his own lives of Cuthbert,[51] but initially without the strong sense of Ecgfrith's personal responsibility for his own destruction which he later developed in the *Ecclesiastical History*. The earlier *Metrical Life* has: 'the great sun having completed a year within its customary months, Ecgfrith is killed by the hostile sword of the Picts, and the bastard brother [Aldfrith] succeeded to the honour of the royal kingdom'.[52] This was written, of course, when Ecgfrith's (half-)nephew had succeeded to the throne following Aldfrith's death in 705, and Bede had a more critical vision of these events when he returned to the subject over a decade later,[53] when he developed the story in his *Prose Life* along the same general lines as he would in the *Ecclesiastical History*, using some of the same language by which to place responsibility on Ecgfrith's wickedness.[54]

Bede then set out the consequences of Ecgfrith's actions, using a quotation from Virgil's *Aeneid*. Colgrave and Mynors listed five passages in which quotations occur from this work in the *Ecclesiastical History*, but two are mere echoes.[55] Of the remaining three, in III, 11 Bede used Virgil's depiction of the audience awaiting the opening line of Aeneas's narration of the sack of Troy, which opens book I, to develop suspense as a group of monks awaited the outcome of having used some of the soil from Oswald's place of death to heal a sick man, while V, 12 orchestrates Dryhthelm's vision with a quotation from Aeneas's visit to the underworld.[56] Each was used for rhetorical effect, therefore, and this example was no exception, with Bede utilising a quotation from a passage which spelled out the consequences of a terrible sacrilege perpetrated by Diomedes and Ulysses, which roused the anger of Minerva and brought down divine vengeance on the heads of the Greeks as a whole.[57] Just as their particular acts had dire consequences for their whole people, so too did Ecgfrith's: Bede detailed the loss of recently conquered land back to the Picts and the collapse of Northumbrian hegemony over the Irish in Britain (Dalriada) and 'some part of the British nation' (Strathclyde, or part thereof, is generally assumed[58]). The English were variously slain or fled from Pictish territory and Bishop Trumwine, 'a most reverend man of the Lord', retired from Abercorn because of its proximity to lands now controlled by the Picts and dispersed the community, retiring himself to Streanæshalch (?Whitby), then ruled by Ecgfrith's sister, Ælfflæd, and his mother, Eanflæd, where he was eventually buried in the church of St Peter. The rhetorical significance of Hild's house was, therefore, here re-emphasised at the close of Bede's narration of Ecgfrith's death, reinforcing the relevance of previous passages on the old abbess's death and Cædmon's special, God-given talents to Ecgfrith's own destruction, and implying that Bede was here seeking to separate a God-beloved people, the Northumbrians, and the merits, in particular, of several of their great royal churches and monasteries, from the iniquities of the individual ruler. Aldfrith succeeded his half-brother and Bede could use the fact of his scriptural learning here to establish his greater virtue, but it was a smaller realm which he then restored, suggesting that Ecgfrith's iniquity had lasting impacts upon the body politic. Thereafter, Bede turned away from Northumbrian affairs to work-in contemporary Kentish affairs, noting the death of King Hlothhere and various difficulties thereafter until the kingdom came into the hands of Wihtred, his nephew, whom Bede – presumably on the basis of his Kentish informant, Abbot Albinus – considered 'the rightful king'. Like other Late Antique authors, Bede liked to group political problems into particular passages and this provides a characteristic example of the style.

The remainder of this book then consists of six closely linked chapters recounting the story of St Cuthbert from his consecration as bishop (IV, 27 (25)), through the exceptional virtues of his early life as a monk, his role as a hermit and several miracles attached thereto, the universal pressure for his consecration, then the story of his knowledge of his own death-date and the event itself, fortified (in IV, 30 (28)) by the story of his intact condition some eleven years later and, finally, post-mortem miracles (IV, 31, 32 (29, 30)). The effect is very largely to shift attention away from Ecgfrith's terrible end to the God-beloved Christian hero, but these passages also serve to enhance Cuthbert's reputation as a man close to God, so put into stark relief Ecgfrith's perverse refusal to listen to his advice in 685. Through Cuthbert, Bede was stressing that it was not Northumbria's churchmen who had failed, for the 'signs' of God's love for them and His special favour remained clearly manifest. The failure was royal: Ecgfrith, alone, had distanced himself from God-beloved figures around him and ignored their warnings, rushing to his own destruction.

What was Ceolwulf expected to take away from this, Bede's principal, royal example of what he had termed in the Preface *mala de pravis* ('the evil deeds of perverse men')? The message seems reasonably clear: Ecgfrith's mistakes were to expel and/or ignore the advice of his senior clergy in pursuit of his own ill-advised and wicked ambitions; the result was a terrible retribution wrought by the Lord. In the context of the events of 731, this should be read as making the case for the king listening to his senior clerics and behaving in ways they might consider appropriate to a Christian king, rather than engaging in political in-fighting with them or ravaging his neighbours like a pagan king of old, as Ecgfrith had done. Juxtaposition of Ecgfrith's behaviour and particularly his death with those of the monastics, Æthelthryth, Hild, Cædmon and Cuthbert, had considerable power to persuade his audience to walk in paths which Bede considered righteous. Ceolwulf's eventual retirement to the monastic life certainly conforms to the rationale which Bede here seems to have been pursuing, but it would be rash to suppose that there was necessarily a causal connection between the arguments underlying Bede's *EH* and the life chosen for himself by the king of the day, two years after its author's own death and six years after this work's completion.

King Aldfrith was presented initially as a figure of renewal, healing the dissension and turmoil of Ecgfrith's reign. He was 'a man very learned in the Scriptures' who 'nobly recovered the kingdom from its shattered condition, albeit within narrower boundaries', but Ecgfrith's successor also received somewhat ambivalent treatment from Bede, who (as already noted) distanced himself from his claim to royal kinship. His regnal years were used to contextualise Bishop Eata's death and the succession to Hexham of John of Beverley (V, 2), whose miracle stories make up the most substantial group of chapters in the final book. In Aldfrith's third regnal year he then described Cædwalla's retirement to Rome (V, 7), by which Bede was setting out royal behaviour of a kind which he considered particularly appropriate in the present, following on from his more general comments concerning English individuals making the pilgrimage to Rome in his *Greater Chronicle*, which he had there individualised through the person of his own abbot, Ceolfrith. Bede then (V, 12) depicted Dryhthelm relating his visions of the afterlife to Aldfrith, 'a most learned man in every way, who listened freely and carefully', and arranged for him to be admitted to Melrose Abbey (see below). Next the king acted as host to Adamnan, from Iona, on a mission to learn about the Roman dating of Easter (V, 15), who donated to him a copy of his work on the holy places, which Bede later abridged.

Aldfrith comes comparatively well out of these several entries but is nowhere singled out for exceptional approval or praise. Bede dealt with his death in a bare and matter-of-fact account which opens V, 18, which then proceeds to detail miracles associated with the West Saxon bishop, Hædde. The lack of connection between the Northumbrian succession, on the one hand, and Hædde's death, 'signs' of his sanctity and the succession of his diocese thereafter – to include notice of Aldhelm – is very apparent and Bede seems here deliberately to avoid making any extended comment on Aldfrith, in part owing to the sensitivity of the current dynastic situation but also perhaps because of that aspect of his reign to which he had so far made no allusion, to which he turned in his extended retrospect concerning Wilfrid (V, 19). The bishop had been restored in Aldfrith's second regnal year but then had been expelled again five years later, 'by the king himself and several bishops', eliciting another of Wilfrid's journeys to Rome and complete vindication at the hands of the papacy. On his return, despite the support of Archbishop Berhtwold and Æthelred, once king of Mercia and now abbot of Bardney, 'Aldfrith, king of the Northumbrians, scorned to receive him, but he did not survive for long'. Aldfrith had, therefore, failed to accept a papal decision on Wilfrid's behalf and, although his rapid decease thereafter was not explicitly associated with that event, an implicit connection between his obstinacy and death is inescapable.

Like Ecgfrith, therefore, Aldfrith had failed to accept the advice of the godly – here the pope of the day. While Coenred of the Mercians, with whom Wilfrid had been reconciled, went on to renounce his throne and retire 'even more nobly' to Rome (V, 19), Aldfrith died in office without the opportunity to make any such settlement of his own spiritual life and in a moral condition which was necessarily marred, in Bede's eyes, by his obstinacy. Again, Ceolwulf was being offered the vision of a king whose behaviour was ambivalent. Aldfrith was exceptionally learned and open to warnings concerning the life to come offered by Dryhthelm, both of which had considerable value in Bede's estimation, but his obstinacy when it came to papal instruction concerning a member of the episcopacy was a serious issue. Once again, Ceolwulf was being offered the example of a past king whose behaviours Bede considered to be flawed in the area of relations with his duly appointed bishop.

One aspect of Bede's *Ecclesiastical History* which has come out of this discussion is the presumption that he intended his audience to take away from particular passages a very immediate message relevant to themselves in the here and now. It is as if he viewed successive kings as the captains of a ship of state: following the excellence of Oswald's stewardship, Oswiu's captaincy had led that ship into the shallows but it had survived the threat, regaining deep water by virtue of the captain's timely rediscovery of God; Ecgfrith's had, however, then holed it below the waterline by his obstinacy and unwillingness to accept good advice; Aldfrith's captaincy, despite his undoubted religiosity, had failed to rekindle divine approbation, falling down on the issue of papal advocacy of Wilfrid.

To test this presumption more fully, I now propose to turn to ways in which Bede constructed connections between his narration of history and the present, both across the more distant past and also in the most recent section of this work, in book V, to examine the overall strategies that he was pursuing herein. We will again be interested in the messages that he anticipated that his audience might take away from his work, but at the forefront will be Bede's sense of the contemporaneity and currency of his *historia*, to the audience which he had in mind as he wrote it.

The immediate: the present in the *Ecclesiastical History*

Across the *Ecclesiastical History*, Bede made comparatively frequent connections between his treatment of the past and the present, using such terms as *hodie* ('today'),[59] *in praesenti* ('at the present time')[60] and *nunc* ('now').[61] These begin in book I, 1, the geographical and ethnographical introduction, which is very largely written in the present tense, with notice of, for example, the current (*nunc*) Anglo-Saxon vernacular name of Richborough, the five languages spoken *in praesenti* ('in the present'), and matrilineal Pictish inheritance customs practised *usque hodie* ('even today'). When dealing with very distant events both in time and place, Bede often reinforced the immediacy of his narrative by alluding to particular current landmarks in the context of the past, whether or not these were likely to have been familiar to his immediate, Northumbrian audience. So, for example, he noted that the thick stakes encased in lead which he had Cassivelaunus's troops using to defend the Thames crossings against Julius Caesar were visible *usque hodie* ('even today': I, 2), which few of his immediate audience will have seen for themselves unless they happen to have crossed the Thames on their way, perhaps, to Canterbury or the Channel crossings. Similarly, the cities, lighthouse (at Dover, presumably), bridges and roads which characterised Roman government of Britain still testified to that rule *usque hodie* (I, 11). Ceolwulf and his associates may well have been better acquainted with the Antonine and Hadrianic walls (I, 12), both of which Bede proclaimed to be visible *usque hodie* (I, 12), at least in parts. Likewise he gave the name of the place *hodie* where Coifi's idols had stood a century or more earlier (II, 13), so giving it a present locale within southern Northumbria and rendering more credible his story of Edwin's great council called to determine whether or not he should accept Christianity, the details at least of which were probably to a large extent fictional.[62] This was not, of course, a practice on Bede's part restricted to Anglo-Saxon England: he elaborated his vision of the English Settlement (in I, 15), in which he described the regional peoples whom he considered to be descended variously from the Jutes, Saxons and Angles, by stating that the district of *Angulus* (Angeln, now on the Danish/German borders) had remained deserted by virtue of the English emigration, *ab eo tempore usque hodie* ('from that time even to the present'). This was apparently hearsay, rather than specific information from a named individual, and may have been nothing more than a story then current in England, but it makes the point that Bede made no effort to limit such observations to information which his intended audience was likely to be able to verify through personal experience.

Bede's purposes in making such connections across time can be illustrated to good effect by detailed attention to a particular passage. Let us take book II, 16: Paulinus had built, Bede told his audience, 'an extraordinary stone church' at Lincoln, the walls of which stood *hactenus* ('up to now'), even despite the collapse of the roof; the efficacy of the site was demonstrated by 'signs' which had occurred every year (so, implicitly at least, up to the present) as miracles continued to occur there; he then offered a description of Bishop Paulinus, which he had had from one Abbot Deda of Partney, who had in turn derived it from 'a certain old man' who had been baptised by Paulinus, probably before 633 and certainly before 644, so bringing this Italian very much to life for his audience a century later. 'He had also', Bede added, 'James the Deacon associated with him in his ministry . . . who remained *ad nostra usque tempora*' ('even to our time': he survived at least to the mid-660s so close to Bede's own birth date); lastly, Bede added the proverb still repeated *usque hodie* regarding the peace and tranquillity of the land under Edwin's kingship (see p. 150).

The intended effect seems to be twofold. In the first place, Bede was attempting to make connections between his narrative and the web of knowledge among his immediate audience which he had anticipated as a means of rendering his narrative of a comparatively distant past less foreign than it might otherwise have seemed and so both more accessible and more credible. By so doing he was, in effect, attempting to underpin the veracity of his stories where these were beyond verification via recourse to other sources of information, in the expectation that to substantiate particular parts of his account might carry with it the inference that the whole story was true. Secondly, he seems to have been emphasising the interconnection of past events with the present, in terms both of causal explanation and of the overarching unity of a history in which the dominant factor was consistently, in Bede's view, the immanence of the Lord. Such interconnections had considerable value to a presentation of the past as a set of exemplary behaviours, each of which involved interaction with a just and benevolent God, but one who was impatient of human failings in general, and of royal failings in particular.

Bede's insistence on the currency of past events goes well beyond his use of particular words, pervading much of his narrative. So, for example, King Eadwulf (II, 15) 'in our time' could recall seeing the temple used by Rædwald in East Anglia, the golden cross taken south by Paulinus *c.*633 was 'still preserved' in Kent at the time of writing 'to this day' (III, 1), the year of the two apostate kings (633–4) 'remains unfortunate and very hateful to all good [men]', the place of Oswald's cross is still shown 'today' (III, 2), Bothelm, whose miracle story Bede recounted concerning it, 'is still living', Oswald's arm and hand, cut off in 642, 'remain incorrupt right up to the present' (III, 6), and the soil from the place of his death heals both men and beasts 'to this day' (III, 9). This is a recurring and comparatively frequent refrain, therefore, of some potency, which had the effect of reinforcing his message in the present and assuring his audience of the relevance of his narration of the often distant past to their own lives.

Another rhetorical device which Bede used on occasion was direct speech, through which past figures were depicted as if speaking directly to Bede's own audience, and this was again a strategy used with some frequency to bring together past and present. This was a common feature of works of many different kinds accessible to Bede, including the *Aeneid*, the Bible and the version of Eusebius's *Ecclesiastical History* translated and extended by Rufinus, so Bede had strong precedents for adopting this style. On occasion, he was conforming to the practice used by a source, as, for example, in his treatment of the Synod of Whitby (III, 25), which he developed from Stephen's *Life of Wilfrid*,[63] which made dramatic use of the same technique, resulting in one of Bede's chapters which features this device most prolifically, but elsewhere Bede himself seems to have introduced direct speech, often quite sparingly but always for dramatic effect. So, for example, he placed a prayer of just six words in Aidan's mouth (III, 16), in response to which Bamburgh was saved by the Lord from Penda's attempts to fire it, and Oswiu's petition to the Lord (III, 24) when *in extremis* as a consequence of Penda's attacks presages Bede's depiction of the ensuing conflict as a characteristically Christian triumph by a 'David' figure over a type of the biblical 'Goliath'. On other occasions, Bede used direct speech as a strategy through which to encourage his audience to credit his stories. A typical example is the role of the doctor, Cynefrith, whom Bede deployed in verification of the incorrupt state of Æthelthryth when her tomb was reopened. Cynefrith was quoted as if verbatim describing the state of an incision which he had made to drain a tumour shortly before her death (IV, 19), which appeared healed when the body was exhumed, rather than the 'open gaping wound' with which she had been buried. Other miracle stories in which Bede used the same strategy include the healing of a man possessed by an unclean spirit by the soil from Oswald's place of death (III, 11), Egbert's assertion that Cedd and a company of angels had been seen descending from heaven to take the soul of his brother Chad back with him (IV, 3), the vision of the apostles experienced by the little Saxon boy at Selsey (IV, 14), and Adamnan's warnings concerning the destruction of Coldingham (IV, 25).

The use of direct speech is not surprising, particularly as Bede had already used the same strategy in his prose *Life of Cuthbert*, for example, but the way it was deployed reinforces the underlying sense of a text which used depictions of the past as a vehicle capable of delivering moral messages in the present. It was carefully deployed and it conveys a sense of theatre, so injecting an illusion of the audience as immediate witnesses of history into a work which is otherwise a succession of stories which they were expected to hear from the lips of a single narrator. Judicious use of direct speech makes the *EH* more variable as a piece of extended prose than it would otherwise have been, so better capable of retaining attention, and the sense of direct communication between past and present arguably assisted absorption of its messages. Such rhetorical ploys reveal Bede as an accomplished writer in command of his medium, as one would expect.

Book V: agenda and discourse

To this point, we have been exploring Bede's strategies as author via scattered instances of particular types. Another approach is to take a section of the work and examine what he was attempting to achieve and the means he utilised to that end. Book V is perhaps the section of the *Ecclesiastical History* least used by historians attempting to write the history of the period, in part because of his reticence regarding matters which might be dynastically sensitive as he moved into the lifetimes of the current generation of the political élite, but that said, he may never have intended to speak at much length about current events: as he explained in the Preface, his intention had been to concentrate *priorum gestis sive dictis* ('on the deeds or words of men of old'). If his work was intended to a large extent as a gallery of examples, both good and bad, then there was no particular merit in seeking such from the more dangerous recent past when there were plenty of less contentious instances to be had from an earlier date. In that context it is, perhaps, somewhat surprising that Bede did offer his final book, the chronology of which is, very broadly, the period from the death of Bishop Cuthbert in the late 680s to the present. It is, however, in no sense a connected narrative covering the previous forty-five years or so, even though much chronological data was included, but a book which is managed internally by reference to specific themes, through which, once again, Bede sought to convey particular messages to his present audience.[64] Given its comparative neglect in recent years and the marginality of descriptions of current events, it may be appropriate here to focus on this last book as an example of how Bede set about treating the past, in such a way as to underscore his methods and promote his overall objectives.

Book V is divided into twenty-four chapters of highly variable length,[65] the longest of which, containing Ceolfrith's letter to the Picts, is the second longest in the whole work.[66] Surprisingly, perhaps, given the comparative lack of interest of recent scholarship, book V is one of the longest books of the five (see table 1), despite its comparatively modest number of chapters, in part because it has several exceptionally long passages.[67] Excluding the Preface, overall the *Ecclesiastical History* has some 8956 lines in the Colgrave and Mynors edition, averaging around sixty-four lines per chapter. Book V has nine chapters longer than the average and four over twice as long.

As already noted above, Book IV ends with a succession of Cuthbert's miracles, offered as 'signs' of his closeness to God, so also, of course, of Ecgfrith's culpability in ignoring his advice in IV, 26 (24). Book V then opens with a miracle story associated with Cuthbert's successor on Farne, one Œthelwald, which serves to sustain the vision of Cuthbert's hermitage as a site of particular potency into the present and God's continuing support for his successor. There are significant connections made here, with Bede contextualising Œthelwald as an erstwhile monk and priest at Ripon – which was Wilfrid's first monastic foundation, of course – and crediting the story to Guthfrith, *venerabilis Christi famulus et presbyter* ('a venerable servant of Christ and priest') at Lindisfarne, who later became abbot there, and whom Bede had presumably met on his visit(s). The transfer of personnel from one house to another is characteristic of the period but the effect here is to associate both Ripon and Lindisfarne with the forthcoming miracle, to their joint benefit.[68] The actual miracle story was then recounted entirely in direct speech,[69] so giving the illusion that Bede was transcribing verbatim the story which he had had from Guthfrith (which he had probably heard years earlier) and rendering it the more immediate to his audience as readers and listeners. God is omnipresent in this passage, answering the needs of His servants, so confirming that they were indeed righteous: Cuthbert is depicted as *vir Domini* ('the man of the Lord'); Œthelwald, who was *amantissimus Deo* ('best-beloved by God') and *vir Dei* ('the man of God'), prayed *ad patrem Domini nostri Iesu Christi* ('to the father of our Lord Jesus Christ') that He would calm the sea and enable his visitors to gain the shore safely through the storm. The actual miracle is reminiscent of ones which Bede had already ascribed to Germanus (I, 17) and Aidan (III, 15), but all are variants ultimately of biblical miracles,[70] so compare the hero-figure with either Christ or St Paul to his obvious benefit. Bede concluded the chapter by remarking that Œthelwald remained on Farne for twelve years – the apostolic number – and was buried in St Peter's on Lindisfarne 'near the bodies of the aforesaid bishops', being Cuthbert and Eadberht, to whose proximate burials he had referred at the close of IV, 30 (28) as a place of continuing healing miracles.

The effect of this opening chapter is to ground Bede's final book in the virtues of God's beloved agents, still active in the recent past despite the decease of particular hero-figures such as Cuthbert, whose ministry God had validated by such wondrous 'signs' at the close of the previous book. Through Œthelwald, the cult sites of Farne and Lindisfarne, which had been established as places of particular veneration initially by association with Aidan then revalidated by connection with Cuthbert, were presented as of continuing potency. Given that Bede was writing for a king who may have been known to have had a particular interest in these cults, this opening of book V perhaps had some capacity to engage with the predilections of his audience.

Bede then turned to achieve a similar effect on behalf of the community of Hexham, where the embattled Acca was, of course, bishop in 731, through a succession of miracle stories associated with Bishop John (of Beverley), attributed to *maxime vir reverentissimus ac veracissimus Bercthun* ('the truly very reverend and most truthful man Berhthun'), whom he described as *nunc* ('now') abbot of *Inderavuda* ('In the wood of the Deirans', later identified as Beverley[71]). The miracle which follows utilises direct speech and positions John as both healer and teacher of a dumb youth, whose incapacity was emphasised by his scabby appearance, which was likewise cured on his learning to speak. Words were, of course, central to Bede's conception of the relationship between God and Man, having even initiated the whole process of Creation in Genesis,[72] and John's achievement in humanising this type of Caliban-figure was here compared with those of the apostles Peter and John, healing a lame man.[73]

Through John, again, Bede then validated the embattled Bishop Wilfrid as well, who had been restored to Hexham *c.*705 (V, 3), and the see of York, where John was then appointed as replacement of the deceased Bosa, 'a man of great sanctity and humility'. Once more, Bede attributed this to Berhthun as an eye witness, but this time it not only contains what purports to be the direct speech of John, Berhthun himself and the unfortunate sick person, a young nun called Cwenburh, but is as if recounted throughout by Berhthun, in a style similar to the story told by Guthfrith of Œthelwald in chapter 1. This has, therefore, direct speech reported within an account set out in direct speech, which is not uncommon in this work and has considerable potential to bring the story alive. The technique may well have been one which was familiar to Bede and his audience from its use in oral literature. The miracles which follow vary little: all are healing miracles which ultimately derive from biblical types; V, 4 is another included as if taken down verbatim from Berhthun which utilises biblical number (forty days, three weeks) and bears a close resemblance to one Bede had already told elsewhere;[74] V, 5 again uses direct speech and likewise replicates in essence a story Bede had told previously;[75] V, 6 was accredited to a different source, Herebald, 'now' abbot of Tynemouth, who was the putative beneficiary of John's prayers in this story, which was again delivered entirely as if in the direct speech of its chief character.

These miracle stories collectively portray John as especially beloved of God and of quasi-apostolic status, comparable to St Peter.[76] Through the image he had constructed and validated by 'signs', Bede was effectively investing in the sanctity of Hexham, York and Beverley, with all of which John was himself closely associated, and also, of course, Wearmouth/Jarrow, where John had ordained Bede himself as first deacon then priest, as he would recount in V, 24. His own status as a priest, as well as author and scholar, was therefore relevant here. Bede closed this group of miracles at the end of V, 6, by noting John's tenure of episcopal office for thirty-three years, which is again a biblical number,[77] his departure for 'the kingdom of heaven' in 'the year from the incarnation of the Lord 721' and his burial at Beverley, where he had retired latterly to 'complete his days in worthy intercourse with God', having first consecrated 'his priest Wilfrid to the bishopric of the church of York'.[78] By so doing, Bede was making important connections between the sanctity of a figure whose death had occurred only a decade previously, the practice of retirement from high office, and the Northumbrian episcopate in the present, with Wilfrid (II) still in office.

A particular feature of these opening chapters of book V is Bede's repeated references to St Peter: he took care to remark that both Œthelwald and then John had been buried in churches dedicated to the saint and explicitly compared Bishop John with SS Peter and John in V, 2, then his healing miracle with Christ's healing of St Peter's mother-in-law in V, 4. These are powerful but implicit strategies by which Bede was effectively validating the Northumbrian church leadership and its principal cult centres in the present, and, indirectly at least, his own apparently self-appointed role as moral or spiritual adviser to the court. Wearmouth's church was, of course, also dedicated to St Peter.

Bede continued in chapter 7 with a rather different type of story, which omits miracles but has parallels with John's retirement to a monastery in old age. This was an instance, however, which Bede perhaps considered more apt in the context of Ceolwulf as audience, being the story of Cædwalla's departure from England to Rome in 689 and his baptism then death there, which he told at some length and rendered the more relevant to the Northumbrian court by dating it via the regnal years of Aldfrith.[79] Again, there is considerable play on the name Peter: that was the baptismal name given the king – which fact Bede offered himself – then it recurs twice in the epitaph on his tomb, which is quoted in full, and he was buried in St Peter's at Rome, which again recurs. Bede displays considerable interest in the notion of pilgrimage to Rome, as his own abbot, Ceolfrith, had attempted. He added notice at the close of this chapter of Ine's subsequent departure following a reign of thirty-seven years, stressing that 'in these times many from the race of the English, nobles and commoners, lay and clerics, men and women, were accustomed to do the same', which mirrors earlier comment in the *Greater Chronicle*.[80] That royal exemplars were being offered may imply that Bede was concerned to engage Ceolwulf personally with this practice. However, his treatment of Oftfor's visit to Rome in IV, 23, which 'in those days was considered to be an act of great merit', may suggest some ambivalence on Bede's part as regards this practice in the present.[81]

Theodore's death (in 690) was then introduced, in chapter 8, by reference to the date of Cædwalla's (689), and Bede took the opportunity to venerate the old archbishop, portraying him as long aware of the timing of his own death.[82] He described his burial in St Peter's at Canterbury, his contribution to the English Church and his epitaph, parts of which he quoted, alongside an apposite extract from the Scriptures. The remainder of the chapter rehearsed the succession at Canterbury of Berhtwold in 692, his consecration in Gaul the following year and his subsequent consecration of 'many bishops', including Tobias, bishop of Rochester, whom Bede particularly approved as 'a man well-versed in erudition and with a command of the Latin, Greek and English languages'. This is a comparatively brief chapter, however, which does no more than the minimum for Theodore's memory, and it is noticeable that Bede had made no reference to his activities since book IV, 21 (19), perhaps having himself somewhat ambiguous feelings concerning a figure whom, on the one hand, he viewed as a major architect of the English Church in the present, responsible for much of its learning and the expansion of its episcopacy to the current modest levels, yet, on the other, as having opposed papal judgement in the matter of Wilfrid's exclusion from his see. And Theodore was of little immediate relevance to the Northumbrian court, so although notice of his death was presumably felt to be obligatory by Bede, it is kept short and to the point, without even the full epitaph included, in contrast to both Cædwalla and Wilfrid. That said, Bede was following Eusebius's practice in providing the succession of key bishoprics and he took this opportunity to carry Canterbury's down to 731, when Berhtwold would himself die of old age,[83] so bridging the years separating Theodore from the present and rendering his demise part of a wider story of current relevance.

From the subject of Theodore, Bede turned (V, 9, 10) to Egbert in Ireland, whom he depicted planning to sail to the continent to undertake the conversion of Germanic peoples, or else go to Rome, but he was putatively prevented from either course of action by divine intervention. The contrivance of Egbert's frustrated missionary aspirations was used by Bede to introduce a series of other missionaries to the continent, including Wihtberht (V, 9), Willibrord (V, 10, 11), the two Hewalds (V, 10) and Swithberht (V, 11), through whom he was able further to depict English – largely Northumbrian – clerics living in Ireland as active in spreading the Gospels in partnership with the Franks and the papacy. Again there is a strong sense of God manifest and active in the world, so, for example, providing the 'signs' of miracles to mark the martyrdoms of the Hewalds, and of the union of interest in conversion shared by a group of English clerics in exile in Ireland with successive popes. By including these stories, Bede was able to present key figures of northern English Christianity as agents of the papacy in its universal mission to convert the heathen. Such offered the opportunity to bring the Anglo-Saxon conversion, which Bede depicted as instigated by Gregory, aided by the Franks and protected by English kings, full circle, with Northumbrian monks and priests now the shock troops of Christianisation in northern Europe. As already suggested above, Egbert was here perhaps being presented as if a latter-day, English type of Gregory the Great. Willibrord still lived on at Utrecht in 731, and his story, alongside those of his compatriots, had considerable potential to enhance the reputation of the Northumbrian Church in the present.[84]

With this achieved, Bede turned next (V, 12, 13, 14) to a sequence of near-death type miracle stories.[85] These are individual tales which are easily assimilated by reader or listener to provide a potent message, warning of the terrible reality of hell, so the necessity of a moral life and attention to contrition and absolution, both earlier and in the face of death. All three are contextualised effectively, two being placed in Northumbria and one in Mercia alongside and in contact with well-known figures such as kings Aldfrith and Coenred and abbot (later bishop) Æthelwold, with even Bede himself acknowledging acquaintance with the central figure of the last tale. Such requires the audience to accept the reality of these individuals and so credit their stories.

Dryhthelm's vision begins the trio (V, 12), and is far by far the longest, longer even than the other two combined,[86] providing graphic images of an afterlife which he had putatively visited under the guidance of an angelic figure. The story, which Bede claimed to have had from Dryhthelm's confidante, the monk Hæmgisl, was presented once more in direct speech, as if taking down Dryhthelm's own words, with the putative conversations between himself and his guide included verbatim. There are some parallels between this and a story concerning Fursa which Bede had already told (III, 19), and another which was recounted of a monk at Wenlock,[87] and all arguably rely heavily on tales told by Gregory in his *Dialogues*.[88] Dryhthelm was presented at the start of this story as a married man, head of a household and a father of upright character, whose near-death experience led him to retire to the monastic life, entering Melrose with the aid of King Aldfrith, so this is yet another instance of a mature layman with responsibilities putting down the trappings of secular life in favour of the tonsure. The reader is led to assume that Dryhthelm himself benefited from the austerity which he had adopted, alongside the many others whom he encouraged to seek their own salvation by his story or example,[89] but this is a morality tale aimed at those of the laity who already considered themselves to be leading a 'good', Christian life. Such would have an obvious impact among those gathered around the king of the day, and indeed for the king, who may have been expected to perceive Dryhthelm as a metaphor for himself.

The next story is rather different, in that its subject is now a member of the actual court and the king's inner circle, which perhaps explains Bede's adoption of a Mercian exemplar and his insistence on the virtues of the king, beside the sinfulness of his follower. This case was positioned in the period 704–9, so safely distant from the family connections of the Mercian king of the day.[90] The warrior concerned was depicted as foolishly ignoring the repeated advice given him by King Coenred, as well as the visions that he himself experienced. The end result was his impenitent death and consequent passage to hell. Bede attributed this story to 'the venerable Bishop Pehthelm', who was bishop of Whithorn at the time of writing but had been an associate of Aldhelm in Wessex. Again it is told with plentiful use of direct speech, which brings the exchanges between king and warrior sharply into focus and particularly underlines the account of the visions that the sick man putatively experienced. There are several important messages here: one was the responsibility of the king for the moral welfare of his people, which Bede shows Coenred as actively pursuing, albeit to no avail; another is the need for constant vigilance, to be ever mindful of the possibility of death and the need to be at peace with the Lord each day; yet another lies in the status of the books which the unfortunate man was shown in his visions. Bede used two terms here, one, *libellus*, for the very small book containing his good deeds, the other, a massive *codex*, containing all his sins. *Libellus* is a word which he used comparatively infrequently in this work,[91] as an alternative to *liber* ('book') particularly for smaller works or saints' lives. So the term appears first in the Preface for the anonymous *Life of Cuthbert*, then for works of Gregory the Great (II, 1), and for the *Life of Fursa* and *Life of Æthelthryth* to which he referred in III, 19 and IV, 10, 11, before being used sparingly for his own shorter works in V, 24. The vision, however, places these two very different types of book in the hands of supernatural beings – one set ostensibly angels, the other devils – offering an image of the written word codified and used as evidence in the process of judgement by God of the individual soul. Such is a common topos, of course, but the authority here invested in 'the book' in the hands of supernatural beings may have implications for the status claimed for Bede's own books, including his *Ecclesiastical History*, which similarly codifies the behaviours of men.

The subject of this 'Mercian' story was left anonymous by Bede and he made a virtue of leaving the central character of his final story similarly unidentified, even while specifying that the events had occurred recently in Bernicia. This, however, was a monk, rather than a member of the laity, who ignored the good advice of his brethren in a 'noble monastery' and lived a life of 'drunkenness and the other pleasures of a neglectful life', rather than attending services in church, but was tolerated by his peers for the sake of his skill as a smith. This miscreant then saw a vision of hell on his death bed and died impenitent and without the last rites. This story reinforces, therefore, the 'Mercian' story which he had just recounted. Its more local provenance, the fact that it was supposedly already circulating and might already be known to his audience, and its apparently more recent occurrence, all enhanced the effect of this story and encouraged readers or hearers to do penance for their sins and to reform their lives.

This small group of out-of-body stories has powerful messages, therefore, and a particular immediacy for Bede's intended audience as regards punishments in the afterlife for sinful behaviour, neglect of good advice and the efficacy of church ritual. As already discussed, Bede shared Gregory's sense of the nearness of the end of time and such tales of individuals misusing the space allotted them to place their spiritual affairs in order had a much broader context, should God terminate the sixth age of the world. These were universal lessons, as appropriate to a court audience as any other. At this point, however, he reverted to his pre-existing theme of the Northumbrians as a people of the Lord, telling the story of how Adamnan, abbot of Iona, was convinced of the correctness of Roman practices via consultation with King Aldfrith's advisers (which presumably means some section of the Northumbrian clergy), then, failing to convert his own community on Iona, persuaded others of the Irish to adopt Catholic ways. Bede's treatment of Adamnan is arguably somewhat misleading,[92] perhaps even defective, but the story here fits alongside his previous discussion of the various English missionaries whom he grouped around Egbert in V, 9, 10, 11 and sustains his vision of Northumbria as a focus from which Roman Christianity was being exported by various agencies to the surrounding nations.

Bede then used the remainder of this chapter (V, 15) to introduce Adamnan's book on the holy places, which had putatively been dictated to him by a Gaulish visitor and which Bede had since himself abbreviated. The next two chapters consist of extracts from this abbreviation, inserted here on the basis of their value to an audience living on the outer reaches of the Christian world. In one sense, these insertions are a departure from the story of English Christianity but they have a significant function: they are written in the present tense, which confers a particular immediacy upon them, and they bring the whole story of Christ into sharp focus. Just as Bede had elsewhere provided background or landscape definition to many stories set in a distant past, so here he was providing a contemporary space in which the Lord's passion and the resurrection could be envisaged and the whole Christian message, to the extent that it was founded on an 'historical' account of distant events, made immediate. The general impact is to reinforce the overall premise of the *Ecclesiastical History*, that the Christian God is an immanent force in the world in the present, to be ignored only at extreme peril.

In chapter 18, Bede then caught up with the dynastic history of Northumbria, detailing the death of Aldfrith (705) and succession of his son, Osred, the difficulties of which he suppressed, then moved rapidly on with an account of the death of Bishop Hædde of the West Saxons, miracles associated with the spot where he died and the subsequent succession to Hædde's diocese, which led in turn to an appreciation of Aldhelm, then an account of the temporary revival of the see of the South Saxons, which he reported as vacant once more *usque hodie* ('even today'). In some senses, it is easy to read this chapter as little more than a bundle of unconnected items which Bede felt required inclusion. Their arrangement is arguably dependent in part on his attempt to put together several sources – Pehthelm is named and the South and West Saxon material apparently derived otherwise either from Bede's correspondence with Bishop Daniel or from Canterbury. The recurring vacancy within the see of the South Saxons was an issue for Bede, who clearly felt that it should be filled and that lengthy vacancies ought not be tolerated, so this was further advice to Northumbria's rulers in the present. The inclusion of an outline of miracles associated with Hædde also, however, has the capacity to recall for Bede's audience the story of the ending of another Northumbrian king, namely Oswald, whose place of death similarly was dug out leaving a great hole, the soil from which was considered to have healing qualities for both men and beasts (III, 9). It is difficult to view the insertion here of distant, West Saxon miracles as mere coincidence. Rather, this may have been intended to remind his audience, in a passage which referred directly but with extreme brevity to the death of King Aldfrith, of the 'signs' of divine approval which had continued to be associated with Bede's principal royal exemplar post-mortem, of whose example Aldfrith was being depicted, largely by default admittedly, as having fallen short.

Chapter 19 opens with Coenred and Offa departing Britain for Rome (see above), and there receiving the tonsure and dying, a sequence of events which Bede portrayed as an effective means by which kings might enter heaven, which had a real significance for his intended audience. The remainder of this long chapter was given over to that other great traveller to Rome, Bishop Wilfrid, who died in the same year that they departed. Wilfrid's extended treatment, which depends heavily on Stephen's *Life*, serves as a powerful justification of his career, validating his activities by reference to the papacy and portraying him as a veritable apostle, for example as a missionary among the South Saxons. Those who opposed him included both Ecgfrith and Aldfrith. Little further comment on their behaviours was necessary in a work which held the papacy in such high esteem but it will not have escaped his audience that both perished forthwith: indeed, the imminence of Aldfrith's death following his refusal to readmit Wilfrid was explicit. Wilfrid's career was, therefore, fully justified by Bede in this chapter, and he depicted Archbishop Berhtwold and both Æthelred and Coenred of the Mercians as eventually accepting the papal judgements. There is perhaps a message herein for Bede's own audience in the present concerning the status of Acca, who was portrayed as the especial confidant of Wilfrid and whom Bede had the elderly bishop singling out and addressing in direct speech in the later stages of this chapter.

Following brief mention of the death of Abbot Hadrian, which opens the next chapter, Bede then picked up his reference to Acca's relationship with Wilfrid and refocused his attention on the younger man, telling a little of his history and ascribing to him complex if somewhat stereotypical achievements and qualities as a man of the Lord. As already established,[93] Bede was highly complimentary regarding his diocesan. He did not generally value grandiose church building and ornamentation in this work, preferring the personal austerity which he had ascribed to such as Aidan and Cuthbert, but the models were to hand in the *Book of Pontiffs* and the *Life of Wilfrid*,[94] and here Bede praised Acca for enriching the fabric of his church, raising fresh altars, establishing new chapels and providing sacred vessels, lamps and other adornments. He also employed a skilled cantor over many years to raise the standard of the choir, which seems to have been something very close to Bede's own heart but was also a very public aspect of a church's activities. Acca was himself, Bede declared, a skilled chorister and a learned theologian who collected passions of the martyrs and other books, who had joined Wilfrid following a childhood spent among the household clergy of the 'very saintly and God-beloved' Bosa, bishop of York, 'in the hope of finding a better way of life', and had visited Rome with Wilfrid and profited considerably from the experience. While the bulk of Bede's commendations of Acca are set in the past tense, he also emphasised their application to the present and even the future. So, for example: 'For he took trouble, as he still does today', and '[Acca] was very knowledgeable concerning the institutional rules of the church, and he will not cease to be even until he will receive the reward of pious devotion [i.e. "goes to heaven"].' This is over and away the strongest and most extended praise of any living person in the whole work. Given the number of Bede's dedications of works of exegesis to Acca, this is not perhaps surprising. The two men seem to have shared numerous interests and were apparently very close.[95] However, in the context of a work dedicated to King Ceolwulf, it is difficult to put aside the suspicion that Bede was here effectively urging reconciliation between the court party and Acca, whose flight from Hexham at some point during 731 is generally read as resulting from the political turmoil of that year.

Twenty-one is the longest chapter in book V, being Ceolfrith's letter to King Nechtan of the Picts concerning the Roman method of calculating Easter. Its introduction by the phrase *litteras scriptas in hunc modum* ('letters written in this manner') suggests that there should be some doubt as to whether this was the actual text of the letter or merely Bede's recollection of it,[96] from memory perhaps, in the event of no copy having been retained. Whichever, he chose not only to include it apparently verbatim but also to introduce it with a proem of unusual length, and close with comment regarding the outcome, which includes a passage in direct speech as if taken down from the lips of Nechtan himself. This serves as another of Bede's several assertions that Northumbrian churchmen had become the committed agents of the papacy, as missionaries to the heathen elsewhere in Britain and in Germany, or as champions of Roman practices vis-à-vis the Celtic world: chapters 9, 10, 11, 15 and 19 of book V had already provided important elements of this vision and Ceolfrith's letter enabled Bede to position the ruler of his own community at the forefront of such efforts, beside Egbert, Adamnan's anonymous Northumbrian advisers, Willibrord and Wilfrid. In partnership with the numerous miracles he had already included as associated with key clerics, the effect is once again to invest moral authority in certain of the great churches and monastic communities of Northumbria – in this instance most specifically Bede's own house of Wearmouth/Jarrow. This lengthy passage also offered Bede the opportunity to deploy another's arguments regarding the Paschal controversy – whether or not he himself had actually inputted to them in the first place, which perhaps added to the authority with which he was here able to assert the Roman position. It is often supposed that the Easter question was long over by 731, but its frequent occurrences in the *Ecclesiastical History* may suggest that it was still of some significance at the time of writing, not necessarily in the sense that alternative methods of computing the date were still in use but rather as a means of paralleling the attention given to various heresies in Eusebius's *Ecclesiastical History*. Conformity on such issues was a key test, in Bede's eyes, of the Catholicism of the English people, which they had passed with flying colours.

This chapter fits naturally, therefore, beside the following one, chapter 22, in which Bede brought to a conclusion several of the themes running across this work through Egbert's conversion of the Ionan community to Roman practices. Just as Gregory had been prompted by God to send missionaries to England in 596, so Egbert's initiative was 'by the Lord's guidance'. Like Augustine, then Aidan and Chad, Egbert was portrayed both as a teacher and as one who led by example, very much after the model which

Bede had adopted from Gregory's *Pastoral Care*. For Bede the context was fundamental:

> This event occurred through a marvellous dispensation of divine mercy, that race [i.e. the Scots] had taken pains to communicate to the people of the English its own knowledge and understanding of the divine, freely and without reserve, and now, through the race of the English, it has reached a more perfect way of life in those areas where it was lacking. In contrast the Britons, who were unwilling to share with the English that knowledge of the Christian faith which they had, still persist in their errors and stumble in their ways, so that no tonsure occurs on their heads and they celebrate the solemn festivals of Christ other than within the fellowship of Christ's Church, while the English people are now both believers and in all areas instructed in the rules of the Catholic faith.

As many commentators have observed, this is a cusp moment in Bede's *Ecclesiastical History*, linking as it does to his oft-stated condemnation of the Christianity of the Britons (see particularly I, 22; II, 2) and his recall of the mission headed by Aidan, through which the Northumbrians and many others of the English were portrayed as having come to the Lord. Egbert's persuasion of Iona to accept Roman practices offered Bede the opportunity to bring his story of the English conversion full circle and portray the English in turn as agents of Rome and of the Lord, correcting the flawed customs of otherwise virtuous Christians on the outer edge of their own world. By making references to Egbert's role as early as book III, 4, when describing the community established by Columba in the sixth century, Bede had clearly telegraphed the later event, so again making connections between a distant past and the present and placing the story of Northumbrian Christianity within a divinely inspired circle of virtuous interactions between the North-umbrians and the Scots. The connectedness of these stories and the sense in which they were being used to frame the past were re-emphasised in V, 22 by notice of the eighty years separating Aidan's despatch from Iona from its conversion by Egbert, and Bede deployed once more the metaphor of light, as had occurred at various points already across this work. The chapter closes with an extended treatment of Egbert's death on an Easter Day on Iona which would have lain outside the limits of the previous, 'Celtic' method of compu-tation, attended by repeated reference to God and Christ: Egbert was *vir Domini* ('the man of the Lord'); he had 'consecrated [Iona] to the peace of Christ'; he celebrated a mass in memory of 'the resurrection of the Lord'; he then 'migrated to the Lord' on the same day, continuing to celebrate in the hereafter with 'the Lord and His apostles'; he 'crossed from this world to the Father', leaving the monks rejoicing in 'the protection of the Father', as 'he went to be with the Lord', and, finally, quoting St John, the *'reverentissiumus pater* (most reverend father) Egbert rejoiced that he should see the day of the Lord; he saw and was glad'. This quotation, which comes from Christ's confrontation with unbelieving Jews in the Temple,[97] effectively claims for Egbert the status of a Christ-figure.

In chapter 23, Bede then proceeded to update events since Egbert's triumph in 716.[98] He recorded the deaths of King Wihtred of Kent (725) and Bishop Tobias of Rochester (726), named their successors, then described the two fearful comets which putatively appeared in 729, which Bede interpreted conventionally as portents of disaster. It was in this context that the Saracen attack on Gaul was included, which was arguably that which culminated in defeat at the hands of Charles Martel in 732 or 733 so was necessarily an addition to the work post 731, reiteration of the death of Egbert (here *sanctus vir Domini*: 'a saintly man of the Lord'), and King Osric's death on 9 May, having appointed Ceolwulf his successor, and the problems which that then ushered in.[99] Berhtwold's death in 731 and the consecration as archbishop of his successor, the Mercian Tatwine, then leads into a description of the present situation, detailing first the areas of responsibility of the several southern bishops and the southern 'overkingship' of Æthelbald, king of the Mercians, then turning to the kingdom of the Northumbrians, which is presented as if a single entity under King Ceolwulf, and its four bishoprics. Three paragraphs remain. The first describes the Picts and Scots as currently at peace with the English – which perhaps really means the Northumbrians – while the Britons remain hostile but impotent, 'being opposed by divine and human power alike'. The second notes the widespread adoption of the monastic life by Northumbrians, 'in these favourable times of peace and prosperity', the outcome of which Bede was not prepared to anticipate. The third effectively concludes the work with pious thanksgiving, bringing the whole story to a close 'about 285 years after the arrival of the English in Britain, in the year 731 since the Lord's incarnation'. Chapter 24 then adds first the recapitulation (see above, pp. 82–95), then Bede's statement concerning his own life and listing of his own works, through which he apparently sought to reinforce his authority as author.

Book V does, therefore, play an important role in Bede's overall work and detailed examination allows us to identify how the individual passages connect with his broader agenda. In one sense, what Bede was doing was offering an ecclesiastical history of the type with which he was familiar via Eusebius and Rufinus, so an episodic record of events of Christian interest plus the succession of particular sees and kingships, for example, but this is not on its own an adequate explanation of the bulk of his text and much of the more strictly 'historical' material tends to be fitted in here and there alongside and between other passages of a more discursive nature. Rather, as he explained in his Preface, the author does seem to have been using ecclesiastical history as a vehicle for putting over his own views on a variety of current issues. His text betrays two major strands. One is his insistence that the Northumbrian clergy in the present and recent past were at the very centre of the Catholic faith, with their status confirmed by 'signs' of divine approbation in the form of miracles which validate, particularly, the cult sites of Farne, Lindisfarne, Hexham, York and Beverley. The emphasis on St Peter, stories about Northumbrian efforts in the area of Christian mission and a portrayal of specific individuals as the God-beloved shock troops of Catholicism – including all of Wilfrid, Egbert, Willibrord and Ceolfrith – establishes this clerical circle as equivalent to the apostles of the distant past at the very core of Bede's conception of the Roman Christian establishment. There is a strong emphasis on the virtues which Gregory the Great had foregrounded in *Pastoral Care*, and particularly both the learning and lack of egotism which he expected of applicants to the priesthood, combined with practice by the clergy of what they themselves preached.

The second strand consists of advice to the secular élite, and in particular King Ceolwulf himself, to listen to such virtuous churchmen and their spokespersons (implicitly including Bede himself, of course) and accept their advice, to live a good life, to protect and lead their people in the paths of righteousness, to respect and prioritise the Church and to fear the Lord, whose punishment of those who had been insufficiently virtuous and/or had failed to repent was everlasting. Royals who had resigned and journeyed to Rome – Cædwalla, Ine, Coenred and Offa – were particularly lauded as having died 'good' deaths, while those who had neglected papal advice and/or excluded properly appointed bishops – as Aldfrith, taking on this role from Oswiu and Ecgfrith in book IV – died less well, with consequences in the hereafter which Bede diplomatically failed to elaborate, other than via three consecutive stories focused on non-royals. At the close is a reiteration of the current popularity of monasticism, which has tended in recent years to be read in tandem with Bede's *Letter to Egbert*, but could, perhaps, equally be viewed in the context of what had gone before, so less critical of the current trend than has been suggested, and more as a model for retirement from the morally ambivalent life typical of kingship. Bede's fifth book is, therefore, centred on how his countrymen should live life and might achieve salvation, with a particular emphasis on relations between laity and clergy, so between those who fight and those who pray.

The immediacy of these messages is repeatedly emphasised by connections between the past and the present, in the pair of chapters centred on Jerusalem as much as those focused on northern Europe. Through such mechanisms Bede sought both to hold his audience's attention and to underline the authority of the Christian message in general, and of his own thesis in particular. So we find Bede using a variety of strategies – including particular terminology, reference to living individuals as witnesses and informants, and cross-references within the text. In addition he made frequent use of direct speech, particularly in his miracle stories, to maintain the illusion that his characters were speaking directly to his audience. Throughout, he deployed God and Christ as the dominant agents in human history, using divine intervention as a means of validating particular events and narrating the resultant mix as his own, very particular history.

In conclusion

Several aspects of Bede's message have been analysed in chapter 4, by approaching the *Ecclesiastical History* less as a 'history' in our conception of the term and more as a collection of moral fables. This approach has facilitated our foregrounding of ways in which divine agency should be viewed as a potent force – even the critical force – throughout the whole work, with Bede offering what he himself, as a biblical scholar, perceived as the lessons to be drawn from an account of the English experience of conversion. Since his audience was in the first instance the Northumbrian élite, what he used was a primarily Northumbrian past, and it is instructive to read the work while consciously striving to identify what lessons Bede intended his audience to take away from each part of his narrative. His presentation of the deeds and fortunes of past kings can thereby be read as a series of parables in which advice regarding élite behaviour was embedded, framed in terms not of what Bede as an individual thought either good or bad, but of what he supposed God had, in the past, either approved, so rewarded, or disapproved, so punished. While 'good' behaviour was discussed far more explicitly than 'bad', particularly in the context of kings Edwin and Oswald in books II and III, Bede's treatments of the reigns of Oswiu, Oswine, Aldfrith and more particularly Ecgfrith all provide evidence of types of royal behaviour which were presented as flawed, so failed to attract the divine support which kings naturally required. Similarly, many of his miracle stories were told so as to validate particular individuals, and also in some instances their spiritual descendants, as in accordance with God's will and beloved of the Lord.

Alongside, we have explored some of the rhetorical strategies that Bede used to bring home his messages to a contemporary audience, including the stress on the connectedness of past and present, the use of direct speech as a means of driving his messages home to his audience, and the care with which he placed, for example, the defeat and death of King Ecgfrith in a very particular literary and moral context by control of the subject matter of surrounding chapters.

Finally, we have focused on how these strategies worked in the context of his final and longest book, V, showing how Bede used his survey of the recent past as a vehicle via which to preach particular messages to his audience. Embedded here are two fundamental assertions, backed up with proofs that these are not just Bede's own judgements but God's. One is the proposal that Northumbria in the present boasted churchmen who should be viewed as at the very heart of the Catholic Church: Bede considered that key individuals should be numbered among its shock-troops in the continuing project, begun by the apostles and continuing under the leadership of the papacy, to spread Catholicism to the far corners of the world. The second is a body of advice as to how rulers should behave. Bede's assumption seems to have been that they had failed in recent decades always to match the moral excellence of particular clerical figures, but had fallen away into moral ambivalence and disregard of the divine will. His advice to them rests implicitly on the tenets which Gregory had developed in his *Pastoral Care*. So secular leaders should strive to live and die well, advise their own followers for good, protect the righteous, be charitable and generous, avoid complacency and act always in accordance with divine will, keeping themselves in constant readiness for the coming of the day of judgement, ever fearful of the Lord.

5 Text and context: Bede, Ceolwulf and the *Ecclesiastical History*

A tale of origins framed dynamically as the Providence-guided advance of a people from heathendom to Christianity; a cast of saints rather than rude warriors; a mastery of historical technique incomparable for its time; beauty of form and diction; and, not least, an author whose qualities of life and spirit set a model of dedicated scholarship.[1]

Just how influential was its immediate political context to the ways in which Bede laid out and interpreted the past? This final chapter will explore the parameters within which we should view Bede's *EH* as a text carrying contemporary messages and reflective of a particular set of political circumstances, and seek to balance this aspect of the work and its authorship against consideration of Bede as first and foremost a religious writer with a self-imposed mission to bring the leaders of the Northumbrians, and through them the whole people, to God.

From text to context

Bede's dedication to Ceolwulf necessarily serves as the starting point in any attempt to place the *Ecclesiastical History* in the cultural-political context in which it was written but this privileging of the king of the day was not entirely exceptional. Bede had previously often written for a prominent individual and named him or her as dedicatee, albeit these were invariably churchmen, so he had an established predilection for this practice. Other authors, including authors of 'historical' works, similarly on occasion dedicated texts to kings or other great men in the secular world. We have already noted the attention paid King Sisebut in Isidore's early *Chronicle* (above, p. 71), which Bede knew. Thereafter the continuator of the *Chronicle of Fredegar* remarked that Count Childebrand had hitherto (to 751–2) made sure to have the deeds of the Franks recorded, but his own fresh contribution was by authority of the latter's son, Count Nibelung.[2] A couple of decades later, Paul the Deacon dedicated his *Roman History* to Adalperga, wife of Arichis of Benevento in a thirty-line preface in letter form.[3] Although Bede obviously could not know the later works, his sits comfortably within the literary tradition which they represent. While this dedication was unique within his corpus, therefore, it walks a comparatively well-populated path.

Bede's dedication, alone, might therefore be dismissed as conventional and merely what one should expect of a work on this subject and at this time. It is only when we consider Bede's unprecedented concern with the behaviour of kings across significant sections that it becomes clear that he was breaking away in important respects from his more normal subject matter, which had hitherto rarely touched upon kingship, and entering into areas of considerable interest to secular society.[4] Other learned men of the period engaged with the leaders of lay society and issues of interest to them in various ways – and Aldhelm is merely the most obvious example, with some at least of whose work Bede was familiar.[5] Let us accept, therefore, that Bede was, indeed, aiming this work at a broader than usual tranche of élite English society, including both religious and laity and centred on the Northumbrian royal court of the day.

The *Ecclesiastical History* was completed, and perhaps even written in its entirety, across the years 729–31, during a period of dynastic upheaval in Northumbria, as is reflected, albeit very mildly, in the text (V, 23). Given this political context, there is some value in testing, to the limited extent possible, whether or not Bede betrayed in any sense a factional interest in recent dynastic issues, by positioning himself either inside or outside the dominant royal clique of the moment, headed by King Ceolwulf.

Some aspects of this issue have already emerged from previous discussion. So, for example (see above, pp. 131–3), Bede seems to have rethought his choice of virtuous exemplars as offered in the *Greater Chronicle* c.725, to foreground hero-figures connected rather less with King Edwin and other of Oswiu's Deiran connections, investing far more heavily than he had hitherto in the kingship of Oswald and the sanctity of Aidan: clearly, the *Greater Chronicle* and *Ecclesiastical History* were written in very different circumstances, for different reasons and aimed at different audiences. The earlier piece was part of a much longer didactic work, *Concerning the Reckoning of Time*, which Bede wrote quite explicitly for his own brethren, in the reign of one of Oswiu's putative grandsons. The presentation of the English within the overall work was arguably tailored to the perceptions and positioning of Bede's own abbot and brethren within that overall political context, and perhaps reflects quite closely Bede's own preferred vision of the past. To have promoted key figures from the Scottish mission as exemplars within this work might have undermined the status of Wearmouth/Jarrow, which was itself a highly Rome-centric foundation, and even rendered Bede's position on the Paschal controversy more ambiguous than he might have wished. The *EH*, on the other hand, was certainly completed, and perhaps even written in its entirety, after Osric had lost power, and was dedicated to a king from a hitherto marginalised branch of the Bernician royal family, who should be thought of as a dynastic opponent of Oswiu's descendants. Additionally, it was written for a broader audience than Bede's own brethren, so the immediate political context was arguably of greater significance to this later work.

In addressing the current king, Bede perhaps felt that he needed to beware of such issues as might be considered politically or dynastically contentious in the present, and there is an argument, in principle at least, for such factors having exercised a pervasive influence over the writing of this entire narrative, to include the paucity of references to, and more particularly praise of, his recent predecessors.[6] Such influences are perhaps most noticeable in discussion of the recent past, but that was not necessarily the sole arena where they might be anticipated, since dynasts and their adherents had long memories and might care a great deal about the commemoration of the deeds of their own particular ancestors, for example, and the reputations of those whom they opposed. Bede need not, therefore, have been constructing the *Ecclesiastical History* quite as he would have had current politics been entirely outside his ken. He perhaps felt it necessary to accommodate the sensitivities of his particular audience as best he could.

To move from the general to the specific, it is well established that Bede was extraordinarily shy of commenting on Northumbria over his own adult lifetime, rather passing over numerous careers of the great and the good and several political or dynastic crises of previous decades with a touch so light that even their very occurrence becomes problematic. He certainly seems to have taken care to avoid commenting on recent candidates to the throne in any way that might have had a capacity to offend either Ceolwulf on the one hand, or his opponents on the other. This may well have influenced the presentation of King Oswiu herein (see above, pp. 155–7), which is far less supportive than might have been expected of the long-reigning and wide-ruling conqueror of Penda, perhaps because he was the progenitor of that branch of the royal lineage which had recently been displaced. Had King Osric, for example, still been on the throne in 731, one might have envisaged a very different portrayal of his putative grandfather.

The ambiguities of Bede's presentation of the past deepen with the introduction of King Aldfrith (685–705) in book IV, 26 (24), in which he distanced himself from the view that he was half-brother to Ecgfrith, and Oswiu's son, even while acknowledging his exceptional knowledge of the Scriptures.[7] At issue was not the matter of Aldfrith's illegitimacy, which seems to have been acknowledged by all parties and which Bede had earlier taken as read, even while his son was in power, but of his royal paternity.[8] At Aldfrith's death, Stephen of Ripon informs us that the otherwise unknown 'Eadwulf succeeded him for a short time' but that he was driven out after two months in favour of Aldfrith's young son, Osred, following a dangerous episode during which the latter's supporters were besieged in Bamburgh.[9] But Bede omitted to note this crisis, of which he was presumably aware,[10] portraying the succession of Osred, aged about eight, as if entirely uncontested, in the opening sentence of V, 18, and entirely suppressing the otherwise unknown contender. Were his family, in 731, Ceolwulf's rivals, perhaps? Or was Eadwulf, unbeknown to us, a member of the same faction as Ceolwulf, perhaps even close kin,[11] whose failure in 705 Bede diplomatically passed over? We simply do not know, but either circumstance might lie behind the one thing of which we can be reasonably sure, that Bede glossed over the event.

Where Wearmouth/Jarrow had positioned itself politically and dynastically in recent years is clearly an issue here. In his metrical *Life of Cuthbert*, written by 716 and arguably some years earlier, Bede referred to the young King Osred in highly honorific terms, validating his tenure of the throne and terming him 'a new Josiah, with faith and intellect greater than his early years'.[12] This metaphor was probably stimulated in part by their similarity in age when each attained the kingship, but it was highly supportive, given Josiah's depiction (in II Kings 22–3) as the Old Testament king most obedient to the Laws of Moses and particularly active against both idolatry and apostasy. Taken on its own, it is not clear whether this reveals a deep-rooted alignment of Bede's house with this branch of the royal family or nothing more sinister than conventional praise of the king of the day in a work intended primarily for consumption at another religious house. However, Ceolfrith's correspondence with Nechtan of the Picts perhaps confirms that Wearmouth/Jarrow's abbot was trusted by the king to deal with highly delicate matters of policy with a neighbouring people with whom the Northumbrians had been on hostile terms periodically since the 680s. Nechtan only came to the throne around 709 and Ceolfrith retired from his abbacy in 716, so this letter was written within a seven-year period. Bede himself noted warfare between the Northumbrians and Picts therein, in 711. Ceolfrith's mission was highly sensitive, therefore, so we can be reasonably confident that Wearmouth/Jarrow was high in the confidence of King Osred and its abbot was in some sense representing the court in this correspondence.

In the *EH*, in contrast, completed a decade and a half after Osred had been displaced by Ceolwulf's brother Coenred, Bede unsurprisingly omitted any such praise of Aldfrith's son, contenting himself with using Osred's regnal years to contextualise the synod by the River Nidd and the retirement and departure for Rome of Coenred, king of the Mercians (both in V, 19). There is no characterisation of him as an individual or as king in this work, for good or ill, although there was to be by others elsewhere: some thirty years after his death Boniface denounced him as debauched,[13] and most of a century later Æthelwulf criticised his rule and accused him of killing his own nobles and forcing others into monasteries,[14] but such hostile commemorations may simply have been the price of dynastic failure.

Even Osred's death in 716 and the succession of Coenred to the Northumbrian throne occur in the *EH* only to date and otherwise contextualise Egbert's activities in Iona (V, 22). Bede's use of *occisus* ('killed') does suggest that Osred met a violent end,[15] but the details are wholly obscure and the evidence is insufficient for us to be confident that Ceolwulf's brother was responsible. Coenred's kingship is absent from the brief notice of these events in the recapitulation and he fails to recur in the main text other than as antecedent to the almost equally obscure King Osric (718–29). In practice, Coenred was again never characterised in any way, either supportively or otherwise, and barely appears in the *Ecclesiastical History*. Perhaps this was to avoid having to describe the manner of either his acquisition of the throne or his loss thereof, either of which could have been an unpalatable affair and potentially embarrassing to his brother, Ceolwulf, but the fact remains that Bede had the opportunity to praise Coenred and/or some aspect of his career but chose not to. Osric in turn occurs exclusively in terms of his regnal years (V, 23), which were used to date the death of Wihtred of Kent in 725, and then notice of his death in 729 (V, 23 and the recapitulation). Osric was much later described as King Aldfrith's son,[16] but while it has generally been deemed acceptable to credit this late evidence,[17] and it is at least plausible to imagine Aldfrith adopting the first element of his putative father's name as a legitimising process when naming at least two of his sons, it must be stressed that this is very far from contemporary evidence and cannot be relied upon too heavily until we have a far better understanding than at present of this author's sources.[18] That said, once more Bede neglected the opportunity to establish himself as either an admirer or a detractor of a recent king, covering his reign without overt comment.

It was, however, Osric's death and Ceolwulf's succession that ultimately contextualised Bede's authorship of the *Ecclesiastical History*. Osric 'ceased life' on 9 May 729 (V, 23),[19] having, Bede claimed, 'appointed as his successor to the kingdom Ceolwulf, the brother of that king Coenred who had ruled before him'. This seems very carefully scripted indeed by an author keen to avoid causing offence, either to the party in power or to that which had so recently been excluded. Beyond Osric's death-date, Ceolwulf's relationship with Coenred and his novel tenure of the throne, it is perhaps better not to treat this comment as overly factual, and particularly the claim that Osric had actually nominated Ceolwulf, given that he probably still had a brother living whose claims he might have been expected to have supported.[20] Several versions of the *Anglo-Saxon Chronicle* later described Osric as 'slain',[21] although, of course, this is again far from contemporary evidence, the origin of which may well have been Bede's recapitulation. It must be said that it is quite likely that Ceolwulf was in some sense responsible for Osric's death: Bede must have shared with his audience a general knowledge of the processes by which the current king had come to power, but we have insufficient evidence to make the case. The fact remains, however, that Bede had every reason to present Ceolwulf's reign as both legitimate and consensual and it may well be that his lack of close kinship with the previous incumbent had already encouraged Ceolwulf's party to develop the claim that he had been nominated by his predecessor. Bede then added:

> concerning whose rule [i.e. Ceolwulf's] both the beginning and the course have overflowed with so many and such great convulsions and

set-backs that one cannot yet know what to write about them or guess what the outcome will be.

This is our author at his most enigmatic, telling his audience nothing directly but acknowledging that they already shared his awareness that the last two years had been tumultuous. It is a reasonably safe guess that Bede was referring to a period of dynastic and factional conflict, such as had previously occurred in 716–18, and which was still far from settled across 731, a year in which Ceolwulf was deposed and forcibly tonsured but then regained his throne. On such issues Bede understandably avoided direct comment, but he made remarkably little effort to support Ceolwulf here, despite his eventual dedication of the whole work to him as king. Indeed, his absence from the recapitulation, which runs up to June 731 and includes mention of both the current archbishop and the king of Mercia, is remarkable.

What of the actual timing? Assuming that the single sentence in *EH* V, 23 regarding the Saracens either is a later interpolation or refers to events earlier than 732,[22] the *Ecclesiastical History* seems to have been completed no earlier than the end of June 731, since the consecration of Archbishop Tatwine on 10 June at Canterbury was the last event recorded. Assuming for the moment that this was part of the first draft of Bede's text, it effectively establishes the earliest date at which this can then have been sent to Ceolwulf, prior to a comparatively complex sequence of later events. Whether or not the abortive coup against Ceolwulf had already occurred when Bede finally completed his work is unclear, but it seems safe to assume that Ceolwulf was on the throne when he wrote the Preface – otherwise the dedication seems entirely incongruous. Assuming, therefore, that Tatwine's consecration was already included in the earlier draft of the *EH*, there are two possibilities.

Scenario I. Bede completed the first draft of his *Ecclesiastical History* no earlier than late June 731, to accommodate the consecration of Archbishop Tatwine, and submitted it to King Ceolwulf for approval. When, following a period of consideration (let us suppose July and August), the manuscript was returned to him he made such alterations or additions as seemed appropriate and added the Preface, before sending it back, surely no earlier than September. Only then was Ceolwulf the victim of a coup and forcibly tonsured, but recovered power still within the year, with Acca taking flight from Hexham, perhaps in consequence.

Scenario II. The alternative is to postulate a slightly different sequence, with Bede still completing the first draft no earlier than late June, submitting it to the court and receiving it back, but now allowing for the coup and Ceolwulf's recovery of power to run concurrently with Bede's finalisation of his text and addition of the Preface. The manuscript was then presented once again to Ceolwulf following his recovery of power, at some point in the autumn or early winter.

The weakness of the first scenario is that it requires a comparatively complex sequence of events to be compressed into a six-month period, but that is far from impossible, even though it has tended to encourage commentators to favour the second option.[23] There is no reason to think that drastic revision of the first draft was undertaken, so it is quite possible to imagine Bede turning the work around in no more than perhaps a week, but in the last resort we cannot be sure. There is in fact little evidence capable of swaying us either way, but such as there is tends to focus on Acca. Bede's exceptionally strong affirmation of his diocesan as a model churchman in book V, 20, with emphasis on the currency of his exemplary behaviour (*et hodie facit*: 'and still does today') and, uniquely, the assertion of confidence in his future Catholic orthodoxy – 'and he will not cease to be so until he gains the reward of his piety and devotion' – arguably reflect concern for the political difficulties of his old friend in the early summer. Acca was then depicted as if currently occupying Hexham in the closing summary of V, 23, which it was suggested above (pp. 82–3) may have formed the final passage of the first draft as initially despatched to the king, so written in late June. That this was not corrected in the process of completion later in the year might perhaps lead us to favour the view that Acca's flight had not then occurred: *Acca in Hagustaldensi* ('Acca in [the diocese of] the community of Hexham') seems a very specific statement signifying his actual presence. Acca is the only figure who we can reasonably postulate to have been implicated in the plot against Ceolwulf in 731 (and even that is far from certain: see pp. 63–4 above) and even an implicit plea that the king be reconciled to this bishop whom he had inherited from early in Osred's reign (he was appointed in 709) seems improbable once the coup had actually occurred. This observation might, perhaps, encourage us to favour the first of these two dating scenarios. However, Acca is entirely absent from the recapitulation, which it is suggested above was added to the main text in the process of completion, in which case his flight might already have occurred by the time Bede was revising his work. While this is negative evidence, and so far from compelling, it does nothing to encourage confidence in the above reasoning.

We cannot, therefore, be certain of when Bede finally completed his *History* (barring a handful of minor changes spread across the next two to three years), whether before the coup attempt against Ceolwulf in 731 actually went live or following his recovery of power and Acca's flight. Perhaps he actually updated V, 23, when he received back the initial draft, only then including notice of Tatwine's consecration in the final version: we simply cannot be sure, but such would enable us to postulate completion of the first draft in the spring, so make it easier to envisage the comparatively complex sequence of events thereafter all within the year. Bede's initial text had betrayed his consciousness of political unrest in the present and he might be forgiven if he had little confidence in Ceolwulf's prospects as king. His brother had, after all, lasted only two years. Perhaps this explains why Ceolwulf himself features so marginally in the text: other than in the opening lines of the Preface, he is mentioned only in V, 23, in two separate passages, in reference first to his elevation and then, secondly, to his current tenure of the throne. There is a total lack of affirmative comment or praise of Ceolwulf included prior to Bede's addition of the Preface to the main body of the text very late in the process of production. Supposing that Bede might have been prepared to rewrite his Preface had the dynastic situation thereafter changed dramatically, to provide a dedication to whoever had replaced him, the remainder of the work would have been capable of inclusion in such a project with minor alteration to just two sentences within a single chapter. On this view, Ceolwulf's hold on the text certainly looks tenuous, even despite his centrality as the figure whom Bede was ostensibly addressing.

Not so, however, Bede's 'Oswaldian' emphasis. Even were Ceolwulf to be written out in this guise and replaced with an alternative dedicatee, the philo-Irish/Ionan positioning of much of Bede's narrative was not capable of easy alteration. It is tempting to imagine that the centrality of Oswald and Aidan within the *Ecclesiastical History* was related in some way to the loss of the Northumbrian throne by the heirs of Oswiu, and their replacement by claimants without significant connections with the earlier Deiran royal family, the Gregorian mission headed by Paulinus and the latter-day cults of Gregory and Edwin at Whitby. If so, then we might infer that Bede had concluded that a successful challenge was less likely to come from the recently displaced lineage than from some other, equally 'Bernician' descendant of Ida, who might likewise take a benign view of a conversion story centred on Iona and Lindisfarne, Oswald and Aidan. That said, V, 22 and then the recapitulation are far less 'Oswaldian' than central sections of main text. In V, 22, Bede's quotation from Paul's Epistle to the Romans 10:2, positions the traditions of the Ionan church as if those of the Jews who refused to be persuaded by the apostles. Jewish opponents of Christianity had attracted his outright condemnation in earlier works, by reference to their 'inborne malice', for example in *On the Acts of the Apostles*,[24] although he had always recognised that the Jewish people in the New Testament included both a 'good' community gathered around the apostles and the recalcitrant remainder, who in the *EH* parallel the British in their refusal to accept Catholic customs. The positioning of Iona here was intellectually consistent with Bede's treatment of these issues elsewhere, but there is a certain tension with his earlier valuation of their spiritual and moral excellence, particularly in book III, which may imply that his agenda had shifted at this point. Perhaps this reflects his eagerness to magnify Egbert's achievement as of apostolic proportions, rather than any real intention to shift his position on the integrity of Oswald and Aidan to Northumbria's conversion story.

In contrast, the marginalisation of the 'Oswaldian' past in the recapitulation seems both more consistent and more purposeful. That 'Oswaldian' take on England's conversion history certainly does not accord with what emerges as Bede's own preferred view half a dozen years earlier, when he wrote the *Greater Chronicle*, so it does seem likely that Bede's adoption of this very different vision of the past in the central sections of the *EH* reflects his perception of the preferences of his audience, rather than his own personal position on these issues. For reasons that we can only guess at, he seems to an extent at least to have felt able to abandon this stance when he came to write the recapitulation.

Perhaps it would be helpful at this point to précis Bede's shifts of focus as an historian over a period of years. Setting aside the *Lesser Chronicle* as insufficiently instructive in this respect, his *Greater Chronicle*, written *c.*725, used a particular sequence of English exemplars through whom to establish the English as full members of Christ's Catholic community in the present. The individuals named betray a commitment on Bede's part to a particular subset of characters drawn from Northumbria's conversion story, reflective of a historical perspective in the present which centred on Rome, the Gregorian mission and then Northumbrian furtherance of the Catholic agenda. Bede had earlier remarked, again in his *On the Acts of the Apostles*, that the Holy Spirit 'fills only those who share in the unity of the Catholic and Apostolic Church',[25] and the stance he adopted in the *Greater Chronicle* seems entirely consistent with such comment. Comparison with the *Ecclesiastical History* reveals total amnesia in the earlier work regarding the Ionan mission and a willingness to accept papal condemnation of the Irish as heretics, so incapable of missionary activity of any value. In contrast, the main text of the *EH* itself comprises a subtle blending of Roman and Scottish missionary traditions. The Gregorian mission retained its primacy, in chronological terms, but Bede invested the Ionan input with the greater spiritual value, despite its acknowledged shortcomings in terms of the dating of Easter and certain other practices. He then wove the two together via his account of the Synod of Whitby in III, 25, creating a Northumbrian Church which combined the strengths of each tradition but in obedience to Rome. While such heroes of the *Greater Chronicle* as Edwin, Æthelthryth, Willibrord, Cuthbert, Ceolfrith and Egbert all figure in the *EH*, they are balanced out and in some instances even diminished by comparison with several alternative heroes, most obviously Oswald and Aidan, to offer a past which feels markedly different.

If the recapitulation was then appended by Bede somewhat later to the main text, in the process of amending his great historical opus, then yet another shift now becomes visible. We can see him here in retreat from the vision of history enshrined in the main text, with all of Oswald, Aidan and Colman losing significance and the emphasis reverting back towards the more 'Romanist' stance which he had first adopted *c.*725. Attention is refocused onto several of the hero-figures of the *Greater Chronicle*. Edwin (with Paulinus) and Egbert regain their centrality, with Theodore also gaining a high profile.

Given just how little we know about the political backdrop to the *Ecclesiastical History*, it is impossible to assign these apparent shifts in Bede's historical perspective with any real confidence to particular changes within the dynasty. Nevertheless it does seem plausible to suppose that his inconsistency may well have had political roots, if only because there seems scant sign of a better reason for such dramatic shifts of perspective on an issue concerning which one might reasonably have expected Bede to have adhered consistently to a 'Romanist' line. In particular, it seems fair to associate the fundamental shift in emphasis between his selection of exemplary figures from the past in his *Greater Chronicle, c.*725, and the main text of the *Ecclesiastical History*, with the loss of the throne by the lineage in power when the first was written. Although Aldfrith was not descended from that alliance, it is worth reminding ourselves that his putative father, Oswiu, had married King Edwin's daughter and was eventually buried at *Streanæshalch* (?Whitby), where his father-in-law's cult was established in the later years of Aldfrith's reign.[26] In 655, Oswiu had had his infant daughter, Ælfflæd, consecrated as a nun, and she and her mother had taken over the management of this house following Hild's death in 680. As the place of his father's burial, presided over by his own half-sister, Aldfrith and then his heirs might be expected to have taken a particular interest in this house and its major cults, of St Gregory and King Edwin. Authors of the period certainly seem to have felt free to make connections between their own stories and its key personnel. So Abbess Ælfflæd appears as Cuthbert's interlocutor in the anonymous *Life of Cuthbert*, enquiring concerning the succession to Ecgfrith's throne,[27] and is then portrayed in Stephen's *Life of Wilfrid* as a figure of great piety and considerable political influence in court circles in the last years of Aldfrith's life and the early years of the reign of his son, Osred.[28]

Edwin's cult does, therefore, look to have been promoted from within royal circles in the early eighth century, and to have had royal support. Oswald's cult was also being promoted actively in these years, but not as far as one can judge by those closely associated with Osred's regime. Those responsible included bishops Wilfrid and Willibrord – the one only newly reconciled to the court, the other on the continent, Abbot Eappa at distant Selsey (Sussex), and Oswiu's daughter and son-in-law in Mercia, as well, one might assume, as the communities at Lindisfarne and Bamburgh. The change of dynasty in 729 perhaps resulted in the replacement of Edwin as the favoured cult of the court, with the hitherto 'country' cult centred on Oswald. This would suggest that alternative takes on the past were readily available to Bede throughout but his selection from those available was conditioned by his anticipation of their popularity with his intended audience, at the time of composition, at least as much as his own preferences.

The considerable differences between the main text of the *Ecclesiastical History* and the recapitulation need only mean that Bede had earlier miscalculated Ceolwulf's reaction to his first draft. If his foregrounding of stories surrounding Holy Island was intended to have appealed to Ceolwulf himself, he had perhaps over-estimated the king's ability to access these and had failed to anticipate the possibility that a busy king might pass the work over to clerics with very different visions of the past, to proffer comment. Such would account for the somewhat defensive stance which Bede then adopted in his Preface, deploying there as he does a whole gamut of 'Romanist' sources (such as Abbot Albinus and Bishop Daniel) and external figures of authority (including Gregory the Great, Gregory II, Theodore and Hadrian), alongside

Catholic sources from Northumbria itself with connections to the Ionan mission (the anonymous *Life of Cuthbert*, the monks of Lastingham). That is, however, only one of several possible explanations of these differences, none of which is capable of proof.

In practice, the extent to which we can explore the factional politics of Bede's own day is very limited indeed and capable of little more than revealing the extent of our ignorance, but let us briefly pursue this course, if only to illustrate its limitations. There are retrospective signs of tension between King Osred and his political opponents in Æthelwulf's *De Abbatibus*, but this was written most of a century later and offers very little of real substance. Æthelwulf termed Aldfrith the *nothus germanus* ('bastard brother') of Ecgfrith, and presented his son Osred as 'resplendent in reputation and distinguished among the nations' but tyrannous towards members of the Northumbrian élite. Among the latter was the nobleman Eanmund, the founding figure of Æthelwulf's own monastic community, who abandoned his military career and turned to the religious life to escape factional conflict. He did this in company with others and under the guidance of Bishop Eadfrith of Lindisfarne (698–721), an Irish priest named Ultan, who inculcated literacy among the company, and that Egbert whose exploits in Iona Bede highlighted *c.*725 and again in 731.[29] That Eanmund had fallen foul of King Osred seems a reasonable conclusion. That he sought the aid of both the current bishop of Lindisfarne and the *peregrinus* Egbert might imply that these men were also hostile to Osred, so perhaps supportive of the candidacy to the throne of Northumbria of Coenred and ultimately his brother, Ceolwulf, although the involvement of the local bishop in establishing a monastery was virtually obligatory. We might profit, therefore, from an exploration of the political sympathies of Eadfrith and Egbert, and Bede's attitudes towards both.

That Egbert was in exile for political reasons might offer some potential to explain his lengthy presence in Ireland, but such a scenario is problematic, given that Bede developed this paragon as an exemplary figure in works written both within Osric's reign and then in that of Ceolwulf, and had himself earlier complimented Osred. This makes it difficult to see this well-known exile as antagonistic towards either Osred or Osric, unless one supposes Wearmouth/Jarrow to have been such a committed institutional opponent of the latter that its best-known author was prepared to risk the king's wrath in championing a political opponent in exile. Although his *Greater Chronicle* was clearly intended primarily for internal consumption, Bede's construction of a set of exemplars inclusive of King Edwin makes it very likely that he was here operating in ways sympathetic to the regime currently in power. To have written along lines which were openly subversive implies a scenario so distant from Bede's extreme caution when framing his account of recent history in the *EH* that it is best discarded as implausible. Egbert's involvement in Eanmund's affairs is, therefore, best viewed as non-partisan, and he should perhaps be seen predominantly as a figure outside of Northumbrian dynastic politics, but widely recognised as an expert on monasticism so someone likely to be consulted by any member of the Northumbrian élite in the process of establishing a new house.

There seems, however, rather more substance to the premise that tensions existed between Lindisfarne and either or both of Osred and Osric. In this context, it may be significant that when Ceolwulf eventually resigned his kingship in favour of the monastic life in 737,[30] this was in favour of a retirement which the northern annals utilised by Simeon of Durham located at Lindisfarne.[31] Much later authors eventually claimed that Ceolwulf donated not only considerable estates but even his royal treasure, although the detail of his gifts, at least, could be apocryphal. While this is far from being contemporary evidence, it has generally been accepted that Ceolwulf did retire to Lindisfarne just two years after Bede's own death and he may well have enriched it. The choice of Holy Island does have some potential to connect with the earlier co-operation of King Osred's apparent enemy, Eanmund, with the then bishop of Lindisfarne, Eadfrith, who was presumably responsible for extending Lindisfarne's protection over the new monastic cell. One might conclude, therefore, that these three – Ceolwulf, Eanmund and Bishop Eadfrith – could have been in some sense political associates, early in the eighth century. That Eadfrith at Lindisfarne and Acca at Hexham were predisposed to support different dynastic factions may simply reflect underlying tensions between their sees, given that Hexham had been carved out of the pre-existing diocese of Holy Island and had at times threatened to replace it entirely. Wilfrid's reacquisition of Hexham c.706 is unlikely to have been welcome at Lindisfarne, and Acca was presumably his choice of successor.

In exploring Bede's own position, therefore, we might usefully take stock of his treatment of Bishop Eadfrith, on the grounds that this could perhaps have some capacity to reveal his own attitude towards the faction which had supported Coenred in 716–18 and later Ceolwulf. Eadfrith was a prominent figure in northern Northumbria who was well known to Bede, having been a close associate of Bishop Cuthbert, then prior of Melrose before his elevation to the bishopric in 698, holding this office for around twenty-three years. That he can be identified as the author and illustrator of the Lindisfarne Gospels might also have made Eadfrith an attractive subject for comment by an author with Bede's interests, who found room for several far more distant figures with literary achievements (such as Aldhelm) in his *Ecclesiastical History*. It may be pertinent, therefore, that Eadfrith simply does not appear in the *Ecclesiastical History*, despite having earlier been the honoured dedicatee of Bede's prose *Life of Cuthbert*.[32] The fact that he repeatedly mentioned both his predecessor, Eadberht (688–98),[33] and his successor, Æthelwold (721–40),[34] places this silence in context: indeed, Eadfrith is the sole omission among Lindisfarne's bishops in the *EH*. Had Bede been writing in 731 for a faction which had earlier included Eadfrith, and which had recently triumphed under Ceolwulf, then we might perhaps have expected this bishop to have featured honourably. His total neglect makes it impossible today to determine whether or not Bede's history was heavily influenced by the connections to which Æthelwulf later alluded, in the *EH*. Rather, if anything his policy seems to have been excluding. We have already noted Ceolwulf's marginality within the text and the failure to develop his character or his political and dynastic pedigree, with even Ida – from whom he apparently claimed descent – appearing only belatedly in the recapitulation. To the admittedly very limited extent to which we are able to judge, Bede cannot be shown to have been a member of the faction directly supporting Ceolwulf, or keen to prioritise favourable mention of its members, but that cannot be ruled out. Indeed, it is extremely difficult to postulate the membership of such factions on the basis of evidence available to us today, although these were arguably common knowledge at the time of composition.

Whatever else he was doing, therefore, when writing the *Ecclesiastical History*, Bede was not composing a blatantly partisan text for the current dynast in power, validating his claim to the throne or extolling the virtues of his various supporters across recent years. Rather, the reader is left with an impression of extreme reticence regarding contemporary politics, allied with comparative inclusiveness in terms of the religious communities and bishops who receive praise. Repeated reference to the twin comets of 729, in V, 23 and V, 24, carries a sense of Bede's unease at the current political situation, which might imply that Coelwulf's reign had opened in blood, but it does not actively require that interpretation. Clearly, Bede preferred to make as few enemies as possible and spread praise and affirmation very widely indeed, across the religious community at least, steering round public events and behaviours which he may well have condemned in private. The vision which he had presented in the *Greater Chronicle* was markedly less inclusive. Excluding only his comments regarding the Britons, his principal approach as he closed his later work seems to have been to make the best of whatever he could, to construct examples of good behaviour where these seemed apposite, but to retain a diplomatic silence where caution required and lay out the majority of his examples of behaviour displeasing to God both as implicitly as possible and from earlier generations. This was perhaps in large part a matter of political sensitivity, in case of offending Ceolwulf or other men of power, but he may also have had other issues in mind, including Wearmouth/Jarrow's need as an institution to develop new friendships within the current élite and not cause offence within the ranks of those wielding political influence. If Bede's own community was closely associated with Acca, as his several dedications of religious works might suggest, and had been close to Aldfrith's sons, as his own earlier comment on Osred and the letter to Nechtan written by abbot Ceolfrith may imply (see above, p. 190), then post-729 the house may have been shorn of effective political protection, and hostility between the bishop of Hexham and Ceolwulf might have had some real potential to harm its collective interests. Wearmouth/Jarrow's unusual combination of two different sites founded at different dates but under single management perhaps rendered Bede's monastery more vulnerable to political change than other and more conventionally organised examples may have been. Indeed, it is perfectly possible that Bede was writing in response to a request from his own abbot, Hwætberht, or even Acca himself, as a means of honouring the king of the day, such that would lay on him the onus of reciprocating in turn by providing gifts, patronage and protection to the monastery. But if so, then he executed his brief with extraordinary deftness of touch and without going out of his way to manipulate his account of recent events in such a way as to place the current regime in a particularly positive light. Recent review of post-Nicene historical works is inclined to interpret them as narrative myths written so as to offer a preferred story concerning the origins of a particular ecclesiastical community, developed in accordance with local schools of thought,[35] but the exceptionally low profile of Wearmouth/Jarrow itself in the *EH* would suggest that this was written according to a somewhat different agenda.

Bede was addressing the king, in his Preface at least, so the king's views presumably mattered, but they are very difficult indeed to reconstruct. We know very little about King Ceolwulf of the Northumbrians beyond his regnal years (729–37), his retirement to a monastery (as above) and some specific family connections. Bede notes that he was the brother of King Coenred (716–18) and his putative dynastic descent was later given in several texts from Ida's reputed son Ocga,[36] making him only a very distant cousin of Osred, and also perhaps Osric (assuming he was Osred's brother), whose descent was putatively via another of Ida's sons, Æthelric.[37] A serious challenge was gathering impetus to the long dominance of this lineage, which first appears at the death of Aldfrith, in 705,[38] then at each subsequent royal death until Osric's in 729,[39] when the dynasty was finally overthrown. Whether or not that outcome was still at issue when Bede completed the *Ecclesiastical History* is not entirely clear, but there are some indications, above, that the transfer of power in 729 was decisive, leaving Ceolwulf facing challenges from other sections of the royal house thereafter but less so Aldfrith's. Ceolwulf apparently gained the support of his paternal first cousins, Egbert, who he made bishop, then archbishop of York (732–5; 735–66) and his brother Eadberht, who succeeded as king (737–58) once Ceolwulf himself had accepted the tonsure. This was a high price to pay so it may well be that their support was crucial to Ceolwulf's survival of the crisis of 731, and it may even be that they had then temporarily overthrown him, before coming to an agreement which enabled him in the short term to regain his throne, then depart peacefully into the cloister to an agreed timetable. In the last resort, we simply do not know what role they played but their reward certainly implies that their impact on events had been significant.

One shred of evidence comes in the so-called 'Moore Memoranda', consisting of several items in the same hand as the main text of the *Ecclesiastical History* in the Moore MS, which were inserted into the last, otherwise blank page, apparently by an early Wearmouth/Jarrow copyist of the latter.[40] The last of these, translated and modernised, reads as follows:

In the year 547, Ida began to reign from whom originates the royal family of the Northumbrians; he held and remained ruling 12 years. After him Glappa, 1 year; Adda, 8; Æthelric, 4; Theodoric, 7; Fridwald, 6; Hussa, 7; Æthelfrith, 24; Edwin, 17; Oswald, 9; Oswiu, 28; Ecgfrith, 15; Aldfrith, 20; Osred, 11; Cenred, 2; Osric, 11; Ceolwulf, 8. Paulinus baptised 111 years ago; the eclipse 73 years ago; Penda was killed 79 years ago; Ecgfrith's battle 63 years ago; Ælfwine's [death] 58 years ago; the monastery at Wearmouth just 64 years ago; comets seen 8 years ago; the same year Father Egbert crossed to Christ; the Angles [came] into Britain 292 years ago.

Peter Hunter Blair argued that this had been written in 737 at Wearmouth/Jarrow closely following Ceolwulf's resignation, and suggested it should be read as a brief aide-mémoire to the cardinal points of chronology across a period of 190 years, dated by reference to the present (i.e. 737).[41] It therefore arguably reveals what a member of the Wearmouth/Jarrow *scriptorium* then considered the crucial events of the past, around which all else should properly be marshalled. The descent of the Bernician, then the Northumbrian, kingship from Ida opens the sequence, listing all the kings with their regnal years but excluding the two apostates of 633,[42] and any kings who had ruled only Deira, so the Deiran royal line to Ælle and then Oswine. At the moment of Ceolwulf's succession by a cousin, Ida's role as the fount of royal legitimacy was clearly a matter of some significance, as the principal method of validating the succession, which perhaps explains the fashion in which his kingship appears. As in the *Ecclesiastical History*, Eadwulf (705) does not appear, either for reasons of political sensitivity or on account of the brevity of his reign. Such otherwise reflects the stranglehold on the crown achieved to this date by lineages claiming descent from Ida, and provides a dating scheme for the totality of Northumbrian history which connects with Bede's *EH* but does not entirely depend upon it.[43] Paulinus then represents the earliest horizon in the conversion story of the Northumbrians, who featured, of course, prominently in all of Bede's *Greater Chronicle*, the main text of the *Ecclesiastical History* and the recapitulation. The eclipse of 664 was equally included in all three as a 'sign' or portent sent by the Lord. References to Penda's death (655) and Ecgfrith's battle (against Wulfhere, *c.*674) suggest a desire to commemorate moments at which Oswiu and his son had triumphed over invasions by the Mercians,[44] who were presumably viewed as the Northumbrians' most powerful rivals in the present. The prominence given Ælfwine's death suggests that this was seen as an event of particular political significance, perhaps because it left Ecgfrith without a legitimate heir and opened the door to the succession of Aldfrith and company, who appear in the regnal list but not in subsequent comment. Notice of Wearmouth's foundation seems natural in a note written within that house, as is commemoration of the Anglo-Saxon *adventus* at the close, which had been the first of only two 'English' events inserted into Bede's *Lesser Chronicle* in 703 (see above, pp. 113–15), and which necessarily contextualised all else herein. In addition, like Bede, this author saw fit to pick out the death of Egbert as a key event, linked to the appearance of comets and conditioned by use of *pater* ('father'), which of course coincided with Ceolwulf's securing the Northumbrian throne. This was, therefore, an aide-mémoire which was, like the *Ecclesiastical History*, written very much from within the Northumbrian élite and at a particular moment in time: it carried the stamp of Ceolwulf's kingship and the displacement of Aldfrith's lineage in subtle ways which connect with Bede's work, but it gives due prominence to the military successes of Oswiu and Ecgfrith, which Bede was inclined to play down or even exclude, perhaps in deference to Ceolwulf, for whom he proposed in 731 to set out the behaviours of both these kings as examples of royal behaviours which had incurred divine displeasure, even while his brethren continued to commemorate their successes.

One more source may here be explored as having something to add to the picture; this is the so-called 'Anglian Collection' of royal genealogies,[45] which contains four Northumbrian lineages: I, for Ecgfrith (670–85); II, for Ceolwulf (729–37); III, for Eadberht (737–58); and IV, for Alhred (765–74). This material has variously been viewed as either Mercian or Northumbrian in origin, but the Northumbrian material clearly derives from a knowledge-able source, probably in some sense or other the Northumbrian court and/or one or more of the several Northumbrian monasteries where an interest in such matters was maintained. What is worth noting in the present context is the absence of Aldfrith, Osred and Osric from these genealogies, despite their collective tenure of the throne for some forty-two years. Their presence in the *Ecclesiastical History* implies widespread knowledge of their putative lineage, which may mean that their omission from this collection was intentional. These lists may therefore reflect a Northumbrian establishment which pre-ferred to forget the lineage of Ceolwulf's predecessors since Ecgfrith, who was depicted by a near contemporary as having died without male heirs of his body or legitimate brothers so posed little genealogical threat to the various dynasts of the later eighth century.[46] Aldfrith's descendants, in contrast, may well have still posed some threat in the mid-century.[47] The selection of genealogies for this collection may, therefore, have involved some deliberate amnesia. As has repeatedly been stressed, genealogies were highly political in their inspiration and should not be read over-literally. We should perhaps note not just what they do say but also what they omit.

Another approach would be to consider where Ceolwulf might have been before 729, which is nowhere indicated. The trials and tribulations of the Mercian dynast Æthelbald, in exile in the Fens and elsewhere a decade or so earlier, is a prominent feature of the *Life of Guthlac*, and the Bernician dynasty had a long history of taking refuge in Ireland,[48] in Dalriada[49] and in Pict-land.[50] Ceolwulf was Coenred's brother, so presumably his political heir. Given the probability that dynastic rivalry – perhaps even a state of feud – existed between them and Osric, Ceolwulf's presence in Northumbria in the period 718–28 seems improbable. One reading of the *Ecclesiastical History* would be to associate Ceolwulf in these years with memories of, and stories embroidered around, Oswald, so with that Bernician royal figure of the past who was represented by Bede as having returned in triumph from exile among the Scots to renew his people, refound Christianity within Northumbria, restore its borders and re-establish its supremacy over its neighbours under the special protection of God. Egbert's presence at Iona just might be relevant. Perhaps Ceolwulf was even related in some way to Oswald and/or Egbert: we just do not know. Bede's presentation of the past in his *Ecclesiastical History* may, therefore, have embraced current political sensitivities in ways which would have been immediately apparent to his contemporary audience, but if so the parallel was never made clear, to the point whereby it is now impossible to establish with any degree of certainty and can be no more than inference, at best. We simply do not have enough information to pursue the matter very far. Ceolwulf *may* have been in exile, in Dalriada or elsewhere, up to 729 and probably did eventually retire to become a monk at Lindisfarne, so *may* perhaps have been known to Bede as an enthusiast for this house and its cults in 729–31, which included, of course, all of Cuthbert (who was in any case a favourite of his own), Oswald and Aidan. Bede *may*, therefore, have placed their stories at the very centre of his work in deference to Ceolwulf's political pre-eminence in the present, but in the last resort we just do not know whether this or some other motive lay behind the reorientation of his vision of the past since *c.*725.

What we can conclude, therefore, is very limited. Bede was confronted in 729 by a change of regime in Northumbria, now headed by a king whose branch of the royal family had apparently been excluded since the failure of their last attempt to seize power in 716–18. We do not know where Ceolwulf had been in the interim but his takeover had real potential to upset current claims on the conversion history of the region, and existing visions thereof within the several religious houses whose memories collectively made up those strands of history which were most likely to be written down.

Bede may also, of course, have felt the need to exercise due caution when making reference not just of the king but to the great houses of the Northumbrian nobility, many probably with royal connections, who collectively dominated politics in his day. He was, for example, entirely reticent in the *Ecclesiastical History* regarding Egbert, the bishop of York from 732, whom he addressed with such apparent affection and with every sign of familiarity by letter in 734, yet Egbert was Ceolwulf's first cousin and of royal blood so of a very prominent family. Might this imply some concern on Bede's part regarding the current political situation and relations between these great men? The figure of Berhtfrith provides an example through which to explore Bede's position. Berhtfrith appears in Stephen's *Life of Wilfrid* virtually as king-maker in the succession crisis of 705, when he successfully championed Osred's cause against Eadwulf, and was named as 'a prince second only to the king' in the description of the synod by the River Nidd, and given a substantial speech.[51] Bede, in contrast, omitted him from the main text of the *EH*. He had read Stephen's work and may well have viewed Berhtfrith as too closely associated with the now discredited reign of Osred to warrant inclusion in a work dedicated to Ceolwulf. Somewhat surprisingly, however, he appears in the recapitulation, in 711, in reference to a campaign against the Picts. Supposing this to have been added after Bede had received comments back from court regarding the first draft, then it may be that he was advised to include Berhtfrith. An appreciation of the well-known, shifting alliances characteristic of the English aristocracy in the fifteenth century should be enough to remind us that factional fighting in the early eighth may well have involved all sorts of inconsistencies on the part of the warlords involved. This is not to make a case for any particular reading of Berhtfrith in the *EH*, but just to highlight the problem of trying to understand Bede's treatment of leading lay Northumbrians, in all its fluidity.

Bede perhaps felt it necessary, therefore, to represent the past in ways which accorded with the needs of the new regime, and he may have courted acceptance thereby, on behalf of his own community. There is no sense, however, of anything which might be considered sycophantic towards the current rulers of Northumbria, and Bede's silence regarding Bishop Eadfrith and then perhaps also the future Bishop Egbert may suggest that he was disinclined to glorify figures who might be construed to have been associates of Ceolwulf over recent decades. His decision to undertake the *Ecclesiastical History* might actually have been stimulated as much as anything by the shift in the political establishment which occurred in 729: there is after all no reason to suppose it had been begun at any earlier date, albeit some of the raw materials had already then been in his possession for several years. There is a case for his having discussed the notion at an earlier stage with some at least of his correspondents, particularly Albinus at Canterbury, but this need not have come to much, if anything, at the time. Wearmouth/Jarrow was a considerable establishment, in terms of both its complement of brethren and its estates, and of some real political significance. Its first abbot, Benedict Biscop, had been a well-born thegn of King Oswiu, then an adviser to King Ecgfrith, a man with influential connections at Rome and other continental centres and a friend and associate of Archbishop Theodore and the wider Canterbury community. Abbot Ceolfrith was also a member of the Northumbrian élite from a family intimately acquainted with the king of the day, who had likewise travelled to Rome. King Aldfrith had provided Wearmouth/Jarrow with at least one manuscript and Abbot Ceolfrith's letter to Nechtan implies that he was trusted by Osred's regime to correspond with neighbouring courts on politically sensitive issues. Bede's works collectively demonstrate the connections which the dual house maintained not just with Acca and Lindisfarne but also with other centres both within and without the Northumbrian kingship. Wearmouth/Jarrow clearly required access to patronage, secular power, and the élite products which went with such access – as Bede's own legacy of pepper and incense should remind us.

Acquisition of power by a new branch of a royal family frequently affected the fortunes of religious houses in Anglo-Saxon England.[52] Wearmouth/Jarrow may have felt the need to re-establish its position vis-à-vis the crown post-729 by some new strategy or gesture. And what better than telling the story of the English as a Christian people in a way which centred on the Northumbrians and particularly suited the predilections of their new monarch, was dedicated to the new king in person, and was written by the best-known, most prolific and learned scholar in his realm? In that case, the *Ecclesiastical History* could be read both as addressed to the king, and to a degree even as a vehicle for special pleading on behalf of particular individuals and/or communities who might currently be politically endangered – including Acca, Hexham and Wearmouth/Jarrow itself. The comparative self-denial which Bede practised in this work regarding references to his own house and its leadership in recent events is then explicable in terms of his desire to avoid emphasising their association with earlier regimes and to smooth the path for their acceptance by Ceolwulf in the present.[53]

In practice, the incoming dynast seems to have preferred to refocus royal patronage on a pre-existing house rather than found a new one.[54] Holy Island had been eclipsed by the rejection of Iona's authority in 664, by the resurrection of the see of York and then by the establishment of such new diocesan centres as Hexham, Ripon and Whithorn. Particularly once Cuthbert had died (in 687), Lindisfarne was vulnerable: there are hints that the monastery suffered in the year immediately following Cuthbert's death, prior to the appointment of a replacement; it was arguably marginal to royal patronage, had lost its role as the diocesan centre for all Northumbria and found itself having to share the oversight of even Bernicia with a new see established at Hexham, which even at times may have threatened to replace it entirely. While it had successfully defended itself by promoting the cult of Cuthbert and making alliances with whichever other houses – including Wearmouth/Jarrow – were willing, it seems safe to conclude that Lindisfarne was ripe for royal reinvestment in the early eighth century by some dynast without particular ties elsewhere. Ceolwulf presumably found there a long and distinguished tradition sustained by popular and well-promoted cults and linking back to heroic deeds a century or so earlier which were capable of being cast in terms commensurate with his own portrayal as a figure of moral renewal. The attractions seem plausible even though the details are opaque.

Bede's dedication to Ceolwulf, with which he ultimately prefaced his *Ecclesiastical History*, acknowledged that he had earlier submitted the first draft of his text to the king for his *legendum ac probandum* ('accreditation and examination').[55] He wanted the seal of royal approval, therefore. It is plausible to suppose that he was prepared to amend his narrative to gain it, and the addition of the recapitulation, with its several new pieces of information and real shift of emphasis, may have been part at least of such a process. Although we can do little more than surmise, it does seem very possible that Bede had substantially rethought the way in which he would present the story of the

English conversion post-729, giving a far greater role than he might otherwise have done to the Scottish mission and the establishment of Lindisfarne, to accommodate Ceolwulf's partiality for this monastic community and its first royal patron, Oswald, whose cult was perhaps the most popular and wide-flung of any royal saint of the day. This resulted in a text which departed significantly from the conversion story which he had recently outlined in its bare essentials in his *Greater Chronicle*. The new version incorporated an extended account of the Irish mission to Northumbria and gave it a central role. The key outcome of this rethinking of the Northumbrian conversion story is book III of the *Ecclesiastical History*, which foregrounds the Ionan contribution in terms which contrast with his recent amnesia regarding their input. Although Bede was very careful to stress the shortcomings of specific views held by the Irish missionaries and their adherents, his is in general a highly positive take which heaps exceptional praise on them, and includes them within the moral focus of the entire narrative. This represents a significant shift away from his earlier practice of highlighting only the Roman contribution, along with star performers among (primarily) their Northumbrian adherents, while excluding the Irish contribution via a combination of papal condemnation and what can perhaps best be described in terms of studied omission. While Bede's English exemplars in the *Greater Chronicle* were somewhat exclusive, the *Ecclesiastical History* was far more inclusive of all things Northumbrian, which perhaps had some value in the context of King Ceolwulf as dedicatee.

Such a reading has some potential to explain late changes to the text. As already noted, Benedict Biscop may have been excised from book III, or perhaps the opening section of IV, while Bede's love affair herein with Oswald and a desire post-731 to reinforce connections between his Wilfridian associates – particularly Acca – and the royal saint may have encouraged the insertion of a new chapter (IV, 14) that is omitted from the *c*-type of manuscripts, which may have derived from an earlier version. Also missing were two entries in the recapitulation in V, 24, for the years 697 and 698. The earlier deals with Queen Osthryth's murder by the Mercians, but she only otherwise appeared in this work as the figure responsible for Oswald's cult at Bardney, within Mercia.[56] The later is notice of Berhtred's death in battle with the Picts, the meaning of which in a current setting is obscure, albeit this is very much a 'Bernician' and 'northern' event of some potential interest to Ceolwulf's court. Berhtred may, of course, have been closely connected with Ceolwulf but he was not otherwise named, unless he should be identified as that Berht who had led an army to Ireland at Ecgfrith's command in 684 (IV, 26 (24)), although he may, of course, have been connected in some sense with the slightly better-known Berhtfrith, who Bede likewise remarked only in the recapitulation (above).

All of this is, however, fragile in the extreme. The problem with this interpretation, like any other, is that we are overly reliant on Bede's own works to establish the context in which he wrote. We cannot be entirely confident that Ceolwulf was already known to be an enthusiast for Lindisfarne when Bede set out to write his *Ecclesiastical History*, given that he only retired to a monastery two years *after* Bede's own death and that house was only identified as Holy Island at a much later date. Indeed, it would be possible to argue the very different case that it was the centrality of Lindisfarne to Bede's *Ecclesiastical History* that actually encouraged Ceolwulf to enter, and only his exemplification of kings receiving the tonsure that encouraged him to do so in his turn. Similarly, it *could* have been Bede's influence which encouraged his cousin and successor, Eadberht, to accept the tonsure in 758, but that could also have occurred for entirely different reasons.

In the last resort, we can identify significant differences between Bede's main two versions of the past, written respectively *c.*725 and 731, and that the main text of the *EH* is the least consistent of his several assays: Oswald and Aidan are omitted from the *Greater Chronicle* and *Martyrology* and they also seem to have lost their centrality by the time Bede came to write the recapitulation at the close of the *EH*. The recapitulation reads less like an epitome of the whole work than as a compromise between Bede's earlier vision of the past and that which he had adopted in the *Ecclesiastical History*, so as an attempt at reorientation of the overall tenor, given that the tone has changed and there are entirely new events brought in. That the recapitulation was written after the first draft of the work was returned by Ceolwulf, as a means of incorporating additions or amendments required by the king with the minimum of rewriting, is a possibility which has been mooted above (pp. 94–5), but this is no more than one of several options. And the Preface and V, 24 aside, it seems fairly certain that the *Ecclesiastical History* was conceived and written with pretty much the shape and organisation with which it eventually emerged, with book III and the particular treatment of the Ionan mission which it encompasses very much integral to the whole work.

It seems reasonable to postulate, therefore, that Bede was consciously developing Oswald, Aidan and figures whom he chose to depict as their spiritual heirs at the core of this work against a particular political backdrop, so within a comparatively restricted time-span, and in so doing was knowingly updating his much briefer excursions into the same territory in his pre-existing work. This may imply that the *Ecclesiastical History* was conceived, planned and executed entirely within the period 729–31, so under Ceolwulf as king and as a response to the new dynastic situation, but that entire case remains very much a matter of inference. In the last resort, we can only speculate as to whether or not his dedication to Ceolwulf provides the key to understanding Bede's thinking behind the *Ecclesiastical History*.

This concluding chapter offers, therefore, some ideas concerning the political context in which the *Ecclesiastical History* was written, which are little more than conjecture but which may at least provide a new starting point for further discussion of these issues. What we can be reasonably clear about, however, is that both David Kirby and then Walter Goffart were on the right lines when they proposed to explore the contemporary political context of

Bede's *EH*: rejection of Goffart's arguments in favour of Bede as a mouthpiece of anti-Wilfridian sections of the Northumbrian church does not mean that we should merely revert to previous visions of Bede as a cloistered monastic somehow insulated from the power struggles of his own day.[57] Beside its undoubted intellectualism and theological interests, the *Ecclesiastical History* does contain echoes of what were arguably fast-changing contemporary politics. These do provide hints at the context in which this work was produced but they do not provide an adequate justification for Bede's commitment of considerable time and energy to the enterprise when that could have been expended on other, more narrowly religious projects. Rather, the *EH* was conceived by Bede as a part of his normal religious concerns and as a project on the grand scale, designed to offer an immediate, secular audience a gallery of examples, both good and bad, drawn from their own insular history, rather than continental or biblical backdrops, from which they were being invited to learn. Why? Surely, because Bede was pursuing an essentially Gregorian vision of his role as a religious thinker and had a joined-up vision of the world in which he lived, wherein kings and the secular élite had a particular responsibility for the good of the whole community via their relationship with the one God. Bede expected his new work to be accessed as an English equivalent of the greater ecclesiastical histories which had gone before, but his pastoral concerns were arguably foremost, as he himself asserted. He was attempting to set out history to the Northumbrian élite in the form of parables which read in simplified terms: 'x in the past did this, which pleased/ displeased God, who in response rewarded/punished x'. His intention was that this should be understood by his audience as guidance to their own current and future behaviours: 'If you act badly, like x, in the past, then God will react in the same way as before, as I have shown, so you would do better to follow the good examples set out and turn away from the bad.'

The *Ecclesiastical History* should, therefore, be read primarily as an extended form of sermon aimed to engender moral reform among Bede's contemporaries – particularly the secular élite – and so improve the relationship between the Northumbrians, as a people, and the Christian God. Consistently, that is its principal purpose, which overshadows and on occasion renders obscure more mundane issues regarding the actual affairs of kings. For the historian the problem is how we should read such a text, and how reliable are all the many details for which Bede provides us with the only evidence. Clearly, the numerous characterisations that Bede offered, promoting some figures of the past as saints and others as sinners, should not be allowed to pass the processes of critical reading in the present. But there is also so much that is lost. The historical context of Bede's hints and innuendos, exclusions, partial inclusions and particular emphases were arguably far more comprehensible to a politically aware, contemporary audience, who shared much of his knowledge of recent events at least, than to a modern readership which is reliant primarily on Bede's own work for access to a very distant past, knowledge of which is in most respects now lost. The very quality of his work, its lucidity and fluency, and the extraordinary subtlety of a narrative powered less by anything which we could view as an historical agenda than by moral concern all now stand between us as consumers and the context in which he wrote.

Towards conclusions

On one level, it seems safe to conclude that Bede saw himself as writing a chapter in the universal ecclesiastical history of the sixth age of the world, as an addendum to that of Rufinus, to include a story of the conversion of the English under willing kings, the foundation of dioceses and monasteries and the succession of bishops. In that sense, this was a history, in terms then conventional, of the English as one of God's chosen peoples, led in large part by Northumbria's rulers. But he was also using ecclesiastical history as a vehicle to present the Northumbrian élite of the day with a whole gallery of both good and bad examples of behaviour drawn from a predominantly regional past, which Bede supposed might be more appropriate to the present generation than those offered by the Scriptures as a spur to good behaviour. That this audience was a somewhat 'Bernician' subset of the whole Northumbrian élite perhaps required that Bede shift his ground from the much smaller body of exemplars which he had used to position his people within the Catholic mainstream in his *Greater Chronicle* just a few years earlier, for an audience confined to his own brethren. It is quite likely, but by no means proven, that the new emphasis that he now placed on Oswald and Aidan, in particular, reflected the interests of Ceolwulf as a dynast. That said, the very marginality of the king's presence within the body of the text, as opposed to the Preface, may imply that Bede, while writing, had serious doubts regarding Ceolwulf's ability to retain the throne, so was inclined to preach to a somewhat more generic, but still Bernicia-centric audience concerning the responsibilities incumbent upon those who held power, while retaining the ability to reorientate his work towards the particular faction in control at as late a stage as possible. The addition of the recapitulation provided Bede with an opportunity to reinforce his dedication with some complimentary entry regarding Ceolwulf: that he did not but ended with an entry which recognised the *imperium* of a Mercian king suggests that the fortunes of the Northumbrian ruler may have been at comparatively low ebb at this point.

It seems fair to conclude that Bede's narration of the past was to a large extent subordinated to his concern with the present and immediate future. As modern readers, approaching Bede's *Ecclesiastical History* almost 1300 years after it was written, we are at a substantial disadvantage when compared with the immediate audience for whom he was writing, who had a very different vision of the world and far greater knowledge of contemporary politics, and the family connections and antagonisms by which politics were largely defined. Subtleties of meaning, which may, for example, easily have included oblique references to particular living individuals or recent, but not explicitly described, events, are very largely now beyond recall, simply because we are so dependent on this work to contextualise the world at which it was directed. This should not, however, be allowed to detract from our consciousness of its currency when written, for the *Ecclesiastical History* was a piece of comparatively systematic advocacy which centred on how its intended audience should and should not behave, so as to maximise divine approbation and avoid, for example, the fate of the Britons, as spelled out across book I, the second chapter of book II, and the final narrative passage in V, 23. Bede was not informed in a modern sense by secular concerns, since his was a very different, providential theory of history. His interest in Northumbrian politics and its array of historical characters centred on their meanings as construed in terms of relations between God and His people. It was in this context that he set out the deeds of several recent southern kings and the power vouchsafed them by the Lord. Bede was offering the secular leadership of Northumbria a series of exemplars drawn from their own past and developed by reference to the leaders of neighbouring peoples, whom he presented as having secured divine favour by following particular types of career: Cædwalla of the West Saxons is perhaps the most extreme case but the rise of Mercian kings to Southumbrian supremacy was the more recent phenomenon. *Imperium* was explicitly God-granted, for His purposes. In contrast to his later *Letter to Egbert*, general support for the moral integrity of the episcopacy and the vast majority of Northumbria's clergy and monastic communities was apparently intended to persuade the secular leadership that the need for moral reform centred primarily on themselves rather than their clerical associates.

Bede's fundamental role all his adult life was as a teacher and this was the text through which he sought to reach out beyond the limits of his accustomed monastic and clerical audience, to share his vision with the secular élite as well, advising them how to proceed so as best to please the Lord. This was not a particularly factional message: Bede did not, for example, concern himself with the glorious achievements of the antecedents of King Ceolwulf since Ida. Nor was he in the business of justifying Ceolwulf's claim on the throne. Rather, this was an essentially moral tale, delivered via a much-extended type of sermon, but we need to bear in mind that Bede believed that political achievement, like spiritual fulfilment, depended primarily on the ongoing interplay between Man and God. This does not mean that he was lecturing Ceolwulf on the art of government, like some precursor to Machiavelli's *The Prince*, for his advice was both less specific and more concerned with principles than that. What his audience was expected to take away from the text was, in part, a sense of the historical traditions underlying the present under God's steering hand, in part, a series of lessons embedded within exposition of the behaviours of the rulers and clergy of earlier generations, which offered a vision of what actions He might reward or punish in the present. What Ceolwulf and others had done in the past was less important, from Bede's perspective, than the extent to which he would now throw himself into a leadership role under Bede's own guidance and so secure the protection of God for himself and his people and gain redemption. All of runs of chapters focusing on such past heroes as Oswald, Aidan, Cuthbert and John of Beverley, lengthy single chapters (as depicting the lives of Gregory, Chad and Wilfrid) or consecutive paired chapters (as Hild and Æthelthryth) serve to emphasise both the types of behaviour which were being encouraged and the benevolence of God towards those who in the past had behaved in such ways. Clerical exemplars were clearly intended to make a considerable contribution to the lessons to be learned.

In some senses, like Gildas's *Concerning the Ruin of Britain*, this was a work more closely connected with pastoral care and moral reform than a type of text that we, today, would conceive of as history. That said, it is all too easy for modern readers to underestimate the sense of divine agency universally manifest in this conception of the world. It is a providential vision of the past, as one should expect of a monastic author nearing the close of a long and distinguished career in exegesis: it was never intended to be a passive recording of events but to be read as ideologically driven, with the issue of salvation always in view. It was quite explicitly encouraging the present generation to emulate the best behaviours offered from the past and eschew the failings of their forebears, so as to reverse a slide in the affairs of Northumbria's leaders since the golden era associated with King Oswald, which might otherwise ultimately place their very status as a people of the Lord in jeopardy. This was Bede posing as prophet and guardian of the special relationship between God and His people, worrying about the present and the immediate future for his compatriots.

Few of his proposals were entirely new, of course. Bede's admiration, for example, for various types of royal retirement had strong roots in Cuthbert's preference as he neared death for the ascetic life on Farne over his duties on Holy Island, Abbot Ceolfrith's departure as a pilgrim for Rome and Bishop John's resignation from York in favour of the monastic life at Beverley.[58] Ceolwulf did himself, just a few years later,[59] follow the example set by a succession of non-Northumbrian kings, appoint his own successor and retire from political life to a monastery,[60] and that successor, his cousin Eadberht, eventually did the same in 758, in favour of his son Oswulf, receiving the tonsure at York following what was perhaps the most successful reign by a Northumbrian king since Ecgfrith's defeat and death.

These behaviours could mean that Bede's underlying moral message had been appreciated by his target audience to the point that it eventually affected political behaviour, but that must remain open to question since, as already noted, we simply cannot pretend to know any king's motives. Tonsure at Lindisfarne may, after all, have looked very attractive to a dynasty whose reign had been as heavily contested as Ceolwulf's seems to have been. That said, the great drought noticed in the same annals and for the same year, which 'rendered the land infertile',[61] just may have encouraged Ceolwulf to seek divine aid for his people, by such an act of renunciation as Bede seems to have recommended to him via earlier exemplars drawn from English history. That

Eadberht later followed his example surely reinforces the point. 'Was Bede's agenda understood by his intended audience?' is, therefore, a question which merits the answer 'Yes, it just might have been.' Yet, the very immediacy of the work that Bede had contrived in terms of his dedication to the king of the day arguably gave it a very limited shelf-life. Oswulf's murder in 759 brought to the Northumbrian throne a figure with no known connection with Ceol-wulf, and no reason to take note of a work dedicated to him, and urging him towards behaviours pleasing to the Lord. In such circumstances, the *Ecclesiastical History* may well have lost whatever currency it had to date achieved in the immediate forum for which it was intended, and its continuing circulation came to depend largely on unforeseen clerical and monastic audiences both in England and on the continent. Their interest was arguably for reasons which were largely tangential to the purposes for which Bede had actually written, and more concerned with the *EH* as a reservoir of saintly behaviour, of one kind or another, and as a document of record. In the latter guise, Bede's major historical work rapidly became a monolith which henceforth served to define the period, effectively disguising the very fluidity with which very different and even quite oppositional perceptions of the past were competing for attention as he was writing.

Notes

Introduction

1 Quoted in *The Times*, 20 June 2000, p. 3, and *The Guardian*, 21 June 2000, p. 3, respectively. To be fair to Livingstone, it has to be said that historians and archaeologists have at times over the last 150 years made not dissimilar comments.
2 Quoted in *The Times*, 5 October 1996, p. 9.

1 (Re-)Reading Bede: an author and his audience

1 J. Barnes, *Flaubert's Parrot*, London: Jonathan Cape, 1984, quote from the Picador edition by Pan Books Ltd, 1985, 130.
2 L. Sherley-Price (trans. and intro.), revised by R. E. Latham, ed. D. H. Farmer, *Bede: A History of the English Church and People*, Harmondsworth: Penguin, 1968; J. McClure and R. Collins (ed. and intro.), *Bede: The Ecclesiastical History of the English People*, Oxford: Oxford University Press, 1994, which offers the translation of Bruce Colgrave, from *EH*, which is today the standard text.
3 Alcuin, in the late eighth century, is the nearest comparison, but he wrote much of his output in Frankia and very many of his far more numerous works are comparatively short letters. Otherwise, the only parallels are with the slightly earlier Aldhelm and the much later Ælfric, neither of whom wrote as much as Bede.
4 R. H. Hodgkin, *A History of the Anglo-Saxons* I, Oxford: Oxford University Press, 1935, 355, traces this expression back to several earlier writers.
5 To give an example, my own history students are directed to read Bede's *History of the Abbots* and the prose *Life of Cuthbert*, but only to examine specific passages from *Concerning the Reckoning of Time* or *Homilies*.
6 It is important to note that Wearmouth/Jarrow was not founded as a double monastery but in two comparatively separate episodes, eight years apart and in rather different political circumstances. King Ecgfrith, who granted the necessary extensive estates on both occasions, was the dominant figure in Anglo-Saxon England in 673, when he acted as protector to a Church Synod at Hertford, but he had recently been defeated by the Mercians in 681 and lost control of Lindsey. The unity of the twin monastery seems to have been more a product of Ceolfrith's dual abbacy than of any initial design. Dual-sited monasteries did exist elsewhere but were not commonplace and the communities of Wearmouth/Jarrow seem to have been understandably nervous of their ability to retain both sites under single management.
7 This detail is in *EH* V, 24. Although Bede seems to have been familiar with the Rule of St Benedict, he expressly stated that the monastery's founder, Benedict Biscop, collected advice on the organisation of monastic life from seventeen continental monasteries. For discussion of the issue, see P. Wormald, 'Bede and

Benedict Biscop', in *FC* 141–69 at 143–4, and C. Cubitt, *Anglo-Saxon Church Councils, c.650–850*, London: Leicester University Press, 1995, 129ff.

8 Twenty-five was the canonical age, but we cannot know how common exceptions were.

9 Had Bede been of royal birth, we might have expected the fact to have leaked out in some form; had he been effectively unfree then his family would presumably not have had the power to decide that he should enter the monastery; but both are assumptions based on supposition. More detailed attempts to postulate his family background, such as the common argument that he was of non-noble origin, seem to me to exceed the very little evidence which is available. For Bede's views on the status of monastic inmates vis-à-vis their status by birth, see his treatment of Abbot Eosterwine in 'Bede: Lives of the Abbots of Wearmouth and Jarrow', in D. H. Farmer (ed.) and J. F. Webb (trans.), *The Age of Bede*, Harmondsworth: Penguin, revised edn 1988, 8; C. Plummer, *Venerabilis Baedae Opera Historica*, Oxford: Clarendon Press, 1896, I, 371.

10 Undertaken by Professor Rosemary Cramp but only finally published after this volume had gone to press. See R. J. Cramp, 'Excavations at the Saxon Monastic Sites of Wearmouth and Jarrow, Co. Durham: An Interim Report', *Medieval Archaeology* 13 (1969) 21–66, a summary of the 1971 season published in *Medieval Archaeology* 17 (1973) 148–53 and Cramp, 'Monkwearmouth and Jarrow: The Archaeological Evidence', in *FC* 1–18.

11 Little survives of the seventh-century church: see the description in H. M. Taylor and J. Taylor, *Anglo-Saxon Architecture*, Cambridge: Cambridge University Press, 1965, I, 432–46. See also P. Wormald, 'Monkwearmouth and Jarrow', in J. Campbell (ed.), *The Anglo-Saxons*, London: Phaidon Press, 1982, 74–5.

12 At V, 14. For discussion see P. Meyveart, 'Bede the Scholar', in *FC* 47.

13 For the church, see Taylor and Taylor, *Anglo-Saxon Architecture* I, 338–49, who argue against even the present chancel, which originated as a separate small church east of and on the same alignment as St Paul's, being of seventh-century date. Their suggestion is that the nave which was demolished as unsafe in 1782 was Benedict's church. Foundations of its north wall are visible in the present Victorian nave. The two churches were eventually conjoined by the construction of the tower.

14 Cramp, 'Monkwearmouth and Jarrow', 16; the 'imperial' connections were usefully explored by I. Wood, *The Most Holy Abbot Ceolfrid*, JL (1995) 13–15.

15 *Chronica Minor Auctore Minorita Erphordiensi*, ed. O. Holder-Egger, in *Monumenta Germaniae Historica Scriptorum* 24, Hanover: Hahn, 1879, 172–204, at 180.

16 The issue was raised but not resolved by B. Ward, *The Venerable Bede*, 2nd edn, London and New York: Continuum, 1998, 57.

17 D. A. Bullough, *Alcuin: Achievement and Reputation*, Education and Society in the Middle Ages and Renaissance 16, Leiden: Brill, 2004, 110–17, discusses the issue without coming to any particular conclusion.

18 Felix's near-contemporary *Life of St Guthlac* depicted him as retiring to the hermitage of Crowland with two young male attendants. While perhaps indicative of his high status and royal birth necessitating servants, this remains open to other interpretations, but there is certainly less cause to go down that road in his case than Alcuin's: the reference is in B. Colgrave (ed.), *Felix's Life of Saint Guthlac*, Cambridge: Cambridge University Press, 1956, XXVI. That such practices by hermits were on occasion at least frowned upon is illustrated by M. de Jong, *In Samuel's Image: Child Oblation in the Early Medieval West*, Leiden: E. J. Brill, 1996, 16.

19 W. Trent Foley and A. G. Holder, *Bede: A Biblical Miscellany*, Liverpool: Liverpool University Press, 1999, 57–80.

20 A. G. Holder, 'The Feminine Christ in Bede's Biblical Commentaries', in *BV* 109–18.

21 *Liber Vitae Ecclesiæ Dunelmensis*, ed. J. Stevenson, *Surtees Society* 13(2) (1841), 10. That the list of abbots opens with Biscop, and of kings with Edwin (who was Ecgfrith's maternal grandfather), has encouraged the view that this document may have originated at Wearmouth/Jarrow but the majority opinion now favours Lindisfarne.

22 B. Colgrave (ed. and trans.), *Two Lives of St. Cuthbert*, Cambridge: Cambridge University Press, 1940, xxxv, 265, fn. 37.

23 D. Dumville, 'The Anglian Collection of Royal Genealogies and Regnal Lists', *Anglo-Saxon England* 5 (1976) 23–50, at 37. That this Beda was depicted as father to one Beoscep seems improbably similar to the connection between Bede and Benedict Biscop, albeit their spiritual relationship is herein rendered genetic and reversed, suggesting that this genealogy may be derivative of contemporary literature and far from genuine; J. Bateley (ed.), *The Anglo-Saxon Chronicle, A Collaborative Edition, 3, MS A*, Cambridge: D. S. Brewer, 1986, 20. This late ninth-century text was clearly written with a considerable acquaintance with Bede's work and the use of his name here may have been apocryphal.

24 H. Ström, *Old English Personal Names in Bede's History, an Etymological–Phonological Investigation*, Lund Studies in English 8, Lund: C.W.K. Gleerup, 1939, 63.

25 *EH* V, 24: *cura propinquorum datus sum educandus reuerentissimo abbati Benedicto* ('by the care of relatives given to be educated to the most reverend abbot Benedict'). Alcuin suggested that it was his parents who had 'made him enter' Jarrow: P. Godman, *Alcuin, The Bishops, Kings, and Saints of York*, Oxford: Clarendon Press, 1982, lines 1293–4.

26 Stephen's *Life of St. Wilfrid*, cap. 3, named him Biscop Baducing: B. Colgrave, *The Life of Bishop Wilfrid by Eddius Stephanus*, Cambridge: Cambridge University Press, 1927, 31. Even Biscop ('bishop') has been considered an unlikely name to confer within a noble warrior family. The name 'Benedict' was apparently adopted by Biscop, presumably out of respect for the abbot whom Gregory the Great so revered. Bede's friend Hwætberht acquired the name Eusebius, presumably on becoming abbot, but neither of these instances are of an Old English name, which implies that Bede's was his birth name.

27 *Monumenta Germaniae Historica, Legum III, Concilia Aevi Karolini*, ed. E. Werminghoff, Hanover and Leipzig, 1906, II, 1, 409, quoting from Bede's commentary on Luke, and II, 1, 759.

28 *PL* 95, col. 1574.

29 D. Rollason (ed. and trans.), *Simeon of Durham, Libellus de Exordio atque Procursu Istius, Hoc est Dunhelmensis, Ecclesie: Tract on the Origins and Progress of this the Church of Durham*, Oxford: Clarendon Press, 2000, I, 14.

30 Quoted by Colgrave and Mynors, *EH* lxxiv.

31 Godman, *Alcuin*, lines 79, 1260, 1388.

32 F. Wormald (ed.), *English Kalendars before A.D. 1100*, Publications of the Henry Bradshaw Society 72, Woodbridge: Boydell Press for the Henry Bradshaw Society, 1988, *passim*.

33 The Latin original was printed most recently with parallel translation in *EH* 580–7, and a translation alone in McClure and Collins, *Bede*, 300–3.

34 The modern practice is enshrined in Plummer's scholarly 'Introduction' to his edition: Plummer, *Baedae Opera* I, ix–x, lxxiii–lxxvii, and has been followed by most later commentators, but it dates back to the twelfth century: see for example, Rollason, *Simeon of Durham* I, 14.

35 Gregory of Tours, *Ten Books of History* (commonly known today as *History of the Franks*) X, 31, lists the bishops of Tours down to himself as nineteenth in succession, lays claim to having rebuilt the cathedral and recovered the relics of its saints, then, like Bede, lists the works he had authored: books of history and of miracles, a commentary on the psalms and a work on church services; Jerome

focuses on his own works, which has much in common with Bede's listing of his own in *EH* V, 24; S. Mason (trans. and commentary), *The Life of Josephus*, Leiden: Brill, 2001.

36 E.g. F. Ruehl (ed.), *Eutropius, Breviarium ab urbe condita*, Leipzig: Teubner, 1887, Preface. The dedication opens: *Domino Valenti Gothico Maximo Perpetuo Augusto Eutropius* . . . ('To the Lord Valens Gothicus, Great and Perpetual Augustus, Eutropius . . .').

37 Colgrave, *Two Lives of St. Cuthbert*, 142–3.

38 D. Hurst (ed.), *Bedae Venerabilis Opera* II, *Opera Exegetica* 2a, *CCSL* 119a, Turnhout: Brepols, 1969, 237.

39 C. W. Jones (ed.), *Bedae Venerabilis Opera* VI, *Opera Didascalica* 2, *CCSL* 123b, Turnhout: Brepols, 1977, 265.

40 See C. B. Kendall, 'Bede's *Historia Ecclesiastica:* The Rhetoric of Faith', in J. J. Murphy (ed.), *Medieval Eloquence*, Berkeley: University of California Press, 1978, 151–2.

41 Bede's closure with a prayer to God perhaps replicates Gregory of Tours's ending of his *History* with the words 'Here ends in Christ's name'. Different early texts of the *EH*, however, have Bede's prayer variously at the end of the whole or at the close of the Preface.

42 Bede followed St Augustine's *Concerning Christian Doctrine* in seeing number in a biblical context as carrying symbolic meaning. His greatest excursus in this area is in his *Commentary on the Temple*, but significant biblical numbers, such as 3, 4, 7, 12, are a commonplace of the *Ecclesiastical History*. It is difficult to establish a 'standard' age at which child oblates entered the religious life in early medieval Europe: Mayke de Jong suggests that under the Rule of St Benedict such were normally quite young, and always under the age of fifteen, at which the rules of adult entry apply: *In Samuel's Image*, 26–8.

43 L. T. Martin and D. Hurst (trans.), *Bede the Venerable: Homilies on the Gospels, Book One, Advent to Lent*, Kalamazoo, MI: Cistercian Publications, 1991, 125–31; a Latin text is provided in D. Hurst (ed.), *Homelia I, 13, S. Benedicti Biscopi*, in *Beda Venerabilis Opera* III, *Opera Homiletica*, Turnhout: Brepols, 1955, 88–94.

44 D. Whitelock (ed.), *English Historical Documents* I, 2nd edn, London: Routledge, 1979, 758–69.

45 *Ibid.*, 758–70, at 762, ch. 14.

46 Caution was urged by D. Whitelock, 'Bede and His Teachers and Friends', in *FC* 20–2.

47 There is a useful discussion of the issue in McClure and Collins, *Bede*, xiii–xiv.

48 Brethren from Jarrow were present at Wearmouth following the departure of Ceolfrith in 716 to elect his successor: Whitelock, *English Historical Documents*, 766, cap. 29.

49 L. T. Martin (ed. and trans.), *The Venerable Bede: Commentary on the Acts of the Apostles*, Kalamazoo, MI: Cistercian Publications, 1989, XXVII, 15. Bede was also, of course, an expert on the tide around Britain, which may imply that he had personally observed it at several points around the coast: F. Wallis (trans., intro. and comment.), *Bede: The Reckoning of Time*, Liverpool: Liverpool University Press, 1999, 29 (at 85)

50 As revealed by the *Letter to Egbert* of late 734.

51 As is at least implicit in the Preface of Bede's prose *Life of Cuthbert*, ed. Colgrave, *Two Lives of St. Cuthbert*, 145: this refers to Herefrith's travelling 'hither' but Bede bringing 'what was written into the presence of your brotherhood', presumably on Holy Island.

52 The text is provided in translation by Wallis, *The Reckoning of Time*, appendix 3.3.

53 *Ibid.*, appendix 3.2.

54 In W. T. Foley and A. G. Holder, *Bede: A Biblical Miscellany*, Liverpool: Liverpool

University Press, 1999, 39–51, at 39–40. This work provides an apposite example of Bede's address to his bishop: 'To the most blessed lord who is always to be venerated with profoundest charity, the holy bishop Acca'.

55 Whitelock, 'Bede and His Teachers and Friends', in *FC* 19.

56 William of Malmesbury quoted a letter from Pope Sergius to Abbot Ceolfrith but seems to have been responsible for the incorporation of Bede's name into the text, which is not present in what is thought to be his original: R. A. B. Mynors, R. M. Thomson and M. Winterbottom (ed. and trans.), *William of Malmesbury, Gesta Regum Anglorum* I, Oxford: Clarendon Press, 1998, 58; M. Thomson, *William of Malmesbury*, Woodbridge: Boydell Press, 1987, 172–3.

57 Anon., *Life of Abbot Ceolfrith*, 35–8, Whitelock, *English Historical Documents*, 768–9. Alcuin remarked that his incorrupt body was eventually exhumed and brought back to 'his native land': P. Godman (ed.), *Alcuin: The Bishops, Kings and Saints of York*, Oxford: Clarendon Press, 1982, lines 1299–1300, 102–3.

58 C. H. Talbot, *Anglo-Saxon Missionaries in Germany*, London: Sheed and Ward, 1954, 154–77.

59 W. Goffart, *Narrators of Barbarian History (550–800): Jordanes, Gregory of Tours, Bede and Paul the Deacon*, Princeton: Princeton University Press, 1988, 240–1 makes the same point but for rather different reasons.

60 *EH* 580–7, at 580–1. Plummer, *Baedae Opera* I, lxxii, has *collectori* in reference to Cuthwin rather than Colgrave and Mynor's *conlector*, but prefers the meaning of the latter. That Cuthbert had already featured as dedicatee in Bede's *On the Art of Metre* implies that he may have been a particularly favoured pupil of the older man.

61 W. F. Bolton, '*Epistola Cuthberti de Obitu Bedae*: A Caveat', *Medievalia et Humanistica*, N.S. 1 (1970), 127–39, arguing that the authenticity of the *Letter* should not be taken for granted, nor Bede's death date.

62 See, for example, *De Die Judicii* ('Concerning the Day of Judgement'): M. J. B. Allen and D. G. Calder, *Sources and Analogues of Old English Poetry: The Major Latin Texts in Translation*, Woodbridge: Boydell and Brewer, 1976, 208–12. Although this is not listed in *EH* V, 24, it is generally presumed to be an authentic work of Bede: see, for example, M. Lapidge, *Bede the Poet*, JL (1993), 1–5, who noted that others of his poems also concerned themselves with the moment of death, contrasting the trauma of hell with the bliss of heaven. That said, the pastoralism of the opening of *De Die Judicii* is exceptional in the context of Bede's work and some caution regarding his authorship might be appropriate. Assuming Bede to have been the author, reference to Acca may imply that it does not post-date completion of *EH* V, 24, which might otherwise explain its omission.

63 See, for example, Bede's treatment of Wilfrid in *EH* V, 19, in which the bishop is presented as sharing with Acca a vision of the archangel Michael predicting the length of time remaining to him, which Cuthbert is likely to have known. Such episodes rely heavily on Gregory's narration of St Benedict foretelling the time of his own death in *Dialogues* II, 37, and ultimately on Christ's foreknowledge of his own death.

64 Bede's prose *Life of Cuthbert*, iv, in Colgrave, *Two Lives of St. Cuthbert*, 164–7. Cuthbert's role as a herdsman suggests that the parallel is with the shepherds and the nativity. The episode derives from the anonymous *Life*, 5, and Bede's *Metrical Life*, 4.

65 *EH* IV, 23.

66 St Boniface, for example, is revealed by his surviving letters as a significant source of pepper, spices, incense, myrrh and wine reaching English houses and diocesans, including York: E. Emerton (trans. and intro.), *The Letters of Saint Boniface*, New York: Columbia University Press, 1940, 11.

67 Whitelock, *English Historical Documents*, 831–2.

68 D. Whitelock, *After Bede*, JL (1963), 3.

69 W. Böhne, 'Das älteste Lorscher Kalendar und seine Vorlagen', in F. Knöpp (ed.), *Die Reichsabtei Lorsch: Festschrift zum Gedenken an ihre Stiftung 764*, Darmstadt: Hess. Histoc. Komma., 1977, 171–220, at 185; Donald Bullough agrees that 'the Wearmouth-Jarrow stamp [of this calendar] is unmistakeable': 'York, Bede's Calendar and a Pre-Bedan English Martyrology', *Analecta Bollandiana* 121 (2003), 328–55, at 351.

70 Wormald, *English Kalendars, passim.*

71 The Letter of Boniface to Archbishop Egbert of York, 746–7, is translated in Emerton, *Letters of St Boniface*, 110–11 and Whitelock, *English Historical Documents*, 823–4: 'I beseech you to copy and send me some treatises from the work of the teacher, Bede, whom lately, as we have heard, the divine grace endowed with spiritual understanding and allowed to shine in your province, so that we also may benefit from that candle.' Boniface's letter to Hwætberht is translated by Emerton, *ibid.*, 111–12, and Whitelock, *ibid.*, 824–5. For the second letter to Egbert of 747–51, see Emerton, *ibid.*, 145–6. For a Latin text, see M. Tangl, *Die Briefen des heiligen Bonifatius und Lullus*, Monumenta Germaniae Historica, Epistolae Selectae 1, Berlin: Weidmann, 2nd edn, 1955, nos. 75, 76, 91. It is interesting to note that precisely the same images occur in some modern treatments of Bede: see, as one example among many, E. P. Echlin, 'Bede and the Church', *Irish Theological Quarterly* 40 (1973) 351: 'Bede burned as a candle in a dark time before a darker time – and the light that radiated from his scriptorium on the Tyne was the best tradition of the church.'

72 Whitelock, *English Historical Documents*, 831–2; Tangl, *Die Briefen des heiligen Bonifatius und Lullus*, nos. 116, 126, 127.

73 Whitelock, *English Historical Documents*, 834–5; Tangl, *Die Briefen des heiligen Bonifatius und Lullus*, no. 125.

74 See discussion of these issues by D. W. Rollason, *Bede and Germany*, JL (2001).

75 Godman, *Alcuin*, xxxix–xlvii.

76 *Ibid.*, xxxix–xli. Alcuin's treatment of Cuthbert in lines 646–740 rests entirely on Bede's work.

77 *Ibid.*, 102–5 for quotations and see footnote to lines 1291–1318.

78 D. Kirby, *Bede's Historia Ecclesiastica Gens Anglorum, Its Contemporary Setting*, JL (1993), 14–15; see below, p. 212.

79 *Denotatio dedicationis ecclesiae Sancti Salvatoris constructae in monasterio Fuldae*, in E. Dümmler (ed.), *Hrabani Mauri Carmina*, Monumenta Germaniae Historica, Poetae Latini Aevi Karolini II, Berlin: Weidmann, 1884, 205–8.

80 Despite its inclusion of the abbots Benedict, Eosterwine, Ceolfrith and Hwætberht, which may suggest that it originates from the abbacy of Cuthbert, when Bede's commemoration was at its height, and it has tentatively been dated 750–5: Böhne, 'Das älteste Lorscher Kalendar und seine Vorlagen', 174–5.

81 Wormald, *English Kalendars before A.D. 1100*, 2–13, at 5 (Bodleian Library, Digby Ms 63, ff. 40–45vo); the calendar fragment in an eighth-century Northumbrian hand edited and analysed by P. P. Siffren does not include entries for May, so Bede's presence cannot be tested, but parallels between this and Willibrord's calendar, which does not include Bede (perhaps because he was then still alive) may suggest that he would not have appeared herein: 'Das Walderdorffer Kalendarfragment saec. VII und die Berliner Blätter eines Sakramentars aud Regensburg', *Ephemerides Liturgicae* 47 (1933) 201–44.

82 M. Lapidge, 'Latin Learning in Ninth-Century England', in M. Lapidge, *Anglo-Latin Literature, 600–899*, London: The Hambledon Press, 1996, 426–7.

83 R. Cramp, 'Monkwearmouth and Jarrow: The Archaeological Evidence', in *FC* 17.

84 Ælfric described the work in 992 as one 'which King Alfred translated from Latin into English' and it was assumed by William of Malmesbury that Alfred

was the author: see the discussion of D. Whitelock, *The Old English Bede*, Sir Israel Gollancz Memorial Lecture, London: Oxford University Press, 1962.

85 S. Keynes and M. Lapidge, *Alfred the Great*, Harmondsworth: Penguin, 1983, 33.

86 *The Old English Version of Bede's Ecclesiastical History of the English People*, trans. T. Miller, New York: Old English Text Society, 1988, 2; compare with Colgrave's translation of the original: 'you wish to see my *History* more widely known, for the instruction of yourself and those over whom divine authority has appointed you to rule', Preface, 3.

87 The final chapter in the Old English version is V, 22, not V, 24, and the recapitulation of events is omitted, as are two of the less clear cut items on the list of works: 'On Isaiah, Daniel . . .', and 'Also a book of letters . . .'.

88 Whitelock, *Old English Bede*, 61–3.

89 Whitelock, *English Historical Documents*, 146–7.

90 *Ibid.*, 173.

91 Following Bede's treatment of these figures in his recapitulation in V, 24, but not the main body of his narrative, in Penda's case at least.

92 For Tatwine, see M. Lapidge, 'Tatwine', in *BEASE* 440. For fuller discussion of the relationship between Bede and the *Anglo-Saxon Chronicle*, see J. Bately, 'Bede and the Anglo-Saxon Chronicle' in *SSH* I, 233–54.

93 See M. Lapidge, 'Surviving booklists from Anglo-Saxon England', in M. Lapidge and H. Gneuss (eds), *Learning and Literature in Anglo-Saxon England*, Cambridge: Cambridge University Press, 1985, 33–89, at 45–7, 49–50 and 52–3.

94 Wormald, *English Kalendars before A.D. 1100*, 29–41, 113–25, 127–39, 155–67, 183–95, 197–209, 225–37. Five of these are considered to be West Saxon, with the most northerly deriving perhaps from Worcester.

95 M. Lapidge, *Anglo-Saxon Litanies of the Saints*, Publications of the Henry Bradshaw Society 106, Woodbridge: Boydell Press for the Henry Bradshaw Society, 1991, 115–19: *Sancte Beda ora. Omnes sancti confessors orate.*

96 R. R. Darlington (ed.), *The Vita Wulfstani of William of Malmesbury*, Camden Society, 3rd Series, 40, London, 1928, I, 14 (p. 20).

97 R. A. B. Mynors, R. M. Thomson and M. Winterbottom (ed. and trans.), *William of Malmesbury: Gesta Regum Anglorum* I, Oxford: Clarendon Press, 1998, 15.

98 *Ibid.*, I, 54, the verbatim quotation of the passage following as I, 55.

99 See above, note 56.

100 Mynors *et al.*, *William of Malmesbury* I, 62.

101 C. N. L. Brooke, 'Geoffrey of Monmouth as a Historian', in C. N. L. Brook (ed.), *Church and Government in the Middle Ages: Essays Presented to C. R. Cheney*, Cambridge: Cambridge University Press, 1976, 77–91; N. Wright (ed.), *The Historia Regum Britanniae of Geoffrey of Monmouth*, Cambridge: D. S. Brewer, I, 1985, xviii; N. J. Higham, *King Arthur: Myth-Making and History*, London: Routledge, 2002, 222–6.

102 D. Greenway (ed. and trans.), *Henry, Archdeacon of Huntingdon, Historia Anglorum: The History of the English People*, Oxford: Clarendon Press, 1996, 7.

103 *Ibid.*, lxxxvi.

104 The earliest is a group of manuscripts preserving a *Vita Venerabilis Bedae, Presbyteri, et Geruensis Monachi* ('Life of the Venerable Bede, Priest, and Monk of Jarrow'), to be found for example in BL Cotton Nero E.i, the bulk of which dates to not long after 1000 and which consists of a large collection of saints' lives, some of which are earlier than Bede: the Bedan text offers details of his illness and death, drawn from Cuthbert's letter. This is printed by Migne in *PL* 90, cols 41–54; Oxford, Bodleian Barlow MS 39 is a thirteenth-century manuscript containing the *Ecclesiastical History*, plus a brief life drawing exclusively on Bede's biographical passage; another is printed in the Bollandist *Acta Sanctorum* VI, 720, deriving in part from Simeon of Durham's *Historia Dunelmensis Ecclesiae*

(Rollason, *Simeon*), in part from *EH* V, 24, in part from Cuthbert's letter. This is also printed by Migne in *PL* 90, cols 59–68. Another version of Bede's life was entered into the 'Golden Legend' by Jacob of Voragine *c.*1260

105 Mynors *et al.*, *William of Malmesbury* I, 61.

106 W. M. Aird, *St. Cuthbert and the Normans*, Woodbridge: Boydell Press, 1998, 131–6

107 D. Rollason, *Northumbria 500–1100: Creation and Destruction of a Kingdom*, Cambridge: Cambridge University Press, 2003, 287–90.

108 Rollason, *Simeon* I, 1. At xlii–xliv, Rollason establishes the date of composition as 1104–7 × 1115, and argues for authorship by a team led by Simeon.

109 Aird, *St. Cuthbert and the Normans*, 136.

110 Rollason, *Simeon* I, 42.

111 W. T. Mellows (ed.), *The Chronicle of Hugh Candidus*, Peterborough: Peterborough Natural History, Scientific and Archaeological Society, 1941, 31, 32; for a Latin text, see W. T. Mellows with La Geste de Burch (ed.), *The Chronicle of Hugh Candidus, A Monk of Peterborough*, London: Oxford University Press on behalf of the Friends of Peterborough Cathedral, 1949, 64 (*Et in Girum sanctus Beda presbyter*).

112 A. J. Piper, *Durham Monks at Jarrow*, JL (1986).

113 M. R. James, 'The Manuscripts of Bede', in *BLTW* 232.

114 L. T. Smith (ed.), *The Itinerary of John Leland*, London: Centaur Press Ltd, 1964, V, 128.

115 T. Towers, 'Smith and Son, Editors of Bede', in *FC* 357–65.

116 C. Hunter, *The History of the Cathedral Church of Durham*, Durham: printed for John Richardson, bookseller, 2nd edn, 1742, 59–61; P. Sanderson, *The Antiquities of the Abbey or Cathedral Church of Durham*, Durham: printed by J. White and T. Saint at Mr Pope's Head, 1767, 47–9.

117 Colgrave, *Two Lives of S. Cuthbert*, 7.

118 *BLTW*, xiv, xvi.

119 *The Times*, 26 April 1935, p. 8.

120 *Ibid.*, 28 May 1935, pp. 10, 17. Bede might well have savoured the biblical numbers involved.

121 *FC* 5–18.

122 See the letter to *The Times*, 21 April 1903, 5, and the extended description of the event by an eyewitness in the same paper, 11 October 1904, 8; 12 October 1904, 7.

123 *The Times*, 18 May 1935, which concludes: 'If the style is the man, Bede stands before us in his simplicity and humility, his devotion to truth and accuracy, his love of learning and literature, his capacity for hard work, his profound faith in God. He was deeply religious, and withal a humanist . . . In an age in which scholarship scarcely existed he was every inch a scholar, and drew his learning from every available source. Well did he earn his proud title – the Father of English History.' The sermon was the subject of further comment in *The Times* on the following day, 20 May 1935, 16 and the restoration of the Bede Altar was further commented upon on 22 May 1935, 10.

124 *JL*.

125 *BASE*, containing seven papers.

126 Five of the papers were subsequently published, with three additional pieces, as *BV*.

127 *BLVTP*.

128 Dante, *The Divine Comedy* X: Bede might perhaps have been displeased to find himself following Isidore, who received significantly more notice than himself, as the tenth of twelve figures.

129 C. Babington (ed.), *Polychronicon Ranulphi Higden Monachi Cestrensis*, London:

Longman (Rolls Series), 1865. J. Taylor, *The Universal Chronicle of Ranulph Higden*, Oxford: Clarendon Press, 1966, 58, 85, 171, notes Ranulph's widespread use of Bede's *Ecclesiastical History*.

130 C. W. Jones, *Bedae Pseudepigrapha: Scientific Writings Falsely Attributed to Bede*, London: Oxford University Press, 1939, 1.

131 M. Lapidge, *Bede the Poet*, JL (1993), 1.

132 Smith, *Itinerary* II, 25; V, 39, 54, respectively.

133 C. de Hamel, 'Archbishop Matthew Parker and His Imaginary Library of Archbishop Theodore of Canterbury', http://www.lambethpalacelibrary.org/ news/Friendsreport2002/lecture.html

134 S. Birkbeck, *The Protestants evidence taken out of good records; shewing that for fifteene hundred yeares next after Christ, divers worthy guides of Gods Church, have in sundry weightie points of religion, taught as the Church of England now doth: distributed into severall centuries*, London: printed by Augustine Mathewes and Thomas Cotes for Robert Milbourne, 1634, 202: 'in diverse maine grounds of Religion, he [Bede] was an Adversarie to your *Trent Faith*'.

135 Anon., *Sundry strange Prophecies of Merline, Bede, Becket, And others; Foretelling many things of consequence that have happened in England, Scotland, and Ireland, since these late Wars*, London: printed for Matthew Walbancke, 1652, 165

136 Colgrave and Mynors, *Bede*, lxxi.

137 Plummer, *Baedae Opera*, cxxxi–cxxxii. T. Stapleton, *Fortresse of the Faith first planted among us Englishmen, and continued hitherto in the vniuersall Church of Christ*, St Omers: John Heigham, 1565.

138 J. Milton, *Britain under Trojan, Roman, Saxon Rule*, Kennet's England, 1719, reprinted London: Alex. Murray & Son, 1870. He began the work in 1649 but publication was long delayed.

139 D. Wheare, *The Method and Order of reading both Civil and Ecclesiastical Histories*, 3rd edn made *English* and Enlarged by E. Bohun, London, 1710, 260–1, 277.

140 T. Salmon, *The History of Great Britain and Ireland; from the First Discovery of these Islands to the Norman Conquest*, 2nd edn London: Printed for John Wyat, 1725, Preface, A3.

141 J. Adams, *The Flowers of Modern History*, London: printed for G. Kearsley, 1796, 44.

142 J. Berkenhout, *Biographia Literaria; or a Biographical History of Literature containing the Lives of English, Scottish and Irish Authors* I, London: printed for J. Dodsley, 1777, 5.

143 D. Hume, *The History of England from the Invasions of Julius Caesar to the Revolution in 1688*, London, Longman, Brown, Green and Longmans, I, 1848, particularly 28–31: Hume wrote in the period 1754–62.

144 S. Turner, *History of the Anglo-Saxons*, 3 vols, London, 1799–1805.

145 E. A. Freeman, *Old English History for Children*, London: Macmillan, 1869, 57–9; J. R. Green, *The Making of England*, London: Macmillan, 1881: see for example 219ff; Green, *A Short History of the English People*, London: Macmillan 1892, I, 71–4, which contains paraphrases of both Bede's own commentary on his own life and Cuthbert's recollections of his death.

146 Lord Macaulay, *History of England*, 1848: the quotation is from the 1867 edition, London, Longmans, Green and Co., 3.

147 *Ibid.*, 5.

148 J. M. Kemble, *The Saxons in England*, London: Longman, Brown, Green and Longmans, 1849, 26.

149 *Ibid.*, 27. There are noticeable parallels herein with the recent comments of Ken Livingstone, as quoted in the Introduction, above.

150 W. Stubbs (ed.), *Select Charters and Other Illustrations of English Constitutional History*, Oxford: Clarendon Press, 1870, 8.

151 O. Dobiache-Rojdestvensky, 'Un manuscrit de Bede à Leningrad', *Speculum* 3 (1928) 314–21; the manuscript was printed in facsimile by O. Arngart, *The Leningrad Bede*, Copenhagen: Rosenkilde and Bagger, 1952.

152 Plummer, *Baedae Opera* I, lxxvii–lxxix. Church was dean of St Paul's (1871–90), Lidden a canon there; both were leading members of the Oxford Movement, Tractarians and Anglo-Catholics, and Church in particular was a man of influence, a friend of Newman and confidant of Gladstone. The Anglicanism of Anglo-Saxon England was brilliantly parodied by W. C. Sellars and R. J. Yeatman, *1066 and All That*, London: Methuen, 1930, republished in an illustrated edition in 1993 with an introduction by Frank Muir, Stroud: Sutton, 7. Sellars and Yeatman famously referred to Bede as 'the Venomous Bead (author of *The Rosary*)'.

153 C. Oman, *A History of England in Seven Volumes*, I, *England before the Norman Conquest*, London: Methuen, 1910, 319.

154 See the judgement of the Revd C. Jenkins, 'Bede as Exegete and Theologian, in *FC* 152–200, at 199: 'It will probably occur to patristic students that Bede's handling of theological problems is at most times somewhat conventional and recalls methods and arguments which they have constantly encountered in earlier works.'

155 R. H. Hodgkin, *A History of the Anglo-Saxons*, Oxford: Oxford University Press, 1935.

156 *Ibid.*, 257–355.

157 F. M. Stenton, *Anglo-Saxon England*, Oxford: Clarendon Press, 1943, 186.

158 *Ibid.*, 187.

159 As is exemplified by J. Campbell, 'Bede I', in *EASH* 1–27.

160 See most recently P. Fowler, *Farming in the First Millennium AD*, Cambridge: Cambridge University Press, 2002, which has an extensive bibliography.

161 As B. Yorke, *Kings and Kingdoms of Early Anglo-Saxon England*, London: Seaby, 1990; D. P. Kirby, *The Earliest English Kings*, London: Unwin Hyman, 1991, both of which attempt to extract a secular history, very largely from Bede's *EH*.

162 As N. Brooks, *The Early History of the Church at Canterbury*, Leicester: Leicester University Press, 1984.

163 As, respectively, J. Hines, 'The Becoming of the English: Identity, Material Culture and Language in Early Anglo-Saxon England', *Anglo-Saxon Studies in Archaeology and History* 7 (1994) 49–59; S. Hollis, *Anglo-Saxon Women and the Church*, Woodbridge: Boydell Press, 1992.

164 As J. Campbell, *Bede's Reges and Principes*, *JL* (1979), reprinted in *EASH* 85–98; A. Thacker, 'Some Terms for Noblemen in Anglo-Saxon England', *Anglo-Saxon Studies in Archaeology and History* 2 (1981) 201–36; S. Fanning, 'Bede, *Imperium* and the Bretwaldas', *Speculum* 66 (1991) 1–26. Such approaches and others have been much assisted by J. M. Wallace-Hadrill's posthumously published *Bede's Ecclesiastical History of the English People: A Historical Commentary*, Oxford: Clarendon Press, 1988.

165 J. McClure, 'Bede's Old Testament Kings', in *IR*, 76–98; J. Campbell, 'Bede's Words for Places', in *EASH* 99–119.

166 For a seminal exploration of élite culture outside the monastery, see P. Wormald, 'Bede, Beowulf and the Conversion of the Anglo-Saxon Aristocracy', in *BASE* 32–95, although this depends heavily on an eighth-century dating of *Beowulf* which is no longer generally upheld; for an attempt to separate the dynamics of the conversion process from Bede's perceptions of this history of his own people, see N. J. Higham, *The Convert Kings: Power and Religious Affiliation in Early Anglo-Saxon England*, Manchester: Manchester University Press, 1997.

167 Most incisively by W. Goffart, *The Narrators of Barbarian History (A.D. 550–800)*, Princeton: Princeton University Press, 1988, 235–328.

168 See *The Times*, 22 May 1935, 15.

169 Plummer, *Baedae Opera*, I, v.

170 Not to imply that Plummer had ignored this aspect, which he acknowledged in his Preface, ii, but the theme was never thereafter developed.

171 Sister M. Thomas Aquinas Carroll, *The Venerable Bede: His Spiritual Teachings*, Washington, DC: The Catholic University of America Press, 1946, vii.

172 *Ibid.*, 2.

173 D. Knowles, *Saints and Scholars: Twenty Five Medieval Portraits*, Cambridge: Cambridge University Press, 1946, ch. 2.

174 P. Meyvaert, 'Bede the Scholar', in *FC* 40–69, but note that Meyvaert left holy orders part way through his academic career.

175 Ward, *The Venerable Bede*, who opened her own discussion of 'Bede and his times' on p. 1 with an extended quotation from David Knowles.

176 Plummer, *Baedae Opera* I, cxlv–clix.

177 This issue is discussed in detail by M. Gorman, 'The Canon of Bede's Works and the World of Ps. Bede', *Revue Bénédictine* 111 (2001) 399–445, listing Bede's works at 402–5.

178 The most trenchant comment coming from W. T. Foley, 'Introduction', in W. T. Foley and A. G. Holder (trans. and ed.), *Bede: A Biblical Miscellany*, Liverpool: Liverpool University Press, 1999, xxvii: 'myopic concern for Bede's historical writings about early England has not only made full appreciation of his biblical scholarship impossible, it has also obscured much about the character of historical writings themselves, including the *Ecclesiastical History*.'

179 Ward, *The Venerable Bede*, 115.

180 Although the point is less well made as regards the *Ecclesiastical History* than regards his more technical works, the explicit aim of several of which was to educate his younger brethren.

181 Wallis, *The Reckoning of Time*, 66 (157–8). See also his *Letter to Plegwin*, 14, *ibid.*, 412–13, which reacts to an accusation of heresy made informally against his earlier but briefer work, *On Times*, 16, by unnamed individuals in the presence of Bishop Wilfrid, as regards the length of these several ages.

182 See, for example, the appearance of two comets in 729, 'striking great terror into numerous beholders' (*EH* V, 23), and the general sense of a current pause in history, characterised by general peace and prosperity, in the same chapter, as if a prelude to dramatic changes in the near future. Gregory had similarly anticipated a speedy end to the sixth age in his letter to Æthelberht, quoted by Bede in *EH* I, 32 and Gregory of Tours likewise commented on the issue in his Preface to the *Ten Books of History*.

183 At the end of the penultimate paragraph of the same chapter, Bede wrote: *Quae res quem sit habitura finem, posterior aetas uidebit*. Colgrave's translation reads: 'What the result will be, a later generation will discover', although *aetas* could mean 'age', here in the sense of either a 'lifetime' or a 'life stage'. 'Generation' may not quite convey the breadth of Bede's potential meaning, which was equally capable of interpretation in the sense of 'within the next life-stage of the reader or hearer'. *Posterior* can translate as 'next' as well as 'later' or 'latter'. The future envisaged by Bede, therefore, need not be read as so necessarily distant as 'later generation' might imply.

184 See his brief letter to Abbot Albinus: *Epistola ad Albinum*, in Plummer, *Baedae Opera* I, 3, which invites him to have a copy made from the attached original, which was presumably to be returned, but there is no expectation herein that this was for other than Albinus's own consumption. No early manuscript of this letter survives, however, so its authenticity is not assured.

185 Gregory of Tours, *Ten Books of History* X, 31: Gregory was here describing the

Trivium and *Quadrivium*, that is the two categories into which contemporary learning was divided under seven headings.

186 See discussion by C. W. Jones, 'Bede's Place in Medieval Schools', in *FC* 263.

187 C. W. Jones, *Bedae Venerabilis Opera*, VI, *Opera Didascalica*, Preface, vi *et seq.*

188 The point is well made by Campbell, 'Bede I', in *EASH* 10–13.

189 C. W. Jones, *Saints' Lives and Chronicles*, Ithaca, NY: Cornell University Press, 1937, 80, assumes that Ceolwulf had enjoyed a monastic education but there is no contemporary or even near-contemporary evidence for this. Given that he was forcibly tonsured in 731, it seems improbable that Ceolwulf had earlier already been a monk.

190 See, for example, M. de Jong, 'The empire as ecclesia: Hrabanus Maurus and biblical *historia* for rulers', in Y. Hen and M. Innes (eds.), *The Uses of the Past in the Early Middle Ages*, Cambridge: Cambridge University Press, 2000, 191–226, at 195, referring specifically to Lothar.

191 See Rollason, *Simeon* I, 13: 'because he [Ceolwulf] was grounded in liberal studies, Bede dedicated to him the Ecclesiastical History of the English People which he had written, praising his diligence in reading and listening, to the holy scriptures and the deeds of his predecessors'. The translation of Ceolwulf's relics was in the mid-ninth century: J. Blair, 'A Handlist of Anglo-Saxon Saints', in A. Thacker and R. Sharpe (eds.), *Local Saints and Local Churches in the Early Medieval West*, Oxford: Oxford University Press, 2002, 520. There is further comment on Ceolwulf's retirement in *The History of St Cuthbert*, 7: T. Johnson South (ed.), *Historia De Sancto Cuthberto*, Cambridge: D. S. Brewer, 2002, 48–9, but this may well not have been written before the second half of the eleventh century: *ibid.*, 35.

192 A. W. Haddan and W. Stubbs (eds.), *Councils and Ecclesiastical Documents Relating to Great Britain and Ireland* III, Oxford: Clarendon Press, 1871, 362–76. For discussion, see Cubitt, *Anglo-Saxon Church Councils*, 99–124

193 M. Lapidge and M. Herren (eds.), *Aldhelm: The Prose Works*, Ipswich: Brewer, 1979, 155–60, letter 4.

194 He was later remembered as a keen 'soldier for the Kingdom of Heaven' among the monks at Lindisfarne (Rollason, *Simeon* I, 16), but not as a learned man, although he may have been a monk for well over two decades, since his death was noted in the *Historia Regum* under the year 764: Whitelock, *English Historical Documents*, 267, although that does not, of course, constitute a near-contemporary record.

195 Take the example of Owine, in *EH* IV, 3, who preferred to work outside while others read within, although he need not necessarily have been entirely illiterate on this reckoning.

196 B. Colgrave (ed.), *The Life of Bishop Wilfrid by Eddius Stephanus*, Cambridge: Cambridge University Press, 1927, xxi.

197 *Ibid.*, 60, at p. 131.

198 Bede's provision of written versions of some of the core texts of Christianity in the vernacular may imply that some non-Latin speakers could read, but they could equally have accessed these texts aurally and then committed them to memory.

199 *EH* V, 21, but see p. 181 below for discussion.

200 Emerton (ed. and trans.), *The Letters of Saint Boniface*, 2nd edn, New York: Columbia University Press, 2000, LVIII, 130–1.

201 C. Grocock, 'Bede and the Golden Age of Latin Prose in Northumbria', in J. Hawkes and S. Mills (eds.), *Northumbria's Golden Age*, Stroud: Sutton, 1999, 371–82.

202 *EH* V, 24.

203 To whom he addressed his *Commentary on the Revelation of St. John the Divine*,

written between 710 and 716, and *Concerning the Reckoning of Time*, completed *c.*725.

204 Acca was by far Bede's commonest dedicatee, being named in, or in letters pertaining to, such major works as the *Commentary on the Catholic Epistles*, *Commentary on the Acts of the Apostles* and the *Commentary on the First Book of Samuel*.

205 S. Connolly, *Bede: On Tobit and On the Canticle of Habbakuk*, Dublin: Four Courts Press, 1997, 65.

206 The nearest comparator being his homily on the *Magnificat*: see Ward, *The Venerable Bede*, 77.

207 *EH* IV, 23: 'She compelled those under her direction to devote so much time to the study of the Holy Scriptures and so much time to the performance of good works.'

208 And more particularly West Saxon women: B. Yorke, 'The Bonifacian Mission and Female Religious in Wessex', *Early Medieval Europe* 7.2 (1998) 145–72.

209 K. Biddick, *The Shock of Medievalism*, Durham, NC: Duke University Press, 1998, 97–101: I assume that Dr Biddick identifies herself with this persona.

210 *Ibid.*, 100.

211 At least in the opinion of Cuthbert, in his *Letter on the Death of Bede*, in Colgrave and Mynors, *Bede*, 582–3, who included verbatim an Old English poem on death which his elderly master putatively recited during his final illness. Bede's treatment of Cædmon's poetry, which he discusses in *EH* IV, 24 (22), sustains the impression of considerable interest in this medium.

212 D. Kirby, 'Bede's Native Sources for the *Historia Ecclesiastica*', *Bulletin of the John Rylands Library* 48 (1966) 341–71.

213 *EH* IV, 24 (22).

214 A. White, *A History of Whitby*, Chichester: Phillimore, 2nd edn, 2004, 57, dismisses the correlation of Bede's *farus* here with Greek *pharos*, meaning 'lighthouse', 'since the words are sufficiently unlike for the connection to be philologically implausible', but offers no alternative translation. In fact, Bede had already used the term in *EH* I, 11, and his meaning is unambiguous.

215 See discussion by P. S. Barnwell, L. A. S. Butler and C. J. Dunn, 'The Confusion of Conversion: Streanæshalch, Strensall and Whitby and the Northumbrian Church', in M. Carver (ed.), *The Cross Goes North*, Woodbridge: Boydell and Brewer, York Medieval Press, 2003, 314. The meaning 'treasure' might fit well with 'cavity', in relation to a cave in the cliffs beneath the monastery. The early eleventh-century ealdorman Eadric Streona provides a parallel to this usage, meaning 'the acquisitive'. The suggestion that *Streanæshalch* might be read as representing two centres of a single monastery further complicates the issue, perhaps unnecessarily, since the only other example of a double-sited monastery – Wearmouth/Jarrow – has two site-specific names, not one, but see I. Wood, *The Most Holy Abbot Ceolfrid*, JL (1995) 22, fn. 42.

216 Barnwell *et al.*, 'The Confusion', 325.

217 *EH* IV, 23 (21): 'Now these two monasteries are nearly thirteen miles apart.' This is entirely accurate in terms of Whitby and Hackness but highly inaccurate as a measure of the distance between Strensall and Hackness, which are some 28 miles (45 km) apart.

218 For an effective defence of the traditional attribution, see C. Hough, 'Strensall, Streanæshalch and Stronsay', *Journal of the English Place-Name Society* 35 (2002–3) 17–24.

219 *EH* IV, 23 (21): 'a light which poured in from above filled the whole place. As she watched the light intently, she saw the soul of the handmaiden of the Lord being borne to Heaven in the midst of that light, attended and guided by angels . . . she had seen her ascend in the midst of a great light and escorted by angels to the abode of eternal light'. It may also be appropriate to note that late Roman

towers were located along this coast, the nearest known example being at Goldsborough, a headland less than 5 miles (8 km) north of Whitby. Bede or one of his informants could easily have misinterpreted such a ruined tower as a derelict lighthouse. For the suggestion that *sinus* here is a reference to Hild's mother's bosom, see P. Hunter Blair, 'Whitby as a Centre of Learning in the Seventh Century', in M. Lapidge and H, Gneuss (eds.), *Learning and Literature in Anglo-Saxon England: Studies Presented to Peter Clemoes on the Occasion of His Sixty-Fifth Birthday*, Cambridge: Cambridge University Press, 1985, 9–12.

220 According to his *Letter to Egbert*, Bede had himself translated both the Lord's Prayer and the Creed from Latin into English for the benefit of priests without sufficient command of Latin to use it effectively themselves.

221 *EH* I, 32, on pp. 89 and 59, respectively.

222 E.g. Brown's *Bede the Venerable*; Browne's *The Venerable Bede*; Carroll's *The Venerable Bede*; Ward's *The Venerable Bede*; and the collection of conference papers published in 2005 called *Bède le Vénérable entre tradition et postérité* (*BLVTP*).

223 Although he was by the 730s increasingly aware that apparently contradictory material on occasion required rationalisation via spiritual meanings and that there had been problems of textual transmission of the Bible from Greek and Hebrew into Latin.

224 See, for example, P. Hunter Blair, *An Introduction to Anglo-Saxon England*, Cambridge: Cambridge University Press, 1956, 325, who suggested that his 'fundamental approach to history differs little from modern works of narrative history' and that the *EH* should be seen as 'a masterpiece of historical narrative' which is 'a source of accurate information'. For the difficulties today of understanding the spirituality of a seventh- or eighth-century cleric, see B. Ward, 'The Spirituality of St. Cuthbert', in *CCC* 67.

225 Knowles, *Saints and Scholars*, 17, used as an opening, extended quotation with obvious approval by Ward, *Bede*, 1. It is extraordinarily hard to justify use of such a term as 'simple' of a writer as diverse, mature and complex as Bede, so this must presumably be read as a primarily religious response to his work.

226 As K. Kumar, *The Making of English National Identity*, Cambridge: Cambridge University Press, 2003, 41–2, 46.

227 Wallis, *Reckoning of Time*, 405–15. The accusation derived from his preference for Jerome's calculation of the length in years of several of the ages of the world over that of the older *Septuagint*: there is an excellent discussion in W. Levison, 'Bede as Historian', in *BLTW*.

228 Plummer, *Baedae Opera* I, xliv. For a gentle critique of Plummer's stance, see J. M. Wallace-Hadrill, *Bede's Ecclesiastical History of the English People: A Historical Commentary*, Oxford: Clarendon Press, 1988, xv–xxxv.

229 See Wallace-Hadrill, *Bede's Ecclesiastical History*, xvii–xix.

230 Plummer, *Baedae Opera* x.

231 R. Baldick (selected, trans. and intro.), *The Memoirs of Chateaubriand*, Harmondsworth: Penguin, 1965, 333.

2 The *Ecclesiastical History*: Bede's purposes and ours

1 Revd J. Adams, *The Flowers of Modern History*, London: printed for G. Kearley, a new edition, enlarged, 1796, 44.

2 To date the most rounded review of Bede's purposes is that of J. Campbell, 'Bede I', in *EASH* 1–27, initially published in T. A. Dorey (ed.), *Latin Historians*, London: Routledge and Kegan Paul, 1966, 159–90.

3 Excluding, that is, the addition of IV, 14 and a small number of very minor amendments, which are visible in terms of differences between the Moore and Leningrad versions, some of which may well not have been Bede's amendments

at all. These are conveniently listed by D. Rollason, *Bede and Germany*, JL (2001) 4–7. David Dumville has recently suggested both that the differences are more numerous than this and that the manuscripts are a generation later than hitherto supposed: 'Discussion', in J. Hines (ed.), *The Anglo-Saxons from the Migration Period to the Eighth Century: An Ethnographic Perspective*, Woodbridge: Boydell Press, 1997, 369.

4 As the late, much-lamented Patrick Wormald, 'Bede and Benedict Biscop', in *FC* 155: 'Bede's dynamic was neither learning nor common sense, but idealism.' His was a '*History* that is much more than a factual record: it is also a vision of timeless grace and power'. Similar views had already been expressed by G. Musca, *Il Venerabile Beda strico dell'Alto Medioevo*, Bari: Dedalo Libri, 1973, 213, who speaks of his 'genuina religiosità', and A. Gransden, *Historical Writings in England c.550–c.1307*, London: Routledge and Kegan Paul, 1974, 13–28: 'Bede's mind was dominated by the Christian religion'; 'Bede was a man of profound religious conviction.' Religious conviction does not, of course, preclude political interests or purposes.

5 D. Kirby, 'King Ceolwulf of Northumbria and the *Historia Ecclesiastica*', *Studia Celtica* 14–15 (1980) 168–73.

6 A. Thacker, 'Bede's Ideal of Reform', in *IR* 130–53.

7 *Ibid.*, 134.

8 See discussion in C. Cubitt, *Anglo-Saxon Church Councils c.650–c.850*, London: Leicester University Press, 1995, 99–124; J. Blair, *The Church in Anglo-Saxon Society*, Oxford: Oxford University Press, 2005, 100–17.

9 S. DeGregorio, 'Bede's *In Ezram et Neemiam* and the Reform of the Northumbrian Church', *Speculum* 79 (2004) 1–25, the last point at 12: 'Would that some Nehemiah come in our own days and hold our errors in check, kindle our breasts to love of the divine.' If this was written post–729, then Ceolwulf does not seem to have impressed Bede as a Nehemiah-figure, but it may derive from a little earlier. For a wider survey of Bede's later exegesis in the same vein, see S. DeGregorio, ' "Nostrorum socordiam temporum": the reforming impulse of Bede's later exegesis', *Early Medieval Europe* 11(2) (2002), 107–22, and 'Bede's *In Ezram et Neemiah*: A Document in Church Reform?', in *BLVTP* 97–107. For the view that Bede interested himself in reform significantly earlier, see P. Meyvaert, 'The Date of Bede's *In Ezram* and His Image of Ezra in Codex Amiatinus', *Speculum* 80(4) (2005) 1128. Reference to 'the negligence of our own time' occurs also in Bede's significantly earlier *Thirty Questions on the Book of Kings*, 30: W. T. Foley and A. G. Holder (eds.), *Bede: A Biblical Miscellany*, Liverpool: Liverpool University Press, 1999, 136.

10 Bede, *Expositio Apocalypseos*, ed. R. Gryson, in *CCSL* 121a (2001).

11 *EH* II, 1.

12 *EH* IV, 5.

13 *EH* IV, 12: this was initially a division into two *c.*678, dividing Northumbria between York (the Deirans) and Hexham/Lindisfarne (the Bernicians), but Lindsey also obtained a see for the first time, having previously fallen under Wilfrid when King Ecgfrith controlled it.

14 Hexham was divided from Lindisfarne *c.*681 and a see for the Picts also founded at Abercorn but the latter was abandoned when the first bishop, Trumwine, retired south after Ecgfrith's great defeat in 685: *EH* IV, 26.

15 On which Bede commented laconically in his summation: *EH* V, 23, being York, Lindisfarne, Hexham and Whithorn.

16 *EH* 560, fn. 1. See also Wallace-Hadrill, *Bede's Ecclesiastical History*, 200.

17 *EH* V, 23.

18 Campbell, 'Bede I', 19, 26.

19 C. W. Jones, *Saints' Lives and Chronicles in Early England*, Ithaca, NY: Cornell University Press, 1947, 82.

20 So, for example, Campbell, 'Bede I', 5, who called it, among other things, 'a chronological hagiography'.

21 Rollason, *Bede and Germany*, JL (2001), 14–15.

22 I. Wood, *The Missionary Life: Saints and the Evangelisation of Europe 400–1050*, Harlow: Longman, 2001, 42. One should note that he then adds, 43: 'There is, of course, more to the *Ecclesiastical History* than Christianisation.'

23 *Ibid.*, 43.

24 At the close of *EH* I, 22. I discussed the role of mission and the nature of conversion in an Anglo-Saxon context in *Convert Kings, passim*.

25 A translation is available in Whitelock, *English Historical Documents*, no. 167, 795–7.

26 W. Levison, 'Bede as Historian', in *BLTW*, 146.

27 D. P. Kirby, 'Bede, Eddius Stephanus and the "Life of Wilfrid" ', *English Historical Review* 98 (1983), 101.

28 Plummer, *Baedae Opera* II, 316. The single miracle which he included is in *EH* V, 19.

29 Wallis, *The Reckoning of Time*, 405–15, and see the discussion, xxx, xxxi.

30 W. Goffart, *The Narrators of Barbarian History (A.D. 550–800): Jordanes, Gregory of Tours, Bede, and Paul the Deacon*, Princeton: Princeton University Press, 1988, 235–328; 'The *Historia Ecclesiastica*: Bede's Agenda and Ours', *Haskins Society Journal* 2 (1990), 29–45; 'L'Histoire ecclésiastique et l'engagement politique de Bède', in *BLVTP* 149–58.

31 Goffart, *Narrators*, 245–8, by which he meant his two chronicles, his hagiographical works, his *Martyrology*, the *History of the Abbots* and the *Ecclesiastical History*.

32 *Ibid.*, 236. Campbell, 'Bede I', 15, contrasts Bede's reticence concerning his own adult lifetime with Gregory of Tours's focus on his own.

33 Goffart, *Narrators*, 240, 252–3.

34 *Ibid.*, 258. The northern predominance in this hagiographic and historical output is unfortunately strengthened by the erroneous assumption that the *Life of Guthlac* was of Northumbrian authorship: 248–9, fn. 73.

35 Described by Bede, *EH* IV, 19 (17), who also included a Latin hymn or poem he had previously written on the subject as the following chapter. Æthelthryth also occurs in *Concerning the Reckoning of Time*: Wallis, *Bede*, 232. For discussion, see S. J. Ridyard, *The Royal Saints of Anglo-Saxon England*, Cambridge: Cambridge University Press, 1988, 176–81.

36 Goffart, *Narrators*, 260–6. There is, however, no evidence that Wilfrid was in any sense central to the process and the nuns at Ely had their own reasons for developing the cult of their foundress: A. Thacker, 'The Making of a Local Saint', in A. Thacker and R. Sharpe (eds.), *Local Saints and Local Churches in the Early Medieval West*, Oxford: Oxford University Press, 2002, 68. Bede, likewise, had reasons for commemorating Æthelthryth, who was the putatively virgin wife of the first patron of his own house, whom he had already celebrated in the *Greater Chronicle*.

37 Goffart, *Narrators*, 260. The monks at Hexham had developed Oswald's cult at Heavenfield, and Wilfrid's protégés in Sussex were also interested in his sanctity. However, Æthelred of Mercia's wife was Oswald's niece and Bede attributes Oswald's cult at Bardney primarily to her: *EH* III, 11. There is no obvious connection with Wilfrid, although Æthelred certainly did patronise him on occasion and sought to exploit his conflicts with the Northumbrian establishment.

38 Colgrave, *Two Lives of St. Cuthbert*, 13, dates composition within the period 699–705 and it is difficult to disagree with this. The anonymous *Life* was arguably designed to encourage the development of Cuthbert's cult at Holy Island following the elevation of his body in 698. The cult was presumably fostered to sustain

the ongoing credibility of the site in a period of ambiguity regarding its diocesan status and the legitimacy of its foundation story, but there is no evidence that it was conceived as directly anti-Wilfridian.

39 B. Colgrave, *The Earliest Life of Gregory the Great by an Anonymous Monk of Whitby*, Lawrence: University of Kansas Press, 1968, 48, dates composition *c.*704–14, but without excessive confidence. The cult of Gregory was apparently being encouraged by Archbishop Theodore (668–90), which arguably accounts for the shrine at Canterbury. Its presence at Whitby is hardly surprising, given the centrality of that monastery to the triumph of Catholic practices in the north and its long period of rule by the descendants of King Edwin, the patron of Gregory's mission to Northumbria.

40 Although in fact Hild died *c.*680, but her successors were equally members of Oswiu's dynasty and close kin to Edwin.

41 Goffart, *Narrators*, 267.

42 *Ibid.*, 270.

43 Eadwulf only reportedly secured Northumbria for two months: B. Colgrave (ed.), *The Life of Bishop Wilfrid by Eddius Stephanus*, Cambridge: Cambridge University Press, 1927, LIX, LX. Stephen asserted that it had been Aldfrith's dying wish that his successor should reconcile himself with Wilfrid, but this may well be apocryphal.

44 The River Nidd is a tributary of the Ouse which runs through Knaresborough. Given that the archbishop was probably travelling up Roman Dere Street, the meeting may perhaps have occurred nearer Cattal or Hunsingore than Nidd itself, which is far to the west.

45 Colgrave, *Life of Wilfrid*, LX.

46 *EH* V, 23.

47 W. Jaager (ed.), *Bedas metrische Vita sancti Cuthberti*, Leipzig: Mayer and Müller, 1935, XXI, translates as: 'Now his [Aldfrith's] venerable offspring wears the purple and justly holds the reins of the sceptre, passed on by his father and a new illustrious Josiah, with faith and intellect greater than his years, governs the land.' Osred was about nine in 705 so only about twenty when he died in 716. My thanks to Martin Ryan for this translation.

48 Goffart, *Narrators*, 280, on the assumption that Coenred would have been hostile to a foundation of King Ecgfrith. Wearmouth/Jarrow had also been favoured by Aldfrith, of course, so may well have been by his son(s).

49 *Ibid.*, 281–4. The quotations are highlighted by Colgrave, *Life of Wilfrid*, 2, 14.

50 Goffart, *Narrators*, 284.

51 *Ibid.*, 285.

52 *Ibid.*, 286–90.

53 *Ibid.*, 291.

54 *Ibid.*, 292–3.

55 *Ibid.*, 294.

56 *Ibid.*, 295.

57 *Ibid.*, 296.

58 Goffart, 'L'Histoire ecclésiastique', 152.

59 Goffart, *Narrators*, 298–9, quote at 299.

60 *Ibid.*, 306; 'L'Histoire ecclésiastique', 153.

61 Goffart, *Narrators*, 308, 316: the term 'Quartodecimans' was an antique term referring to those who celebrated Easter on the fourteenth day of the lunar month irrespective of whether or not it fell on a Sunday, which the Irish did not do.

62 *Ibid.*, 309.

63 *Ibid.*, 311–12.

64 *Ibid.*, 320, 324.

65 *Ibid.*, 325–7.

66 *Ibid.*, 328.

67 See, for example, I. Wood, *The Most Holy Abbot Ceolfrid*, JL (1995) 8, and S. Coates, 'Ceolfrid: History, Hagiography, and Memory in Seventh- and Eighth-Century Wearmouth-Jarrow', *Journal of Medieval History* 25 (1999) 69–86, who, at 82–3, supports the view that the *Life of Cuthbert* had to be rewritten by Bede on account of Wilfrid.

68 Goffart's argument, in 'L'Histoire ecclésiastique', 150, fn. 4, that Bede's effusive dedications to Acca were merely literary convention, falls when attention is paid to his treatment in the *EH*: see for example, M. Lapidge, 'Acca of Hexham and the Origins of the *Old English Martyrology*', *Analecta Bollandiana* 123 (2005) 29–78, who considered them good friends.

69 *EH* III, 13; IV, 14.

70 *EH*, V, 19.

71 *EH*, V, 20.

72 Goffart, *Narrators*, 273, notes the difficulty: 'It is a perplexing fact that Bede had the same patron as Wilfrid's biographer.' He attempts to resolve this issue in his second essay, 'Bede's Agenda', while still retaining his core thesis, but this does not convince.

73 Wallis, *The Reckoning of Time*, 233, in which he was termed 'venerable'; *EH* V, 11.

74 S. Connolly, *Bede: On the Temple*, Liverpool: Liverpool University Press, 1995, 2. Although O'Reilly (in *ibid.*, xvii) dates this work 729–31, we cannot be certain that it does not relate to the latter part of Osric's reign, as Wood seems to suppose: *Ceolfrid*, 12.

75 Colgrave and Mynors, *Bede*, 573.

76 As M. Lapidge, 'Acca', in *BEASE* 4.

77 This author could, of course, have been Bede.

78 Whitelock, *English Historical Documents*, 265: such an obit does of course post-date Ceolwulf's own retirement to the monastic life, at which point Hexham may have been the freer to celebrate its controversial bishop.

79 As Lapidge, 'Acca of Hexham', 68–9, who envisages Acca in retirement at Hexham having the time and literary resources to compile the *Old English Martyrology*.

80 Richard of Hexham considered the tutelary saints of his house as 'Andrew the Apostle and Wilfrid, bishop and martyr' but named Acca, Alcmund and Eata as additional patrons: Richard of Hexham, *History of the Acts of King Stephen*, in *The Church Historians of England*, trans. J. Stevenson, London: Seeleys, 1856, 44.

81 *EH* V, 6.

82 Goffart, *Narrators*, 307, uses 'The Abasement of Bishop Wilfrid' as a sub-heading.

83 *EH* III, 13, 25, 28; IV, 2, 3, 5, 12, 13, 15, 16 (14), 19 (17), 23 (21), 24 (22), 29 (27); V, 11, 18, 19, 20.

84 Colgrave, *Life of Wilfrid*, 10.

85 Campbell, 'Bede I', 19–20.

86 This epitaph does not occur in Stephen's *Life of Wilfrid*. Wallace-Hadrill, *Bede's Ecclesiastical History*, 194, is sympathetic to the view that Bede himself composed the epitaph for Ripon, but it is at least as likely that one of the presumably numerous, literate monks there undertook the task. That said, Bede is known to have provided epigrams for distant churches: M. Lapidge, 'Some Remnants of Bede's Lost *Liber Epigrammatum*', *English Historical Review* 90 (1975) 798–820.

87 See, for example, Gregory, Augustine, Chad, Hild and Theodore: *EH* II, 1; II, 3; IV, 3; IV, 23 (21); V, 8.

88 Böhne, 'Das älteste Lorscher Kalendar', 185, 216: the burial of Wilfrid was commemorated in combination with those of Egbert (archbishop of York) and Mellitus (archbishop of Canterbury) on 24 April, but his death has traditionally been celebrated on 12 October, although Stephen provided no date. This

discrepancy may be explicable in terms of his death at Oundle (Northants) but burial at Ripon, which may have occurred only in the following spring.

89 S. Duncan, '*Signa de Caelo* in the Lives of St. Cuthbert: The Impact of Biblical Images and Exegesis in Early Medieval Hagiography', *Heythrop Journal* 41 (2000) 399–412.

90 Colgrave, *Two Lives of Saint Cuthbert*, particularly 60–4.

91 Colgrave, *Life of Wilfrid*, 3, referring to [Benedict] Biscop Baducing as 'noble and of admirable spirit', makes it clear that the early careers of Wilfrid and Benedict were closely entwined but the latter as the more established and elder seems to have been the senior figure and the more committed to the task of reaching Rome at this initial stage.

92 Whitelock, *English Historical Documents*, 759, cap. 3. No one else could have ordained Ceolfrith, given that Wilfrid was at this date the sole bishop of the Northumbrians, so his presence in this role is unremarkable.

93 *Ibid.*, 760, cap. 8.

94 See, in general, Wood, *The Most Holy Abbot Ceolfrid*, 9–12.

95 The view has been championed by J. McClure, 'Bede and the *Life of Ceolfrid*', *Peritia* 3 (1984), 71–84, but is by no means established, particularly since this work does not occur in the listing of his works in *EH* V, 24. See the critique by Goffart, *Narrators*, 277, fn. 195.

96 *Ibid.*, 403: *Narrabant autem nobis reverse comites Deo dilecti patris nostri* ('However the companions of our father, chosen by God, on their return to us used to narrate').

97 Compare T. Mommsen (ed.), *Chronica Minora, saec. IV, V, VI, VII* III, Berlin: Weidmann, 1898, 320, with Plummer, *Baedae Opera* I, 400.

98 As Goffart reaffirmed in his recent 'L'Histoire ecclesiastique', 152.

99 For that matter, it remains doubtful whether or not Bede actually knew the Whitby *Life of Gregory* at all. The obvious connection lies in their respective treatments of Gregory and the English slaves in the Roman market, but Bede's is not necessarily derivative of the earlier *Life* and he attributes it to a popular story descending from ancient times (see p. 80), so the assumption that the two are textually linked needs additionally to confront Bede's own attribution of the story to hearsay.

100 W. T. Foley, *Images of Sanctity in Eddius Stephanus' Life of Bishop Wilfrid: An Early English Saint's Life*, Lewiston: The Edwin Mellen Press, 1992, 17 and *passim*.

101 *Ibid.*, 105.

102 The use of biblical models of kingship was, of course, already widespread in literature which Bede had read, including Gregory of Tours: Y. Hen, 'The Uses of the Bible and Perception of Kingship in Merovingian Gaul', *Early Medieval Europe* 7(3) (1998) 277–89.

103 Although it is often said that Bede was reticent regarding examples of bad behaviour, as H. Mayr-Harting, *The Coming of Christianity to Anglo-Saxon England*, London: Batsford, 3rd edn, 1991, 43–4, it would be more accurate to say that he was reticent regarding English clerical bad behaviour. There is a plenitude of wickedness recounted regarding the Britons, which serves as the central exemplar of immorality and disobedience to God, plus frequent comment which is, implicitly at least, critical of members of the English laity.

104 J. McClure and R. Collins (ed. and trans.), *Bede: The Ecclesiastical History of the English People*, Oxford: Oxford University Press, 1994, 348: 'For you have, I believe, in King Ceolwulf a most active helper in so just an undertaking. From his own love of religion he will be constantly and determinedly anxious to help with anything that relates to the rule of piety.'

105 To take two examples distant in time from one another, J. M. Lappenberg, *A History of England under the Anglo-Saxon Kings* I, trans. B. Thorpe, London:

John Murray, 1845, 212: 'of his love for piety and learning, we have the most honourable testimony of the Venerable Beda'; D. P. Kirby, *Bede's Historia Ecclesiastica Gens Anglorum: Its Contemporary Setting*, JL (1992), 5, argued that Bede perceived in him 'a love of religion'. While this is possible it is by no means established.

106 For a survey of the several incidents see C. Stancliffe, 'Kings who opted out', in *IR* 154–76. That Ceolwulf apparently stepped aside to make way for Archbishop Egbert's brother, his cousin, might suggest an agreed approach to the tenure of power within the wider family but it might equally denote his inability to face down competition for the kingship. Whether or not he was a committed member of the religious is unknowable but the solution adopted did avoid a repeat of the turmoil of 731 in a way that provided him with a comparatively secure and comfortable retirement.

107 *EH* 572–3. Given that this continuation to the recapitulation ended in 734, prior to Bede's death in 735, it could easily have been his work.

108 See p. 11.

109 Although it occurs seven times in adverbial form, of the rule of Popes Gregory and Eleutherius, kings Æthelberht and Edwin, Abbot Ceolfrith and Bishop Chad, and the deeds of Bishop Felix: *EH* II, 1; V, 24; II, 5; II, 20; V, 21; IV, 3; II, 15.

110 The Preface and V, 10, respectively, the latter in the context of Bede's only narration of 'English' martyrdom.

111 I, 32 and V, 21, respectively.

112 J. C. Martin (ed.), *Isidori Hispalensis Chronica*, Turnhout: Brepols, 2003, 2, 415–17.

113 This is an approximate figure which depends in detail on how particular instances are dealt with: I have, for example, counted the name Hewald twice in V, 10, and excluded Æthelthryth (IV, 17) on the grounds that she is here called 'queen', although she was also an abbess.

114 Take, for example, IV, 25 (27) to 30 (32), all of which relate to Cuthbert, although he was only named in the first.

115 G. H. Brown, 'Le commentaire problématique de Bède sur le premier livre de Samuel', in *BLVTP* 87–95, particularly 93–5.

116 See, for example, R. Ray, 'Bede's *Vera Lex Historiae*', *Speculum* 55(1) (1980) 11: 'Bede hoped that Ceolwulf would measure himself by "the famous men of our nation", especially the godly Northumbrian kings of the seventh century.'

117 Campbell, 'Bede I', 14, 25. The role of a king as spiritual guide was set out explicitly by Boniface in his *Letter to Æthelbald* of 746–7: Emerton, *Letters of Boniface*, LVII, 127–30. Bede arguably had a very similar vision of kingship.

118 Assuming the Preface to be a late feature of the work, written after the bulk at least of the text was otherwise complete.

119 *EH* IV, 20 (18). It had putatively been written 'many years ago', perhaps when Bede learned of the incorrupt state of her body at her elevation, in the mid to late 690s. The hymn begins with a reproof of Virgil, whose secular, heroic theme of the fall of Troy was to be replaced herein by the sacred subject of virginity in the context of Christ's appearance on earth.

120 D. Hurst (ed.), *In primam partem Samuhelis*, in *CCSL* 119, Turnhout: Brepols, 1962, 1. There is a translation offered in B. Ward, *The Venerable Bede*, London: Continuum, 2ⁿᵈ edn, 1998, 49–50.

121 M. D. Laynesmith, 'Stephen of Ripon and the Bible: Allegorical and Typological Interpretations of the *Life of St. Wilfrid*', *Early Medieval Europe* 9(2) (2000) 163–82.

122 See S. Connolly, *Bede: On the Temple*, Liverpool: Liverpool University Press, 1995, *passim.*

123 *EH* I, 14: 'Yet those who survived could not be awakened from the spiritual death which their sins had brought upon them either by the death of their kinsmen or by fear of their own death.'

124 *EH* II, 1: 'Pope St. Gregory, who had reigned in great glory over the apostolic Roman see . . . was taken up to reign for ever in the kingdom of heaven.'

125 *EH* II, 1.

126 Gennadius, 'Lives of Illustrious Men', in *Nicene and Post-Nicene Fathers*, series III, vol. 3, 1892, 385–404, at 389. For a Latin text, see O. Von Gebhardt and E. C. von Richardson (eds.), *Hieronymus Liber de viris inlustribus, Texte und untersuchungen zur Geschichte der altchristlichen Literatur*, Leipzig: J. C. Hinrich's Buchhandlung, 1896, series XIV, vol. 1.

127 So, for example, Bede's Prologue to *On the Temple*, addressed to Acca, commenting that: 'it seemed good to me to send to your holiness for perusal the little work that I had recently written in the allegorical style on the construction of the temple of God': Connolly, *Bede: On the Temple*, Prol. 3, p. 3. There is an excellent discussion by A. G. Holder in his *Bede: On the Tabernacle*, Liverpool: Liverpool University Press, 1994, xvii–xx.

128 This emphasises the point made above, p. 44, that the *EH* was not a work which a secular audience is likely to have been capable of reading or understanding without considerable assistance from well-educated clerics.

129 L. Feldman (trans.), *Judean Antiquities*, Leiden: Brill, 1999, Preface, 3.

130 I. W. Raymond, *Seven Books against the Pagans*, New York: Columbia University Press, 1936, 395–8; for a Latin text, see *Orose Histoires (Contre les Païens)*, 3 vols., ed. M.-P. Arnoud-Lindet, Paris: Les Belles Lettres, 1990, III, 43.

131 Ward, *The Venerable Bede*, 111–12.

132 Although he described it at the close in *EH* V, 24 as *historia ecclesiastica Brittaniarum, et maxime gentis Anglorum* ('the ecclesiastical history of the British [provinces], and particularly of the people of the English'), but this comes after his notice of the acceptance of the Roman calculation of Easter by the Picts, many of the Irish and some of the Britons (V, 15, 21, 22) and the expansion outwards was arguably intended to reflect this process. That said, an emphasis on Britain as a theatre appropriate to mission in the second half of the sixth century comes across in book I and then again in the recapitulation of V, 24. The sense in which Bede viewed his work as insular in context needs, therefore, to be borne in mind but the bulk of his focus is English.

133 Eutropius, *Breviarium ab urbe condita*, ed. F. Ruehl, Leipzig: Teubner, 1887.

134 R. Philip and S. J. Amidon (ed. and trans.), *The Church History of Rufinus of Aquileia*, Oxford: Oxford University Press, 1997, offer only the last two books. Rufinus translated the ten books of Eusebius but reduced them to nine, then added his own books x and xi, to take the story up to the death of Theodosius (January 395).

135 R. Markus, *Bede and the Tradition of Ecclesiastical Historiography*, JL (1975), 3.

136 He used the phrase again in II, 1 as a description of this work.

137 Josephus had similarly structured his *Judean Antiquities* around the succession of high priests, kings and other rulers.

138 J. Elfassi, 'L'Occultation du paganisme dans la *Chronique mineure* de Bède le Vénérable', in *BLVTP* 63–9.

139 W. Levison, 'Bede as Historian', in *BLTW* 133.

140 As argued by J. M. Wallace-Hadrill, 'Bede and Plummer', in *FC* 369.

141 M. Winterbottom (ed. and trans.), *Gildas, The Ruin of Britain and Other Documents*, Chichester: Phillimore, 1978: see particularly IV, 2: 'I shall not speak of the ancient errors, common to all races, that bound the whole of humanity fast before the coming of Christ in the flesh.' For a discussion, see M. Miller, 'Bede's Use of Gildas', *English Historical Review* 90 (1975) 241–61, but the central focus

of her essay is on the attempt to reconstruct what happened, as opposed to the strategy of borrowing.

142 For Bede's source and purposes here, see C. W. Jones, 'Polemius Silvius, Bede, and the Names of the Months', *Speculum* 9 (1934) 50–6.

143 Wallis, *Reckoning of Time*, 53. The whole matter is dealt with in chapters 11–15. For a discussion, see *ibid.*, 284–7.

144 *EH* 3, fn. 3. This use of Gregory's text signposts Bede's treatment of very similar issues in terms of the authority of his own narrative.

145 Plummer, *Baedae Opera* I, B2.

146 It is somewhat extreme to take the view that the very idea was Albinus's, as Jones, *Saints' Lives and Chronicles*, 81. Nor was Albinus a bishop as he supposed.

147 W. T. Foley and A. G. Holder (trans.), *Bede: A Biblical Miscellany*, Liverpool, Liverpool University Press, 1999, 89. Trent Foley discusses the date of this letter, noting existing arguments in favour of 713/14–17 and *c.*725 respectively, but neither is ultimately capable of proof. Suffice it to say that Bede's acquaintance with Nothhelm already went back some considerable time in 731.

148 The *On Eight Questions*, which is generally but less certainly attributed to Bede, is in some manuscripts also directed towards Nothhelm, but this is omitted from the listing of his works in *EH* V, 24. For discussion, see Foley and Holder, *Bede*, 145–7.

149 Wallis, *Reckoning of Time*, 227.

150 The issue is discussed by F. A. Markus, 'The Chronology of the Gregorian Mission: Bede's Narrative and Gregory's Correspondence', *Journal of Ecclesiastical History* 14 (1963) 16–30.

151 *EH* V, 20.

152 L. Feldman (trans. and commentary), *Judean Antiquities*, 1–4, Leiden: Brill, 1999, Preface, 2; S. Mason (trans. and commentary), *The Life of Josephus*, Leiden: Brill, 2001. Epaphroditus has not otherwise been identified.

153 Gregory, *Dialogues* I, 9.

154 *EH* II, 1.

155 This Cyneberht is probably the same figure as Bede addressed in a surviving epigram: M. Lapidge, 'Some Remnants of Bede's Lost *Liber Epigrammatum*', *English Historical Review* 90 (1975) 805–6.

156 Colgrave, *EH* 7, adopted the singular in treating of this sentence, so adducing the sense to Bede as individual: 'I have simply sought to commit to writing what I have collected', but the Latin is consistently in the plural, suggesting that Bede intended here a collective subject made up of himself plus his informants.

157 As Plummer, *Baedae Opera* I, xliv–xlv; in II, 3–4, notes Bede's previous use of the phrase in his commentary on Luke and remarks that he 'is nearly always careful to mark where he is writing only "fama uulgante" by using such words as "fertur", "perhibetur", &c.'.

158 Jerome, *Perpetual Virginity of the Blessed Mary*, PL 23, cols 187–8: *Denique excepto Joseph, et Elisabeth, et ipsa Maria, paucisque admodum, si quos ab his audisse possumus aestimare, omnes Jesum filium aestimabant Joseph: intantum, ut etiam Evangelistae opinionem vulgi exprimentes, quae vera historiae lex est, patrem cum dixerint Salvatoris, ut ibi, et venit in spiritu in Templum (haud dubium quin Simeon) et cum inducerent parentes ejus puerum Jesum, ut facerent de illo secundum consuetudinem legis* ('Finally, with the exception of Joseph, and Elizabeth, and Mary herself and a few others, if we can assume they heard from them, all considered Jesus to be the son of Joseph, to such an extent that the Evangelists, following the opinion of the vulgar, that is **the/a true law of history**, call him the father of the Saviour, such as, "And he (that is, Simeon) came by the Spirit into the temple: and when the parents brought in the child Jesus, to do for him after the custom of the law" ').

Bede had already used the phrase in his *Commentary on St. Luke, CCSL* 120, 67 (Luke 2:33–4): *Et erat pater eius et mater mirantes super his quae dicebantur de illo, et benedixit illis Symeon. Patrem saluatoris appellat Ioseph non quo uere iuxta Fotinianos pater fuerit eius sed quo ad famam Mariae conseruandam pater sit ab omnibus aestimatus. Neque enim oblitus euangelista quod eam de spiritu sancto concepisse et uirginem peperisse narrarit sed opinionem uulgi exprimens quae* **vera historiae lex** *est patrem Ioseph nuncupat Christi* ('And his father and mother were amazed at these things that were said about him, and Symeon blessed them. Joseph is called the father of the Saviour not because in truth he was his father as the Photinians have it, but observing the reputation of Mary he was considered by all to be the father. It should not be forgotten that the Evangelist narrated that she conceived through the Holy Spirit and gave birth as a virgin but following the opinion of the vulgar, which is **the true law of history**, he names Joseph as the father of Christ.') I am grateful to Martin Ryan for these translations.

159 Jones, *Saints' Lives and Chronicles*, 83.
160 R. Ray, 'Bede's *Vera Lex Historiae*', *Speculum* 55(1) (1980) 1–21.
161 *Ibid.*, 10.
162 *Ibid.*, 14.
163 W. M. Lindsay (ed.), *Isidori Hispalensis Episcopi Etymologiarum sive Originum Libri XX*, Oxford: Clarendon Press, repr. 1957, I, 41.
164 As Campbell, 'Bede I', 26: 'the veneration which he has so long so rightly been accorded ought to be tempered by some mistrust'.
165 Ray remarks on this, p. 20, but cannot quite counter the conclusion that Bede recognised that his veracity here lay less in terms of the historicity of specific events than in his overriding message regarding the Irish bishop as a model prelate.
166 *EH* II, 1.
167 M. L. W. Laistner (ed.), *Bedae Venerabilis Expositio Actuum Apostolorum et Retractatio*, Cambridge, MA: The Medieval Academy of America, 1939, 32–3 (VII, 16, lines 31–3); Ray remarks on this, p. 8.
168 See the discussion of Ward, *Venerable Bede*, 113–14.
169 See Bede's interpretation, for example, of their initial meeting outdoors on account of the king's 'traditional superstition', which presumably reflects his rendering of either oral or written communications from Albinus at Canterbury, via Nothhelm. This, in turn, presumably rests on oral tales developed locally over several generations, which are unlikely to have been committed to writing earlier than Bede's *EH*, and may well be apocryphal, or have even been reinterpreted so heavily by Bede as to be unrecognisable. Despite the obvious weakness of this material's historicity, it has regularly been quoted virtually verbatim in modern works, as, to take just one example of many, H. Mayr-Harting, *The Coming of Christianity to Anglo-Saxon England*, London: Batsford, 3rd edn, 1991, 62: 'King Ethelbert met the party on the island of Thanet – in the open air for fear that indoors they might get the better of him with their magical arts.' That Bede should be treated as a secondary source for the Augustinian mission was argued both by I. N. Wood, 'The Mission of Augustine of Canterbury to the English', *Speculum* 69 (1994) 1–17, and Higham, *Convert Kings*. That said, Martin Ryan points out to me that the routine miracle of the mass normally occurs indoors, and Æthelberht might well have been aware of such through his wife's attendance at St Martin's, in which case the story may have a basis in reality.
170 See J. Sharpe, *Dick Turpin: The Myth of the English Highwayman*, London: Profile, 2004, *passim*.
171 Ward, *Venerable Bede*, 114.
172 See the treatment of this issue by Jones, *Saints' Lives and Chronicles*, 85, although his comments regarding Bede and Eddius should be treated with some caution.

173 For recent comment, see W. D. McCready, *Miracles and the Venerable Bede*, Toronto: Pontifical Institute of Mediaeval Studies, 1994, 195–213.

174 Wallace-Hadrill, *Bede's Ecclesiastical History*, 199, questioned the common assumption that this pertains to events post-dating 731, suggesting it might refer to a victory in 721, of which Bede might have been aware from the *Book of Pontiffs*. That this had occurred several years before the comets of 729, however, does not support this interpretation.

175 W. Levison, 'Bede as Historian', in *BLTW* 136–7; Jones, *Saints' Lives and Chronicles*, 31–2; Wallace-Hadrill, *Bede's Ecclesiastical History*, 200.

176 Although it arguably contains as its first element a Scottish personal name, the suffix implies that the place-name was formed in Old English, which suggests that it may have been within Northumbria, at some stage at least.

177 I made the case elsewhere that this probably refers to Hatfield near the Humber, rather than the Hertfordshire example: N. J. Higham, *The Kingdom of Northumbria: AD 350–1100*, Stroud: Sutton, 1993, 139.

178 *EH* IV, 12: *pulsus est* occurs in both contexts.

179 *EH* V, 23.

180 For recent discussion of eclipses as portents, see E. Grant, 'Medieval and Renaissance Scholastic Conceptions of the Influence of the Celestial Region on the Terrestrial', *Journal of Medieval and Renaissance Studies* 17 (1987) 1–23; J. D. North, 'Medieval Concepts of Celestial Influence: A Survey', in P. Curry (ed.), *Astrology, Science and Society: Historical Essays*, Woodbridge: Boydell, 1987, 5–17; Wallis, *Reckoning of Time*, 306. Bede had interpreted the comets of 729 in his longer narrative as having a relevance to the whole of Christendom, not just as signs to be associated with two English deaths. The two sixth-century eclipses are not fictional, being confirmed by modern calculation as occurring in 538 on February 15 (Bede has 16) and in 540 on June 20 (with which Bede concurs): http://sunearth.gsfc.nasa.gov/eclopise/SEcat/SE0501–0600.html. Neither is recorded in either of Bede's chronicles but he presumably derived them from some now lost, near-contemporary chronicle.

181 Bede presumably derived Ida's twelve-year reign from a king-list: D. P. Kirby, 'Bede and Northumbrian Chronology', *English Historical Review* 78 (1963) 514–27, at 515.

182 Gregory's death opens book II. The correct date is 604.

183 This brief and anonymous entry refers back to the much fuller report of Northumbrian victory in I, 34, with which Bede closed book I.

184 For Gregory's letter to Augustine on the organisation of the new English Church, see *EH* I, 29.

185 As is made clear in the main text: *EH* III, 21, 24.

186 Egbert was the only figure in the recapitulation to be termed either 'man of God' or 'Saint'.

187 He used this term of Claudius early in the recapitulation: *EH* V, 24, and of a series of English kings in *EH* II, 5. For discussion of his usage, see B. A. E. Yorke, 'The Vocabulary of Anglo-Saxon Overlordship', *Anglo-Saxon Studies in History and Archaeology* 2 (1981) 171–200; S. Fanning, 'Bede, *Imperium* and the Bretwaldas', *Speculum* 66 (1991) 1–26; N. J. Higham, *An English Empire: Bede and the Early English Kings*, Manchester: Manchester University Press, 1995, 21–40, 47–68.

188 Penda was *rex Merciorum* (or similar) in *EH* III, 7, 9, 17, 18, 21, 24, the last two both in two instances. His paganism was also particularly stressed, as III, 9.

189 As Eadbald, Oswiu, Egbert, Hlothhere and Wihtred, all of whom *obiit*, Osred (*interfectus*), Æthelberht, Eorcenberht, Wulfhere, Aldfrith and Ceolred (*defunctus est*) and Oswald, Oswine and Ecgfrith (*occisus*). Even Berhtred (*interfectus*) was described as *dux regius Nordanhymbrorum*.

190 The same verb, *uastare*, was used of Penda's devastation of Northumbria: *EH* III, 24.

191 See particularly *EH* V, 23.

192 That one at least of his followers in exile in Ireland had earlier spent time at Melrose suggests a Northumbrian origin for all of Egbert and his companions, but we cannot be sure: *EH* V, 9.

193 It amounts to 14 per cent of the total number of entries.

194 Although she was mentioned in *EH* III, 11 and IV, 21 (19), this is the sole reference to her death.

195 Although it would be highly appropriate were he to be the same individual whom Ecgfrith had, wrongfully in Bede's opinion, sent to Ireland: *EH* IV, 26 (24).

196 Which is primarily the view promoted by Patrick Wormald in his seminal works, 'Bede and Benedict Biscop', in *FC* 141–69, and 'Bede, "Beowulf" and the Conversion of the Anglo-Saxon Aristocracy', in *BASE* 62.

197 Particularly Alan Thacker, in his 'Bede's Ideal of Reform', in *IR* 130–53.

198 As Goffart, initially in *Narrators*, 235–328.

199 As D. P. Kirby, 'King Ceolwulf of Northumbria and the *Historia Ecclesiastica*', *Studia Celtica* 14–15 (1979–80) 168–73.

200 Stephen's *Life* only survives in two medieval manuscripts and is unlikely ever to have existed in much larger numbers, in contrast to Bede's *EH*: Colgrave, *Life of Bishop Wilfrid* xiii–xvi.

201 In *EH* IV, 26 (24).

202 In *Pastoral Care*: for a discussion, see C. Leyser, *Authority and Asceticism from Augustine to Gregory the Great*, Oxford: Clarendon Press, 2000, 171–6.

203 Campbell, 'Bede I', 25.

3 Structure, organisation and context

1 Spike Milligan, *The Looney*, Harmondsworth: Penguin, 1958, 1, lampooning a theme initially developed by Bede, *EH* I, 1; III, 6, for which see above p. 131.

2 Expressed in terms of the number of chapters per book (34, 20, 30, 32 (30) and 24, respectively), book II is only approximately 59 per cent of book I; the variation is somewhat less in terms of numbers of lines of text, whereby the shortest book (again, II) is approximately 67 per cent the length of the longest (now, V).

3 R. Gryson (ed.), *Bedae Presbyteri, Expositio Apocalypseos*, in *CCSL* 121a, 2001, comment at 133 and text at 233: Preface, lines 134–5. For a translation, see E. Marshall, *In Apocalypsin: The Explanation of the Apocalypse by the Venerable Bede*, Oxford: James Parker & Co., 1878, at http://www.apocalyptic-theories.com/theories/bede/bede.html.

4 Bede referred to Augustine by name, *ibid.*, lines 136–7: K.-D. Daur (ed.), *Sancti Aurelii Augustini Contra Adversarium Legis et Prophetarum*, in *CCSL* 49, 1985, I, 24.

5 For a discussion, see C. Grocock, 'Bede and the Golden Age of Latin Prose', in J. Hawkes and S. Mills (eds), *Northumbria's Golden Age*, Stroud: Sutton, 1999, 372–3.

6 Forty-six also approximates to the number of books in the Vulgate, although Bede, of course, had access to several different formats of the Bible, the organisation of which was not uniform. Bede used Constantius's *Life of St. Germanus* in *EH* I, 17–21. The anonymous *Life of Cuthbert*, which served as Bede's primary source for both his lives, was organised in four books, perhaps in deference to the *Life of St. Martin* by Sulpicius Severus, so Bede's adoption of another Gallic

model for his own works on Cuthbert seems plausible. The alternative, that this number derives from the years of the rebuilding of the Temple, was proposed by M. D. Laynesmith, in the context of Stephen's portrayal of Wilfrid's episcopacy inaccurately as fifty-six years in length: 'Stephen of Ripon and the Bible: Allegorical and Typological Interpretations of the *Life of St. Wilfrid*', *Early Medieval Europe* 9(2) (2000) 168, and this clearly offers another perspective on Bede's organisation of this work, and also, of course, of Constantius's *Life*.

7 It is an approximation, since some texts have numerous and on occasion quite lengthy additions which have been included. Part columns are here counted as if whole, but these distortions are not such as to affect materially the comparisons being offered here.

8 Bede's concern with the unity of Wearmouth/Jarrow was arguably the decisive factor. Book I focuses particularly on Benedict Biscop, who is presented as founder of both sites. His death is heavily anticipated in I, 13, but actually occurs in book II, overshadowing the other events of book II under the joint abbacies of his successors, enabling the author to remind his audience of his role as founder of both in later contexts: Plummer, *Baedae Opera* I, 364–87, with the second book opening on 377. Chapterisation is continuous across the two books, as in the three books of *On the Apocalypse of St. John*, which is perhaps why division into books is ignored in the translation which is most commonly read, by J. F. Webb, in D. H. Farmer (ed.), *The Age of Bede*, Harmondsworth: Penguin, revised edn, 1988, 185–208.

9 *EH* I, 5, quoting briefly from Vegetius, *Epitoma re militaris* I, 24, on the construction of turf walls by the Roman military.

10 In his *Greater Chronicle*, 4427, Bede quoted an entire sentence on the subject from Gennadius, *De viris illustribus*, 89: see Wallis, *Reckoning of Time*, 222.

11 Lindsay, *Isidori Hispalensis Episcopi Etymologiarum*, V, 39.

12 See, for example, D. P. Kirby, *Bede's Historia Ecclesiastica Gentis Anglorum: Its Contemporary Setting*, in *JL* II, 1.

13 *EH* I, 34, quoting Genesis 49:27.

14 *EH* IV, 24: 'some clean animal chewing the cud' is used as a simile for Cædmon, but this is an allusion to Mosaic law rather than a quotation.

15 *EH* V, 23.

16 Wallis, *Reckoning of Time*, 167, under the year 2493. Jerome, *Chronicon*, ed. R. Helm, *Eusebius Werke* 7.1, Griechischen christlichen Schriftsteller 24, Leipzig: J. C. Hinrichs, 1913, 46a, 1–6.

17 *Bede: On the Tabernacle*, ed. and trans. Holder, II, 3, 7, 9, 10.

18 *Bede: On the Temple*, trans. Connolly, I, 13, 18.

19 Bede, *In primam partem Samuhelis*, ed. Hurst, in *CCSL* 119, 157, 160.

20 Bede, *In Lucam*, ed. Hurst, in *CCSL* 120, 29.

21 So compare God's expulsion of Adam and Eve from the Garden of Eden with the Britons' loss of Britain on account of their wickedness.

22 *EH* V, 23, quoting from Psalms 96 (97), 29 (30).

23 See pp. 55–6.

24 Now see O. Szerwiniack, 'L'Histoire ecclésiastique ou le rêve d'un retour au temps de l'innocence', in *BLVTP* 159–76.

25 Assuming that the two chapters added to book IV be excluded.

26 W. Levison, 'Bede as Historian', in *BLTW* 141: the five books 'do not differ in the numbers of chapters and length so much as to give the reader a sense of disproportion'.

27 Ward, *Venerable Bede*, 114–29.

28 *Ibid.*, 114. Bede's interest in the ages of man already occurs in his earliest work on time in 703.

29 Wallis, *Reckoning of Time*, 157–8, although she translates the *quasi senilis aetas* of

the fifth age as 'maturity, if you will', perhaps because Bede's passage from *iuvenali aetate* ('the age of youth') in the fourth age to senility in the fifth seems somewhat extreme.

30 Only the events of *EH* I, 1, 2 certainly pre-date the sixth age.

31 Ward, *Venerable Bede*, 115.

32 *Ibid.*

33 *Ibid.*

34 Augustine's development of this notion is discussed by Wallis, *Reckoning of Time*, 356.

35 These seven parts are the four Gospels, Acts, Epistles and Apocalypse: C. Tischenddorf (ed.), *Codex Amiatinus: Novum Testamentum Latine interprete Hieronymo*, Leipzig: Avenarius et Mendelssohn, 1854.

36 To which he refers in *On the Tabernacle* II, 11, 13; *On the Temple* I, 8, 15; II, 19, 23, 24; *In primam partem Samuhelis*, in *CCSL* 119, 51; *In Esram et Neemiam*, *PL* 91, col. 901; *In Lucam*, in *CCSL* 120, 339; *Expositio Apocalypseos*, in *CCSL* 121a, 485.

37 Wallis, *Reckoning of Time*, 96–9, cap. 34.

38 *De natura rerum*, *PL* 90, col. 202.

39 *On the Temple* I, 7, the translation is by Connolly, *Bede: On the Temple*, 26.

40 The lines have been counted manually from *EH*. The totals are offered as approximations but should be broadly accurate.

41 As I, 23, 24, 28, 29, 30, 31, 32; II, 4, 8, 10, 11, 17, 18, 19; III, 29; IV, 5, 17 (15), 20 (18); V, 7, 8, 16, 17, 21.

42 Ed. Jones, in *CCSL* 123c, 579–611.

43 I am grateful to Martin Ryan for this translation.

44 The date is one day out from that offered in *EH* III, 27 (3 May 664). The eclipse actually occurred on 1 May.

45 This last entry seems to date the work to 703, yet modern editions of the text provide dates of 708 and 709 respectively. The earlier date must necessarily be preferred. For discussion see M. Ohashi, '*Sexta aetas continent annos praeteritos DCCVIIII*', in *Time and Eternity: The Medieval Discourse*, ed. G. Jaritz and G. Moreno-Riaño, International Medieval Research 9, Turnhout: Brepols, 2003, 55–61.

46 Following Isidore's chronicle in *Etymologies* on which Bede's *Lesser Chronicle* is based: Lindsay, *Isidori Hispalensis Episcopi Etymologiarum* V, 39: Bede reduced the incidence of 'barbarian' territorial successes (such as the Vandal occupation of Africa) included by Isidore, plus mention of Persian conquests which the latter had attributed to the reign of Phocas, adding two mentions of the Angles, plus St Benedict, whom his source omitted. There are minor discrepancies in the regnal years in the printed editions. Bede's final sentence similarly closes Isidore's.

47 Notice of the arrival of the English does not occur in all manuscripts so it is possible that it was an interpolation, but this is by no means certain.

48 All brief quotations here are to the excellent translation, with commentary, by Wallis, *Reckoning of Time*, but such full sentences which are not so referenced have been translated from the Latin *de novo* to try to be as literal as possible (see below).

49 It is here that Bede's anti-chiliastic agenda is clearest. For discussion see Wallis, *Reckoning of Time*, 360–3.

50 Following Isidore's development of the notion of a single dating system from the Creation, which relied on Eusebius's synchronisation of biblical and secular time: see Wallis, *Reckoning of Time*, 357–8.

51 One cannot be precise about the number of entries, which depend in detail on what is considered to constitute a discrete 'fact' and the sense in which a group of related events may be treated as one.

52 Wallis, *Reckoning of Time*, 211.

53 So, for example, providing the names Alban, Aaron and Julius from Gildas as insular martyrs attributable to Diocletian's persecution to add to the wider story

which was here an amalgam of the works of Jerome and Orosius and *The Book of Pontiffs*.

54 Winterbottom, *Gildas, The Ruin of Britain*, XIX–XXIII, although the name Vortigern does not occur in Winterbottom's edition, which derives from the text established in the nineteenth century by Theodore Mommsen. It is, however, present in the late twelfth-century text at Avranches: *Abrincensis bibliothecae civicae*, n. 162.

55 *EH* I, 14–21, particularly 15, 20.

56 Wallis, *Reckoning of Time*, 226, slightly amended.

57 Maurice was given a twenty-one-year reign by Bede. From 'Augustine' to 'to Christ', Bede took this material verbatim from *The Book of Pontiffs*. He last took material from this work relating to the year 716, which was, of course, the year in which several of his brethren visited Rome, which may have facilitated his acquisition of a contemporary version. The end-date of the *Greater Chronicle* is calculated from his notice that Leo [III] had then ruled eight years (beginning in 717), although if this came from written material transmitted ultimately from the continent then composition may well have been completed only in 726.

58 Wallis, *Reckoning of Time*, 226.

59 Although only Æthelfrith is named in I, 34, Ælle not appearing until the close of II, 1.

60 This and other long quotations from the *Greater Chronicle* in this chapter are comparatively literal translations by the author which are intended to retain as much as possible of Bede's rhetorical treatment of his subjects. The Latin text is printed and edited by T. Mommsen, *Monumenta Germaniae Historica, Auctorum Antiquissimorum Tomus* XIII, *Chronicorum Minorum Saec. IV, V, VI, VII*, III, Berlin: Weidmann, 1898, 223–333.

61 This was the sole use of the term in the *Greater Chronicle*.

62 Whether Bede's dates are correct or marginally incorrect has been argued at length by D. P. Kirby, 'Bede and Northumbrian Chronology', *English Historical Review* 78 (1963) 514–27; S. Wood, 'Bede's Northumbrian Dates Again', *English Historical Review* 98 (1983) 280–96.

63 *EH* IV, 3, 19 (17), 20 (18), 22 (20); 27 (25)–32 (30), respectively.

64 *Greater Chronicle* 4639, see above, note 60.

65 Although he also occurs in *EH* III, 13; V, 10, 19.

66 Willibrord had been an oblate at Ripon, then spent a considerable period in Ireland, in part with Egbert, before being despatched by the latter to Frisia in 690, then was ordained by the pope in 695. Alcuin believed himself to have been related to him and wrote his *Life* for a Gaulish bishop of Sens, Beornrad: *Alcuin, The Life of Saint Willibrord*, trans. C. H. Talbot, in *Soldiers of Christ: Saints and Saints' Lives from Late Antiquity and the Early Middle Ages*, ed. T. F. X. Noble and T. Head, London: Sheed and Ward, 1995, 191–211.

67 Edwin was Ecgfrith's maternal grandfather.

68 Alcuin, *The Life of Saint Willibrord* I, in B. Krusch and W. Levison (eds.), *Passiones vitaeque sanctorum aevi Marovingici, Monumenta Germaniae Historica* V, Hanover: Hahan, 1910. For a translation, see note 66 above.

69 *EH* III, 13.

70 He was later culted at Ripon but the evidence comes from the eleventh century and post-dates much translation of relics: D. W. Rollason, 'Lists of Saints' Resting-Places in Anglo-Saxon England', *Anglo-Saxon England* 7 (1978) 61–94, no. 6; J. Blair, 'A Hand-List of Anglo-Saxon Saints', in A. Thacker and R. Sharpe (eds.), *Local Saints and Local Churches in the Early Medieval West*, Oxford: Oxford University Press, 2002, 532.

71 Bede termed Egbert 'an Englishman' (*EH* III, 4) and 'of noble birth' (III, 27); Alcuin described him as of 'this race of ours', which may imply that he was

Northumbrian: P. Godman, *Alcuin: The Bishops, Kings, and Saints of York*, Oxford: Clarendon Press, 1982, line 1008. Alcuin also described him as a bishop (line 1013), but it is far from clear of what, unless he had acquired an Irish or Scottish see. This may be the implication of his possible appearance in the witness list of the so-called 'Law of Adamnan' established at the Irish Synod of Birr in 697, as 'the wise Bishop Ichtbrict': K. Meyer (ed. and trans.), *Cain Adamnain: An Old-Irish Treatise on the Law of Adamnan*, Oxford: Clarendon Press, 1905, cap. 28. For comment on the latter, T. O'Loughlin (ed.), *Essays in Commemoration of the Law of the Innocents*, Dublin: Four Courts Press, 2001, *passim*.

72 Wallis, *Reckoning of Time*, 228. For a view of the Irish and British churches as seriously influenced by Pelagianism during this period, see M. W. Herren and S. A. Brown, *Christ in Celtic Christianity: Britain and Ireland from the Fifth to the Tenth Century*, Woodbridge: Boydell and Brewer, 2002, *passim*.

73 Colgrave, *Life of Wilfrid*, XII, XIV, XV; see his comments, pp. 157, 159.

74 M. Lapidge and M. Herren (ed. and trans.), *Aldhelm: The Prose Works*, Cambridge: Brewer, 1979, letters III, V and XII at pp. 154–5, 160–4 and 168–70, respectively.

75 L. T. Martin and D. Hurst (trans.), *Bede the Venerable: Homilies on the Gospels, Book One, Advent to Lent*, Kalamazoo, MI: Cistercian Publications, 1991, 125–31.

76 A. Thacker, 'Bede and the Irish', in *BV* 37–40, who suggests that Bede was motivated by the wish to avoid exposing the crudity of the papal arguments; K. Harrison, 'A Letter from Rome to the Irish Clergy', *Peritia* 3 (1984) 222–9.

77 The omission of Oswald was noted by A. Thacker, '*Membra Disjecta*: The Division of the Body and the Diffusion of the Cult', in C. Stancliffe and E. Cambridge (eds.), *Oswald: Northumbrian King to European Saint*, Stamford: Paul Watkins, 1995, 112, who also remarks his absence from the 'original' version of Bede's *Martyrology*.

78 Wallis, *Reckoning of Time*, 230. Note the use of another of Bede's rare superlatives here of an abbot despatched to Canterbury from Rome.

79 *EH* III, 9, but see all of the first thirteen chapters of book III. For discussion of Oswald, see Stancliffe and Cambridge, *Oswald*, in particular papers by Stancliffe and Thacker.

80 *EH* III, 15–17.

81 *EH* III, 19.

82 *EH* III, 21, 22.

83 *EH* III, 22, 23; IV, 3.

84 Their omission was noted by Thacker, 'Bede and the Irish', 50.

85 *Anonymous Life of St. Cuthbert* in *Two Lives of St. Cuthbert*, ed. Colgrave, I, 5.

86 Genesis 35. The topos of ascent to heaven derives ultimately from the description of the death of Elijah in II Kings 2:11 but see also Luke 24:51. The arms of angels carrying souls to heaven recur in Alcuin's rewriting of Bede's history, lines 1247, 1362: Godman, *Alcuin*.

87 Compare the shepherds of Luke 2:8 with those of *Anonymous Life of St. Cuthbert* I, 5.

88 *Vita sancti Cuthberti metrica*, ed. W. Jaager, Palaestria 198, Leipzig: Mayer and Müller, 1935, 5.

89 *Ibid.*, 4, line 19.

90 *Anonymous Life of St. Cuthbert* III, 1; Bede's *Prose Life of Saint Cuthbert*, 14, 20.

91 Bede's *Prose Life of Saint Cuthbert*, 4.

92 *Ibid.* 14, 20.

93 See discussion of A. Thacker, 'Bede's Ideal of Reform', in *IR* 146–50.

94 H. Quentin, *Les martyrologes historiques du moyen âge: étude sur la formation du martyrologe romain*, Paris, 1908, ch. 2. For a recent translation, see F. Lifshitz, 'Bede, Martyrology', in T. Head (ed.), *Medieval Hagiography: An Anthology*, New York and London: Routledge, 2000, 169–97.

95 M. Lapidge included Cuthbert as well: 'Acca of Hexham and the Origins of the

Old English Martyrology', *Analecta Bollandiana* 123 (2005) 29–78, at 49. The difficulties of reconstructing Bede's text make certainty impossible, however.

96 A. Thacker, 'Memorializing Gregory the Great: The Origin and Transmission of a Papal Cult in the Seventh and Early Eighth Centuries', *Early Medieval Europe* 7 (1998) 59–84; *EH* II, 1: *apostolatus eius*.

97 *EH* IV, 23.

98 The seminal discussions are by Thacker, 'Memorializing Gregory the Great' and '*Peculiaris Patronus Noster*: The Saint as Patron of the State in the Early Middle Ages', in J. R. Maddicott and D. M. Palliser (eds.), *The Medieval State: Essays Presented to James Campbell*, London: Hambledon Press, 2000, 1–24, at 18.

99 *Ibid.*, 18–19.

100 Wilfrid was initially patronised by Ecgfrith's elder half-brother, King Alhfrith of the *Deiri*, who was arguably his rival for the succession until his disappearance and apparent death following rebellion against his father, Oswiu, soon after 664.

101 As was recognised by Goffart, *Narrators*, 306: 'Bede's golden past is just as Irish as it is Roman, and Columba of Iona receives no less reverent attention than Pope Gregory of Rome.' This is perhaps a slight exaggeration but it makes the point effectively.

102 *EH* IV, 18 (16).

103 *EH* V, 24.

104 *EH* V, 21.

105 See p. 93: the ratio of entries in the recapitulation to chapters in each book ranges from 1:2.5 to 1:3, excluding book III, which has a ratio of 1:4.3.

106 See, for example, Kirby, *Bede's Historia Ecclesiastica*, 2.

107 W. Levison, 'Bede as Historian', in *BLTW* 145.

108 *Ibid.*; Plummer, *Baedae Opera*, I, 365: *tempore cuius supra beatae memoriae Uitaliani papae* ('in the time above of Pope Vitalian of blessed memory'). In his notes (II, 357) Plummer remarked 'These words . . . cannot be part of the original text of Bede, but must be due to some scribe who forgot that the Hist. Eccles. was written after the Hist. Abb.', but this neglects the possibility that it was either a genuine error on Bede's part or an uncorrected detail following extensive rewriting.

109 *EH* IV, 18: *cuius supra meminimus* ('whom we have mentioned above'). To suggest that Bede intended this as a reference to his treatment of Benedict in his *History of the Abbots* seems implausible: Plummer, *Baedae Opera* II, 233–4: 'Either . . . this is a mere slip, or Bede is referring to the Hist. Abb. I only know, however, four MSS which contain both works . . . and in all these the Hist. Abb. follows . . . the H.E.'; see also *EH* 388, fn. 1. A less clear-cut example of failed cross-referencing is Bede's mention of Pehthelm in V, 18, of whom he promised to write more 'in the proper place' but in fact barely mentioned him again in his summary of the bishops of Northumbria in V, 23.

110 Although there are difficulties around the dating of this journey, given Stephen's claim that Wilfrid was present at the execution of Aunemundus (whom he calls Dalphinus), bishop of Lyons, who was still alive in late 660. Stephen's account is probably in error on this issue, having taken the opportunity to associate the young Wilfrid with the death of a leading Gaulish cleric to the advantage of his hero's saintly credentials, when in fact he only knew him in life: P. Fouracre and R. A. Gerberding, *Late Merovingian France: History and Hagiography 640–720*, Manchester Medieval Series, Manchester: Manchester University Press, 1996, 174–5.

111 *EH* III, 25. The term 'Synod of Whitby' is conventional and should not be taken to indicate that this was in any sense a formal meeting of the English Church. W. Levison preferred the phrase 'the debate of Whitby': *England and the Continent in the Eighth Century*, Oxford: Clarendon Press, 1946, 50.

112 *History of the Abbots*, 3, 4.
113 Chapters 24, 27, 28, 29, 30, 31 and 32.
114 Chapters 4, 8, 10, 11, 17, 18 and 19.
115 Chapters 5, 10, 11, 17 (15) and 20 (18).
116 Chapters 7, 8, 16, 17, 19 and 21.
117 Although he did use a Latin *Life* of St Fursa in III, 19.
118 Such include the use of *Quae diximus* in IV, 28, *retulimus* in V, 9, and *superius* in V, 22. There are also occasional instances of such terms as *infra* ('below') in this context, such as *de ultimis infra dicendum est* ('concerning the last it will be discussed below') in book IV, 23 of the ordinations of John of Beverley (to which he returned in V, 2) and Wilfrid II (V, 6).
119 *EH* IV, 3, referring back to III, 4 and his youth in Ireland.
120 *EH* IV, 5, referring back to his appointment by Archbishop Honorius in III, 20.
121 *EH* IV, 6, referring back to III, 30.
122 *EH* IV, 23, referring back to III, 24.
123 *EH* IV, 26, referring back to III, 24.
124 *EH* IV, 26, referring back to III, 15, 24, 25.
125 *EH* IV, 27, referring back to III, 26.
126 Hild was baptised alongside others of Edwin's court, by Paulinus, but later went on to manage a monastery founded under the authority of Iona/Lindisfarne and was said to be an adherent of the Ionan method of dating Easter in 664. Ælfflæd grew up under her tutelage, so presumably shared her preferences, at least in her youth.
127 *EH* II, 14
128 *EH* II, 20.
129 *EH* IV, 23.
130 *EH* IV, 27.
131 *EH* V, 22.
132 *EH* xlvii–lii.
133 *EH* III, 7: the phrase was recently reused by Clare Stancliffe as a title for her essay on Oswald: 'Oswald, Most Holy and Most Victorious King of the Northumbrians', in Stancliffe and Cambridge, *Oswald*, 1995, 33–83.
134 *EH* III, 9, replicating the terms used in II, 5.
135 As seems clear from the evidence for an early cult which Bede offers in *EH* III, 2, 9, 10, 11, 12: Thacker, '*Membra Disjecta*', 100–4. The cult was of sufficient political value to be contested by the Mercian élite, hence the translation of his putative body to Bardney in Lindsey before 704 by his niece, Queen Osthryth, and the retirement of King Æthelred, her widower, to become abbot there.
136 Implicitly, Oswiu was presented as a David figure versus Penda as Goliath in *EH* III, 24, but Bede did not reinforce the parallel, here or elsewhere, by, for example, quoting from I Samuel 17.
137 The total is necessarily an approximation, dependent on who is included and who is excluded. Here names which occur only in genealogies are omitted, as is Jaruman, bishop of the Mercians, on the grounds that he is more likely to have been Irish than English, but otherwise a comparatively inclusive approach has been taken, including apparently 'English' individuals with names which are 'British'.
138 Henry Mayr-Harting's interpretation of this as Bede's 'witty parody' of Isidore of Seville and Irish learning is best set aside: *The Coming of Christianity to Anglo-Saxon England*, London, Batsford, 3rd edn 1991, 50; the figurative meaning is explored by C. B. Kendall, 'Imitation and the Venerable Bede's *Historia Ecclesiastica*', in M. H. King and W. M. Stevens (eds), *Saints, Scholars and Heroes:*

Studies in Medieval Culture in Honour of Charles W. Jones, Collegeville, MN, 1979, I, 161–90 at 181.

139 *EH* I, 12, following Gildas.

140 See the discussion in Wallace-Hadrill, *Bede's Ecclesiastical History*, 47–8. Goffart, *Narrators*, 240, argues convincingly that Bede intended Æthelfrith be viewed as the counterpart of Augustus in Orosius's narrative, so in terms of his conquests of the Britons as a parallel with the *pax Romana* by which Christ's birth was contextualised.

141 Saul was Israel's first king and war-leader against the Philistines and Amalekites; Benjamin was referred to as a skilled warrior by his father, Jacob: Genesis 49:27. St Paul asserted that Saul was of the house of Benjamin (Acts 13:21), of which Bede was presumably aware. For a general discussion, see J. McClure, 'Bede's Old Testament Kings', in *IR* 90–1.

142 Bede referred to that hostility somewhat tangentially in *EH* II, 12.

143 Edwin's *imperium* was represented as the first of any English king to encompass Anglesey and Man and his occupation of Elmet may well have been known by this audience, although it was not actually mentioned by Bede, while Oswald slew Cædwalla, the British king, and enjoyed an even greater *imperium*.

144 The scholarly world is divided over the historicity of Gregory's meeting with the English slaves: see Wallace-Hadrill, *Bede*, 51; Higham, *Convert Kings*, 63.

145 I Samuel 31:1–6, which Bede, of course, knew well.

146 The parallel term, *nefandus*, had been used of the Saxons by Gildas, *De Excidio Britanniae* XXIII, 1, as Bede will probably have noted, having certainly read and utilised this section of the text.

147 Bede described Oswald's army as *parvus* ('small') but the British host as *inmensus* ('immense').

148 C. Cubitt, 'Universal and Local Saints in Anglo-Saxon England', in A. Thacker and R. Sharpe (eds), *Local Saints and Local Churches in the Early Medieval West*, 439, fn. 70.

149 Oswine likewise occurs in the Calendar of Willibrord but in a later hand; for Bede's perspective, see particularly *EH* III, 14; for a discussion, see Higham, *Convert Kings*, 227–31.

150 Compare his treatment of Egbert in III, 27 with that of Aidan in III, 5.

151 *EH* III, 26: Colgrave and Mynors assumed him to be Irish (*EH* 308, fn. 3) but Professor Richard Coates assures me that the name should be construed as British, making this another example to place beside Bede's notice of the British-named Chad and Cædmon as if 'English' Northumbrians.

152 Which he presumably preferred not to quote, perhaps because it referred back to the accusation against the Irish of the Quartodeciman heresy, reference to which Bede had already resisted in *EH* II, 19.

153 *EH* II, 3.

154 Bede, *Life of St. Cuthbert*, in *Two Lives of St. Cuthbert*, ed. Colgrave, XV, XXV.

155 *EH* III, 4, 27; IV, 3, 26; V, 9, 10, 22, 23, 24.

156 *EH* V, 9, quoting from Jonah 1:12, wherein Jonah had similarly attempted to avoid God's command by taking ship elsewhere.

157 The Epistle of Paul the Apostle to the Romans 10:2, depicting the Columban monasteries as if the Jews, who would ultimately, in Bede's view, be evangelised by Christian gentiles.

158 Ceolfrith's letter comprises by far Bede's longest and best-argued excursus on the Paschal issue in this work and occurs as V, 21, immediately prior to his narration of Egbert's conversion of Iona, which in a sense it therefore contextualises. Ceolfrith's authorship of the letter is not obviously crucial to its impact: indeed, it could have been anonymous and virtually as effective rhetorically,

other than as an implicit statement of the centrality of Wearmouth/Jarrow to Northumbrian orthodoxy on the Paschal question, and its reputation even among neighbouring courts.

159 See, for example, Goffart, *Narrators*, 253, who deemed the *EH* a 'Northumbrian narrative enlarged to English dimensions'.

160 For a résumé of his career see A. Orchard, 'Boniface', in *BEASE* 69–70. He is thought to derive from Crediton and to have been educated and trained in Hampshire. The only alternative is to suppose that he had made very little impact by 731, so might not have been mentioned to Bede by Bishop Daniel, which is also possible.

161 Böhne, 'Das älteste Lorscher Kalendar', 185. He occurs in combination with Wilfrid and Mellitus.

4 Message and discourse

1 Godman, *Alcuin*, 95, lines 1207–8.

2 Resulting in such excellent studies, *inter alia*, as B. Yorke, *Kings and Kingdoms of Early Anglo-Saxon England*, London: Seaby, 1990, and D. P. Kirby, *The Earliest English Kings*, London: Unwin Hyman, 1991.

3 M. H. Abrams, *The Mirror and the Lamp: Romantic Theory and the Critical Tradition*, New York: Norton, 1958, 6.

4 As E. Freund, *The Return of the Reader*, London: Methuen, 1987, 2.

5 For an argument to the same purpose but regarding Stephen, see M. D. Laynesmith, 'Stephen of Ripon and the Bible: Allegorical and Typological Interpretations of the *Life of St. Wilfrid*', *Early Medieval Europe* 9(2) (2000) 163–82.

6 See above, p. 69.

7 That Bede may have 'adapted' his sources on occasion to provide the history he preferred seems very likely. See, for example, his omission of that part of the *Libellus responsionum* which refers to the cult of St Sixtus, inclusion of which would have posed problems for his representation of the Gregorian mission as quite independent of pre-existing British Christianity. William McCready queried his importation of miracles from other narratives into an English context and offered a useful discussion of his attitude towards historicity: *Miracles and the Venerable Bede*, Toronto: Pontifical Institute of Mediaeval Studies, 1994, 214–29.

8 Benedicta Ward began her own appreciation of St Cuthbert by foregrounding comparable issues: 'The Spirituality of St Cuthbert', in G. Bonner *et al.*, *St. Cuthbert, His Cult and His Community to AD 1200*, Woodbridge: Boydell Press, 1989, 65–7.

9 As late seventh-century law-codes suggest. See, for example, the laws of Hlothhere and Eadric, in L. Oliver, *The Beginnings of English Law*, Toronto: University of Toronto Press, 2002, 125–33.

10 Excluding occurrences of *deus* which are generic rather than specific to the Christian God.

11 Excluding six appearances in the Preface but including the variant, *Xristus*, which occurs twice in IV, 20.

12 To which one might add numerous occurrences of 'the Lord' (*Dominus*) used either of Christ or of God, often in dating clauses from the incarnation. Jesus (*Iesus*) also occurs in twenty-three separate passages, but all but five in association with *Christus*, the exceptions being in IV, 17; V, 14, 19, 21, 24.

13 Of a kind of continental artistry with which Bede was clearly very familiar at Wearmouth.

14 As Alan Thacker remarked, 'Bede . . . could scarcely disguise the lineaments of

the Germanic warrior-hero, which lay only just beneath the surface of his carefully contrived portrait': '*Membra Disjecta*', 97.

15 Through whom Bede was, of course, making connections between the brethren at Hexham and St Oswald, so portraying Hexham in a positive light in the present.

16 For a general discussion, see L. Grig, *Making Martyrs in Late Antiquity*, London: Duckworth, 2004, *passim*. Bede only depicted two English individuals in his *EH* as martyrs, the two Hewalds (V, 10), who were killed in continental Germany. Otherwise, he followed the practice developed by Gregory in his *Dialogues* regarding sixth-century Italy, that it is appropriate to substitute asceticism for martyrdom within a fully converted people as an alternative route by which to attain sanctity.

17 Bede actually explained this phenomenon in terms of his charity rather than his warlike qualities: *EH* III, 6, thus demonstrating where his emphasis lay.

18 For Ceolwulf's retirement, see p. 198; for Lindisfarne as a clone of Iona, see Higham, *Convert Kings*, 211.

19 C. Leyser, *Authority and Asceticism from Augustine to Gregory the Great*, Oxford: Clarendon Press, 2000, 171–6. Although Bede does not seem to have quoted from *Pastoral Care* in this work, he was well aware of it, and even commended it as part of his commemoration of Gregory in II, 1: 'He composed another excellent book, which is called *Pastoralis*, in which he set out in the clearest fashion what kinds of person should be chosen to rule the church, and how these governors should live, with what discretion they should instruct listeners of different kinds and how they ought each day to reflect on their own frailty.'

20 Such were the principal qualities highlighted by Gregory in *Pastoral Care* II: for a translation, see J. Barmby (trans.), *The Book of Pastoral Care and Selected Epistles of Gregory the Great*, in Nicene and Post-Nicene Fathers, new series 12, Oxford and New York: James Parker & Co. The Christian Literature Society, 1895, II, 1–72.

21 Gregory the Great, *Dialogues* IV, 7.

22 II Samuel 21:17.

23 The references are collected and discussed by L. L. Morris in *The Marshall Pickering Encyclopedia of the Bible*, ed. W. A. Elwell, London: Marshall Pickering, 1988, II, 1342–4.

24 *EH* III, 2, 9, 10, 11, 12, 13; IV, 16 (14).

25 *EH* V, 2–6; V, 18.

26 The suggestion of Walter Goffart that Bede's depiction of Cædwalla was consciously ironic should arguably be set aside, since his pilgrimage to Rome and baptism there had a real potential to inspire respect from English commentators: *Narrators*, 319.

27 The seminal study of early Anglo-Saxon kings retiring to monasteries is that by Clare Stancliffe, which in broad terms accepts Bede's interpretation of their motives and treats them as evidence of the depth of Christian conversion by the second half of the seventh century: 'Kings Who Opted Out', in *IR* 154–76. For a rather different perspective, with the possibility of political rather than, or alongside, spiritual motivation in the case of Sigeberht of the East Angles, see Higham, *Convert Kings*, 215.

28 R. Davis, *The Book of Pontiffs*, Liverpool: Liverpool University Press, revised 2nd edn 2000, XC, 9 on p. 94.

29 St Boniface exhibited far more explicit disapproval of monks being expected to submit to royal demands: see Emerton, *Letters of St. Boniface*, LXII, 141.

30 Other than the prayers to God which were offered daily at Gilling in after years in atonement for the murder.

31 In *An English Empire*, 10, I singled out Oswiu and the early kingship of Ecgfrith as 'the apogee of English kingship', in the sense that this period saw Northumbrian power at its greatest geographical extent, reaching across the south and as

far north as the Picts. This is not to claim that English kingship had then reached its moral height in Bede's perspective, which it had certainly not, although he did use imagery reminiscent of David and Goliath and invoke Christ as leader of the Northumbrian host in the great battle against Penda in 655, by which Oswiu's moral rehabilitation was established.

32 Other than a passing reference to his reign in the context of Eadhæd's acquisition of the bishopric of Ripon in III, 28.

33 See *EH* 370, fn. 1; Wallace-Hadrill, *Bede's Ecclesiastical History*, 150, and references therein.

34 For a valuable discussion of Wilfrid's successors, see C. Cubitt, 'Wilfrid's Usurping Bishops: Episcopal Elections in Anglo-Saxon England *c.* 600–800', *Northern History* 25 (1989) 18–38.

35 He was mentioned as a priest accompanying Chad on his journey south for consecration in the 660s, in III, 28, then attracted notice for his consecration in the recapitulation of V, 24, in the entry for 678.

36 P. Hunter Blair, 'The *Moore Memoranda* on Northumbrian History', in Sir Cyril Fox and B. Dickins (eds), *The Early Cultures of North-West Europe*, Cambridge: Cambridge University Press, 1950, 243–58.

37 Colgrave, *Life of Wilfrid*, 20, 21.

38 See the discussion of these events in N. J. Higham, 'Bishop Wilfrid in Southern England: A Review of His Political Objectives', *Studien zur Sachsenforschung* 13 (1999), 207–17, but there remains the possibility that Wilfrid's expulsion was primarily the responsibility of Theodore, in pursuit of much smaller dioceses across both Northumbria and Mercia, which the bishops with dioceses equivalent to the two kingdoms then resisted. That view was championed by Wilhelm Levison, *England and the Continent in the Eighth Century*, Oxford: Clarendon Press, 1946, 50, 55.

39 Although Bede added in other missionaries to the South Saxons, such as the Irish monks at Bosham who were entirely omitted by Stephen. He noted that the royal couple were themselves already Christian but had not sponsored wider conversion. This does not, however, necessarily mean, as Goffart argues, that Bede was diminishing Wilfrid. Rather, that he succeeded where others failed implies that Wilfrid's activities were in line with divine providence: *EH* IV, 13; Goffart, *Narrators*, 318–19.

40 For a new discussion of Æthelthryth, see C. E. Karkov, 'The Body of St. Æthelthryth: Desire, Conversion and Reform in Anglo-Saxon England', in M. Carver (ed.), *The Cross Goes North*, York: York Medieval Press, 2003, 397–411.

41 See now, Szerwiniack, 'L'histoire ecclésiastique', 169–70.

42 Only book I, 4 is clearly shorter, but IV, 15, which seems to have been the result of the interpolation of chapter 14 into the text of chapter 13, leaving a short closing passage to become a separate chapter, is of approximately equal length.

43 Ælfwine was termed *rex* ('king') in the opening line of IV, 22 (20) and is generally assumed to have been sub-king over the Deirans under the over-arching, Northumbrian kingship of Ecgfrith.

44 Gregory, *Dialogues* IV, 57.

45 Stephen, *Life of Wilfrid*, 36, which likens the imprisoned Wilfrid to the chained St Peter.

46 For example, Paul's Letter to the Ephesians, III, 1; IV, 1. Bede used *vinciri* and *vinculi*. St John was similarly a captive on Patmos: Revelations 1:9.

47 There are only seven longer chapters out of 140.

48 Including Cædmon's 'British' name and the whole matter of Anglo-Saxon oral literature and vernacular verse, for an introduction to which see K. O'Brien O'Keefe, 'Cædmon', in *BEASE* 81, and references therein.

49 Olivier Szerwiniack associates Bede's depiction of Hild with his portrayal of the

primitive church as an age of innocence to which contemporaries should aspire to return: 'L'Histoire ecclésiastique', 167.

50 *Anonymous Life* III, 6; IV, 8: Colgrave, *Two Lives of St. Cuthbert*, 103–5, 122–3.

51 *Vita sancti Cuthberti metrica*, ed. Jaager, 21; For the *Prose Life*, see *Vita sancti Cuthberti prosaica*, ed. Colgrave, 24.

52 *Metrical Life*, 21. My thanks to Martin Ryan for this translation.

53 *Metrical Life*, 19; *Prose Life*, 27.

54 The *Prose Life*, 27, has Ecgfrith's actions as *ausu temerario* ('in a rash deed'), and *temere* recurs in the *EH* IV, 26, in the same context. The verb *devestare* ('to devastate') in the former is mirrored in the *EH* as *vastare* ('to lay waste').

55 *EH* 592–3; the echoes occur in *EH* II, 13 and V, 1. For comment, see W. Wetherbee, 'Some Implications of Bede's Latin Style', in *BASE* 23–31, particularly at 27–8.

56 *Aeneid* VI, 268.

57 *Ibid.* II, 169.

58 Although the matter is far from clear-cut: Dryhthelm's domicile in Cunningham in Aldfrith's reign seems to imply that the coastal plain of Kyle was then still under Northumbrian control, which suggests that only a comparatively small British territory in what is now western Scotland centred on the Clyde valley could have then lain outside English rule.

59 *Hodie* occurs in forty-one passages of the *EH*, nine times in book I, five in book II, eleven in III, ten in IV and six in V.

60 *Praesens* occurs forty-eight times, on occasion in combination with *tempus* ('time').

61 There are fifty-three occurrences.

62 Higham, *Convert Kings*, 168–9.

63 Colgrave, *Life of Wilfrid*, 10.

64 That Bede wrote in response to immediate 'political' concerns has been championed most effectively by Walter Goffart, for whose most recent views see 'L'histoire ecclésiastique et l'engagement politique de Bède', in *BLVTP* 149.

65 The longest chapter, 21, is fifteen times the length of the shortest, 5.

66 The longest being I, 27, the *Libellus responsionum*, which Bede quoted, arguably with some minor editing to exclude the passage referring to the cult of St Sixtus, from Gregory's correspondence (as note 7 above). Difficulties in locating this at Rome over the next generation may imply that Bede used a copy which had been retained at Canterbury or was circulating independently in northern England. For discussion, see P. Meyvaert, 'Les Responsions de S. Grégoire à S. Augustin de Cantorbéry', *Revue d'Histoire Ecclésiastique* 54 (1959) 879–94, and his 'Le *Libellus Responsionum* à Augustin de Canturbery: un oeuvre authentique de Saint Grégoire le grand', in *Grégoire le Grand*, ed. J. Fontaine, Paris: Editions du Centre National de la Recherche Scientifique, 1986, 543–9. It is worth noting that the two longest chapters in the *EH* are both transcripts of existing work, suggesting that Bede himself preferred chapters which were somewhat shorter. See above, p. 110.

67 Chapters 12, 19 and 24 are all well over twice the average length in this book.

68 Which is yet another factor weighing against Goffart's vision of a Northumbrian church in the present divided trenchantly between Wilfridian and anti-Wilfridian houses: see pp. 58–68 above.

69 Colgrave and Mynors inserted inverted commas appropriately in the Latin text but omitted the second occurrence in the English translation on p. 457, which should be inserted after 'the man of God'.

70 See variously Mark 5:35–41 and Acts 27:13–44.

71 Recently confirmed by J. Blair, 'Beverley, *Inderauuda* and St. John: A Neglected Reference', *Northern History* 38(2) (2001) 315–16.

72 Genesis 1:3: *dixitque Deus* ('and said God'), and *passim*. For discussion see C. B.

Kendall, 'Bede's *Historia Ecclesiastica*: The Rhetoric of Faith', in J. J. Murphy (ed.), *Medieval Eloquence: Studies in the Theory and Practice of Medieval Rhetoric*, Berkeley: University of California Press, 1978, 145–72, particularly 162–3.

73 Acts 3:2–8, as noted by Colgrave and Mynors, *Bede*, 458, fn. 1.

74 *Life of Cuthbert*, 29: Colgrave, *Two Lives of St. Cuthbert*, 253–4.

75 *Ibid.*, 25.

76 See, for example, S. E. Wilson, 'King Athelstan and St John of Beverley', *Northern History* 40(1) (2003) 5: 'John was depicted by Bede as a pious and virtuous bishop.'

77 In the Latin, the biblical nature is in fact emphasised: *XXX tribus* ('30 three').

78 The issue of canon law seems not to have troubled Bede here, although one might certainly expect that he was conscious of it. Boniface similarly appointed his own successor, despite papal prohibition, perhaps following Augustine's example in the early seventh century.

79 As already noted above, note 26, there is no good reason to follow Goffart in interpreting Bede's comments on Cædwalla as ironic. Rather, his balancing of an early life of violence with eventual pilgrimage to Rome and baptism there conforms with the standard allegorical interpretation of the Old Testament Benjamin, of which Bede was certainly aware (as *EH* I, 34).

80 See above, p. 120.

81 Bede likewise cast doubt on the practice in his Homily on Benedict Biscop and St Boniface opposed it vehemently for English women, many of whom he represented as ending up as whores, in his letter to Archbishop Cuthbert: Emerton, *Letters of St. Boniface*, 136–41, at 140.

82 This was a common aspect of sanctity to which Bede had already made allusion regarding Æthelthryth in IV, 19 (17), Cædmon in IV, 24 (22) and Cuthbert in IV, 29 (27).

83 *EH* V, 24.

84 There is a seminal discussion of Bede's treatment of these latter-day English missionaries by R. Hanning, *The Vision of History in Early England, from Gildas to Geoffrey of Monmouth*, New York: Columbia University Press, 1966, 88–90.

85 For general review of the subject, see C. Zaleski, *Otherworld Journeys: Accounts of Near-Death Experience in Medieval and Modern Times*, Oxford: Oxford University Press, 1987, *passim*; A. J. Kabir, *Paradise, Death, and Doomsday in Anglo-Saxon Literature*, Cambridge: Cambridge University Press, 2001, 77–110.

86 In the standard Latin text, it runs to 193 lines, compared with seventy-one and forty for the remaining two.

87 As often noted: see Emerton, *Letters of St. Boniface* II, 25–31. This description occurs in a letter of Winfred to Abbess Eadburg.

88 See particularly IV, 36.

89 The depiction of Dryhthelm immersing himself in the cold waters of the River Tweed at Melrose has much in common with the earlier depiction of Cuthbert's putative practice of night-time sea-immersion: *Anonymous Life of St. Cuthbert* II, 3: Colgrave, *Two Lives of St. Cuthbert*, 78–82.

90 King Æthelbald (716–57) was not descended from Penda, while Coenred (704–9) was his grandson.

91 It occurs in twelve passages in the *EH*, in the Preface and six separate chapters.

92 See Wallace-Hadrill, *Bede's Ecclesiastical History*, 187–8, and see references.

93 See above, p. 63.

94 Davis, *The Book of Pontiffs, passim*; Colgrave, *Life of Wilfrid*, XVII, XXII. Wallace-Hadrill draws attention to the similarities between Acca and Wilfrid: *Bede's Ecclesiastical History*, 195, and Trent Foley suggests that Wilfrid may have consciously modelled himself in such respects on the mid-seventh-century popes and other great continental bishops: W. T. Foley, *Images of Sanctity in Eddius Stephanus'*

Life of Bishop Wilfrid: An Early English Saint's Life, Lewiston: Edwin Mellen Press, 1992, 93–5.

95 Goffart, 'L'Histoire ecclésiastique', 150, fn. 4, argues against Plummer's view that Bede and Acca should be viewed as friends, seeing the numerous dedications to his bishop of Bede's exegetical works as mere formulae, but taken together those addresses and his treatment of Acca in *EH* V, 20 are extremely difficult to dismiss as purely conventional.

96 Wallace-Hadrill, *Bede's Ecclesiastical History*, 196, discusses the possibility that Bede was himself responsible for the letter but with no clear results. Ceolfrith was clearly a learned man who had been exposed directly to Roman practices so it may be better to follow Bede's own ascription of this work to him.

97 John 8:56.

98 Bede offered the date 715 in III, 4.

99 For discussion of which, see above, pp. 191–2.

5 Text and context: Bede, Ceolwulf and the *Ecclesiastical History*

1 Goffart, *Narrators*, 235.

2 J. M. Wallace-Hadrill, *The Fourth Book of the Chronicle of Fredegar, with Its Continuations*, London: Thomas Nelson and Sons Ltd, 1960, xxv–xxvi and XXXIV at pp. 102–3.

3 A. Crivellucci (ed.), *Pauli Diaconi Historia Romana*, Rome: Tip. Del Senato, 1914, Preface.

4 Campbell, 'Bede I', 11: 'Much of the *Ecclesiastical History* was intended to show how the needs of kings could be fulfilled and where their true interests lay.'

5 A. Orchard, *The Poetic Art of Aldhelm*, Cambridge Studies in Anglo-Saxon England 8, Cambridge: Cambridge University Press, 1994, 1–18.

6 As D. P. Kirby, 'King Ceolwulf of Northumbria and the *Historia Ecclesiastica*', *Studia Celtica* 14–15 (1979–80) 168–73.

7 Using the formula *esse dicebatur* ('was said to be') but describing him as *vir in scripturis doctissimus* ('a man very learned in the Scriptures'), and reverting to the same superlative again in V, 12.

8 Bede was very direct on this issue in his *Metrical Life of St. Cuthbert*, terming Aldfrith *Nothus* ('bastard', 'illegitimate one'): Bede, *Vita sancti Cuthberti metrica*, 95–100. In his *Prose Life*, 24, Bede described Aldfrith as 'said to be the son of his [Ecgfrith's] father': Colgrave, *Two Lives of St. Cuthbert*, 236. The *Prose Life* was written no later than 721, since it was dedicated to Bishop Eadfrith who died in that year. When he referred to it in *De temporum ratione* it was as having been written 'some years ago'. Colgrave took this to imply that it was written not much before 721: *Two Lives of St. Cuthbert*, 16; but it is quite possible that Bede actually composed it while Coenred, Ceolwulf's brother, was on the throne, 716–18.

9 Colgrave, *Life of Wilfrid*, 59, 60.

10 In 705 Bede was in his early thirties and already establishing his network of correspondents within Northumbria and perhaps beyond. It seems highly improbable that these events were other than common knowledge in the great religious houses of the period, particularly given the northern synod which occurred very soon after Osred's succession, under the presidency of Archbishop Berhtwold, which representatives from Wearmouth/Jarrow may well have attended.

11 As Goffart assumed: *Narrators*, 271–3.

12 Bede, *Vita sancti Cuthberti metrica*, 21. I am grateful to Martin Ryan for the translation.

13 M. Tangl (ed.), *Die Briefe des heiligen Bonifatius und Lullus, Epistolae Selectae in usum*

scholarum ex Monumentis Germaniae Historicis separatism editae I, Berlin: Weidmann, 1916, no. 73; for a translation, see Emerton, *Letters of St. Boniface*, 129–30. This letter focuses on King Æthelbald of Mercia, not either of kings Osred or Ceolred, whose reigns were here used as object lessons as to what might happen to sinful rulers, which does not suggest that this should be interpreted as a realistic appraisal of either king. The condemnation of Osred in modern works ignores Bede's contemporary comment and neglects the sense that criticism derives either from those seeking to use him for their own rhetorical needs or from the voices of his dynastic opponents. See, for example, Colgrave, *Life of Wilfrid*, 184: 'He seems to have been a youth of thoroughly dissolute character as several contemporary writers testify'. In his most recent essay, Goffart described Osred as one of three *rois fainéant*, but this may well be a matter of our knowing little rather than his doing little: 'L'Histoire ecclésiastique', 151.

14 A. Campbell (ed.), *Æthelwulf: De Abbatibus*, Oxford: Oxford University Press, 1967, ii. The work is dated to the episcopacy of Egbert at Lindisfarne (803–21).

15 *Quo Osredo occiso* ('in which Osred was killed'). This has been read in terms of an assassination: see, for example, Goffart, *Narrators*, 272, but this may be to go beyond the evidence. *ASC(D,E)* add to their notice that 'Osred was slain' the enigmatic phrase 'south of the border': Whitelock, *English Historical Documents*, 171. This addition seems unlikely to refer to open warfare with Mercia and perhaps suggests that he was later thought to have taken flight from Northumbria and to have been killed while attempting to go into exile. Excluding Bede's metrical life, the nearest to contemporary evidence comes from Boniface, whose *Letter to King Æthelbald* of 746–7 used Osred's premature loss of his throne and death as an example of what God had in store for those who oppressed the Church and violated nuns, but this is again written a generation or more later: Emerton, *Letters of St. Boniface*, LVII, 129–30.

16 D. Rollason (ed.) *Simeon of Durham, Libellus de Exordio atque Procursu istius, hoc est Dunhelmensis, Ecclesiae: Tract on the Origins and Progress of This the Church of Durham*, Oxford: Clarendon Press, 2000, I, 13.

17 As D. Rollason, *Northumbria, 500–1100: Creation and Destruction of a Kingdom*, Cambridge: Cambridge University Press, 2003, 192.

18 While the *Anglo-Saxon Chronicle* agrees with Bede that Osred was slain and succeeded initially by Coenred (for two years) then Osric (for eleven years), there is no additional information herein comparable to that offered concerning Æthelbald of the Mercians in the same entry and one might conclude that the Chronicler took this information from the *EH*: G. P. Cubbin (ed.), *The Anglo-Saxon Chronicle: A Collaborative Edition, 6, MS D*, Cambridge: D. S. Brewer, 1996; for a translation see Whitelock, *English Historical Documents*, 171.

19 That the phrase *vita decessit*, 'ceased from life', is unique in this text to this passage highlights Bede's extreme care at this point. He used *mortuus est* in the recapitulation, alongside St Egbert, who *transit*.

20 See Simeon of Durham's *History of the Kings of England*, entry for 750, which refers to Offa, son of Aldfrith, being dragged from sanctuary at Lindisfarne, although the same issues of late evidence clearly apply as above: T. Arnold (ed.), *Simeonis Monachi Opera omnia*, Roll Series, London: Longman, 1885, II, 39–40. For a translation, see Whitelock, *English Historical Documents*, 265.

21 J. Bately (ed.), *The Anglo-Saxon Chronicle: A Collaborative Edition, 3, MS A*, Cambridge: D. S. Brewer, 1986. For a translation, see Whitelock, *English Historical Documents*, 172–3.

22 This is generally read as a reference to Charles Martel's victory in 732 or 733. The most recent editors considered this sentence to have been interpolated (*EH* 557, fn. 5), attracted perhaps by the natural fit between the two comets which were viewed as harbingers of terrible events and the inroads to the Catholic world

of these heathen outsiders, but see also Wallace-Hadrill, *Bede's Ecclesiastical History*, 199.

23 This was somewhat tentatively assumed without explicit discussion by Bede's most recent editors: *EH* xxix.

24 L. T. Martin (trans.) *The Venerable Bede: Commentary on the Acts of the Apostles*, Kalamazoo, MI: Cistercian Publications, 1989, V, 24.

25 *Ibid.*, XIX, 7.

26 B. Colgrave (ed.), *The Earliest Life of Gregory the Great by an Anonymous Monk of Whitby*, Lawrence: University of Kansas Press, 1968, XVIII, XIX, and see introduction, 47–8.

27 *Anonymous Life of St. Cuthbert* III, 6: Colgrave, *Two Lives of St. Cuthbert*, 102–5. She appears elsewhere in this work at IV, 10 and also in Bede's *Life of Cuthbert*, XXIII, XXIV, XXXIV, which derive from the earlier work, all of which suggests that she was considered a figure of real importance when the anonymous work was written, between 699 and 705.

28 Colgrave, *Life of Wilfrid*, LIX, LX.

29 Campbell, *Æthelwulf* II, 2, 3, 5, 6, 8.

30 Colgrave and Mynors, *Bede*, 'Continuation', 573.

31 Rollason, *Simeon of Durham* II, 1. See also Whitelock, *English Historical Documents*, 264, for the later Durham text, *History of the Kings*.

32 The translation of J. F. Webb reads: 'To my holy and most blessed lord and father, Bishop Eadfrid': D. H. Farmer (ed.) and J. F. Webb (trans.), *The Age of Bede*, Harmondsworth: Penguin, 1988, 41.

33 *EH* III, 25; IV, 29, 30.

34 *EH* V, 12, 23.

35 T. C. Ferguson, *The Past is Prologue: The Revolution of Nicene Historiography*, Leiden: Brill, 2005, *passim*.

36 His descent being Ida, Ocga, Eadhelm, Ecgwold, Leodwold, Cuthwine, Coenred/ Ceolwulf, to which some texts add Cutha after Cuthwine: see Whitelock, *English Historical Documents*, table 6, but note that this is non-contemporary evidence.

37 Whose descent was later traced as Ida, Æthelric, Æthelfrith, Oswiu, Aldfrith, Osred/?Osric/?Offa.

38 Although there is no known familial connection between Ceolwulf and Coenred on the one hand and Eadwulf on the other, all three presumably headed factions committed to dislodging Aldfrith's family from the Northumbrian throne.

39 Supposing Osric to have been Aldfrith's son, as discussed above.

40 Hunter Blair, 'The *Moore Memoranda* on Northumbrian History', 243–58.

41 *Ibid.*, 247–52.

42 Whom Bede had commented (*EH* III, 1) had been excluded from such lists thereafter.

43 The date at which Ida began to reign and his regnal years may have derived from the recapitulation of *EH* V, 24, but the succeeding reigns up to Æthelfrith presumably derive from a current king-list. Bede clearly used such but did not reproduce them in his *Ecclesiastical History*.

44 Ecgfrith's victory over the Mercians was mentioned in passing in the *Life of Wilfrid*: Colgrave, *Life of Wilfrid*, 20, but went unmentioned by Bede in the *Ecclesiastical History*, whose references to Ecgfrith's wars omitted this success: *EH* IV, 21 (19), 26 (24).

45 D. N. Dumville, 'The Anglian Collection of Royal Genealogies and Regnal Lists', *Anglo-Saxon England* 5 (1976) 23–50.

46 The *Anonymous Life of St. Cuthbert* III, 6, provides a possibly apocryphal account of a meeting between Cuthbert and Abbess Ælfflæd in 684 which implicitly established his half-brother, Aldfrith, as heir, although this may simply be a matter of political expediency given that Aldfrith was on the throne when the life was

written: Colgrave, *Two Lives of St. Cuthbert*, 102–5. It may be worth noting that a genealogy claiming descent from Ecgfrith and supporting the claims of the late eighth-century Oslaf to the throne was incorporated in the *Historia Brittonum*, written *c*.829, in which case Ecgfrith's second marriage had perhaps produced offspring by 685 but in that case his putative son, one Oslac, would presumably have then been an infant: J. Morris (ed.), *Nennius: British History and the Welsh Annals*, Chichester: Phillimore, 1980, LXI. That said, Oslaf's claim to be descended from Ecgfrith may well be apocryphal and have been developed for political purposes a century later, particularly since the apparent failure of the lineage to attempt the throne earlier (particularly in 705 when Aldfrith's sons were very young) must weigh against the authenticity of this claim.

47 See note 20.

48 As perhaps Oswiu during Oswald's reign and more certainly Aldfrith during Ecgfrith's reign.

49 As Oswald and Oswiu during Edwin's reign.

50 As Eanfrith during Edwin's reign.

51 Colgrave, *Life of Wilfrid*, LX.

52 The case is made in reference to nunneries by B. Yorke, *Nunneries and the Anglo-Saxon Royal Houses*, London: Continuum, 2003, 105, but can easily be extrapolated to all royal monastic houses.

53 The comparatively scanty treatment of Benedict Biscop and Ceolfrith has been outlined above; Hwætberht, abbot since 716, appears only in *EH* V, 24, in the listing of Bede's own works, so should perhaps be considered another casualty of Bede's approach.

54 As many of his predecessors had done, for example Edwin's foundation of York, Oswald's of Lindisfarne, Oswiu's of Whitby, Alhfrith's of Ripon, Œthelwald's of Lastingham and Ecgfrith's of Wearmouth/Jarrow.

55 *EH* has 'perusal and criticism', but this does not quite capture the force of *legere*, which in classical literature is primarily connected with the ambassadorial role. *Probare* can mean either 'examine' or 'approve' and arguably carries both meanings here.

56 *EH* III, 11, although she was named as Æthelred's wife in IV, 21 (19).

57 Goffart, *Narrators*, 235–328; contrast P. Wormald, 'Bede and Benedict Biscop', in *FC* 155, who saw Bede rather more as an Olympian thinker remote from politics: 'Bede's dynamic was neither learning nor common sense, but idealism' and unreflective of society at large.

58 *EH* V, 6.

59 That Ceolwulf's retirement to become a monk in 737 was voluntary is stressed by the anonymous author of a set of annals down to 766, which form a continuation to the *Ecclesiastical History* attached to a small group of late, continental manuscripts which arguably date from a Northumbrian original of this date: see *EH* lxvii–lxix.

60 In the recapitulation, Bede offered the examples of Cædwalla's and Coenred's successive retirements to Rome (688, 709), to which the main text adds Offa accompanying Coenred (V, 19), and the retirement of Æthelred to a monastery in 704, to which the main text adds Sigeberht (III, 18).

61 The translation is from McClure and Collins, *Bede: The Ecclesiastical History*, 296. Compare Charlemagne's reaction to a series of disasters in 805, which was to require three-day fasts of his people: R. Meens, 'Politics, Mirrors of Princes and the Bible: Sins, Kings and the Well-Being of the Realm', *Early Medieval Europe* 7(3) (1998) 345–57.

List of abbreviations

BASE   *Bede and Anglo-Saxon England*, ed. R. T. Farrell, BAR British Series 46 (Oxford: British Archaeological Reports, 1978)

BEASE   *The Blackwell Encyclopedia of Anglo-Saxon England*, ed. M. Lapidge, J. Blair, S. Keynes and D. Scragg (Oxford: Blackwell, 1999)

BLVTP   *Bède le Vénérable entre tradition et postérité*, ed. S. Lebecq, M. Perrin et O. Szerwiniack (Lille: Université Charles de Gaulle, 2005)

BLTW   *Bede: His Life, Times, and Writings*, ed. A. Hamilton Thompson (Oxford: Clarendon Press, 1935)

BV   *Beda Venerabilis: Historian, Monk, and Northumbrian*, ed. L. A. J. R. Houwen and A. A. Macdonald, Mediaevalia Groningana (Groningen: Forsten, 1996)

CCC   *St Cuthbert, His Cult and His Community*, ed. G. Bonner, D. Rollason and C. Stancliffe (Woodbridge: Boydell Press, 1989)

CCSL   *Corpus Christianorum Series Latina*

EASH   *Essays in Anglo-Saxon History*, J. Campbell (London: Hambledon, 1986)

EH   *Bede's Ecclesiastical History of the English People*, ed. B. Colgrave and R. A. B. Mynors (Oxford: Clarendon Press, 1969)

FC   *Famulus Christi: Essays in Commemoration of the Thirteenth Centenary of the Birth of the Venerable Bede*, ed. G. Bonner (London: SPCK, 1976)

IR   *Ideal and Reality in Frankish and Anglo-Saxon Society: Studies Presented to J. M. Wallace-Hadrill*, ed. P. Wormald, D. Bullough and R. Collins (Oxford: Blackwell, 1983)

JL   *Bede and His World: The Jarrow Lectures*, 2 vols (Aldershot: Variorum, 1994)

JL   Jarrow Lecture (Jarrow, Jarrow Parish Council, delivered 1993–)

PL   *Patrologia Latina*

SSH   *Saints, Scholars, and Heroes: Studies in Medieval Culture in Honour of Charles W. Jones*, ed. M. H. King and W. M. Stevens, 2 vols (Collegeville, MN: St John's University, 1979)

Select bibliography

Editions and translation of the works of the Venerable Bede

The following list sets out the most recent editions and, where available, English translations of the works of the Venerable Bede. The list follows the order of Bede's own list in *EH* V, 24.

'The beginning of Genesis up to the birth of Isaac and the casting out of Ishmael: four books': *In principium Genesim*, ed. C. W. Jones, *CCSL* 118a (Turnhout: Brepols, 1967) [whole volume].

'The Tabernacle, its vessels, and the priestly vestments: three books': *De tabernaculo*, ed. D. Hurst, *CCSL* 119a (Turnhout: Brepols, 1969) 1–139; trans. A. G. Holder, *Bede: On the Tabernacle*, Translated Texts for Historians (Liverpool: Liverpool University Press, 1994).

'The First Book of Samuel, to the death of Saul: four books': *In primam partem Samuhelis*, ed. D. Hurst, *CCSL* 119 (Turnhout: Brepols, 1962) 1–272.

'On the building of the temple, an allegorical interpretation like the others: two books': *De templo*, ed. D. Hurst, *CCSL* 119a (Turnhout: Brepols, 1969) 141–234; trans. S. Connolly, *Bede: On the Temple*, Translated Texts for Historians (Liverpool: Liverpool University Press, 1995).

'On the book of Kings: thirty questions': *In Regum librum XXX quaestiones*, ed. D. Hurst, *CCSL* 119 (Turnhout: Brepols, 1962) 289–322; trans. W. T. Foley in W. T. Foley and A. G. Holder, *Bede: A Biblical Miscellany*, Translated Texts for Historians (Liverpool: Liverpool University Press, 1999) 89–138.

'On the Proverbs of Solomon: three books': *In prouerbia Salomonis*, ed. D. Hurst, *CCSL* 119b (Turnhout: Brepols, 1983) 21–163.

'On the Song of Songs: seven (*recte* 6) books': *In Cantica canticorum*, ed. D. Hurst, *CCSL* 119b (Turnhout: Brepols, 1983) 165–375.

'On Isaiah, Daniel, the twelve prophets, and part of Jeremiah: chapter divisions taken from the treatise of St Jerome', see P. Meyvaert, 'Bede's *Capitula lectionum* for the Old and New Testament', *Revue Bénédictine* 105 (1995) 348–80, partic. 362–3.

'On Ezra and Nehemiah: three books': *In Esram et Neemiam*, ed. D. Hurst, *CCSL* 119a (Turnhout: Brepols, 1969) 235–392; trans. S. DeGregorio, *Bede: On Ezra and Nehemiah* (Liverpool: Liverpool University Press, 2006).

'On the Song of Habakkuk: one book': *In Habacuc*, ed. J. E. Hudson, *CCSL* 119b (Turnhout: Brepols, 1983) 377–409; trans. S. Connolly, *Bede: On Tobit and the Canticle of Habakkuk* (Dublin: Four Courts Press, 1997) 65–95.

'On the book of the blessed father Tobias, an allegorical explanation concerning

Christ and the Church: one book': *In Tobiam*, ed. D. Hurst, *CCSL* 119b (Turnhout: Brepols, 1983) 1–19; trans. S. Connolly, *Bede: On Tobit and the Canticle of Habakkuk*, (Dublin: Four Courts Press, 1997) 39–63.

'Also, summaries of lessons on the Pentateuch of Moses, on Joshua and Judges, on the books of the Kings and Chronicles, on the book of the blessed father Job, on Proverbs, Ecclesiastes, and the Song of Songs, on the prophets Isaiah, Ezra, and Nehemiah', see P. Meyvaert, 'Bede's *Capitula Lectionum* for the Old and New Testament', *Revue Bénédictine* 105 (1995) 348–80, partic. 371–2.

'On the Gospel of Mark: four books': *In Marcum*, ed. D. Hurst, *CCSL* 120 (Turnhout: Brepols, 1960) 427–648.

'On the Gospel of Luke: six books': *In Lucam*, ed. D. Hurst, *CCSL* 120 (Turnhout: Brepols, 1960) 1–425.

'Homilies on the Gospel: two books': *Homiliae euangelii*, ed. D. Hurst, *CCSL* 122 (Turnhout: Brepols, 1965) 1–378; trans. L. T. Martin and D. Hurst, *Bede the Venerable: Homilies on the Gospels*, Cistercian Studies 110 and 111 (Kalamazoo, MI: Cistercian Publications, 1991).

'On the Apostle (Paul), I have transcribed in order whatever I found in the works of St Augustine': no printed edition; trans. D. Hurst, *Bede the Venerable: Excerpts from the Works of Saint Augustine on the Letters of the Blessed Apostle Paul*, Cistercian Studies 183 (Kalamazoo, MI: Cistercian Publications, 1999).

'On the Acts of the Apostles: two books': *Expositio Actuum Apostolorum*, ed. M. L. W. Laistner, *CCSL* 121 (Turnhout: Brepols, 1983) 1–99; trans. L.T. Martin, *The Venerable Bede: Commentary on the Acts of the Apostles*, Cistercian Studies 117 (Kalamazoo, MI: Cistercian Publications, 1989); *Retractio in Actus Apostolorum*, ed. M. L. W. Laistner, *CCSL* 121 (Turnhout: Brepols, 1983) 101–63.

'On the seven catholic Epistles: one book each': *In epistolas VII catholicas*, ed. D. Hurst, *CCSL* 121 (Turnhout: Brepols, 1983) 179–342; trans. D. Hurst, *Bede the Venerable: Commentary on the Seven Catholic Epistles*, Cistercian Studies 82 (Kalamazoo, MI: Cisterician Publications, 1985).

'On the Apocalypse of St John: three books': *Expositio Apocalypseos*, ed. R. Gryson, *CCSL* 121a (Turnhout: Brepols, 2001) [whole volume]; trans. E. Marshall, *The Explanation of the Apocalypse by Venerable Beda* (Oxford: James Parker & Co., 1878).

'Also, summaries of lessons on the whole of the New Testament except the Gospels', see P. Meyvaert, 'Bede's *Capitula Lectionum* for the Old and New Testament', *Revue Bénédictine* 105 (1995) 348–80, partic. 355–60.

'A book of letters to various people':

'one of these is on the six ages of the world': *Epistola ad Pleguinam*, ed. C. W. Jones, *CCSL* 123c (Turnhout: Brepols, 1980) 613–26; trans. F. Wallis, *Bede: The Reckoning of Time*, Translated Texts for Historians (Liverpool: Liverpool University Press, 1999) 405–15.

'one on the resting places of the children of Israel': *De mansionibus filiorum Israel*, ed. J.-P. Migne, *PL* 93 (Paris: Migne, 1862) cols 699–702; trans. A. G. Holder in W. T. Foley and A. G. Holder, *Bede: A Biblical Miscellany*, Translated Texts for Historians (Liverpool: Liverpool University Press, 1999) 29–34.

'one on the words of Isaiah': *De eo quod ait Isaias*, ed. J.-P. Migne, *PL* 94 (Paris: Migne, 1862) cols 702–10; trans. A. G. Holder in W. T. Foley and A. G. Holder, *Bede: A Biblical Miscellany*, Translated Texts for Historians (Liverpool: Liverpool University Press, 1999) 39–51.

'one on the reason for leap year': *Epistola ad Helmuualdum*, ed. C. W. Jones, *CCSL*

123c (Turnhout: Brepols, 1980) 627–9; trans. F. Wallis, *Bede: On the Reckoning of Time*, Translated Texts for Historians (Liverpool: Liverpool University Press, 1999) 416.

'one on the equinox, after Anatolius': *Epistola ad VVicthedum*, ed. C. W. Jones, *CCSL* 123c (Turnhout: Brepols, 1980) pp. 631–42; trans. F. Wallis, *Bede: On the Reckoning of Time*, Translated Texts for Historians (Liverpool: Liverpool University Press, 1999) 417–24.

'Also of the histories of the saints':

'A book on the life and passon of St Felix the confessor, which I put into prose from the metrical version of Paulinus': *Beati Felicis confessoris vita*, ed. J.-P. Migne, *PL* 94 (Paris: Migne, 1862) cols 789–98.

'A book on the life and passion of St Anastasius, which was badly translated from the Greek by some ignorant person, which I have corrected as best I could, to clarify the meaning': see C. Vircillo Franklin and P. Meyvaert, 'Has Bede's Version of the *Passio S. Anastasii* Come Down to Us in *B.H.L.* 408', *Analecta Bollandiana* 100 (1982) 373–400.

'I have also described the life of the holy father Cuthbert':

'first in heroic verse': *Vita sancti Cuthberti metrica*, ed. W. Jaager, *Bedas metrische Vita sancti Cuthberti*, Palaestra 198 (Leipzig: Mayer and Müller, 1935).

'and then in prose': *Vita sancti Cuthberti prosaica*, ed. and trans. B. Colgrave, *Two Lives of Saint Cuthbert* (Cambridge: Cambridge University Press, 1940; repr. 1985) 142–307.

'A history of the abbots of the monastery in which it is my joy to serve God, namely Benedict, Ceolfrith, and Hwætberht, in two books': *Historia Abbatum*, ed. C. Plummer, *Venerabilis Baedae Opera Historica*, 2 vols (Oxford: Clarendon Press, 1896) I, 364–87; trans. D. H. Farmer in J. F. Webb and D. H. Farmer, *The Age of Bede* (Harmondsworth: Penguin, 1988) 185–210.

'The history of the Church of our island and race, in five books': *Historia Ecclesiastica Gentis Anglorum*, ed. Plummer, *Venerabilis Baedae Opera Historica*, 2 vols (Oxford: Clarendon Press, 1896) I, 5–360; trans. B. Colgrave in B. Colgrave and R. A. B. Mynors, *Bede's Ecclesiastical History of the English People*, Oxford Medieval Texts (Oxford: Clarendon Press, 1969), 3–571.

'A martyrology of the festivals of the holy martyrs, in which I have diligently tried to note down all that I could find about them, not only on what day, but also by what sort of combat and under what judge they overcame the world': ed. J. Dubois and G. Renaud, *Edition pratique des martyrologes de Bède, de l'Anonyme lyonnais et de Florus* (Paris: Editions du Centre National de la Recherche Scientifique, 1976); trans. F. Lifshitz in T. Head (ed.), *Medieval Hagiography: An Anthology* (London: Routledge, 2001) 179–96.

'A book of hymns in various metres and rhythms': *Liber hymnorum, rhythmi, variae preces*, ed. J. Fraipont, *CCSL* 122 (Turnhout: Brepols, 1965) 405–70.

'A book of epigrams in heroic and elegiac metre': partial edition M. Lapidge, 'Some Remnants of Bede's Lost *Liber Epigrammatum*', *English Historical Review* 90 (1975) 798–820.

'On the nature of things': *De natura rerum*, ed. C. W. Jones, *CCSL* 123a (Turnhout: Brepols, 1975) 173–234.

'On chronology': *De temporibus*, ed. C. W. Jones and T. Mommsen, *CCSL* 123c (Turnhout: Brepols, 1980) 579–611.

'A longer book on chronology': *De temporum ratione*, ed. C. W. Jones and T. Mommsen,

CCSL 123b (Turnhout: Brepols, 1977) [whole volume]; trans. F. Wallis, *Bede: The Reckoning of Time*, Translated Texts for Historians (Liverpool: Liverpool University Press, 1999) 157–237.

'A book about orthography, arranged according to the order of the alphabet': *De orthographia*, ed. C. W. Jones, *CCSL* 123a (Turnhout: Brepols, 1975) 1–57.

'A book on the art of metre': ed. and trans. C. B. Kendall, *Libri II de arte metrica et de schematibus et tropis/Bede's Art of Poetry and Rhetoric: The Latin Text with an English Translation, Introduction, and Notes*, Bibliotheca Germanica series nova 2 (Saarbrucken: AQ-Verlag, 1991) 36–167.

'A small book on figures of speech or tropes, that is, concerning the figures and modes of speech with which the Holy Scriptures are adorned': ed. and trans. C. B. Kendall, *Libri II de arte metrica et de schematibus et tropis/Bede's Art of Poetry and Rhetoric: The Latin Text with an English Translation, Introduction, and Notes*, Bibliotheca Germanica series nova 2 (Saarbrucken: AQ-Verlag, 1991) 168–209.

The following works are not included in Bede's list but are generally considered by scholars to have been written by him.

De locis sanctis, ed. J. Fraipont, *CCSL* 175 (Turnhout: Brepols, 1965) 249–80; trans. W. T. Foley in W. T. Foley and A. G. Holder, *Bede: A Biblical Miscellany*, Translated Texts for Historians (Liverpool: Liverpool University Press, 1999) 5–25.

De octo quaestionibus, ed. M. Gorman, 'Bede's *VIII Quaestiones* and Carolingian Biblical Scholarship', *Revue Bénédictine* 109 (1999) 32–74; trans. A. G. Holder in W. T. Foley and A. G. Holder, *Bede: A Biblical Miscellany*, Translated Texts for Historians (Liverpool: Liverpool University Press, 1999) 149–65.

Epistola ad Albinum, ed. C. Plummer, *Venerabilis Baedae Opera Historica*, 2 vols (Oxford: Clarendon Press, 1896) I, 3.

Epistola ad Ecgberctum, ed. C. Plummer, *Venerabilis Baedae Opera Historica*, 2 vols (Oxford: Clarendon Press, 1896) I, 405–23; trans. D. Whitelock, *English Historical Documents* I, no. 170, and J. McClure and R. Collins, *Bede: The Ecclesiastical History of the English People* (Oxford: Oxford University Press, 1994), 343–57.

Nomina locorum ex Beati Hieronymi Presbiteri et Flavi Iosephi Collecta Opusculis (appendix to *In primam partem Samuhelis*), ed. D. Hurst, *CCSL* 119 (Turnhout: Brepols, 1962) 273–87.

Nomina regionum atque locorum de actibus Apostolorum (appendix to *Expositio Actuum Apostolorum*), ed. M. L. W. Laistner, *CCSL* 121 (Turnhout: Brepols, 1983) 165–78.

Secondary works

Abraham, L., 'Bede's Life of Cuthbert: A Reassessment', *Proceedings of the Patristic, Medieval, and Renaissance Conference* 1 (1976) 23–32

Adams, J., *The Flowers of Modern History* (London: printed for G. Kearsley, 1796)

Aggeler, C., 'The Eccentric Hermit-Bishop: Bede, Cuthbert, and Farne Island', *Essays in Medieval Studies* 16 (1999) 17–25

Aird, W. M., *St. Cuthbert and the Normans* (Woodbridge: Boydell Press, 1998)

Allen, M. J. B. and Calder, D. G., *Sources and Analogues of Old English Poetry: The Major Latin Texts in Translation* (Woodbridge: Boydell and Brewer, 1976)

Amidon, P. R. (trans.), *The Church History of Rufinus of Aquileia, Books 10 and 11* (Oxford: Oxford University Press, 1997)

Arngart, O. S., 'On the Dating of Early Bede Manuscripts', *Studia Neophilologica* 45 (1973) 47–52

Babcock, R. G., 'The *Proverbium antiquum* in Acca's Letter to Bede', *Mittellateinisches Jahrbuch* 22 (1989) 53–5.

Babington, C. (ed.), *Polychronicon Ranulphi Higden Monachi Cestrensis* (London: Longman (Rolls Series), 1865)

Barmby, J. (trans.), *The Book of Pastoral Care and Selected Epistles of Gregory the Great*, Nicene and Post-Nicene Fathers, new series 12 (Oxford: James Parker & Co. for the Christian Literature Society, 1895) II, 1–72

Barnard, L. W., 'Bede and Eusebius as Church Historians', in *FC* 106–24

Barnes, J., *Flaubert's Parrot* (London: Jonathan Cape, 1984)

Barnwell, P. S., Butler, L. A. S. and Dunn, C. J., 'The Confusion of Conversion: Streanæshalch, Strensall and Whitby and the Northumbrian Church', in *The Cross Goes North*, ed. M. Carver (Woodbridge: Boydell and Brewer, York Medieval Press, 2003) 311–26

Bately, J., 'Bede and the Anglo-Saxon Chronicle', in *SSH* I, 233–54

Bateley, J. (ed.), *The Anglo-Saxon Chronicle, A Collaborative Edition, 3, MS A* (Cambridge: D. S. Brewer, 1986)

Beeson, C. H., 'The Manuscripts of Bede', *Classical Philology* 42 (1947) 73–87

Benedikz, B. S., 'Bede in the Uttermost North', in *FC* 334–43

Berkenhout, J., *Biographia Literaria; or a Biographical History of Literature containing the Lives of English, Scottish and Irish Authors* I (London: printed for J. Dodsley, 1777)

Berschin, W., '*Opus deliberatum ac perfectum*: Why Did the Venerable Bede Write a Second Prose Life of Cuthbert?' in *CCC* 95–102

Biddick, K., *The Shock of Medievalism* (Durham, NC: Duke University Press, 1998) 83–101

Biggs, M., 'Bede's Use of Augustine: Echoes from Some Sermons', *Revue Bénédictine* 108 (1998) 201–13

Birkbeck, S., *The Protestants evidence taken out of good records; shewing that for fifteene hundred yeares next after Christ, divers worthy guides of Gods Church, have in sundry weightie points of religion, taught as the Church of England now doth: distributed into severall centuries* (London: printed by Augustine Mathewes and Thomas Cotes for Robert Milbourne, 1634)

Black, J., '*De Civitate Dei* and the Commentaries of Gregory the Great, Isidore, Bede and Hrabanus Maurus on the Book of Samuel', *Augustinian Studies* 15 (1984) 114–27

Blair, J., 'Beverley, *Inderauuda* and St. John: A Neglected Reference', *Northern History* 38(2) (2001) 315–16

Blair, J., 'A Hand-List of Anglo-Saxon Saints', in A. Thacker and R. Sharpe (eds), *Local Saints and Local Churches in the Early Medieval West* (Oxford: Oxford University Press, 2002), 495–566

Blair, J., 'A Saint for Every Minster? Local Cults in Anglo-Saxon England', in A. Thacker and R. Sharpe (eds), *Local Saints and Local Churches in the Early Medieval West* (Oxford: Oxford University Press, 2002), 455–94

Blair, J., *The Church in Anglo-Saxon Society* (Oxford: Oxford University Press, 2005)

Böhne, W., 'Das älteste Lorscher Kalendar und seine Vorlagen', in F. Knöpp (ed.), *Die Reichsabtei Lorsch: Festschrift zum Gedenken an ihre Stiftung 764* (Darmstadt: Hess. Histor. Komm., 1977), 171–220

Bolton, W. F., '*Epistola Cuthberti de Obitu Bedae*: A Caveat', *Medievalia et Humanistica* N.S. 1 (1970) 127–39

Bonner, G., 'Bede and Medieval Civilization', *Anglo-Saxon England* 2 (1973) 71–90

Bonner, G., 'Ireland and Rome: The Double Inheritance of Northumbria', in *SSH* I, 101–16

Bonner, G., 'Saint Bede in the Tradition of Western Apocalyptic', in *JL* I, 153–84

Bonner, G., 'Bede: Scholar and Spiritual Teacher', in J. Hawkes and S. Mills (eds), *Northumbria's Golden Age* (Stroud: Sutton, 1999) 365–70

Brooke, C. N. L., 'Geoffrey of Monmouth as a Historian', in C. N. L. Brooke (ed.), *Church and Government in the Middle Ages: Essays Presented to C. R. Cheney* (Cambridge: Cambridge University Press, 1976) 77–91

Brooks, N., *The Early History of the Church at Canterbury* (Leicester: Leicester University Press, 1984)

Brooks, N., *Bede and the English*, JL (1999)

Brooks, N., 'The English Origin Myth', in *Anglo-Saxon Myths: State and Church, 400–1066* (London: Hambledon, 2000) 79–89

Brown, G. H., *Bede the Venerable* (Boston: Twayne, 1987)

Brown, G. H., 'The Meanings of *interpres* in Aldhelm and Bede', in P. Boitani and A. Torti (eds), *Interpretation: Medieval and Modern* (Cambridge: Cambridge University Press, 1993) 43–65

Brown, G. H., *Bede the Educator*, JL (1996)

Brown, G. H., 'The Preservation and Transmission of Northumbrian Culture on the Continent: Alcuin's Debt to Bede', in P. E. Szarmach and J. T. Rosenthal (eds), *The Preservation and Transmission of Anglo-Saxon Culture*, Studies in Medieval Culture 40 (Kalamazoo, MI: Medieval Institute Publications, 1997) 159–75

Brown, G. H., 'Royal and Ecclesiastical Rivalries in Bede's History', *Renascence* 52 (1999) 19–33

Brown, G. H., 'The Church as Non-Symbol in the Age of Bede', in J. Hawkes and S. Mills (eds), *Northumbria's Golden Age* (Stroud: Sutton, 1999) 359–64

Brown, G. H., 'Le Commentaire problématique de Bède sur le premier Livre de Samuel', *BLVTP* 87–96

Brown, M. P., '*In the Beginning Was the Word*': *Books and Faith in the Age of Bede*, JL (2000)

Browne, G. F., *The Venerable Bede: His Life and Writings* (London: Macmillan for the SPCK, 1919)

Bruce-Mitford, R. L. S., 'The Art of the *Codex Amiatinus*', in *JL* I, 185–234

Bullough, D. A., 'Hagiography as Patriotism: Alcuin's "York Poem" and the Early Northumbrian "Vitae Sanctorum" ', in *Hagiographie, cultures et sociétés IVe–XIIe siècles* (Paris: Etudes Augustiniennes, 1981) 339–59

Bullough, D. A., 'York, Bede's Calendar and a Pre-Bedan English Martyrology', *Analecta Bollandiana* 121 (2003) 329–55

Bullough, D. A., *Alcuin: Achievement and Reputation*, Education and Society in the Middle Ages and Renaissance 16 (Leiden: Brill, 2004)

Campbell, A., 'Some Linguistic Features of Early Anglo-Latin Verse and Its Use of Classical Models', *Transactions of the Philological Society* (1953) 1–20

Campbell, J., 'Bede I', in *EASH* 1–27

Campbell, J., 'Bede II', in *EASH* 29–48

Campbell, J., 'Bede's Words for Places', in *EASH* 99–120

Campbell, J., 'The First Century of Christianity in England', in *EASH* 49–67

Campbell, J., 'Observations on the Conversion of England: A Brief Commemorative Review Article', in *EASH* 69–84

Campbell, J., 'Elements in the Background to the Life of St Cuthbert and his Early Cult', in *CCC* 3–19

Campbell, J., 'Bede's *Reges* and *Principes*', in *JL* II, 491–506

Carroll, M. T. A., *The Venerable Bede: His Spiritual Teaching* (Washington, DC: Catholic University of America Press, 1946)

Chambers, R. W., 'Bede', *Proceedings of the British Academy* 32 (1936) 3–30

Charles-Edwards, T. M., 'Bede, the Irish and the Britons', *Celtica* 15 (1983) 42–52

Chazelle, C., 'Ceolfrid's Gift to St Peter: The First Quire of the *Codex Amiatinus* and the Evidence of Its Roman Destination', *Early Medieval Europe* 12 (2003) 129–57

Coates, S., 'Bede – the Miraculous and Episcopal Authority in Early Anglo-Saxon England', *Downside Review* 113 (1995) 219–32

Coates, S., 'The Bishop as Benefactor and Civic Patron: Alcuin, York, and Episcopal Authority in Anglo-Saxon England', *Speculum* 71 (1996) 529–58

Coates, S., 'The Bishop as Pastor and Solitary: Bede and the Spiritual Authority of the Monk-Bishop', *Journal of Ecclesiastical History* 47 (1996) 601–19

Coates, S., 'Dwellings of the Saints: Monasticism in the Scottish Borders in the Early Middle Ages', *Downside Review* 114 (1996) 166–84

Coates, S., 'Ceolfrid: History, Hagiography and Memory in Seventh- and Eighth-Century Wearmouth-Jarrow', *Journal of Medieval History* 25 (1999) 69–86

Colgrave, B. (ed.), *The Life of Bishop Wilfrid by Eddius Stephanus* (Cambridge: Cambridge University Press, 1927)

Colgrave, B., 'Bede's Miracle Stories', in *BLTW* 201–29

Colgrave, B. (ed.), *Felix's Life of Saint Guthlac* (Cambridge: Cambridge University Press, 1956)

Colgrave, B., 'The Venerable Bede and His Times', in *JL* I 1–18

Colgrave, B (ed.), *The Earliest Life of Gregory the Great by an Anonymous Monk of Whitby* (Lawrence: University of Kansas Press, 1968)

Coronati, L., 'La Dottrina del Tetramento Trociacio in Beda', *Romanobarbarica* 6 (1981) 53–62

Cosmos, S., 'Oral Tradition and Literary Convention in Bede's Life of St Aidan', *Classical Folia* 31 (1977) 47–63

Cowdrey, H. E. J., 'Bede and the "English People" ', *Journal of Religious History* 11 (1981) 501–23

Cramp, R., 'Excavations at the Saxon Monastic Sites of Wearmouth and Jarrow, Co. Durham: an Interim Report', *Medieval Archaeology* 13 (1969) 21–66

Cramp, R., 'Monkwearmouth and Jarrow: The Archaeological Evidence', in *FC* 1–18

Cramp, R., 'Early Northumbrian Sculpture', in *JL* I 133–52

Crivellucci, A. (ed.), *Pauli Diaconi Historia Romana* (Rome: Tip. Del Senato, 1914)

Cross, J. E., 'Bede's Influence at Home and Abroad: An Introduction', in *BV* 17–29

Cubitt, C., 'Wilfrid's "Usurping Bishops": Episcopal Elections in Anglo-Saxon England c.600–c.800', *Northern History* 25 (1989) 18–38

Cubitt, C., *Anglo-Saxon Church Councils, c.650–850* (London: Leicester University Press, 1995)

Cubitt, C., 'Unity and Diversity in the Early Anglo-Saxon Liturgy', *Studies in Church History* 32 (1996) 45–57

Cubitt, C., 'Memory and Narrative in the Cult of Early Anglo-Saxon Saints', in M. Innes and Y. Hen (eds), *The Uses of the Past in the Early Middle Ages* (Cambridge: Cambridge University Press, 2000) 29–66

Cubitt, C., 'Monastic Memory and Identity in Early Anglo-Saxon England', in W. D. Frazer and A. Tyrell (eds), *Social Identity in Early Medieval Britain*, Studies in the Early History of Britain (London: Leicester University Press, 2000) 253–76

Darlington, R. R. (ed.), *The Vita Wulfstani of William of Malmesbury, Transactions of the Camden Society*, 3rd Series, 40 (1928)

Davidse, J., 'The Sense of History in the Works of the Venerable Bede', *Studi Medievali* 23 (1982) 647–95

Davidse, J., 'On Bede as a Christian Historian', in *BV* 1–15

Davis, R., 'Bede's Early Reading', *Speculum* 8 (1933) 179–95

DeGregorio, S., 'The Venerable Bede on Prayer and Contemplation', *Traditio* 54 (1999) 1–39

DeGregorio, S., ' "*Nostrorum socordiam temporum*": The Reforming Impulse of Bede's Later Exegesis', *Early Medieval Europe* 11 (2002) 107–22

DeGregorio, S., 'Bede's *In Ezram et Neemiam* and the Reform of the Northumbrian Church', *Speculum* 79 (2004) 1–25

DeGregorio, S. 'Bede's in *Ezram et Neemiam*: A document in Church Reform', *BLVTP* 97–108

de Hamel, C., 'Archbishop Matthew Parker and His Imaginary Library of Archbishop Theodore of Canterbury', http://www.lambethpalacelibrary.org/news/Friendsreport2002/lecture.html

de Jong, M., *In Samuel's Image: Child Oblation in the Early Medieval West* (Leiden: E. J. Brill, 1996)

de Jong, M, 'The Empire as Ecclesia: Hrabanus Maurus and Biblical *Historia* for Rulers', in Y. Hen and M. Innes (eds), *The Uses of the Past in the Early Middle Ages* (Cambridge: Cambridge University Press, 2000) 191–226

Dickinson, W. W., 'Bede as Literary Architext of the Church: Another Look at Bede's Uses of Hagiograpy in the *Historia Ecclesiastica*', *American Benedictine Review* 45 (1994) 93–105

Dionisotti, A. C., 'On Bede, Grammars and Greek', *Revue Bénédictine* 92 (1982) 111–41

Dobiache-Rojdestvensky, O., 'Un manuscrit de Bède à Leningrad', *Speculum* 3 (1928) 314–21

Druhan, D. R., 'The Syntax of Bede's *Historia Ecclesiastica*', *Catholic University Studies in Medieval and Renaissance Latin* 8 (1938) 1–24

Dümmler, E. (ed.), *Hrabani Mauri Carmina, Monumenta Germaniae Historica, Poetae Latini Aevi Carolini* II (Berlin: Weidmann, 1884)

Dumville, D. N., 'Textual Archaeology and Northumbrian History Subsequent to Bede', in D. M. Metcalf (ed.), *Coinage in Ninth-Century Northumbria*, BAR British Series 180 (Oxford: British Archaeology Reports, 1987) 43–55, repr. in D. N. Dumville, *Britons and Anglo-Saxons in the Early Middle Ages* (Aldershot: Variorum, 1993) 43–55 (original pagination)

Dumville, D. N., 'The Terminology of Overkingship in Early Anglo-Saxon England', in J. Hines (ed.), *The Anglo-Saxons from the Migration Period to the Eighth Century: An*

Ethnographic Perspective, Studies in Historical Archaeoethnology 2 (Woodbridge: Boydell Press, 1997) 345–73

Duncan, A. A. M., 'Bede, Iona and the Picts', in R. H. C. Davis and J. M. Wallace-Hadrill (eds), *The Writing of History in the Middle Ages* (Oxford: Clarendon Press, 1981) 1–42

Duncan, S., '*Signa de Caelo* in the Lives of St Cuthbert: The Impact of Biblical Images and Exegesis on Early Medieval Hagiography', *Heythrop Journal* 41 (2000) 399–412

Eby, J. C., 'Bringing the Vita to Life: Bede's Symbolic Structure of the Life of St Cuthbert', *American Benedictine Review* 48 (1997) 316–38

Echlin, E., 'Bede and the Church', *Irish Theological Quarterly* 40 (1973) 351–63

Eckenrode, T. R., 'The Growth of a Scientific Mind: Bede's Early and Late Scientific Writings', *Downside Review* 94 (1976) 197–212

Eckenrode, T. R., 'The Venerable Bede as an Educator', *The History of Education* 6 (1977) 159–68

Elfassi, J., 'Germain d'Auxerre, figure d'Augustin de Cantorbéry: la réécriture par Bède de la "Vie de Saint Germain d'Auxerre" ', *Hagiographica* 5 (1998) 37–47

Emerton, E. (trans. and intro.), *The Letters of Saint Boniface* (New York: Columbia University Press, 1940)

Eusebius, *The Ecclesiastical History*, trans. and ed. J. E. L. Oulton (London: William Heinemann, 1953)

Fanning, S., 'Bede, *Imperium*, and the *Bretwaldas*', *Speculum* 66 (1991) 1–26

Farr, C. A., 'The Shape of Learning at Wearmouth-Jarrow: The Diagram Pages in the *Codex Amiatinus*', in J. Hawkes and S. Mills (eds), *Northumbria's Golden Age* (Stroud: Sutton, 1999) 336–44

Ferguson, T. C., *The Past Is Prologue: The Revolution of Nicene Historiography* (Leiden: Brill, 2005)

Fletcher, E., 'Benedict Biscop', in *JL* II, 539–54

Foley, W. T. *Images of Sanctity in Eddius Stephanus' Life of Bishop Wilfrid, an Early English Saint's Life* (Lampeter: Edwin Mellen, 1992)

Foley, W. T., 'Suffering and Sanctity in Bede's Prose Life of St Cuthbert', *Journal of Theological Studies* 50 (1999) 102–16

Fowler, P., *Farming in the First Millennium AD* (Cambridge: Cambridge University Press, 2002)

Franklin, C. V., 'The Date of Composition of Bede's *De schematibus et tropis* and *De arte metrica*', *Revue Bénédictine* 110 (2000) 199–203

Frantzen, A. J., 'The Penitentials Attributed to Bede', *Speculum* 58 (1983) 573–97

Freeman, E. A., *Old English History for Children* (London: Macmillan, 1869)

Gebhardt, O. von and Richardson, E. C. von (eds), *Hieronymus Liber de viris inlustribus*, Texte und Untersuchungen zur Geschichte der altchristlichen Literatur (Leipzig: J. C. Hinrich's Buchhandlung, 1896) series XIV, vol. 1

Gleason, M., 'Bede and His Fathers', *Classica et Mediaevalia* 45 (1994) 223–38

Gneuss, H. and Lapidge, M., 'The Earliest Manuscript of Bede's Metrical *Vita S. Cudbercti*', *Anglo-Saxon England* 32 (2003) 43–54

Godman, P. (ed.), *Alcuin: The Bishops, Kings and Saints of York* (Oxford: Clarendon Press, 1982)

Goffart, W., *The Narrators of Barbarian History (A.D. 550–800): Jordanes, Gregory of Tours, Bede, and Paul the Deacon* (Guildford: Princeton University Press, 1988)

Goffart, W., 'The *Historia Ecclesiastica*: Bede's Agenda and Ours', *Haskins Society Journal* 2 (1990) 29–45

Goffart, W. 'L'Histoire écclésiastique et l'engagement politique de Bède', in *BLVTP* 149–58

Gorman, M., 'The Glosses on Bede's *De temporum ratione* Attributed to Byrhtferth of Ramsey', *Anglo-Saxon England* 25 (1996) 209–32

Gorman, M., 'Bede's *VIII Quaestiones* and Carolingian Biblical Scholarship', *Revue Bénédictine* 109 (1999) 32–74

Gorman, M., 'The Canon of Bede's Works and the World of Ps. Bede', *Revue Bénédictine* 111 (2001) 399–445

Gorman, M., 'Source Marks and Chapter Divisions in Bede's Commentary on Luke', *Revue Bénédictine* 112 (2002) 246–75

Gransden, A., 'Bede's Reputation as Historian in Medieval England', *Journal of Ecclesiastical History* 32 (1981) 397–425

Gransden, A., 'Traditionalism and Continuity during the Last Century of Anglo-Saxon Monasticism', *Journal of Ecclesiastical History* 40 (1989) 15–207

Green, J. R., *The Making of England* (London: Macmillan, 1881)

Green, J. R., *A Short History of the English People* (London: Macmillan, 1892)

Greenway, D. (ed. and trans.), *Henry, Archdeacon of Huntingdon, Historia Anglorum: The History of the English People* (Oxford: Clarendon Press, 1996)

Gribomont, J., 'Saint Bède et ses dictionnaires grec', *Revue Bénédictine* 89 (1979) 271–80

Grocock, C., 'Bede and the Golden Age of Latin Prose in Northumbria', in J. Hawkes and S. Mills (eds), *Northumbria's Golden Age* (Stroud: Sutton, 1999) 371–82

Gunn, V., 'Bede and the Martyrdom of Oswald', *Studies in Church History* 30 (1993) 57–66

Hamilton Thompson, A., 'Northumbrian Monasticism', in *BLTW* 60–101

Hanning, R. W., *The Vision of History in Early Britain: From Gildas to Geoffrey of Monmouth* (London: Columbia University Press, 1966)

Hart-Hasler, J. N., 'Bede's Use of Patristic Sources: The Transfiguration', *Studia Patristica* 28 (1993) 197–204

Henderson, G., 'Bede and the Visual Arts', in *JL* II, 507–38

Higden, Ranulph, see Babington, C.

Higham, N. J., *The Convert Kings: Power and Religious Affiliation in Early Anglo-Saxon England* (Manchester: Manchester University Press, 1997)

Higham, N. J., *King Arthur: Myth-Making and History* (London: Routledge, 2002)

Hill, R., 'Holy Kings: The Bane of Seventh-Century Society', *Studies in Church History* 12 (1975) 39–43

Hill, R., 'The Labourers in the Field', in *JL* I, 369–84

Hines, J., 'The Becoming of the English: Identity, Material Culture and Language in Early Anglo-Saxon England', *Anglo-Saxon Studies in Archaeology and History* 7 (1994) 49–59

Hodgkin, R. H., *A History of the Anglo-Saxons*, 2 vols (Oxford: Oxford University Press, 1935)

Holder, A. G., 'Allegory and History in Bede's Interpretation of Sacred Architecture', *American Benedictine Review* 40 (1989) 115–31

Holder, A. G., 'New Treasures for Old in Bede's *De Tabernaculo* and *De Templo*', *Revue Bénédictine* 99 (1989) 237–49

Holder, A. G., 'Bede and the Tradition of Patristic Exegesis', *Anglican Theological Review* 72 (1990) 399–411

Holder, A. G., 'The Venerable Bede on the Mysteries of Our Salvation', *American Benedictine Review* 42 (1991) 140–62

Holder, A. G., 'The Feminine Christ in Bede's Biblical Commentaries', in *BLVTP* 109–18

Holder, A. G., '(Un)Dating Bede's *De Arte Metrica*', in J. Hawkes and S. Mills (eds), *Northumbria's Golden Age* (Stroud: Sutton, 1999) 390–5

Holder-Egger, O. (ed.), *Chronica Minor Auctore Minorita Erphordiensi*, Monumenta Germaniae Historica Scriptorum 24 (Hanover: Hahn, 1879), 172–204

Hollis, S., *Anglo-Saxon Women and the Church: Sharing a Common Fate* (Woodbridge: Boydell Press, 1992)

Hough, C., 'Strensall, Streanæshalch and Stronsay', *Journal of the English Place-Name Society* 35 (2002–3) 17–24

Hughes, K., 'Early Christianity in Pictland', in *JL* I, 267–84

Hume, D., *The History of England from the Invasions of Julius Caesar to the Revolution in 1688* I (London: Longman, Brown, Green and Longmans, 1848)

Humphreys, K. W. and Ross, A. S., 'Further Manuscripts of Bede's *Historia Ecclesiastica*, of the *Epistola Cuthberti de Obitu Bedae*, and Further Anglo-Saxon Texts of Cædmon's Hymn and Bede's Death Song', *Notes and Queries* 22 (1975) 50–5

Hunter, C., *The History of the Cathedral Church of Durham* (Durham: printed for John Richardson, bookseller, second edn, 1742)

Hunter Blair, P., 'The *Moore Memoranda* on Northern History', in C. Fox and B. Dickins (eds), *The Early Cultures of North West Europe* (Cambridge: Cambridge University Press, 1950) 245–57

Hunter Blair, P., *An Introduction to Anglo-Saxon England* (Cambridge: Cambridge University Press, 1956)

Hunter Blair, P., 'The Historical Writings of Bede', *Settimane di Studio del Centro Italiano di Studi sull' Alto Medioevo* 17 (1970) 197–221

Hunter Blair, P., *The World of Bede* (Cambridge: Cambridge University Press, 1970)

Hunter Blair, P., 'From Bede to Alcuin' in *FC* 239–60

Hunter Blair, P., *Northumbria in the Days of Bede* (London: Gollancz, 1976)

Hunter Blair, P., 'Whitby as a Centre of Learning in the Seventh Century', in M. Lapidge and H. Gneuss (eds), *Learning and Literature in Anglo-Saxon England: Studies Presented to Peter Clemoes on the Occasion of His Sixty-Fifth Birthday* (Cambridge: Cambridge University Press, 1985) 3–32

Hunter Blair, P., 'Bede's *Ecclesiastical History of the English Nation* and Its Importance Today', in *JL* I, 19–34

Ireland, C., 'Aldfrith of Northumbria and the Irish Genealogies', *Celtica* 22 (1991) 64–78

Ireland, C., 'Aldfrith of Northumbria and the Learning of a Sapiens', in K. A. Klar *et al.* (eds), *A Celtic Florilegium: Studies in Memory of Brendan O Hehir* (Lawrence, MA: Celtic Studies Publications, 1996) 63–77

Irvine, M., 'Bede the Grammarian in the Scope of Grammatical Studies in Eighth-Century Northumbria', *Anglo-Saxon England* 15 (1986) 15–44

Isola, A., '*De Schematibus et Tropis* di Beda in Rapporto al *De Doctrina Christiana* di Agostino', *Romanobarbarica* 1 (1976) 31–82

James, E., 'Bede and the Tonsure Question', *Peritia* 3 (1984) 85–98

James, M. R., 'The Manuscripts of Bede', in *BLTW* 230–6

Jansen, A. M., 'Bede and the Legends of St Oswald', in *BV* 167–78

Jenkins, C., 'Bede as Exegete and Theologian', in *BLTW* 152–200

John, E., *Reassessing Anglo-Saxon England* (Manchester: Manchester University Press, 1996) 4–65

Jones, C. W., 'Polemius Silvius, Bede, and the Names of the Months', *Speculum* 9 (1934) 50–6

Jones, C. W., 'The Victorian and Dionysiac Paschal Tables in the West', *Speculum* 9 (1934) 408–21

Jones, C. W., *Saints' Lives and Chronicles* (Ithaca, NY: Cornell University Press, 1937)

Jones, C. W., *Bedae Pseudepigrapha: Scientific Writings Falsely Attributed to Bede* (London: Oxford University Press, 1939)

Jones, C. W., 'Bede as Early Medieval Historian', *Medievalia et Humanistica* 4 (1946) 26–36

Jones, C. W., 'Bede's Place in Medieval Schools', in *FC* 261–85

Karkov, C. E., 'Whitby, Jarrow, and the Commemoration of Death in Northumbria', in J. Hawkes and S. Mills (eds), *Northumbria's Golden Age* (Stroud: Sutton, 1999) 126–35

Kemble, J. M., *The Saxons in England* (London, Longman, Brown, Green and Longmans, 1849)

Kendall, C. B., 'Bede's *Historia Ecclesiastica*: The Rhetoric of Faith', in J. J. Murphy (ed.), *Medieval Eloquence: Studies in the Theory and Practice of Medieval Rhetoric* (Los Angeles and Berkeley: University of California Press, 1978) 145–72

Kendall, C. B., 'Imitation and Bede's *Historia Ecclesiastica*', in *SSH* I, 161–90

Keynes, S. and Lapidge, M., *Alfred the Great* (Harmondsworth: Penguin, 1983)

Killion, S. B., 'Bedan Historiography in the Irish Annals', *Medieval Perspectives* 6 (1991) 20–36

Kirby, D. P., 'Bede and Northumbrian Chronology', *English Historical Review* 78 (1963) 514–27

Kirby, D. P., 'Problems of Early West Saxon History', *English Historical Review* 80 (1965) 10–29

Kirby, D. P., 'Bede's Native Sources for the *Historia Ecclesiastica*', *Bulletin of the John Rylands Library* 48 (1965–6) 341–71

Kirby, D. P., 'Northumbria in the Time of Wilfrid', in D. P. Kirby (ed.), *Saint Wilfrid at Hexham* (Newcastle upon Tyne: Oriel Press, 1974) 1–34

Kirby, D. P., '. . . *per universas Pictorum provincias*', in *FC* 286–324

Kirby, D. P., 'King Ceolwulf of Northumbria and the *Historia Ecclesiastica*', *Studia Celtica* 14–15 (1979–80) 168–73

Kirby, D. P., 'Bede, Eddius Stephanus, and the "Life of Wilfrid" ', *English Historical Review* 98 (1983) 101–14

Kirby, D. P., 'Bede's *Historia Ecclesiastica Gentis Anglorum*: Its Contemporary Setting', in *JL* II, 903–26

Kirby, D. P., *The Earliest English Kings* (London: Unwin Hyman, 1991)

Kirby, D. P., 'The Genesis of a Cult: Cuthbert of Farne and Ecclesiastical Politics in Northumbria in the Late Seventh and Early Eighth Centuries', *Journal of Ecclesiastical History* 46 (1995) 383–97

Knowles, D., *Saints and Scholars: Twenty Five Medieval Portraits* (Cambridge: Cambridge University Press, 1946)

Kumar, K., *The Making of English National Identity* (Cambridge: Cambridge University Press, 2003)

Laistner, M. L. W., 'The Library of the Venerable Bede', in *BLTW* 237–66

Laistner, M. L. W. and King, H. H., *A Hand-List of Bede Manuscripts* (New York: Cornell University Press, 1943)

Lapidge, M., 'Some Remnants of Bede's Lost *Liber Epigrammatum*', *English Historical Review* 90 (1975) 798–820

Lapidge, M., 'Surviving Booklists from Anglo-Saxon England', in M. Lapidge and H. Gneuss (eds), *Learning and Literature in Anglo-Saxon England* (Cambridge: Cambridge University Press, 1985) 33–89

Lapidge, M., 'The School of Theodore and Hadrian', *Anglo-Saxon England* 15 (1986) 45–72

Lapidge, M., 'Bede's Metrical *Vita S. Cuthberti*', in *CCC* 77–93

Lapidge, M., *Anglo-Saxon Litanies of the Saints*, Publications of the Henry Bradshaw Society 106 (Woodbridge: Boydell Press for the Henry Bradshaw Society, 1991)

Lapidge, M., 'Bede the Poet', in *JL* II, 927–56

Lapidge, M., 'Latin Learning in Ninth-Century England', in M. Lapidge, *Anglo-Latin Literature, 600–899* (London: The Hambledon Press, 1996) 409–54

Lapidge, M., 'Tatwine', in *BEASE* 440

Lawrence, M., 'Bede as Linguistic Scholar', *American Benedictine Review* 35 (1984) 204–17

Lawrence, M., 'Bede's Structural Use of Wordplay as a Way to Truth', in E. R. Elder (ed.), *From Cloister to Classroom: Monastic and Scholastic Approaches to Truth* (Kalamazoo, MI: Cistercian Publications, 1986) 27–46

Lawrence, M., 'The Two Worlds in Bede's Homilies: The Biblical Event and the Listener's Experience', in T. L. Amos, E. A. Green and B. M. Kienzle (eds), *De Ore Domini: Preacher and Word in the Middle Ages* (Kalamazoo, MI: Medieval Institute Publications, 1989) 27–40

Levison, W., 'Bede as Historian', in *BLTW* 111–51

Loomis, C. G., 'The Miracle Traditions of the Venerable Bede', *Speculum* 21 (1946) 404–18

Lutterkort, K., 'Beda Hagiographicus: Meaning and Function of Miracle Stories in the *Vita Cuthberti* and the *Historia Ecclesiastica*', in *BV* 81–106

Lynch, K. M., 'The Venerable Bede's Knowledge of Greek', *Traditio* 39 (1983) 432–8

Macaulay, Lord C., *History of England* (London: Longmans, Green and Co., 1867)

Mackay, T. W., 'Bede's Hagiographical Method: His Knowledge and Use of Paulinus of Nola', in *FC* 77–92

Mackay, T. W., 'Biblical Criticism in Bedan Manuscripts', in *SSH* I, 209–32

Mackay, T. W., 'Augustine and Gregory the Great in Bede's Commentary on the Apocalypse', in J. Hawkes and S. Mills (eds), *Northumbria's Golden Age* (Stroud: Sutton, 1999) 396–405

McClure, J., 'Bede's Old Testament Kings', in *IR* 76–98

McClure, J., 'Bede and the Life of Ceolfrid', *Peritia* 3 (1984) 71–84

McClure, J., 'Bede's *Notes on Genesis* and the Training of the Anglo-Saxon Clergy', *Studies in Church History: Subsidia* 4 (1985) 17–30

McClure, J. and Collins, R. (ed. and intro.), *Bede: The Ecclesiastical History of the English People* (Oxford: Oxford University Press, 1994)

McCready, W. D., *Miracles and the Venerable Bede* (Toronto: Pontifical Institute of Mediaeval Studies, 1994)

McCready, W. D., 'Bede and the Isidorian Legacy', *Mediaeval Studies* 57 (1995) 41–73

McCready, W. D., 'Bede, Isidore, and the *Epistola Cuthberti*', *Traditio* 50 (1995) 75–94

McGroarty, B., 'Bede's Ecclesiastical Vision for England', *Downside Review* 122 (2004) 211–34

McNamara, J., 'Bede's Role in Circulating Legend in the *Historia Ecclesiastica*', *Anglo-Saxon Studies in Archaeology and History* 9 (1994) 61–9

Markus, R. A., 'The Chronology of the Gregorian Mission to England: Bede's Narrative and Gregory's Correspondence', *Journal of Ecclesiastical History* 14 (1963) 16–30

Markus, R. A., 'Bede and the Tradition of Ecclesiastical Historiography', in *JL* I, 385–404

Martin, J. C. (ed.), *Isidori Hispalensis Chronica* (Turnhout: Brepols, 2003)

Mason, S. (trans. and commentary), *The Life of Josephus* (Leiden: Brill, 2001)

Mayr-Harting, H., *The Coming of Christianity to Anglo-Saxon England*, 3rd edn (London: Batsford, 1991)

Mayr-Harting, H., 'Bede's Patristic Thinking as Historian', in A. Scharer and G. Scheibelreiter (eds), *Historiographie im frühen Mittelalter* (Vienna: Oldenbourg, 1994) 367–74

Mellows, W. T. (ed.), *The Chronicle of Hugh Candidus* (Peterborough: Peterborough Natural History, Scientific and Archaeological Society, 1941)

Mellows, W. T., with La Geste de Burch (eds.), *The Chronicle of Hugh Candidus, a Monk of Peterborough* (London: Oxford University Press on behalf of the Friends of Peterborough Cathedral, 1949)

Meyvaert, P., 'Bede and the *Libellus Synodicus* of Gregory the Great', *Journal of Theological Studies* N.S. 12 (1961) 298–302

Meyvaert, P., 'The Registrum of Gregory the Great and Bede', *Revue Bénédictine* 80 (1970) 162–6

Meyvaert, P., 'Bede's Text of the *Libellus Responsionum* of Gregory the Great to Augustine of Canterbury', in P. Clemoes and K. Hughes (eds), *England before the Conquest: Studies in Primary Sources Presented to Dorothy Whitelock* (Cambridge: Cambridge University Press, 1971) 15–33

Meyvaert, P., 'Bede the Scholar', in *FC* 40–69

Meyvaert, P., 'Bede and Gregory the Great', in *JL* I, 103–32

Meyvaert, P., 'Bede, Cassiodorus, and the *Codex Amiatinus*', *Speculum* 71 (1996) 827–83

Meyvaert, P., ' "In the Footsteps of the Fathers": The Date of Bede's Thirty Questions on the Book of Kings to Nothelm', in W. E. Klingshirn and J. M. Vessey (eds), *The Limits of Ancient Christianity: Essays on Late Antique Thought and Culture in Honour of R. A. Markus* (Ann Arbor: University of Michigan Press, 1999) 267–86

Meyvaert, P., 'Discovering the Calendar (*Annalis libellus*) Attached to Bede's Own Copy of *De temporum ratione*', *Annalecta Bollandiana* 120 (2002) 5–64

Meyvaert, P., 'The Date of Bede's *In Ezram* and His Image of Ezra in the Codex Amiatinus', *Speculum* 80(4) (2005) 1087–1133.

Miller, M., 'Bede's Roman Dates', *Classica et Mediaevalia* 31 (1970) 239–57

Miller, M., 'Bede's Use of Gildas', *English Historical Review* 90 (1975) 241–61

Miller, M., 'Starting to Write History: Gildas, Bede, and Nennius', *Welsh History Review* 8 (1977) 456–65

Miller, T. (trans.), *The Old English Version of Bede's Ecclesiastical History of the English People* (New York: Early English Text Society, 1988)

Milton, J., *Britain under Trojan, Roman, Saxon Rule* (first published 1671: the copy used is from Kennet's England, 1719, reprinted London: Alex. Murray & Son, 1870)

Morris, J. (ed.), *Nennius: British History and Welsh Annals* (Chichester: Phillimore, 1980)

Mynors, R. A. B., Thomson, R. M. and Winterbottom, M. (ed. and trans.), *William of Malmesbury, Gesta Regum Anglorum* I (Oxford: Clarendon Press, 1998)

Newlands, C. E., 'Bede and Images of Saint Cuthbert', *Traditio* 52 (1997) 73–109

O'Brien O'Keeffe, K., 'Orality and the Developing Text of Cædmon's Hymn', *Speculum* 62 (1987) 1–20

O'Carragain, E., *The City of Rome and the World of Bede*, JL (1994)

O'Croinin, D., 'The Irish Provenance of Bede's Computus', *Peritia* 2 (1983) 229–47

O'Croinin, D., ' "New Heresy for Old": Pelagianism in Ireland and the Letter of 640', *Speculum* 60 (1985) 505–16

Ogilvy, J. D. A., 'The Place of Wearmouth and Jarrow in Western Cultural History', in *JL* I, 235–46

O'Hare, C., 'The Story of Cædmon: Bede's Account of the First Old English Poet', *American Benedictine Review* 43 (1992) 345–57

Olsen, G., 'Bede as Historian: The Evidence from His Observations of the Life of the First Christian Community of Jerusalem', *Journal of Ecclesiastical History* 33 (1982) 519–30

Oman, C., *A History of England in Seven Volumes*, I, *England before the Norman Conquest* (London: Methuen, 1910)

Orchard, A., *The Poetic Art of Aldhelm* (Cambridge: Cambridge University Press, 1994)

Orchard, B., 'Bede the Venerable', *Downside Review* 53 (1935) 344–68

Ortenberg, V., 'Virgin Queens: Abbesses and Power in Early Anglo-Saxon England', in R. Gameson and H. Leyser (eds), *Belief and Culture in the Middle Ages: Studies Presented to Henry Mayr-Harting* (Oxford: Oxford University Press, 2001) 59–68

Parkes, M. B., 'The Scriptorium of Wearmouth-Jarrow', in *JL* II, 555–86

Parsons, D., 'Books and Buildings: Architectural Description before and after Bede', in *JL* II, 729–74

Pepperdene, M., 'Bede's *Historia Ecclesiastica*: a New Perspective', *Celtica* 4 (1958) 253–62

Picard, J.-M., 'Bede, Adomnan, and the Writing of History', *Peritia* 3 (1984) 50–70

Piper, A. J., *Durham Monks at Jarrow*, JL II (1986) 691–728

Poole, R., 'St Wilfrid and the See of Ripon', *English Historical Review* 34 (1919) 1–24

Riain, P. O., 'A Northumbrian Phase in the Formation of the Hieronymian Martyrology: The Evidence of the Martyrology of Tallaght', *Annalecta Bollandiana* 120 (2002) 311–63

Ray, R., 'Bede, the Exegete, as Historian', in *FC* 125–40

Ray, R., 'Bede's *Vera Lex Historiae*', *Speculum* 55 (1980) 1–21

Ray, R., *Bede, Rhetoric, and the Creation of Christian Latin Culture*, JL (1997)

Robinson, B., 'The Venerable Bede as Exegete', *Downside Review* 112 (1994) 201–26

Rollason, D. W., 'Lists of Saints' Resting-Places in Anglo-Saxon England', *Anglo-Saxon England* 7 (1978) 61–94

Rollason, D. W., *Saints and Relics in Anglo-Saxon England* (Oxford: Blackwell, 1989)

Rollason, D. W. (ed. and trans.), *Simeon of Durham, Libellus de Exordio atque Procursu Istius, hoc est Dunhelmensis, Ecclesie: Tract on the Origins and Progress of this the Church of Durham* (Oxford: Clarendon Press, 2000)

Rollason, D. W., *Bede and Germany*, JL (2001)

Rollason, D. W., *Northumbria, 500–1100: Creation and Destruction of a Kingdom* (Cambridge: Cambridge University Press, 2003)

Rollason, D. W., Gore, D. and Fellows-Jensen, G., *Sources for York History to AD 1100*, The Archaeology of York 1 (York: York Archaeological Trust, 1998)

Rosenthal, J. T., 'Bede's Use of Miracles in the Ecclesiastical History', *Traditio* 31 (1975) 328–35

Ruehl, F. (ed.), *Eutropius, Breviarium ab urbe condita* (Leipzig: Teubner, 1887)

Salmon, T., *The History of Great Britain and Ireland; from the First Discovery of these Islands to the Norman Conquest*, 2nd edn (London: printed for John Wyat, 1725)

Sanderson, P., *The Antiquities of the Abbey or Cathedral Church of Durham* (Durham: printed by J. White and T. Saint at Mr Pope's Head, 1767)

Schaller, D., 'Der Verleumdete David: Zum Schubkapitel von Bedas "*Epistola ad Pleguinam*" ', in A. Önnerfors, J. Rathover and F. Wagner (eds), *Literatur und Sprache in Europäischen Mittelalter: Festschrift für Karl Langoosch zum 70. Geburstag* (Darmstadt: Wissenschaftliche Buchgeselleschaft, 1973) 39–43

Sellars, W. C. and Yeatman, R. J., *1066 and All That* (London: Methuen, 1930)

Sherley-Price, L. (trans. and intro.), revised by R. E. Latham, ed. D. H. Farmer, *Bede: A History of the English Church and People* (Harmondsworth: Penguin, 1968)

Siffren, P. P., 'Das Walderdorffer Kalendarfragment saec VII und die Berliner Blätter eines Sakramentars auf Regensburg', *Ephemerides Liturgicae* 47 (1933) 201–44

Simonettis, G., 'Osservatione sul Testo di Alcuini Passi della *Historia Ecclesiastica* di Beda', *Siculorum Gymnasium* 29 (1978) 403–11

Sims-Williams, P., 'The Settlement of England in Bede and the Chronicle', *Anglo-Saxon England* 12 (1983) 1–41

Siniscalco, P., 'La Età del Mondo in Beda', *Romanobarbarica* 3 (1978) 297–332

Smith, L. T. (ed.), *The Itinerary of John Leland*, 5 vols. (London: Centaur Press Ltd, 1964)

Sparks, H. F. D., 'A Celtic Text of the Latin Apocalypse Preserved in Two Durham Manuscripts of Bede's Commentary on the Apocalypse', *Journal of Theological Studies* N.S. 5 (1954) 227–31

Stancliffe, C., 'Kings Who Opted Out', in *IR* 154–76

Stancliffe, C., 'Cuthbert and the Polarity between Pastor and Solitary', in *CCC* 21–44

Stansbury, M., 'Source-Marks in Bede's Biblical Commentaries', in J. Hawkes and S. Mills (eds), *Northumbria's Golden Age* (Stroud: Sutton, 1999) 383–9

Stapleton, T., *Fortresse of the Faith first planted among us Englishmen, and continued hitherto in the vniuersall Church of Christ* (St Omers: John Heigham, 1565)

Stenton, F. M., *Anglo-Saxon England* (Oxford: Clarendon Press, 1943)

Stephens, J. N., 'Bede's Ecclesiastical History', *History* 62 (1977) 1–14

Stevens, W. M., 'Bede's Scientific Achievement', in *JL* II, 645–88

Stevenson, Revd J. (trans.), *Richard of Hexham: History of the Acts of King Stephen*, The Church Historians of England (London: Seeleys, 1856)

Stranks, C. J., *The Venerable Bede* (London: SPCK, 1974)

Ström, H., *Old English Personal Names in Bede's History, an Etymological–Phonological Investigation*, Lund Studies in English 8 (Lund: C. W. K. Gleerup, 1939)

Stubbs, W. (ed.), *Select Charters and Other Illustrations of English Constitutional History* (Oxford: Clarendon Press, 1870)

Szerwiniak, O., 'L'Histoire ecclésiastique ou le rêve d'un retour au temps de l'innocence', in *BLVTP* 159–76

Talbot, C. H., *Anglo-Saxon Missionaries in Germany* (London: Sheed and Ward, 1954)

Tangl, M., *Die Briefen des heiligen Bonifatius und Lullus,* Monumenta Germaniae Historica, Epistolae Selectae 1 (Berlin: Weidmann, 2nd edn, 1955)

Taylor, H. M. and Taylor, J., *Anglo-Saxon Architecture*, 2 vols (Cambridge: Cambridge University Press, 1965)

Taylor, J., *The Universal Chronicle of Ranulph Higden* (Oxford: Clarendon Press, 1966)

Thacker, A., 'Some Terms for Noblemen in Anglo-Saxon England', *Anglo-Saxon Studies in Archaeology and History* 2 (1981) 201–36

Thacker, A., 'Bede's Ideal of Reform', in *IR* 130–53

Thacker, A., 'Lindisfarne and the Origins of the Cult of St Cuthbert', in *CCC* 103–22

Thacker, A., 'Monks, Preaching and Pastoral Care in Early Anglo-Saxon England', in J. Blair and R. Sharpe (eds), *Pastoral Care before the Parish*, Studies in the Early History of Britain (London: Leicester University Press, 1992) 137–70

Thacker, A., '*Membra Disjecta*: The Division of the Body and the Diffusion of the Cult', in C. Stancliffe and E. Cambridge (eds), *Oswald: Northumbrian King to European Saint* (Stamford: Paul Watkins, 1995) 97–127

Thacker, A., 'Bede and the Irish', in *BV* 31–59

Thacker, A., 'The Making of a Local Saint', in A. Thacker and R. Sharpe (eds), *Local Saints and Local Churches in the Early Medieval West* (Oxford: Oxford University Press, 2002) 45–74

Thomas, C., 'Bede, Archaeology, and the Cult of Relics', in *JL* I, 347–68

Thomson, R. M., *William of Malmesbury* (Woodbridge: Boydell Press, 1987)

Towers, T., 'Smith and Son, Editors of Bede', in *FC* 366–87

Turner, S., *History of the Anglo-Saxons*, 3 vols (London, 1799–1805)

Uppinder, M. and Townsend, D., ' "Nation" and the Gaze of the Other in Eighth-Century Northumbria', *Comparative Literature* 53 (2001) 1–26

Wallace-Hadrill, J. M. (trans.), *The Fourth Book of the Chronicle of Fredegar with Its Continuations* (London: Nelson, 1960)

Wallace-Hadrill, J. M., 'Gregory of Tours and Bede: Their Views on the Personal Qualities of King', *Frümittelalterliche Studien* 2 (1968) 31–44

Wallace-Hadrill, J. M., *Early Germanic Kingship in England and on the Continent* (Oxford: Oxford University Press, 1971)

Wallace-Hadrill, J. M., 'Bede's Europe', in *JL* I, 71–86

Wallace-Hadrill, J. M., 'Bede and Plummer', in *FC*, 366–85

Wallace-Hadrill, J. M., *Bede's Ecclesiastical History of the English People: A Historical Commentary*, Oxford Medieval Texts (Oxford: Clarendon Press, 1988)

Ward, B., 'Miracles and History: A Reconsideration of the Miracle Stories used by Bede', in *FC* 70–6

Ward, B., 'The Spirituality of St Cuthbert', in *CCC* 65–76

Ward, B., 'Bede and the Psalter', in *JL* II, 869–902

Ward, B., *The Venerable Bede*, Outstanding Christian Thinkers Series (London: Continuum, 1990; repr. 1998)

Watson, E. W., 'The Age of Bede', in *BLTW* 39–59

Wetherbee, W., 'Some Implications of Bede's Latin Style', in *BASE* 23–31

Wheare, D., *The Method and Order of Reading both Civil and Ecclesiastical Histories*, 3rd edn made English and Enlarged by E. Bohun (London, 1710)

Whitbread, L., 'A Study of Bede's *Versus de die iudicii*', *Philological Quarterly* 23 (1944) 193–221

Whitbread, L., 'Bede's Verses on Doomsday: A Supplementary Note', *Philological Quarterly* 45 (1972) 485–6

White, A., *A History of Whitby*, 2nd edn (Chichester: Phillimore, 2004)

Whitelock, D., *The Old English Bede*, Sir Israel Gollancz Memorial Lecture (London: Oxford University Press, 1962)

Whitelock, D., 'Bede and His Teachers and Friends', in *FC* 19–39

Whitelock, D. (ed.), *English Historical Documents* I, 2nd edn (London: Routledge, 1979; reissued 1996)

Whitelock, D., 'After Bede', in *JL* I, 35–50

Whiting, C. E., 'The Life of the Venerable Bede', in *BLTW* 1–38

Wilson, D. M., 'The Art and Archaeology of Bedan Northumbria', in *BASE* 1–22

Wilson, S. E., 'King Athelstan and St. John of Beverley', *Northern History* 40(1) (2003) 5–23

Wood, I. N., 'The Mission of Augustine of Canterbury to the English', *Speculum* 69 (1994) 1–17

Wood, I. N., *The Most Holy Abbot Ceolfrid*, JL (1995)

Wood, I. N., *The Missionary Life: Saints and the Evangelisation of Europe 400–1050* (Harlow: Longman, 2001)

Wood, S., 'Bede's Northumbrian Dates Again', *English Historical Review* 98 (1983) 280–96

Wormald, F. (ed.), *English Kalendars before A.D. 1100*, Publications of the Henry Bradshaw Society 72 (Woodbridge: Boydell Press for the Henry Bradshaw Society, 1988)

Wormald, P., 'Bede and Benedict Biscop', in *FC* 141–69

Wormald, P., 'Bede, Beowulf and the Conversion of the Anglo-Saxon Aristocracy', in *BASE* 32–95

Wormald, P., 'Monkwearmouth and Jarrow', in J. Campbell (ed.), *The Anglo-Saxons* (London: Phaidon Press, 1982) 74–5

Wormald, P., 'Bede, the *Bretwaldas*, and the Origins of the *Gens Anglorum*', in *IR* 99–129

Wormald, P., 'Bede and the Conversion of England: The Charter Evidence', in *JL* II, 611–44

Wright, N., 'Bede and Vergil', *Romanobarbarica* 6 (1981–2) 361–79

Wright, N. (ed.), *The Historia Regum Britanniae of Geoffrey of Monmouth* I (Cambridge: D. S. Brewer, 1985)

Yorke, B., *Kings and Kingdoms of Early Anglo-Saxon England* (London: Seaby, 1990)

Yorke, B., 'The Bonifacian Mission and Female Religious in Wessex', *Early Medieval Europe* 7(2) (1998) 145–72

Index

Routledge History

Medieval Religion: New Approaches

Edited by Constance Hoffman Berman

Constance Hoffman Berman presents an indispensable new collection of the most influential and revisionist work to be done on religion in the Middle Ages in the last couple of decades. Bringing together an authoritative list of scholars from around the world, the book provides a valuable service to students of religious history in providing a compilation of the most important new work. The collection includes considerations of gender, 'otherness', the body, and diversity of beliefs between the eleventh and fifteenth centuries. *Medieval Religion: New Approaches* is essential reading for all those who study the Middle Ages, church history or religion.

ISBN10: 0–415–31686–3 (hbk)   ISBN10: 0–415–31687–1 (pbk)
ISBN13: 978–0–415–31686–6 (hbk)   ISBN13: 978–0–415–31687–3 (pbk)

Medieval Religion: A Sourcebook

Edited by Dominic Bellenger and Roberta Anderson

This book provides a wide-ranging collection of original source material that covers the history of medieval religion from the fall of the Roman Empire to the Renaissance.

Easy-to-read and accessible to students, with introductions to each section explaining the main themes and issues raised, it provides coverage of the key elements of the history of the Western Church in the period, including: the Papacy, saints, monastic orders, popular piety and devotion, and sections on the Eastern Church, Judaism, Islam and Mysticism.

The texts selected are arranged clearly in chronological order and each one is introduced by a brief editorial note to provide context. *Medieval Religion* also includes a comprehensive further reading section. Students of medieval religion will find this a valuable companion in their studies.

ISBN10: 0–415–37027–2 (hbk)   ISBN10: 0–415–37028–0 (pbk)
ISBN13: 978–0–415–37027–1 (hbk)   ISBN13: 978–0–415–37028–8 (pbk)

Available at all good bookshops
For ordering and further information please visit
www.routledge.com

Routledge History

THE TWO CITIES

The Two Cities:
Medieval Europe,
1050–1320

Malcolm Barber

'Meets every conceivable need and effectively renders redundant all earlier textbooks on the high Middle Ages ... inshort, the book is excellent in every respect.' – *History Today*

First published to wide critical acclaim in 1992, *The Two Cities* has become an essential text for students of medieval history. For the second edition, the author has thoroughly revised each chapter, bringing the material up to date and taking the historiography of the past decade into account.

The Two Cities covers a colourful period from the schism between the eastern and western churches to the death of Dante. It encompasses the Crusades, the expansionist force of the Normans, major developments in the way kings, emperors and Popes exercised their powers, a great flourishing of art and architecture and the foundation of the very first universities. Running through it is the defining characteristic of the high Middle Ages – the delicate relationship between the spiritual and secular worlds, the two 'cities' of the title.

This survey provides all the facts and background information that students need, and is defined into straightforward thematic chapters. It makes extensive use of primary sources, and makes new trends in research accessible to students. Its fresh approach gives students the most rounded, lively and integrated view of the high Middle Ages available.

ISBN10: 0–415–17414–7 (hbk)
ISBN10: 0–415–74115–5 (pbk)

ISBN13: 978–0–415–17414–5 (hbk)
ISBN13: 978–0–415–74115–2 (pbk)

Available at all good bookshops
For ordering and further information please visit
www.routledge.com

Routledge History

The Atlas of Medieval Europe
Edited by David Ditchburn
and Angus Mackay

'I recommend the atlas as the most painless and reliable introduction available to medieval history.' – *Jonathan Riley-Smith, University of Cambridge*

'This is an original and engaging atlas of medieval history.' – *Thomas Bisson, Harvard University*

Covering the period from the fall of the Roman Empire through to the beginnings of the Renaissance, this is an indispensable volume which brings the complex and colourful history of the Middle Ages to life.

Key features:

- Geographical coverage extends to the broadest definition of Europe from the Atlantic coast to the Russian steppes
- Each map approaches a separate issue or series of events in Medieval history, whilst a commentary locates it in its broader context
- As a body, the maps provide a vivid representation of the development of nations, peoples and social structures.

With over 140 maps, expert commentaries and an extensive bibliography, this is the essential reference for those who are striving to understand the fundamental issues of this period.

ISBN10: 0–415–01923–0 (hbk)
ISBN10: 0–415–12231–7 (pbk)

ISBN13: 978–0–415–01923–1 (hbk)
ISBN13: 978–0–415–12231–3 (pbk)

Available at all good bookshops
For ordering and further information please visit
www.routledge.com

Routledge History

The Mystic Mind: The Psychology of
Medieval Mystics and Ascetics
Jerome Kroll and Bernard Bachrach

'A truly pioneering, unique study that should attract considerable attention among specialists and a wide range of general readers.' – *Ursula King, University of Bristol and SOAS, University of London*

'This study presents an original and stimulating analysis of the nature and experience of medieval mysticism.' – *Katherine Lewis, University of Huddersfield*

The Mystic Mind is the result of a fascinating collaboration between a medieval historian and a professor of psychiatry, applying modern biological and psychological research findings to the lives of medieval mystics and ascetics. This illuminating study examines the relationship between medieval mystical experiences, and the religious practices of mortification of the body. Laceration of the flesh, sleep deprivation and extreme starvation, while undoubtedly related to cultural and religious motivations, directly produced dramatic effects upon the body and brain functioning of the heroic ascetics, that in turn brought about altered states of consciousness. Applying modern understandings of physiology, the authors demonstrate how heroic asceticism could be used to obtain a desired mystical state, as well as examining and disputing much contemporary writing about the political and gender motivation in the medieval quest for closeness with God.

Drawing upon a database of 1,462 medieval holy persons as well as in-depth studies of individual saints, *The Mystic Mind* is essential reading for all those with an interest in medieval religion or the effects of self-injurous behaviour on the mind.

ISBN10: 0–415–34050–0 (hbk)
SBN10: 0–415–34051–9 (pbk)

ISBN13: 978–0–415–34050–2 (hbk)
ISBN13: 978–0–415–34051–9 (pbk)

Available at all good bookshops
For ordering and further information please visit
www.routledge.com

The Pocket Book of
KINDNESS

The Pocket Book of
KINDNESS

Inspirational thoughts on goodness and generosity

ARCTURUS

ARCTURUS

This edition published in 2018 by Arcturus Publishing Limited
26/27 Bickels Yard, 151–153 Bermondsey Street,
London SE1 3HA

ISBN: 978-1-78828-746-3
AD006310UK

Printed in China

Contents

Introduction

Lady Macbeth described it as "milk"- a pallid, insipid sentiment that weakens her husband's resolve. Franklin D. Roosevelt disagreed: "Human kindness has never weakened the stamina or softened the fibre of a free people", he proclaimed.

Yet, amid the blizzard of accounts of cruelty that blows out daily from our televisions and radios, rarely are we granted the respite of a tale of kindness to lighten the heart. Notable exceptions stand out: Mother Teresa, Florence Nightingale, Androcles, Winnie the Pooh... but they are few and far between. It seems that cruelty is more compelling.

The truth is that simple acts of kindness happen all the time. It is fundamental to our nature to be kind, generous, benevolent, altruistic, philanthropic, empathetic, sympathetic and caring. Kindness is, indeed, a sign of strength, for it comes from a position of confidence and is given without fear of the consequences. As Mahatma Gandhi said, "The simplest acts of kindness are by far more powerful than a thousand heads bowing in prayer."

The word kindness is linked to kin, kindred and the German *kinder*, meaning children. It implies oneness, unity and nurture - the sense that we are all in this together. As this book reveals, amid all the cruelty, kindness is never far from the minds of people, nor from their deeds.

WHAT IS KINDNESS?

Kindness is
the language which the
deaf can hear and the
blind can see.

Mark Twain

Kindness is the sunshine in which virtue grows.

Robert Green Ingersoll

Sweet mercy is nobility's true badge.

William Shakespeare

Amnesty is as good for those who give it as for those who receive it. It has the admirable quality of bestowing mercy on both sides.

Victor Hugo

Pity may represent little more than the
impersonal concern which prompts the
mailing of a check, but true sympathy
is the personal concern which demands
the giving of one's soul.

Martin Luther King, Jr.

Kindness is ever the begetter of kindness.

Sophocles

Kindness is loving people more than they deserve.

Joseph Joubert

Life is mostly froth and bubble,
Two things stand like stone
Kindness in another's trouble,
Courage in your own.

Adam Lindsay Gordon

A kind heart is a
fountain of gladness,
making everything
in its vicinity freshen
into smiles.

Washington Irving

16

A warm smile is the universal language of kindness.

William Arthur Ward

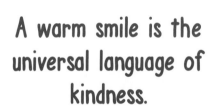

17

Any mind that is capable
of real sorrow is capable
of good.

Harriet Beecher Stowe

Care is a state in
which something does
matter; it is the source
of human tenderness.

Rollo May

Character is made of duty
and love and sympathy,
and, above all, of living
and working for others.

Robert Green Ingersoll

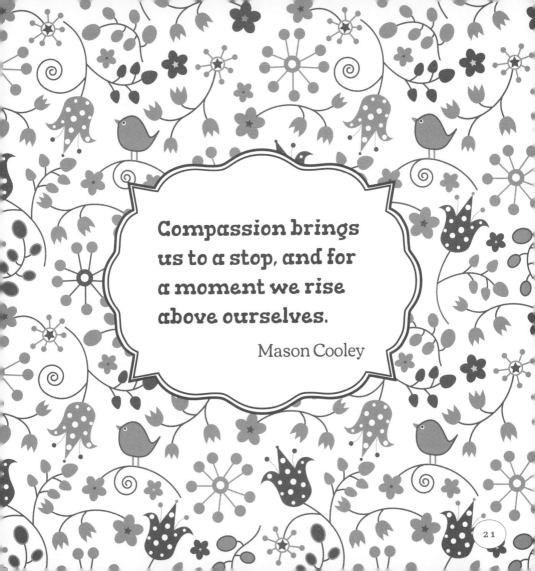

Compassion brings us to a stop, and for a moment we rise above ourselves.

Mason Cooley

21

Compassion is a call,
a demand of nature,
to relieve the unhappy as
hunger is a natural call
for food.

Joseph Butler

Compassion is not weakness, and concern for the unfortunate is not socialism.

Hubert H. Humphrey

Compassion is sometimes the fatal capacity for feeling what it is like to live inside somebody else's skin. It is the knowledge that there can never really be any peace and joy for me until there is peace and joy finally for you too.

Frederick Buechner

Compassion is the antitoxin of the soul: where there is compassion even the most poisonous impulses remain relatively harmless.

Eric Hoffer

Compassion is the basis of morality.

Arthur Schopenhauer

Empathy is the faculty to resonate with the feelings of others. When we meet someone who is joyful, we smile. When we witness someone in pain, we suffer in resonance with his or her suffering.

Matthieu Ricard

For me, forgiveness and compassion are always linked: how do we hold people accountable for wrongdoing and yet at the same time remain in touch with their humanity enough to believe in their capacity to be transformed?

bell hooks

Generosity during life is a very different thing from generosity in the hour of death; one proceeds from genuine liberality and benevolence, the other from pride or fear.

Horace Mann

Generosity is giving more than you can, and pride is taking less than you need.

Kahlil Gibran

Generosity is not giving me that which I need more than you do, but it is giving me that which you need more than I do.

Kahlil Gibran

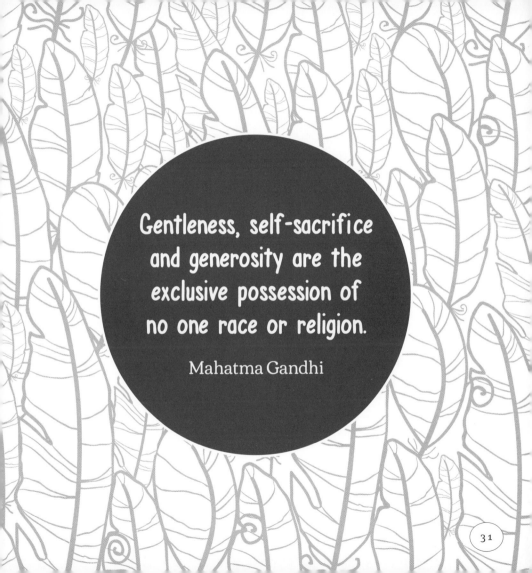

Gentleness, self-sacrifice
and generosity are the
exclusive possession of
no one race or religion.

Mahatma Gandhi

Harshness and
unkindness are relative.
The appearance of them
may be the fruits of the
greatest kindness.

William Godwin

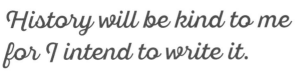

History will be kind to me for I intend to write it.

Winston Churchill

Human it is to have compassion on the unhappy.

Giovanni Boccaccio

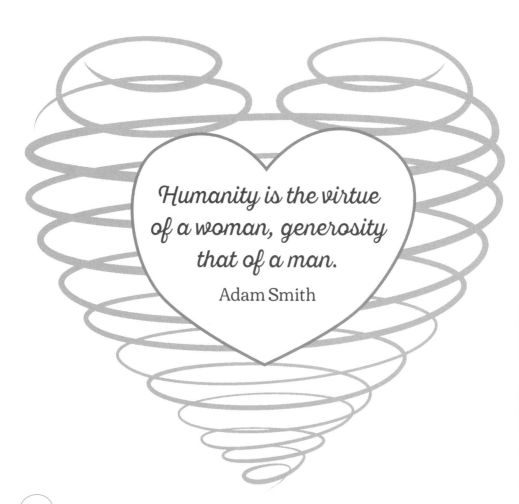

Humanity is the virtue of a woman, generosity that of a man.

Adam Smith

I slept and I dreamed that life is all joy.
I woke and I saw that life is all service. I
served and I saw that service is joy.

Kahlil Gibran

It is kindness
to immediately
refuse what you
intend to deny.

Publilius Syrus

Kindness in ourselves
is the honey that blunts the
sting of unkindness
in another.

Walter Savage Landor

Kindness is a passport
that opens doors and fashions
friends. It softens hearts and
molds relationships that
can last lifetimes.

Joseph B. Wirthlin

Kindness is an everyday byproduct of all the great virtues.

Krista Tippett

Kindness is not about instant gratification. More often, it's akin to a low-risk investment that appreciates steadily over time.

Josh Radnor

Kindness is the essence of greatness and the fundamental characteristic of the noblest men and women I have known.

Joseph B. Wirthlin

41

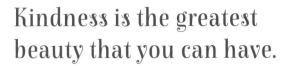

Kindness is the greatest beauty that you can have.

Andie MacDowell

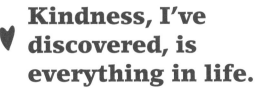

Kindness, I've discovered, is everything in life.

Isaac Bashevis Singer

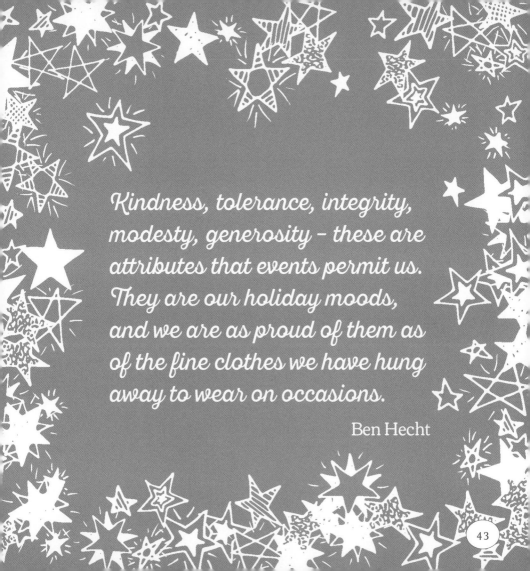

Kindness, tolerance, integrity, modesty, generosity – these are attributes that events permit us. They are our holiday moods, and we are as proud of them as of the fine clothes we have hung away to wear on occasions.

Ben Hecht

43

One of the toughest things for leaders to master is kindness. Kindness shares credit and offers enthusiastic praise for others' work. It's a balancing act between being genuinely kind and not looking weak.

Travis Bradberry

Tenderness is the name for a lover's most exquisite sensation; protection is implied in his most generous and heart-thrilling impulse.

William Godwin

That's what I consider true generosity: You give your all, and yet you always feel as if it costs you nothing.

Simone de Beauvoir

The beauty of a woman
is not in a facial mode
but the true beauty in a
woman is reflected in her soul.
It is the caring that she lovingly
gives the passion that she
shows. The beauty of a
woman grows with the
passing years.

Audrey Hepburn

The deed is everything,
the glory naught.

Johann Wolfgang
von Goethe

The dew of
compassion
is a tear.

Lord Byron

The greatness of a man is measured by the way he treats the little man. Compassion for the weak is a sign of greatness.

Myles Munroe

The heart benevolent
and kind
The most resembles
God.
Robert Burns

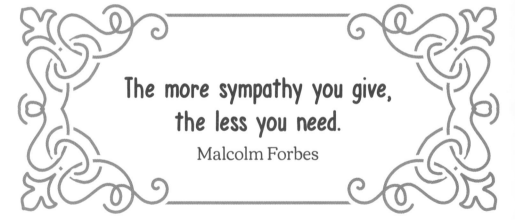

The more sympathy you give,
the less you need.

Malcolm Forbes

The true humanist maintains a just balance between sympathy and selection.

Irving Babbitt

There is an organic affinity
between joyousness and
tenderness, and their
companionship in the
saintly life need in no way
occasion surprise.

William James

There never was any heart
truly great and generous,
that was not also tender
and compassionate.

Robert Frost

'Tis the most tender part of love, each other to forgive.

John Sheffield

*To desire and expect
nothing for oneself
and to have profound
sympathy for others is
genuine holiness.*

Ivan Turgenev

To feel much for others and little for ourselves; to restrain our selfishness and exercise our benevolent affections, constitute the perfection of human nature.

Adam Smith

To remove ignorance
is an important branch
of benevolence.

Ann Plato

True compassion means not only feeling another's pain but also being moved to help relieve it.

Daniel Goleman

What does love look like? It has the hands to help others. It has the feet to hasten to the poor and needy. It has eyes to see misery and want. It has the ears to hear the sighs and sorrows of men. That is what love looks like.

Saint Augustine

When autumn darkness falls, what we will remember are the small acts of kindness: a cake, a hug, an invitation to talk, and every single rose. These are all expressions of a nation coming together and caring about its people.

Jens Stoltenberg

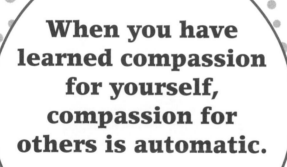

When you have learned compassion for yourself, compassion for others is automatic.

Henepola Gunaratana

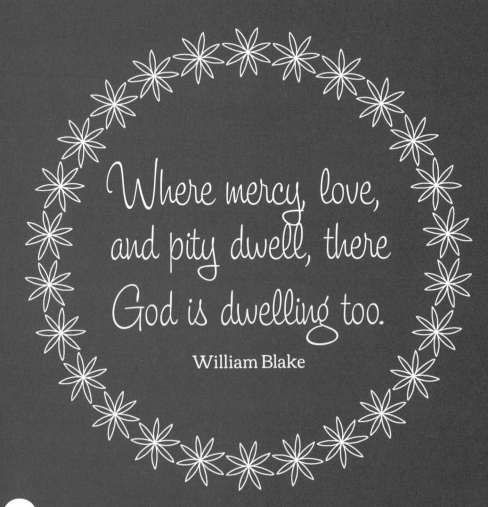

Where mercy, love,
and pity dwell, there
God is dwelling too.

William Blake

Wisdom, compassion and courage are the three universally recognised moral qualities of men.

Confucius

You may call God love, you may call
God goodness. But the best name for
God is compassion.

Meister Eckhart

THE VALUE OF KINDNESS

The simplest
acts of kindness
are by far more
powerful than a
thousand heads
bowing in prayer.

Mahatma Gandhi

A tree is known by its fruit; a man by his deeds. A good deed is never lost; he who sows courtesy reaps friendship, and he who plants kindness gathers love.

Saint Basil

Compassion will cure more sins than condemnation.

Henry Ward Beecher

The best portion of a good man's life, his little, nameless, unremembered acts of kindness and of love.

William Wordsworth

I have always found that mercy bears richer fruits than strict justice.

Abraham Lincoln

I have found that among its other benefits, giving liberates the soul of the giver.

Maya Angelou

69

A laugh, to be joyous, must flow from a joyous heart, for without kindness, there can be no true joy.

Thomas Carlyle

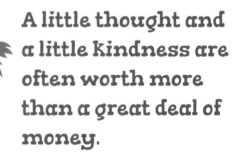

A little thought and a little kindness are often worth more than a great deal of money.

John Ruskin

And as I've gotten older, I've had more of a tendency to look for people who live by kindness, tolerance, compassion, a gentler way of looking at things.

Martin Scorsese

At the end of the day, love and compassion will win.

Terry Waite

Compassion alone stands apart from the continuous traffic between good and evil proceeding within us.

Eric Hoffer

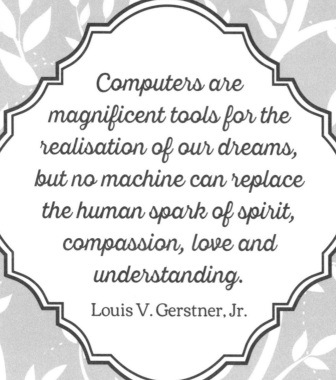

Computers are magnificent tools for the realisation of our dreams, but no machine can replace the human spark of spirit, compassion, love and understanding.

Louis V. Gerstner, Jr.

Constant kindness can accomplish much. As the sun makes ice melt, kindness causes misunderstanding, mistrust, and hostility to evaporate.

Albert Schweitzer

Feeling compassion for ourselves in no way releases us from responsibility for our actions. Rather, it releases us from the self-hatred that prevents us from responding to our life with clarity and balance.

Tara Brach

For it is in giving
that we receive.

Francis of Assisi

**General benevolence,
but not general
friendship, made a
man what he ought
to be.**

Jane Austen

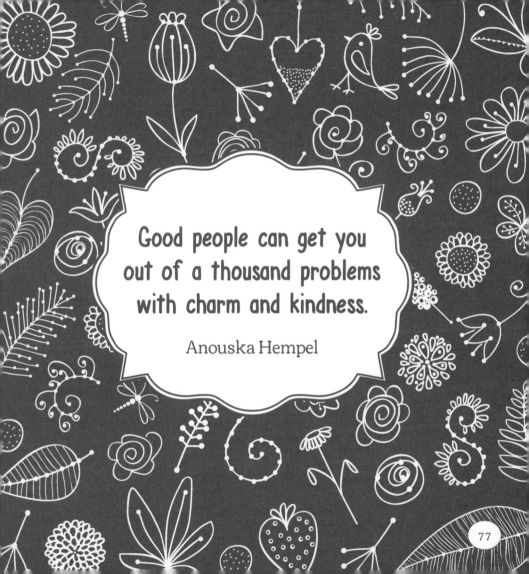

Good people can get you
out of a thousand problems
with charm and kindness.

Anouska Hempel

Here are the values that I stand for: honesty, equality, kindness, compassion, treating people the way you want to be treated and helping those in need. To me, those are traditional values.

Ellen DeGeneres

Honesty is the quality I value most in a friend. Not bluntness, but honesty with compassion.

Brooke Shields

I don't believe that directors need to essentially manipulate actors into doing things. You can suffer for your art, and you can make your own self suffer for your art. You don't need anyone else to do it for you. I work best when there's a safety trampoline of kindness.

Ruth Negga

I feel no need for any other faith than my faith in the kindness of human beings. I am so absorbed in the wonder of earth and the life upon it that I cannot think of heaven and angels.

Pearl S. Buck

I have understood that the most important things are tenderness and kindness. I can't do without them.

Brigitte Bardot

I learned far too
late in life that a long list
of letters after someone's
name is no guarantee of
compassion, kindness,
humour, all the far more
relevant stuff.

Bill Nighy

If a man sets his heart on benevolence he will be free from evil.

Confucius

If what must be given is given willingly the kindness is doubled.

Publilius Syrus

In giving freedom to the slave, we assure freedom to the free – honorable alike in that we give and what we preserve. We shall nobly save, or meanly lose, the last best hope of earth.

Abraham Lincoln

It's not how much we give but how much love we put into giving.

Mother Teresa

Kind words do not cost much.
Yet they accomplish much.

Blaise Pascal

Kindness and faithfulness keep a king safe, through kindness his throne is made secure.

King Solomon

Kindness and politeness are not overrated at all. They're underused.

Tommy Lee Jones

86

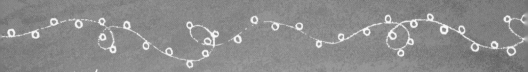

Kindness can become its own motive. We are made kind by being kind.

Eric Hoffer

Kindness eases everything almost as much as money does.

Mason Cooley

Kindness in women, not their beauteous looks, shall win my love.

Washington Irving

Kindness in words creates confidence. Kindness in thinking creates profoundness. Kindness in giving creates love.

Lao Tzu

Kindness is always fashionable, and always welcome.

Amelia Barr

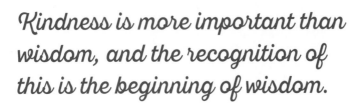

Kindness is more important than wisdom, and the recognition of this is the beginning of wisdom.

Theodore Isaac Rubin

Kindness is really important to me in finding my own prince – so are patience and a sense of humor. Without those qualities he's no Prince Charming!

Anne Hathaway

**Kindness makes a fellow
feel good whether it's being
done to him or by him.**

Frank A. Clark

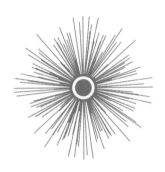

Life is made up, not of great sacrifices or duties, but of little things, in which smiles and kindness, and small obligations given habitually, are what preserve the heart and secure comfort.

Humphry Davy

Love and compassion are necessities, not luxuries. Without them humanity cannot survive.

Dalai Lama

Love and kindness
are never wasted. They
always make a difference.
They bless the one who
receives them, and they
bless you, the giver.

Barbara De Angelis

Many men fail because they do not see the importance of being kind and courteous to the men under them. Kindness to everybody always pays for itself. And, besides, it is a pleasure to be kind.

Charles M. Schwab

Most of the good things that have happened to me, happened by accident when I was trying to help someone else.

Frank A. Clark

No act of kindness, no matter how small, is ever wasted.

Aesop

No one has ever become poor by giving.

Anne Frank

No one has yet realized the wealth of sympathy, the kindness and generosity hidden in the soul of a child. The effort of every true education should be to unlock that treasure.

Emma Goldman

**No one is useless
in this world
who lightens
the burdens of
another.**

Charles Dickens

None is so near the gods as he who
shows kindness.

Lucius Seneca

Nothing can make
injustice just but mercy.

Robert Frost

**One must be
poor to know the
luxury of giving.**

George Eliot

Our human compassion binds us the one to the other – not in pity or patronizingly, but as human beings who have learnt how to turn our common suffering into hope for the future.

Nelson Mandela

Our lack of forgiveness makes us hate, and our lack of compassion makes us hard-hearted. Pride in our hearts makes us resentful and keeps our memory in a constant whirlwind of passion and self-pity.

Mother Angelica

Paradise was made for tender hearts; hell, for loveless hearts.

Voltaire

Remember there's no such thing as a small act of kindness. Every act creates a ripple with no logical end.

Scott Adams

Remember this. Hold on to this. This is the only perfection there is, the perfection of helping others. This is the only thing we can do that has any lasting meaning. This is why we're here. To make each other feel safe.

Andre Agassi

Rich gifts wax poor when
givers prove unkind.

William Shakespeare

The drying up a single
tear has more of
honest fame than
shedding seas of gore.

Lord Byron

The end result of kindness is that it draws people to you.

Anita Roddick

The everyday kindness of the back roads more than makes up for the acts of greed in the headlines.

Charles Kuralt

The Gross National Product measures neither our wit nor our courage, neither our wisdom nor our learning, neither our compassion nor our devotion to our country. It measures everything, in short, except that which makes life worthwhile, and it can tell us everything about America – except whether we are proud to be Americans.

Robert Kennedy

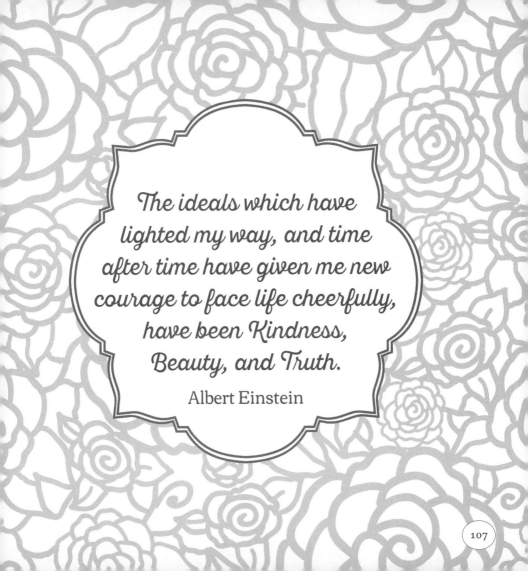

The ideals which have lighted my way, and time after time have given me new courage to face life cheerfully, have been Kindness, Beauty, and Truth.

Albert Einstein

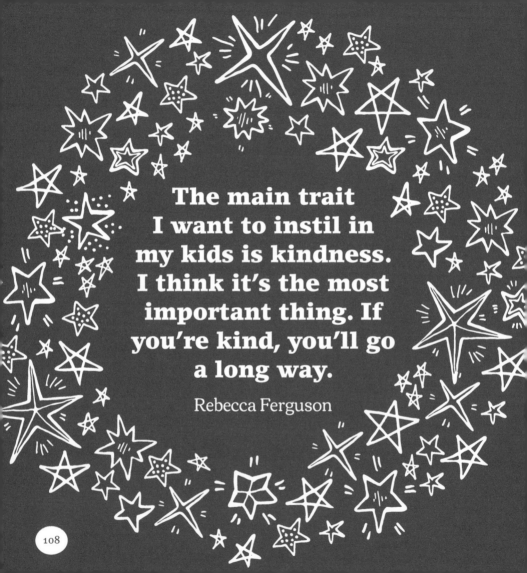

The main trait
I want to instil in
my kids is kindness.
I think it's the most
important thing. If
you're kind, you'll go
a long way.

Rebecca Ferguson

The man who practises unselfishness, who is genuinely interested in the welfare of others, who feels it a privilege to have the power to do a fellow-creature a kindness – even though polished manners and a gracious presence may be absent – will be an elevating influence wherever he goes.

Orison Swett Marden

The manner of giving is worth more than the gift.

Pierre Corneille

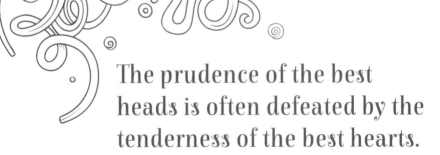

The prudence of the best
heads is often defeated by the
tenderness of the best hearts.

Henry Fielding

The purpose of life is not to be happy. It is to be useful, to be honorable, to be compassionate, to have it make some difference that you have lived and lived well.

Ralph Waldo Emerson

The qualities I most admire in women are confidence and kindness.

Oscar de la Renta

The words of kindness are more healing to a drooping heart than balm or honey.

Sarah Fielding

There are no greater treasures than the highest human qualities such as compassion, courage and hope. Not even tragic accident or disaster can destroy such treasures of the heart.

Daisaku Ikeda

113

There is no charm equal to tenderness of heart.

Jane Austen

There is no exercise better for the heart than reaching down and lifting people up.

John Holmes

There's nothing so kingly as kindness, and nothing so royal as truth.

Alice Cary

Those who are happiest are those who do the most for others

Booker T. Washington

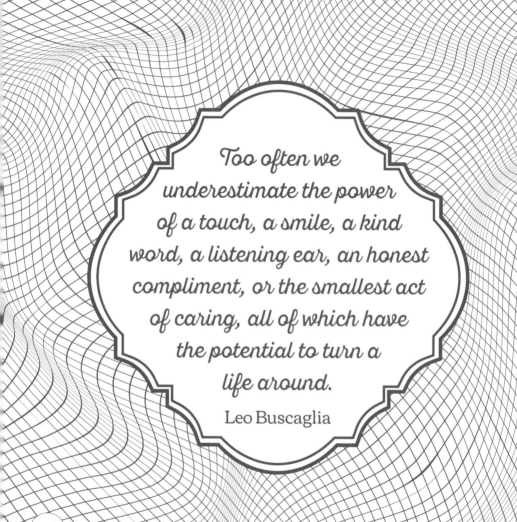

Too often we underestimate the power of a touch, a smile, a kind word, a listening ear, an honest compliment, or the smallest act of caring, all of which have the potential to turn a life around.

Leo Buscaglia

True beauty is born through our actions and aspirations and in the kindness we offer to others.

Alek Wek

True popularity comes from acts of kindness rather than acts of stupidity.

Bo Bennett

We are constituted so that simple acts of kindness, such as giving to charity or expressing gratitude, have a positive effect on our long-term moods. The key to the happy life, it seems, is the good life: a life with sustained relationships, challenging work, and connections to community.

Paul Bloom

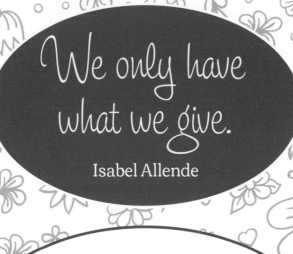

We only have
what we give.

Isabel Allende

What a liberating thing to realize that our problems are probably our richest sources for rising to the ultimate virtue of compassion.

Krista Tippett

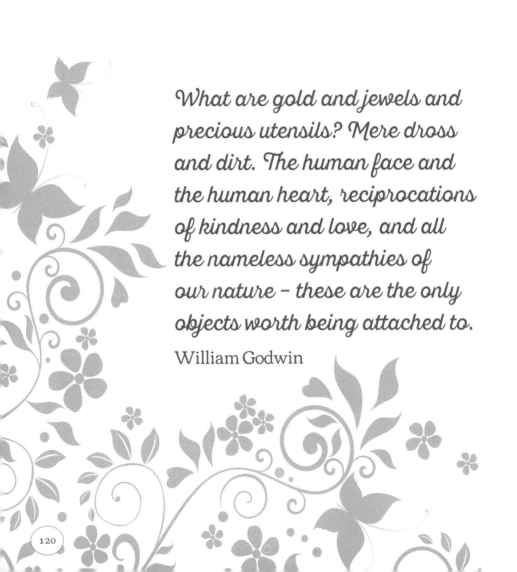

What are gold and jewels and precious utensils? Mere dross and dirt. The human face and the human heart, reciprocations of kindness and love, and all the nameless sympathies of our nature – these are the only objects worth being attached to.

William Godwin

What wisdom can you find that is greater than kindness?

Jean-Jacques Rousseau

Whatever possession we gain by our sword cannot be sure or lasting, but the love gained by kindness and moderation is certain and durable.

Alexander the Great

When death, the great reconciler, has come, it is never our tenderness that we repent of, but our severity.

George Eliot

When I was young, I admired clever people. Now that I am old, I admire kind people.

Abraham Joshua Heschel

When you carry out acts of kindness you get a wonderful feeling inside. It is as though something inside your body responds and says, yes, this is how I ought to feel.

Harold Kushner

When you treat yourself with the kindness and high regard that you would give to one of your spiritual heroes, your body becomes the epicenter of quiet joy rather than a battlefield for the ego.

Debbie Ford

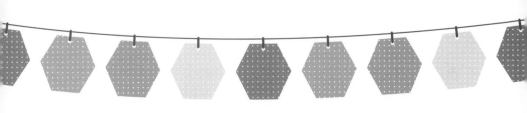

Where there is no human connection, there is no compassion. Without compassion, then community, commitment, loving-kindness, human understanding, and peace all shrivel. Individuals become isolated, the isolated turn cruel, and the tragic hovers in the forms of domestic and civil violence. Art and literature are antidotes to that.

Susan Vreeland

Wise sayings often fall on barren ground; but a kind word is never thrown away.

Sir Arthur Helps

Without tenderness, a man is uninteresting.

Marlene Dietrich

You can accomplish by kindness
what you cannot by force.

Publilius Syrus

**You can be rich in spirit,
kindness, love and all
those things that you
can't put a dollar sign on.**

Dolly Parton

127

You either believe that people respond to authority, or that they respond to kindness and inclusion. I'm obviously in the latter camp. I think that people respond better to reward than punishment.

Brian Eno

KINDNESS
AS SOCIAL
RESPONSIBILITY

It is in our faults
and failings, not in our
virtues, that we touch each
other, and find sympathy.
It is in our follies that
we are one.

Jerome K. Jerome

Kindness is in our power, even when fondness is not.

Samuel Johnson

Life's persistent and most urgent question is 'What are you doing for others?'

Martin Luther King, Jr.

Man's inhumanity to man makes countless thousands mourn!

Robert Burns

A little anger is a good thing if it isn't on your own behalf, if it's for others deserving of your anger, your empathy.

David Simon

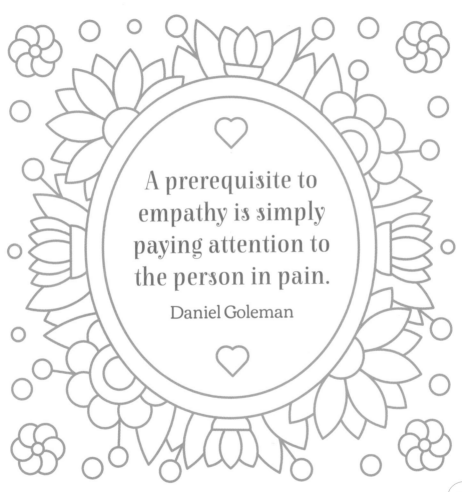

A prerequisite to empathy is simply paying attention to the person in pain.

Daniel Goleman

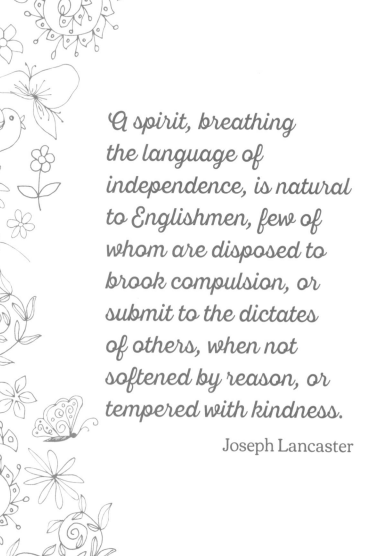

*A spirit, breathing
the language of
independence, is natural
to Englishmen, few of
whom are disposed to
brook compulsion, or
submit to the dictates
of others, when not
softened by reason, or
tempered with kindness.*

Joseph Lancaster

As we grow in our consciousness, there will be more compassion and more love, and then the barriers between people, between religions, between nations will begin to fall.

Ram Dass

Be kind to unkind people – they need it the most.

Ashleigh Brilliant

Cowards are cruel, but the brave love mercy and delight to save.

John Gay

Day after day, ordinary people become heroes through extraordinary and selfless actions to help their neighbours.

Sylvia Mathews Burwell

Desperation, weakness, vulnerability – these things will always be exploited. You need to protect the weak, ring-fence them, with something far stronger than empathy.

Zadie Smith

**Difficult as it is really
to listen to someone in affliction,
it is just as difficult for him
to know that compassion is
listening to him.**

Simone Weil

Do not ask the name of the person who asks you for a bed for the night. He whose name is a burden to him needs shelter more than anyone.

Victor Hugo

Each time a man stands up for an ideal, or acts to improve the lot of others, or strikes out against injustice, he sends forth a tiny ripple of hope, and crossing each other from a million different centers of energy and daring, those ripples build a current that can sweep down the mightiest walls of oppression and resistance.

Robert Kennedy

Every man must decide
whether he will walk in the
light of creative altruism
or in the darkness of
destructive selfishness.

Martin Luther King, Jr.

Give what you have. To someone, it may be better than you dare to think.

Henry Wadsworth Longfellow

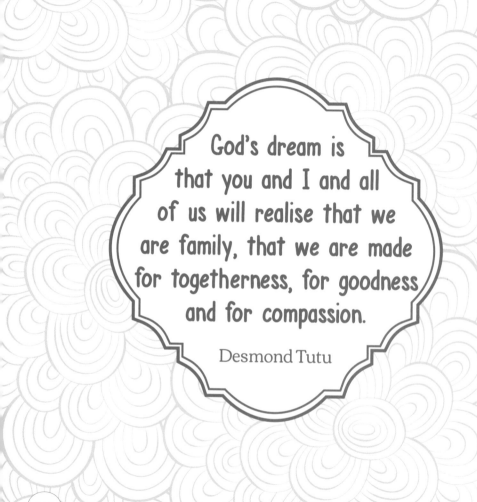

God's dream is
that you and I and all
of us will realise that we
are family, that we are made
for togetherness, for goodness
and for compassion.

Desmond Tutu

Having levelled my palace, don't erect a
hovel and complacently admire your own
charity in giving me that for a home.

Emily Brontë

He has a right to criticize,
who has a heart to help.

Abraham Lincoln

How far you go in life depends on your being tender with the young, compassionate with the aged, sympathetic with the striving and tolerant of the weak and strong. Because someday in your life you will have been all of these.

George Washington Carver

Human kindness has never weakened the stamina or softened the fibre of a free people. A nation does not have to be cruel to be tough.

Franklin D. Roosevelt

Human nature is complex. Even if we do have inclinations toward violence, we also have inclination to empathy, to cooperation, to self-control.

Steven Pinker

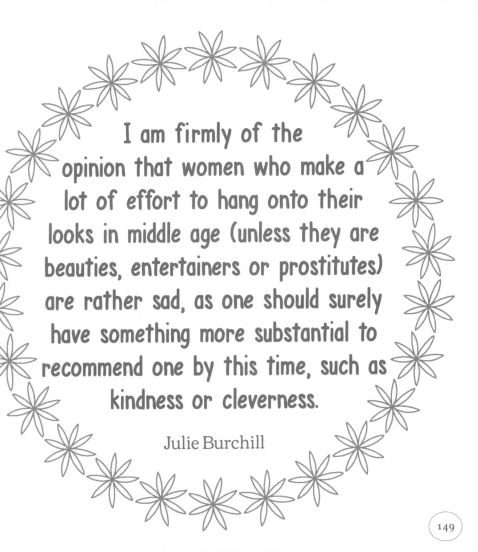

I am firmly of the
opinion that women who make a
lot of effort to hang onto their
looks in middle age (unless they are
beauties, entertainers or prostitutes)
are rather sad, as one should surely
have something more substantial to
recommend one by this time, such as
kindness or cleverness.

Julie Burchill

I have always depended on the kindness of strangers.

Tennessee Williams

I have no idea
what's awaiting me, or
what will happen when this all
ends. For the moment I know this:
there are sick people and they
need curing.

Albert Camus

I like kindness. Who doesn't?
Life is definitely too short for
self-centered, abusive people.

Ellen Greene

*I think one of the best words
in the English language is 'compassion.'
I think it holds everything. It holds love,
it holds care... and if everybody just did
something. We all make a difference.*

Michael Crawford

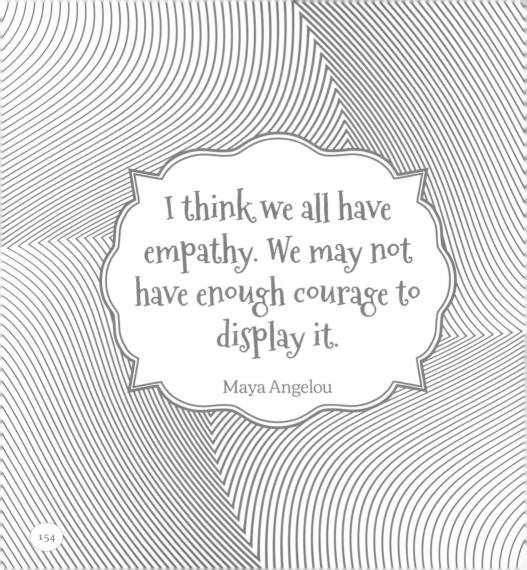

I think we all have empathy. We may not have enough courage to display it.

Maya Angelou

I'm doing everything that I can, working with experts, really studying the statistics to figure out a way we can make it cool or normal to be kind and loving.

Lady Gaga

If our wondrous kindness
is evidence for God, is
our capacity for great evil
proof of the Devil?

Paul Bloom

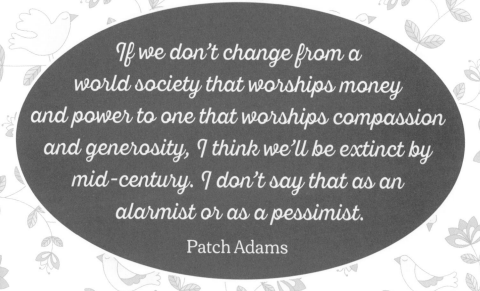

If we don't change from a world society that worships money and power to one that worships compassion and generosity, I think we'll be extinct by mid-century. I don't say that as an alarmist or as a pessimist.

Patch Adams

If you list the qualities that we consider feminine, they are patience, understanding, empathy, supportiveness, a desire to nurture. Our culture tells us those are feminine traits, but they're really just human.

Sydney Pollack

In the face of unspeakable evil, our whole nation must respond with countless acts of kindness, warmth and generosity.

Steve Scalise

It takes generosity to discover the whole through others. If you realize you are only a violin, you can open yourself up to the world by playing your role in the concert.

Jacques Yves Cousteau

It's not our job to play judge and jury, to determine who is worthy of our kindness and who is not. We just need to be kind, unconditionally and without ulterior motive, even – or rather, especially – when we'd prefer not to be.

Josh Radnor

Kindly words do not enter so deeply into men as a reputation for kindness.

Mencius

Kindness has converted more sinners than zeal, eloquence or learning.

Frederick William Faber

162

Never respect men merely for their riches, but rather for their philanthropy; we do not value the sun for its height, but for its use.

Gamaliel Bailey

163

No deep and strong feeling, such as we may come across here and there in the world, is unmixed with compassion. The more we love, the more the object of our love seems to us to be a victim.

Boris Pasternak

Not for ourselves alone are we born.

Marcus Tullius Cicero

Nothing graces the Christian soul so much as mercy; mercy as shown chiefly towards the poor, that thou mayest treat them as sharers in common with thee in the produce of nature, which brings forth the fruits of the earth for use to all.

Saint Ambrose

*Obviously, you would give
your life for your children, or give
them the last biscuit on the plate. But
to me, the trick in life is to take that sense
of generosity between kin, make it apply
to the extended family and to your
neighbour, your village
and beyond.*

Tom Stoppard

Oh! if the good hearts had the fat purses, how much better everything would go!

Victor Hugo

One who knows how to show and to accept kindness will be a friend better than any possession.

Sophocles

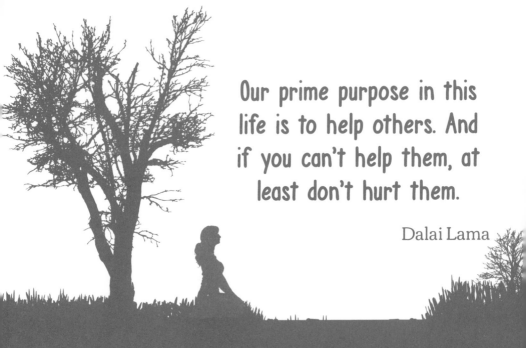

Our prime purpose in this life is to help others. And if you can't help them, at least don't hurt them.

Dalai Lama

Remember that the happiest people are not those getting more, but those giving more.

H. Jackson Brown, Jr.

Somewhere near you,
somebody right now
is trying to help the
indigent and poor –
providing food, shelter,
clothing or simple
kindness.

Tony Snow

Sustainability, ensuring the future of life on Earth, is an infinite game, the endless expression of generosity on behalf of all.

Paul Hawken

Teetotallers lack the
sympathy and generosity
of men that drink.

W. H. Davies

The bravest are the
most tender; the loving
are the daring.

Bayard Taylor

The delicate balance of mentoring someone is not creating them in your own image, but giving them the opportunity to create themselves.

Steven Spielberg

The fact that I might be altruistic isn't because I have a gene for altruism; the fact that I do something for my children at some cost to myself comes from a history that has operated on me.

B. F. Skinner

173

The good in this world far outweighs the evil. Our common humanity transcends our differences, and our most effective response to terror is compassion, it's unity, and it's love.

Loretta Lynch

174

The proper aim of giving is to put the recipient in a state where he no longer needs our gifts

C. S. Lewis

The test of a civilisation is in the way that it cares for its helpless members.

Pearl S. Buck

The Trail of Tears should teach all of us the importance of respect for others who are different from ourselves and compassion for those who have difficulties.

Joseph Bruchac

The way I stand up to bullies is with kindness and love. Because I think that's what they really need. They're misunderstood and probably really upset themselves.

Chrissy Metz

The youngest children have a great capacity for empathy and altruism. There's a recent study that shows even 14-month-olds will climb across a bunch of cushions and go across a room to give you a pen if you drop one.

Alison Gopnik

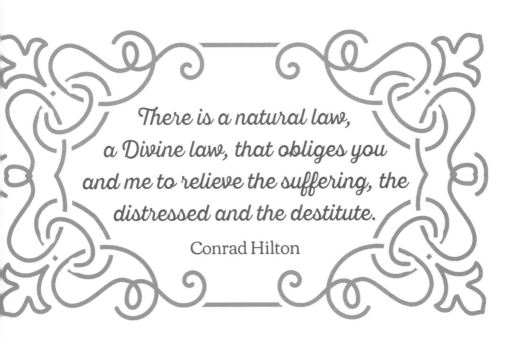

There is a natural law,
a Divine law, that obliges you
and me to relieve the suffering, the
distressed and the destitute.

Conrad Hilton

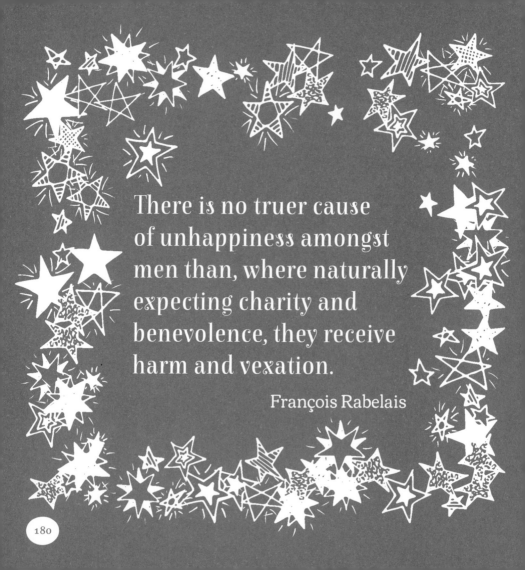

There is no truer cause
of unhappiness amongst
men than, where naturally
expecting charity and
benevolence, they receive
harm and vexation.

François Rabelais

There's no dearth of kindness In the world of ours; Only in our blindness We gather thorns for flowers.

T. G. Massey

'Tis not enough to help the feeble up but to support him after.

William Shakespeare

181

To pity distress
is but human;
to relieve it is
Godlike.

Horace Mann

Today we are afraid of simple words
like goodness and mercy and kindness.
We don't believe in the good old words
because we don't believe in good old values
anymore. And that's why the world is sick.

Lin Yutang

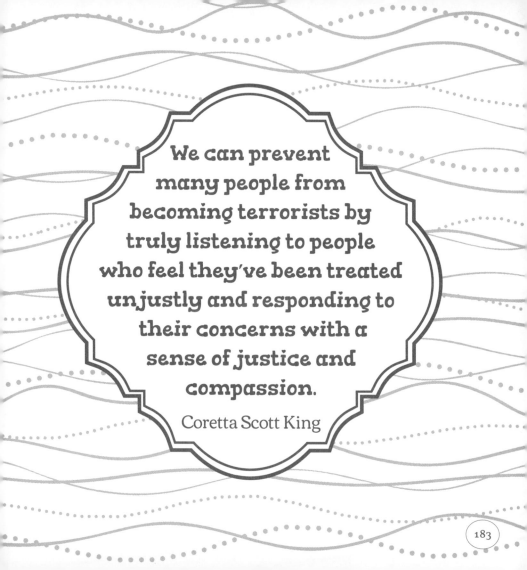

We can prevent many people from becoming terrorists by truly listening to people who feel they've been treated unjustly and responding to their concerns with a sense of justice and compassion.

Coretta Scott King

183

We cannot be kind to each other here for even an hour. We whisper, and hint, and chuckle and grin at our brother's shame; however you take it we men are a little breed.

Alfred Lord Tennyson

We who lived in concentration camps can remember the men who walked through the huts comforting others, giving away their last piece of bread.

Viktor E. Frankl

We're all generous, but with different things, like time, money, talent – criticism.

Frank A. Clark

Wealth is not to feed our egos but to feed the hungry and to help people help themselves.

Andrew Carnegie

What I hope to promote is the idea that we all need each other and that the greatest happiness in life is not how much we have but how much we give. That's a wealth that's priceless.

Herbie Hancock

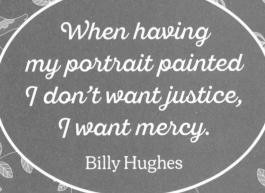

When having
my portrait painted
I don't want justice,
I want mercy.

Billy Hughes

When we're looking for compassion, we need someone who is deeply rooted, is able to bend and, most of all, embraces us for our strengths and struggles.

Brene Brown

When will our consciences grow so tender that we will act to prevent human misery rather than avenge it?

Eleanor Roosevelt

When you are kind to someone in trouble, you hope they'll remember and be kind to someone else. And it'll become like a wildfire.

Whoopi Goldberg

Whether one believes in a religion or not, and whether one believes in rebirth or not, there isn't anyone who doesn't appreciate kindness and compassion.

Dalai Lama

You often say; I would give, but only
to the deserving,

The trees in your orchard say not so,
nor the flocks in your pasture.

Surely he who is worthy to receive his
days and nights is worthy of all else
from you.

Kahlil Gibran

You have not lived today until you have done something for someone who can never repay you.

John Bunyan

We are all here on earth to help others; what on earth the others are here for I don't know.

W. H. Auden

TOUGH LOVE

"I don't feel very much like Pooh today," said Pooh.
"There there," said Piglet. "I'll bring you tea and honey until you do."

A. A. Milne

A person who has good thoughts cannot ever be ugly. You can have a wonky nose and a crooked mouth and a double chin and stick-out teeth, but if you have good thoughts they will shine out of your face like sunbeams and you will always look lovely.

Roald Dahl

A benevolent mind, and the face assumes the patterns of benevolence. An evil mind, then an evil face.

Jimmy Sangster

A good commander is benevolent and unconcerned with fame.

Sun Tzu

'A man must have something to grumble about; and if he can't complain that his wife harries him to death with her perversity and ill-humour, he must complain that she wears him out with her kindness and gentleness.

Anne Brontë

A word of kindness is seldom spoken in vain, while witty sayings are as easily lost as the pearls slipping from a broken string.

George Dennison Prentice

And in our world
  of plenty we must
  spread a smile of joy
Throw your arms
  around the world at
  Christmas time.

Bob Geldof and Midge Ure

Come, gentlemen, I hope we
shall drink down all unkindness.

William Shakespeare

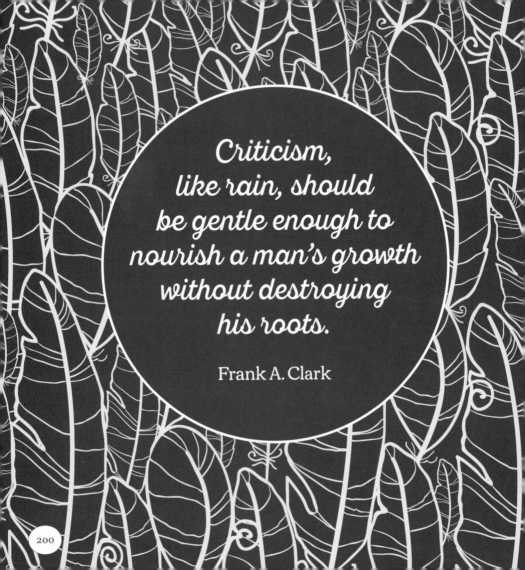

Criticism,
like rain, should
be gentle enough to
nourish a man's growth
without destroying
his roots.

Frank A. Clark

Do you know what it means to come home at night to a woman who'll give you a little love, a little affection, a little tenderness?

It means you're in the wrong house, that's what it means.

Henny Youngman

Entrepreneurs may be brutally honest,
but fostering relationships with partners
and building enduring communities
requires empathy, self-sacrifice and
a willingness to help others without
expecting anything in return.

Ben Parr

Every day, some act of kindness comes my way, even if it's just someone opening the door. It happens every day if you keep an eye out for it. Keeping an eye out, that's the key.

Aaron Neville

For auld lang syne, my dear, for auld lang syne, We'll take a cup of kindness yet for auld lang syne.

Robert Burns

For Brutus, as you know,
  was Caesar's angel.
Judge, *O you gods,* how
  dearly Caesar lov'd him!
This was the most
  unkindest cut of all;
For when the noble Caesar
  saw him stab,
Ingratitude, more strong
  than traitors' arms,
Quite vanquish'd him: then
  burst his mighty heart.

William Shakespeare

Generosity is nothing else than a craze to possess. All which I abandon, all which I give, I enjoy in a higher manner through the fact that I give it away. To give is to enjoy possessively the object which one gives.

Jean-Paul Sartre

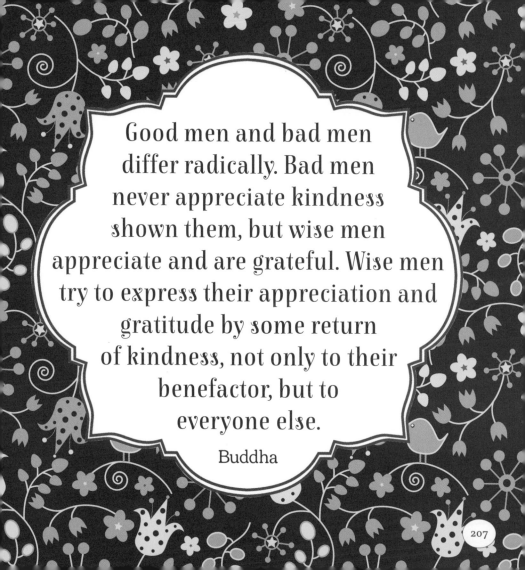

Good men and bad men differ radically. Bad men never appreciate kindness shown them, but wise men appreciate and are grateful. Wise men try to express their appreciation and gratitude by some return of kindness, not only to their benefactor, but to everyone else.

Buddha

Difficulty creates the opportunity for self-reflection and compassion.

Suzan-Lori Parks

Greed has poisoned men's souls, has barricaded the world with hate, has goose-stepped us into misery and bloodshed.

We have developed speed, but we have shut ourselves in. Machinery that gives abundance has left us in want. Our knowledge has made us cynical; our cleverness, hard and unkind. We think too much and feel too little. More than machinery, we need humanity. More than cleverness, we need kindness and gentleness. Without these qualities, life will be violent and all will be lost.

Charlie Chaplin

Grief can be the garden of compassion. If you keep your heart open through everything, your pain can become your greatest ally in your life's search for love and wisdom.

Rumi

Here bring your wounded
   hearts, here tell your anguish;
Earth has no sorrow that
   Heaven cannot heal.

Thomas Moore

*Here is my secret. It is very simple: It is
only with the heart that one can see rightly;
what is essential is invisible to the eye.*

Antoine de Saint-Exupéry

**How beautiful a
day can be
When kindness
touches it!**

George Elliston

Human judges can show mercy. But against
the laws of nature, there is no appeal.

Arthur C. Clarke

By ventilation units where towers
  meet the street
The ragged stand in bags soaking
  heat up through their feet
This was the only kindness, it
  was accidental too...

The Clash

Human kindness is like a
defective tap; the first gush
may be impressive but the
stream soon dries up.

P. D. James

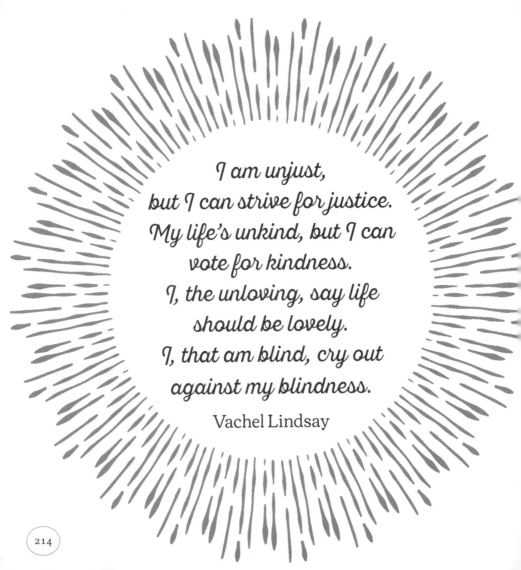

I am unjust,
but I can strive for justice.
My life's unkind, but I can
vote for kindness.
I, the unloving, say life
should be lovely.
I, that am blind, cry out
against my blindness.

Vachel Lindsay

I believe we are still so innocent. The species are still so innocent that a person who is apt to be murdered believes that the murderer, just before he puts the final wrench on his throat, will have enough compassion to give him one sweet cup of water.

Maya Angelou

I expect to pass through life but once. If therefore, there be any kindness I can show, or any good thing I can do to any fellow being, let me do it now, and not defer or neglect it, as I shall not pass this way again.

William Penn

I have learned silence from the talkative, toleration from the intolerant, and kindness from the unkind; yet, strange, I am ungrateful to those teachers.

Kahlil Gibran

I will not call that person happy who knows no rest because of his enemies, who is the butt of fun by all and for whom no one has any empathy, who is as if held on a leash by others, who has lost himself in hedonistic pursuits, who preys on those weaker to him and wags his tail for his superiors.

Munshi Premchand

I've never known any human being, high or humble, who ever regretted, when nearing life's end, having done kindly deeds. But I have known more than one millionaire who became haunted by the realization that they had led selfish lives.

B. C. Forbes

"Pooh, promise me you won't forget about me, ever. Not even when I'm a hundred."

Pooh thought for a little.

"How old shall I be then?"

"Ninety-nine."

Pooh nodded.

"I promise," he said.

A. A. Milne

If nature has made you for a giver, your hands are born open, and so is your heart; and though there may be times when your hands are empty, your heart is always full, and you can give things out of that – warm things, kind things, sweet things – help and comfort and laughter – and sometimes gay, kind laughter is the best help of all.

Frances Hodgson Burnett

If you haven't any charity in your heart, you have the worst kind of heart trouble.

Bob Hope

If you stop to be kind, you must swerve often from your path.

Mary Webb

Ignorant kindness may have the effect of cruelty; but to be angry with it as if it were direct cruelty would be an ignorant unkindness.

George Eliot

In human relationships, kindness and lies are worth a thousand truths.

Graham Greene

It is only after one is in trouble that one realises how little sympathy and kindness there are in the world.

Nellie Bly

It is sometimes difficult to view compassion and loving kindness as the strengths they are.

Sharon Salzberg

It was good to learn so early. They're not going to be kind to you. You have to do it and get on, and then gulp down and get better.

Judi Dench

Just for today, I will let go of anger.
Just for today, I will let go of worry.
Today, I will count my many blessings.
Today, I will do my work honestly.
Today, I will be kind to every living creature.

Mikao Usui

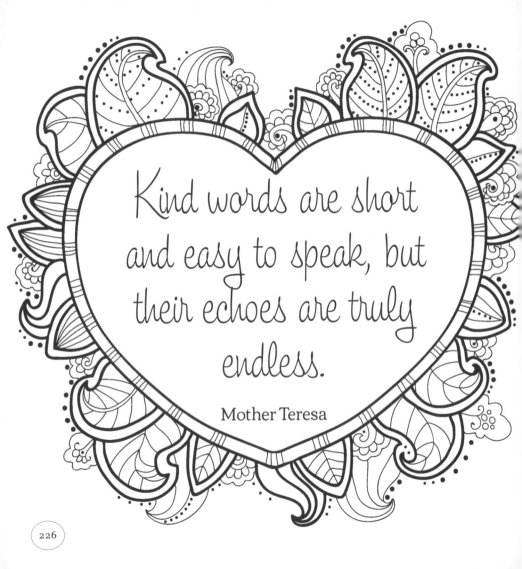

Kind words are short and easy to speak, but their echoes are truly endless.

Mother Teresa

Dame Kindness, she is
so nice!

The blue and red jewels
of her rings smoke

In the windows, the
mirrors

Are filling with smiles.

Sylvia Plath

Kindness is weak when you use it in a self-serving manner. Self-serving kindness is thin – people can see right through it when a kind leader has an agenda.

Travis Bradberry

Like a bridge over troubled water, I will lay me down.

Paul Simon

Love can be unselfish,
in the sense of being
benevolent and generous,
without being selfless.

Mortimer Adler

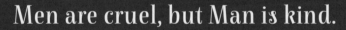

Men are cruel, but Man is kind.

Rabindranath Tagore

Men are more prone to revenge injuries than to requite kindness.

Thomas Fuller

Men who look on nature, and their fellow-men, and cry that all is dark and gloomy, are in the right; but the sombre colours are reflections from their own jaundiced eyes and hearts. The real hues are delicate, and need a clearer vision.

Charles Dickens

Not always actions show
the man; we find who does a
kindness is not therefore kind.

Alexander Pope

Nothing is black
or white, nothing's 'us
or them.' But then there are
magical, beautiful things in
the world. There's incredible
acts of kindness and bravery,
and in the most unlikely
places, and it gives
you hope.

Dave Matthews

Oh, she may be weary
Young girls they do get weary
Wearing that same old shaggy dress
But when she gets weary
Try a little tenderness.

Otis Redding

Oh, why you look so sad, the tears
are in your eyes
Come on and come to me now,
and don't be ashamed to cry
Let me see you through, 'cause
I've seen the dark side too
When the night falls on you, you
don't know what to do
Nothing you confess could make
me love you less, I'll stand by you.

The Pretenders

One could laugh at the world better if it didn't mix tender kindliness with its brutality.

D. H. Lawrence

Only a kind person is able to judge another justly and to make allowances for his weaknesses. A kind eye, while recognising defects, sees beyond them.

Lawrence G. Lovasik

Our brand of democracy is hard. But I can promise that a year from now, when I no longer hold this office, I'll be right there with you as a citizen – inspired by those voices of fairness and vision, of grit and good humour and kindness that have helped America travel so far.

Barack Obama

Resilience is, of course, necessary for a warrior. But a lack of empathy isn't.

Phil Klay

Self-pity comes so naturally to all of us. The most solid happiness can be shaken by the compassion of a fool.

André Maurois

Shall we make a new
rule of life from tonight:
always to try to be a little
kinder than is necessary?

J. M. Barrie

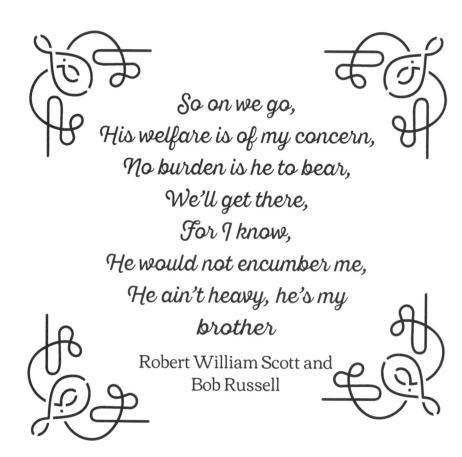

So on we go,
His welfare is of my concern,
No burden is he to bear,
We'll get there,
For I know,
He would not encumber me,
He ain't heavy, he's my
brother

Robert William Scott and
Bob Russell

Sometimes people don't trust the force of kindness. They think love or compassion or kindness will make you weak and kind of stupid and people will take advantage of you; you won't stand up for other people.

Sharon Salzberg

The nicest feeling in the world is to do a good deed anonymously - and have somebody find out.

Oscar Wilde

The pleasure we derive from doing favors is partly in the feeling it gives us that we are not altogether worthless. It is a pleasant surprise to ourselves.

Eric Hoffer

The problem with compassion
is that it is not photogenic.

Sebastian Horsley

The quality of mercy is
  not strain'd,
It droppeth as the gentle
  rain from heaven
Upon the place beneath:
  it is twice blest;
It blesseth him that
  gives and him that takes...

William Shakespeare

There is a rollicking kindness that looks like malice.

Friedrich Nietzsche

There is no sickness worse for me than words that to be kind must lie.

Aeschylus

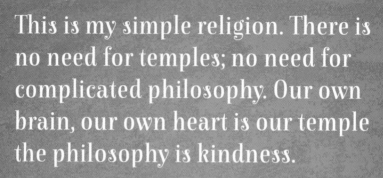

This is my simple religion. There is no need for temples; no need for complicated philosophy. Our own brain, our own heart is our temple the philosophy is kindness.

Dalai Lama

Unseasonable kindness gets no thanks.

Thomas Fuller

Vanity is as ill at ease under indifference as tenderness is under a love which it cannot return.

George Eliot

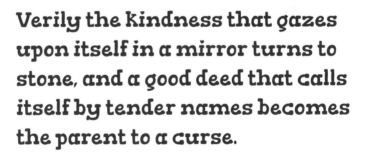

Verily the kindness that gazes upon itself in a mirror turns to stone, and a good deed that calls itself by tender names becomes the parent to a curse.

Kahlil Gibran

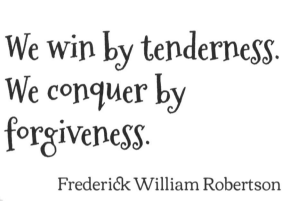

We win by tenderness.
We conquer by
forgiveness.

Frederick William Robertson

**We've put more effort
into helping folks
reach old age than
into helping them
enjoy it.**

Frank A. Clark

When kindness has left people, even for a few moments, we become afraid of them as if their reason had left them. When it has left a place where we have always found it, it is like shipwreck; we drop from security into something malevolent and bottomless.

Willa Cather

When someone is crying, of course, the noble thing to do is to comfort them. But if someone is trying to hide their tears, it may also be noble to pretend you do not notice them.

Lemony Snicket

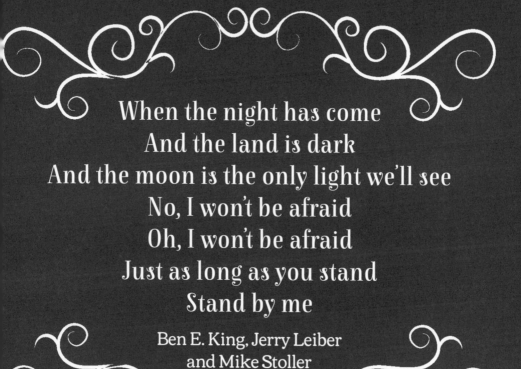

When the night has come
And the land is dark
And the moon is the only light we'll see
No, I won't be afraid
Oh, I won't be afraid
Just as long as you stand
Stand by me

Ben E. King, Jerry Leiber
and Mike Stoller

251

When you're successful,
people have no sympathy.
Nobody wants to catch the
tears of a millionaire.

Boy George

**Where you tend a
rose, my lad, a thistle
cannot grow.**

Frances Hodgson Burnett

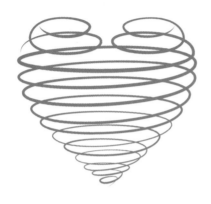

Yet do I fear thy nature;
It is too full o' th' milk of
human kindness.

William Shakespeare

"You have plenty of courage, I am sure," answered Oz. "All you need is confidence in yourself. There is no living thing that is not afraid when it faces danger. The true courage is in facing danger when you are afraid, and that kind of courage you have in plenty."

L. Frank Baum

Sympathy is the first
condition of criticism.

Henri Frederic Amiel

The greatest firmness
is the greatest mercy.

Henry Wadsworth Longfellow

I must be cruel, only to be kind.

William Shakespeare

THE KEY TO
KINDNESS

A man there was, though some did count him mad. The more he cast away, the more he had.

John Bunyan

Be amusing: never tell unkind stories; above all, never tell long ones.

Benjamin Disraeli

Be generous with kindly words, especially about those who are absent.

Johann Wolfgang von Goethe

Be kind to people on the way up – you'll meet them again on your way down.

Jimmy Durante

Be kind whenever possible. It is always possible.

Dalai Lama

Be kind, for everyone you meet is fighting a hard battle.

Philo

"A fight is going on inside you,"
an old man said to his grandson.
"It is a fight between two wolves.
One wolf is evil. He is anger,
greed, envy, destruction and
lies. The other wolf is good. He is
joy, generosity, kindness, hope
and truth. These two wolves are
fighting inside you."
The grandson listened and
thought for a while, then asked,
"But which wolf will win?"
The old man replied,
"The one you feed."

Traditional

'A gentleman has his eyes on all those present; he is tender toward the bashful, gentle toward the distant, and merciful toward the absent.

Lawrence G. Lovasik

A good character is the best tombstone. Those who loved you and were helped by you will remember you when forget-me-nots have withered. Carve your name on hearts, not on marble.

Charles H. Spurgeon

A kindness received should
be returned with a freer hand.

Saint Ambrose

A mistake made by many people
with great convictions is that they
will let nothing stand in the way
of their views, not even kindness.

Bryant H. McGill

Always do good to others. Be selfless. Mentally remove everything and be free. This is divine life. This is the direct way to Moksha or salvation.

Swami Sivananda

An enemy to whom you show kindness becomes your friend, excepting lust, the indulgence of which increases its enmity.

Saadi

As freely as the firmament embraces the world, or the sun pours forth impartially his beams, so mercy must encircle both friend and foe.

Friedrich Schiller

As much as we need a prosperous economy, we also need a prosperity of kindness and decency.

Caroline Kennedy

Because a human being is endowed with empathy, he violates the natural order if he does not reach out to those who need care.

Dayananda Saraswati

Beginning today, treat everyone
you meet as if they were going
to be dead by midnight. Extend
to them all the care, kindness
and understanding you can
muster, and do it with no
thought of any reward. Your life
will never be the same again.

Og Mandino

Behold! I do not give
lectures or a little charity.
When I give I give myself.

Walt Whitman

Being generous often consists of simply extending a hand. That's hard to do if you are grasping tightly to your righteousness, your belief system, your superiority, your assumptions about others, your definition of normal.

Patti Digh

Both man and womankind belie their nature when they are not kind.

Philip James Bailey

Carry out a random act of kindness, with no expectation of reward, safe in the knowledge that one day someone might do the same for you.

Princess Diana

Deliberately seek opportunities for kindness, sympathy, and patience.

Evelyn Underhill

Do not just seek happiness for yourself. Seek happiness for all. Through kindness. Through mercy.

David Levithan

Doing nothing for others is the undoing of ourselves.

Horace Mann

Every minute of every hour of every day you are making the world, just as you are making yourself, and you might as well do it with generosity and kindness and style.

Rebecca Solnit

First and foremost, we need to be the adults we want our children to be. We should watch our own gossiping and anger. We should model the kindness we want to see.

Brene Brown

Getting money is not all a man's business: to cultivate kindness is a valuable part of the business of life.

Samuel Johnson

Guard well within yourself that treasure, kindness. Know how to give without hesitation, how to lose without regret, how to acquire without meanness.

George Sand

Have you had a kindness shown?
Pass it on, pass it on!
'Twas not giv'n for thee alone,
Pass it on, pass it on!
Let it travel down the years,
Let it wipe another's tears;
'Till in heav'n the deed appears
Pass it on, pass it on!

Henry Burton

He that has done you a kindness will be more ready to do you another, than he whom you yourself have obliged.

Benjamin Franklin

He who aspires to paradise should learn to deal with people with kindness.

Abu Bakr

He who confers a favour
should at once forget
it, if he is not to show
a sordid ungenerous
spirit. To remind a man
of a kindness conferred
and to talk of it, is little
different from reproach.

Demosthenes

He who fears to weep, should learn to be kind to those who weep.

Abu Bakr

I cry a lot when I feel empathy. I can feel heartbroken by life, and I cry quite easily, sometimes for no reason. It's healthy, I think.

Bat for Lashes

I know you got
moutains to climb but
Always stay humble
and kind

Lori McKenna

I say to people who care for people who are dying, if you really love that person and want to help them, be with them when their end comes close. Sit with them - you don't even have to talk. You don't have to do anything but really be there with them.

Elisabeth Kubler-Ross

I think it's imperative to have faith or religion, because it's good to have morals, to be kind to others.

Tinie Tempah

I want everyone to know what they deserve in relationships: that they can demand equality and kindness. Because everyone will have a relationship at some point in their life. It's what we all do, every day, and we need to know how to do it.

Olivia Colman

I'm honest and fair, but I don't dispense false kindness.

Steve Easterbrook

I've been searching for ways to heal myself, and I've found that kindness is the best way.

Lady Gaga

If you expect the blessings of God, be kind to His people.

Abu Bakr

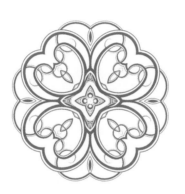

If you have an impulse to kindness, act on it.

Douglas Coupland

If you want to call attention to your good deed then it isn't a good deed, it's a self-serving one. Why? Not only have you patted yourself on the back but you're fishing for others to do the same.

Donna Lynn Hope

If you're not making someone else's life better, then you're wasting your time. Your life will become better by making other lives better.

Will Smith

Illness is the doctor to whom we pay most heed; to kindness, to knowledge we make promise only; pain we obey.

Marcel Proust

287

In giving advice seek to help, not to please, your friend.

Solon

It doesn't hurt to show some empathy.

John Cornyn

It takes a little bit of mindfulness and a little bit of attention to others to be a good listener, which helps cultivate emotional nurturing and engagement.

Deepak Chopra

It's bad enough in life to do without something YOU want; but confound it, what gets my goat is not being able to give somebody something you want THEM to have.

Truman Capote

Justice consists in doing no injury to men; decency in giving them no offense.

Marcus Tullius Cicero

Kind hearts are the gardens,
Kind thoughts are the roots,
Kind words are the flowers,
Kind deeds are the fruits,
Take care of your garden
And keep out the weeds,
Fill it with sunshine,
Kind words and kind deeds.

Henry Wadsworth Longfellow

Kings in this world should imitate God, their mercy should be above their works.

William Penn

Learn to know every man under you, get under his skin, know his faults. Then cater to him – with kindness or roughness as his case may demand.

John McGraw

Let us fill our hearts with our own compassion – towards ourselves and towards all living beings.

Thich Nhat Hanh

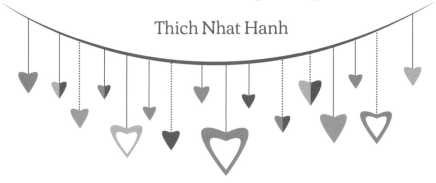

Love one another and help others to rise to the higher levels, simply by pouring out love. Love is infectious and the greatest healing energy.

Sai Baba

Make no judgements
where you have no
compassion.

Anne McCaffrey

Most comedy is based on getting a laugh at somebody else's expense. And I find that that's just a form of bullying in a major way. So I want to be an example that you can be funny and be kind, and make people laugh without hurting somebody else's feelings.

Ellen DeGeneres

My philosophy is that the most important aspect of any religion should be human kindness. And to try to ease the suffering of others. To try to bring light and love into the lives of mankind.

Steven Seagal

My religious philosophy is kindness. Try to be kind. That's something worth achieving.

Pierce Brosnan

Oh be swift to love, make haste to be kind.

Henri Frederic Amiel

One who is kind is sympathetic and gentle with others. He is considerate of others' feelings and courteous in his behavior. He has a helpful nature. Kindness pardons others' weaknesses and faults. Kindness is extended to all – to the aged and the young, to animals, to those low of station as well as the high.

Ezra Taft Benson

One's life has value so long as
one attributes value to the life of
others, by means of love, friendship,
indignation and compassion.

Simone de Beauvoir

Recompense injury with
justice, and recompense
kindness with kindness.

Confucius

Saints were saints
because they acted
with loving kindness
whether they felt like it
or not.

Dan Millman

Since you get more joy out
of giving joy to others,
you should put a good
deal of thought into the
happiness that you are
able to give.

Eleanor Roosevelt

Skip the religion and politics, head straight to the compassion. Everything else is a distraction.

Talib Kweli

Society tends to pit women against each other, but we need to treat each other with kindness and compliment one another instead. Because women's voices are the strongest when they're together.

Normani Kordei

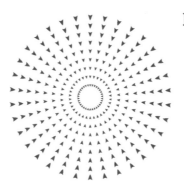

Teach me to feel another's woe,
To hide the fault I see,
That mercy I to others show,
That mercy show to me.

Alexander Pope

*The first thing a kindness
deserves is acceptance,
the second, transmission.*

George MacDonald

The most truly generous persons are
those who give silently without hope of
praise or reward.

Carol Ryrie Brink

The purpose of human life is to serve, and to show compassion and the will to help others.

Albert Schweitzer

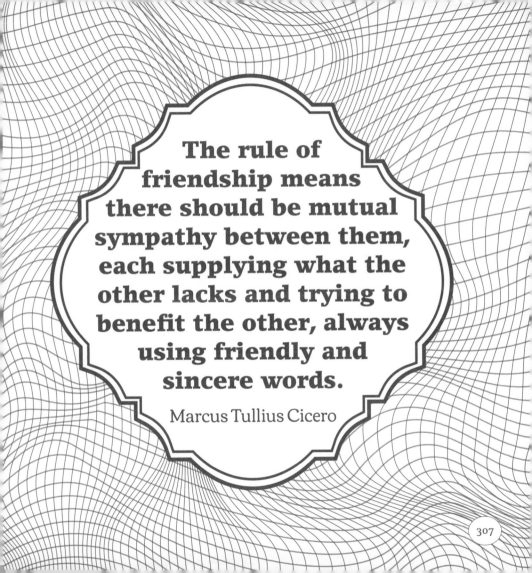

The rule of friendship means there should be mutual sympathy between them, each supplying what the other lacks and trying to benefit the other, always using friendly and sincere words.

Marcus Tullius Cicero

The true greatness of a person, in my view, is evident in the way he or she treats those with whom courtesy and kindness are not required.

Joseph B. Wirthlin

There is no duty more obligatory than the repayment of kindness.

Cicero

There's no use doing
a kindness if you do
it a day too late.

Charles Kingsley

Three things in human life are important. The first is to be kind. The second is to be kind. And the third is to be kind.

Henry James

To be truly stylish, you have to be kind and courteous.

Douglas Booth

To God be humble, to thy friend be kind,
And with thy neighbours gladly lend
   and borrow;
His chance tonight, it maybe thine
   tomorrow.

William Dunbar

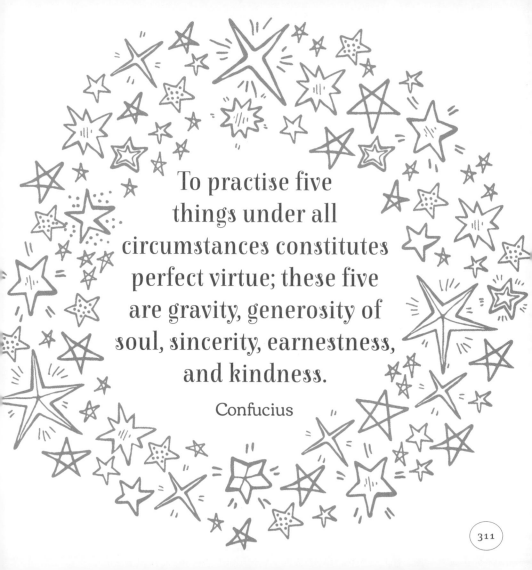

To practise five
things under all
circumstances constitutes
perfect virtue; these five
are gravity, generosity of
soul, sincerity, earnestness,
and kindness.

Confucius

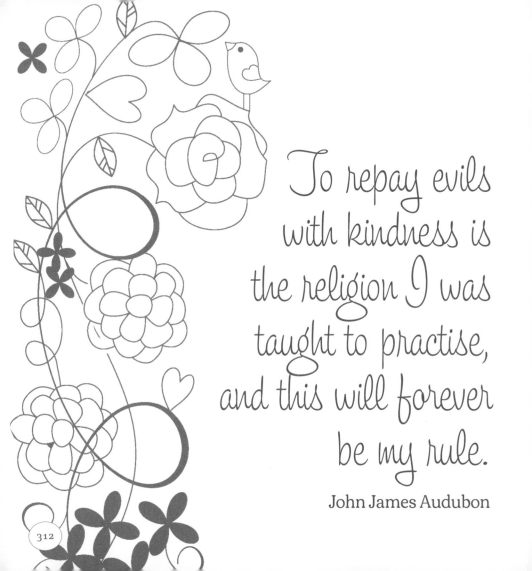

To repay evils
with kindness is
the religion I was
taught to practise,
and this will forever
be my rule.

John James Audubon

312

Try to exercise gentleness, kindness and humour, and you cannot go far wrong.

Sophie Winkleman

We are each made for goodness, love and compassion. Our lives are transformed as much as the world is when we live with these truths.

Desmond Tutu

We ought to be vigilantes for kindness and consideration.

Letitia Baldrige

What we all have in common is an appreciation of kindness and compassion; all the religions have this. We all lean towards love.

Richard Gere

When a thoughtless
or unkind word is
spoken, best tune out.

Ruth Bader Ginsburg

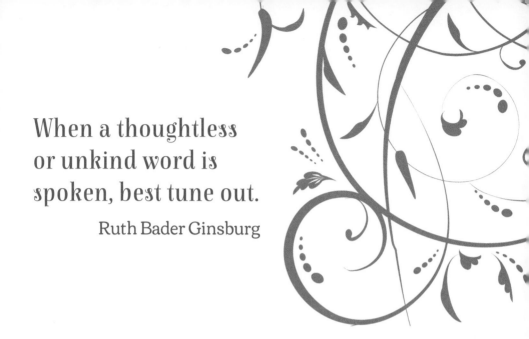

**When you are young you
take the kindness people
show you as your right.**

W. Somerset Maugham

You can give without loving, but you cannot love without giving.

Robert Louis Stevenson

You cannot do a kindness too soon, for you never know how soon it will be too late.

Ralph Waldo Emerson

316

Your days are numbered.
Use them to throw open the
windows of your soul to the sun.
If you do not, the sun will
soon set, and you with it.

Marcus Aurelius

For beautiful eyes, look for the good in others; for beautiful lips, speak only words of kindness; and for poise, walk with the knowledge that you are never alone.

Audrey Hepburn

If you want others to be happy,
practise compassion. If you want to
be happy, practise compassion.

Dalai Lama

What do we live for, if it is not to make life
less difficult for each other?

George Eliot

Wherever there is a
human being, there
is an opportunity
for a kindness.

Lucius Seneca